LAST LION

The Fall and Rise of Ted Kennedy

By the Team at the *Boston Globe:*
Bella English • Neil Swidey • Jenna Russell • Sam Allis
Joseph P. Kahn • Susan Milligan • Don Aucoin

Edited by Peter S. Canellos

Simon & Schuster
New York London Toronto Sydney

Simon & Schuster
1230 Avenue of the Americas
New York, NY 10020

First Simon & Schuster hardcover edition February 2009

SIMON & SCHUSTER and colophon are registered trademarks
of Simon & Schuster, Inc.

For information about special discounts for bulk purchases,
please contact Simon & Schuster Special Sales at
1-800-456-6798 or business@simonandschuster.com

Designed by C. Linda Dingler

Manufactured in the United States of America

1   3   5   7   9   10   8   6   4   2

Library of Congress Cataloging-in-Publication Data
Canellos, Peter.
Last lion : the fall and rise of Ted Kennedy / Peter Canellos and the staff of
the Boston Globe.
p.   cm.
1. Kennedy, Edward Moore, 1932–   2. Legislators—United States—Biography.
3. United States. Congress. Senate—Biography.   I. Globe Newspaper Co.
II. Title.
E840.8.K35C36 2009
973.92092—dc22
[B]   2008050491
ISBN-13: 978-1-4391-3817-5
ISBN-10:   1-4391-3817-6

CONTENTS

THE CONTRIBUTORS

THIS BOOK WAS written by seven members of the *Boston Globe* staff and edited by the paper's Washington bureau chief, Peter S. Canellos.

Bella English joined the *Boston Globe* staff in 1985. She is a feature writer and columnist, and she has covered national and international stories but has especially focused on Boston topics, including politics, women's and children's issues, and the Catholic Church. She lives with her family outside Boston.

Neil Swidey is a staff writer for the *Boston Globe Magazine* and author of *The Assist* (PublicAffairs). His writing has twice won the National Headliner Award and been featured in *The Best American Political Writing, The Best American Crime Reporting,* and *The Best American Science Writing.* He lives with his family outside Boston.

Jenna Russell is a roving regional writer for the *Boston Globe,* reporting news and feature stories from around New England. She previously covered higher education in Boston. Her work has been recognized by the Maine Press Association, the New England Press Association, and the New England Associated Press News Executives Association.

Sam Allis was in the hall when Kennedy gave his memorable speech at the Democratic Convention in 1980 and followed Kennedy while covering Congress for *Time* magazine. In 1997, Allis joined the *Globe* as foreign editor. He is currently the paper's "Sunday Observer" columnist.

Joseph P. Kahn joined the *Boston Globe* staff in 1988. A feature writer for the Living Arts section, he has reported on a wide variety of subjects, from presidential inaugurations and political conventions to local celebrities and Super Bowls. He and his family divide their time between Marblehead, Massachusetts, and an eighteenth-century farmhouse in Maine.

Susan Milligan has covered the Senate for the better part of two decades for the *Boston Globe* and the New York *Daily News*. Since 1999, she has been the *Globe*'s main reporter on Ted Kennedy. She won the Everett M. Dirksen Award for best coverage of Congress in 2004.

Don Aucoin is a reporter at the *Boston Globe* who has covered several political campaigns, including Ted Kennedy's 1994 face-off against Mitt Romney. In 2000–2001, Aucoin was a Nieman Fellow at Harvard University. His work is included in *Best Newspaper Writing*, 2006–2007 edition. He lives with his family outside Boston.

Peter S. Canellos is the *Boston Globe*'s Washington bureau chief, overseeing the paper's national and political coverage. Prior to that he supervised the paper's local news coverage and reported on news and politics. His weekly column, "National Perspective," presents his analysis of the week's events in the world of politics and the national scene.

*"I've described Ted Kennedy as the last lion
of the Senate . . . He remains the single
most effective member of the Senate
if you want to get results."*

—JOHN McCAIN, May 2008

LAST LION

INTRODUCTION

AT 8:19 A.M. on Saturday, May 17, 2008, the dispatcher at the Hyannis Fire Department received a call that generations of rescue workers had anticipated with a mixture of fear and excitement: An emergency at 50 Marchant Avenue. Seemingly everyone in the department knew that address by heart. The Kennedy compound.

The village fire and rescue unit had answered calls at the compound, a sprawling collection of New England–style clapboard homes, many times before. Medics had treated members of the Kennedy clan for broken bones and cut legs after accidents on the beach or the touch-football field. Like everyone else in Hyannis Port, the rescuers recalled their encounters with the Kennedys with both pride and discretion. The family had been through so much, and their hurts—both physical and political—had been felt in Hyannis Port, as well. The Kennedys were protected here.

But it soon became clear to the ten firefighters on duty that Saturday, as they listened to the 911 call being broadcast through the station house, that this was going to be more than a sporting injury. A woman's voice explained to the dispatcher that Ted Kennedy himself, the family patriarch, had fallen ill at the home that once belonged to his parents.

Arriving at the house, the ambulance pulled up beside a billowing tent that had been set up for a reception scheduled for later that day honoring people involved in a charity bike race, hosted by Ted's nephew Anthony Shriver. Uncle Teddy, as he was known to dozens of his nieces and nephews and their progeny, was always eager to help the younger Kennedys with their civic efforts. He saw these good deeds as part of the family's legacy, and himself as the essential caretaker of that legacy.

He had exhorted his own kids, and the many for whom he functioned as a second father, to carry on the tradition of service established by his famous brothers Jack and Bobby, as well as the ritual caretaking that went with it. Even if, in truth, Jack and Bobby had done relatively little hand-to-hand greeting of everyday constituents—and neither particularly enjoyed it—the gregarious Ted had spent forty years hosting and attending charity events, shaking hundreds of thousands of hands and relating the same anecdotes about his fabled Hyannis Port home: these are the stairs down which young Jack would run to the beach; there is the window of Mother's room.

Over time, as the number of people who actually knew Jack and Bobby dwindled, the brothers lived on in Ted's retelling of their lives, and their actual personalities and concerns became almost indistinguishable from his. And while Ted insisted that all the good deeds that people associated with the Kennedys were generated by his brothers and his parents, Joe Sr. and Rose, and that he was merely the custodian of their memories, people lately had begun to think otherwise. Ted, the often discredited, seemingly unworthy younger brother, was shaping Jack's and Bobby's legacies as much as they were shaping his.

When the ambulance arrived at Cape Cod Hospital, just three miles from the compound on the other side of picturesque Lewis Bay, Ted was unconscious. Doctors realized that the 76-year-old senator had had some sort of seizure. His wife, Vicki, his inseparable partner of sixteen years, arrived moments later in a car driven by Hyannis Fire Chief Harold Brunelle, a family friend who had rushed to the compound when he heard about the 911 call.

Chief Brunelle and Vicki found Ted in worse shape than he was when he left the house just minutes before. His morning had begun like so many others. He had used a tennis racket to hit balls to his and Vicki's two Portuguese water dogs, Splash and Sunny. Ted and Vicki took the giant dogs everywhere, from his Senate office to George W. Bush's White House, like the surrogate children of a dream second marriage that neither of them had expected, and that many people had doubted Ted was capable of having. But the surprising fact was that Ted Kennedy, who had once earned the most randy of reputations, had long ago settled down to a cozy domesticity. Splash and Sunny were only the most obvious representations of it.

After playing with the dogs, Ted proceeded with his morning routine, preparing his coffee and orange juice. Just as he was about to sit at his dining room table to read the morning papers, he started to falter. He felt ill and sat down immediately to avoid falling. It was his first seizure. The ambulance arrived five minutes later. But while en route to the hospital Ted suffered a second seizure and lost consciousness entirely.

The emergency team at Cape Cod Hospital rushed to resuscitate him, while neurologists tried to determine what caused the attack. A stroke was the obvious suspect, but initial tests were inconclusive. After less than two hours, the doctors determined that Ted was strong enough to make the trip to Boston, where the more powerful scanners at Massachusetts General Hospital could probe deeper into the senator's brain in hopes of finding the cause of his seizures.

The ambulance drove him another three minutes to Barnstable Municipal Airport—the 600-acre airfield which the Navy used to train torpedo bomber pilots during World War II and where Ted himself had landed thousands of times, always returning home to Hyannis Port. This, too, was the airport at which his nephew John F. Kennedy Jr. had been expected to arrive on his final plane trip in 1999, a tragedy that still reverberated through the family.

In the four decades since Bobby's death, when Ted became the head of the Kennedy family, he had spent thousands of hours attending joyous celebrations like christenings, weddings, and graduations—and an equal amount of time comforting relatives stricken with cancer, beset by accidents, or suffering the loss of loved ones. He had become so associated with those moments of grief that he grew into a living symbol of perseverance amid loss, as famous for his aching eulogies as for his dream-shall-never-die political exhortations. The death of John F. Kennedy Jr. — John-John, the child of Camelot — was, in many ways, the most painful of them all, the extinguishing of a flame that had been lit at Arlington National Cemetery on a cold November day in 1963.

Now, it was Ted himself being carried by stretcher onto a Med-Flight helicopter for the 65-mile trek to Mass. General. It was a gray, wet morning that did not yet hint of warm summer to come, as the helicopter rose above the sea where Ted had spent countless hours on his distinctive 1940s-vintage schooner, the *Mya*.

As the helicopter arced over Plymouth, en route to Boston, phones began ringing in the homes of Kennedy relatives in Massachusetts and around the country, part of an elaborate system that family members had devised to notify each other in the event of yet another crisis. As the word fanned out, those closest to Kennedy quickly began converging on the hospital. His younger son, Representative Patrick Kennedy of Rhode Island, the only other family member still in elective office, got the call in Washington and flew to Boston immediately. His elder son, Teddy Jr., who had lost a leg to cancer as a child and became an activist for people with disabilities, was with his family in Connecticut. His daughter, Kara, also a cancer survivor, was with her family in Maryland. Caroline Kennedy, the niece who had become exceedingly close to her Uncle Teddy after the deaths of her parents and brother, rushed to the hospital immediately from her secluded second home outside New York City.

While the family gathered in a private room, waiting for the initial round of test results, word began to trickle out to the much larger family that had grown up around Ted, the vast network of thousands of former staff members and loyalists reaching all the way to the Supreme Court, where his former Judiciary Committee aide Stephen Breyer was a stalwart of the court's liberal wing.

The news of Kennedy's illness also spread throughout the Senate, where Ted was widely considered the body's most popular member, beloved by Democrats and Republicans alike — despite being a target for derision in many conservative parts of the country. John McCain of Arizona, the presumptive Republican presidential nominee, risked the ire of conservatives by describing Ted as a friend and later calling him "the last lion" of the Senate. Orrin Hatch of Utah, who had entered politics specifically to take on Ted Kennedy but gone on to become one of Kennedy's intimates, was heartsick at the news. So was Christopher Dodd, the Connecticut senator who was also born into a large Irish Catholic political family and had become Ted's daily companion when both were living the bachelor life in the 1980s and early 1990s. And there was John Kerry, for twenty-four years Kennedy's junior colleague from Massachusetts, who had grown closer after Ted worked tirelessly to help Kerry secure their party's presidential nomination in 2004. Perhaps most of all there was Barack Obama, the freshman colleague from Illinois whom Kennedy had personally anointed as keeper of the Camelot flame. Ted had logged tens of thousands of miles exhorting Democrats to vote for Obama, and may have given the untested Obama just enough credibility to get over the hump to the nomination.

Obama was campaigning in Oregon when he got the news and his first reaction, in the glow of his own amazing rise, was to express the kind of upbeat sanguinity that has repeatedly buoyed him politically. "Ted Kennedy is a giant in American political history—he has done more for the health care of others than just about anybody in history and so we are going to be rooting for him and I insist on being optimistic about how it's going to turn out," Obama told reporters.

Meanwhile, at the Kennedy compound, the celebration of the Best Buddies bike race went on, with donors, volunteers, and celebrities, including New England Patriots quarterback Tom Brady, filling the tent. Anthony Shriver, hosting the event on his uncle's lawn, declared, "One thing you can say about the Kennedys is that we're warriors." He added later that day, "I'm 100 percent confident that he'll be fine."

Only three days later, the doctors issued a simple statement announcing the devastating diagnosis: Kennedy had a brain tumor, a malignant mass located in his left parietal lobe, the area of the brain that controls movement on the left side of the body and helps form speech. The news, reverberating among the general public for whom Ted Kennedy had been a fixed point, for good or bad, for decades, set off a surprising reaction: People began to look again at Kennedy as a man, and as a leader of unusual accomplishment.

Mass. General itself, like many other world-class hospitals in Boston and elsewhere around the country, is an unrevealed monument to Ted Kennedy's influence: it was he who quadrupled federal spending on cancer research back in the early 1970s, he who secured the funds for generations of scientists through the National Institutes of Health, and he who relentlessly expanded the federal role in paying for the health care of children, the poor, and the elderly. The dramatic infusions of cash had transformed health care in America, enabling research centers like Mass. General to devise new treatments for the deadliest of diseases.

Without Ted's efforts to boost funding through NIH, Medicare, and many other programs, Mass. General as it is now known would not exist. Nor would the great research hospitals lining Boston's Longwood Avenue. Nor would the outstanding hospitals in other parts of the country, like Duke University Medical Center in North Carolina. Political leaders and historians had long acknowledged Ted's eminent role in expanding health-care treatments, but everyday citizens often failed to make the connection between Ted's health care policies and the great institutions they funded.

Now, facing his own battle, Ted would eventually make a surprising choice, bypassing Mass. General to have surgery performed by the famed neurosurgeon Allan Friedman at Duke, followed by chemotherapy and radiation. As in many decisions, he was guided by memories of his father, Joseph P. Kennedy Sr., who always believed in seeking out the most advanced researchers, wherever he could find them. As in so many other ways, the political and the personal were interwoven into Ted's fight for his life.

Indeed, as he walked out of Mass. General after receiving his diagnosis, with Vicki and his extended family around him, he was a picture of enthusiasm. He was going home.

As the SUV carrying the senator and his wife made the familiar drive down Route 3, over the Sagamore Bridge, and across the Cape on Route 6, friends and constituents arranged themselves on the quiet streets surrounding the Kennedy compound. The people were there to wish their neighbor well, to show their faith in him. Now, in his eighth decade, he had become someone he had never been before: someone you could count on.

It wasn't always so. It wasn't true when he was growing up, when his own father—who loved him dearly—expressed doubts about his intelligence. It wasn't true when he first ran for the Senate, when his own brothers thought he was taking on too much too soon. It wasn't true when tens of millions of voters looked to him as the only possible antidote to the pain of the 1960s, making him the focus of their dream of restoration of Jack's unfulfilled presidency, and he fell short of the task.

It was, some believe, his very failings that were his secret motivation, that made him—the senator with the least need to work hard—drive himself harder than any of his colleagues. But he never explained himself. He always let Jack and Bobby and Joe Sr. and Rose do the explaining. He was driven, he said, to live up to their example. He knew, even as he gazed out at the friends cheering his return to Hyannis Port, and at the supportive wife by his side, that there were other, darker memories in that big old clapboard house. It was there, in 1969, that he had walked into the bedroom of his 81-year-old father, lying nearly immobile and withering away under the effects of a devastating stroke, and said, "Dad, I'm in some trouble. There's been an accident, and you're going to hear all sorts of things about me from now on. Terrible things. . . ."

And friends could only wonder if he knew then that he would spend his life searching for redemption.

PART ONE

THE RISE

"And the last shall be first."

— Inscription on a cigarette case
given by John F. Kennedy to his brother Ted

CHAPTER
1

JOSEPH P. KENNEDY, one of this nation's most politically ambitious fathers, could not have planned it better. On February 22, 1932—the 200th anniversary of George Washington's birth—Joe and Rose Fitzgerald Kennedy's ninth offspring, Edward Moore Kennedy, was born at St. Margaret's Hospital in Dorchester, Massachusetts. It could have been an omen. The proud father, who already had dreams of a Kennedy becoming the first Catholic president, often pointed out the felicitous date to others.

But Ted, as the little boy would be known, was far down on the list of potential Kennedy presidents, and Joe's ambition remained ludicrous in many people's eyes. After all, he and Rose were just two generations off the boat. Their grandparents had arrived in a Boston bursting with Irish immigrants like themselves, fleeing the potato famine. Having settled his family in East Boston, Joe's grandfather Patrick, a barrel maker, died young, leaving a 37-year-old widow with four children and $75 to her name. Bridget Kennedy first worked as a servant and then in a small neighborhood store, which she later managed to buy. Her only son, Patrick Joseph "P. J." Kennedy, worked as a stevedore, but Bridget was able to lend him the money to buy a tavern. Irish pubs were the places where politics and favors were interchangeable, and P. J. Kennedy became a ward boss and a state legislator. He parlayed his political power into business deals, going into the whole-sale liquor business and investing in real estate.

His only son, Joe, grew up in a comfortable home in Boston, and followed the path of many immigrant sons and grandsons on their way to affluence: he attended Boston Latin School, the country's oldest public school, that chose its students through a rigorous exam, and Harvard University.

But in stratified Boston at the turn of the century, many Protestant Brahmins looked down upon even the best-educated Irish Americans, considering them unsuitable for employment in the finest firms and brokerages. It was a closed society that young Joe aspired to, and would spend much of his life chasing. An instinctive businessman for whom deal-making came easily, Joe was determined to best the Yankee elite who snubbed him: he was not shy about seeking wealth and power, in that order.

Rose Fitzgerald, meanwhile, had her roots in the history-rich North End of Boston, across the harbor from her future husband's East Boston. When her grandfather Thomas Fitzgerald arrived in Boston, he worked as a farm laborer in the small town of South Acton, Massachusetts, but soon became a grocer in the city. Growing up in the shadow of Boston's famous Old North Church and Paul Revere's house, Rose's father, John, became an ardent history buff, something he would pass along to his daughter and, eventually, to her youngest son, Teddy. When both of John's parents died in their thirties, leaving nine boys, John's short-lived Harvard days were over. He took a job as a clerk in the Boston Custom House and, with his gift of gab and love of people, became active in local politics. "Honey Fitz," as he was called, would serve in the State Senate and the U.S. House of Representatives while raising his own family in the bucolic Yankee enclave of West Concord. But when he lost his House seat, he moved his family to a large house in the Boston neighborhood of Dorchester and was elected mayor of Boston in 1906.

No matter how successful they became, the Fitzgeralds and the Kennedys, like other "lace-curtain" Irish families, felt like second-class citizens in Yankee Boston. As Rose wrote in her memoir: "Separate 'society columns' were published in the newspapers, one about them, one about us." She knew growing up that she would not be mixing with the Back Bay set. Left out of Protestant clubs, she started her own "Ace of Clubs" for young, well-bred Catholic women, and later joined the Cecilian Club, the Irish version of the Junior League.

Watching their parents advance in the world, despite having their horizons limited by social barriers, both Joe and Rose were seized by a fierce desire to leave their imprint on the world—through their own lives and especially through those of their children. Their ninth child was named after Joe Kennedy's aide, Edward Moore, a family retainer who, along with his wife, Mary, loyally served the Kennedys. The couple often watched over the children when their parents were traveling.

Rose, a devout Catholic, would not use birth control, and by the time she became pregnant with Teddy, at forty-one, friends felt she was crazy to have another child. She was too old. She already had eight. She'd be worn out. Worse, for the fashion-conscious Rose, her figure would be ruined. "I became so incensed and so annoyed at being constantly berated that I determined secretly that no one was going to feel sorry for me or my baby, and so perhaps that is why Ted is so full of optimism and confidence," she wrote in her journal.

Decades later, she would add a postscript: "I have often thought in later years how right I was to trust in God's wisdom and love because, if I did not have Teddy now, I would have no son."

From the moment of his birth, Teddy had a unique vantage point on an extraordinary family; he was swept up in the embrace of eight siblings. Shortly before he was born, big brother Jack, then at the exclusive boarding school Choate, had written his mother: "It is the night before exams so I will write you Wednesday. Lots of love, Jack. P.S. Can I be Godfather to the baby?" And so a month later, 14-year-old Jack stood up at the christening, with Cardinal Cushing officiating. Rosemary, the oldest girl, was godmother.

From the start, Teddy was the adored baby brother. When he was just a month old, Kathleen, the second-oldest daughter, wrote her father: "Everyone is crazy about Ted."

The littlest Kennedy was chubby and cheery, the freckle-faced pet of the family. "Biscuits and Muffins" was his sister Jean's nickname for him. Like many youngest, he was eager to please, and took the teasing—and the occasional brotherly torture—with good humor. He mimicked the exploits of his siblings, skiing with them in Europe, jumping off high rocks on the French Riviera, and sailing in races. When he was five, his beloved eldest brother, Joe Jr., tossed him out of the sailboat and into the cold Atlantic Ocean because Teddy didn't know where the jib was. Joe Jr., twenty-two, hauled him right out of the water, but Teddy never forgot. As with much of his childhood, he chose to remember the good more than the bad—in this case, the rescue rather than the terrifying toss into the ocean.

"I was scared to death practully [sic]," Ted wrote several years later. "I then heard a splash and I felt his hand grab my shirt and then he lifted me into the boat. We continued the race and came in second."

Growing up in Bronxville, a wealthy English-style village with rolling green hills fifteen miles north of Manhattan, Teddy was the victim—or perhaps the beneficiary—of lower expectations. He was born seventeen years after Joe Jr., and Rose and Joe were different parents to him than they were to the older children. "We tried to keep everything more or less equal," Rose once said. "But you wonder if the mother and father aren't quite tired when the ninth one comes along. You have to make more of an effort to tell bedtime stories and be interested in swimming matches . . . I had been telling bedtime stories for twenty years."

Teddy grew up with both a rich kid's sense of superiority and a youngest child's sense of inferiority. He realized early that his role in the family was that of court jester, and he was a natural. He loved jokes and stories, and would entertain the others with his antics, from trying to revive his gasping goldfish to accidentally setting a trash can on fire at the Palace Hotel in the Swiss resort of St. Moritz. He knew his mischief-making was considered charming. In a letter to Santa Claus at age five, he wrote: "Thank you very much for the toys you gave me. You can give me some more anytime you want to . . . Lots of Love, Teddy." When he was seven, he wrote his father that he was going to the World's Fair. "I think I am going to get a pony there and where do you think I could keep it? Maybe in the little tool house."

Teddy was nine when Jack sent his Doberman Pinscher to the family's fourteen-room home in Hyannis Port because he was moving and couldn't keep him. The dog arrived in a crate with a sign that said: "My name is Moe and I don't bite." When Teddy opened the crate, the dog bit him. Teddy immediately sent Jack a telegram: "This dog that doesn't bite just jumped out of his cage and bit me. Teddy."

As he grew older, the youngest became the family Pied Piper, the one who organized group activities and vacations. It was his guarantee that he would get attention. "He had to fight harder, being the baby of the family," his sister Eunice said. "He was always more outgoing and friendly than any of us. He has always been the one most interested in people. He has developed his natural extroversion to the point that all of us envy him and love to be with him."

Teddy was also the most considerate of the Kennedy boys. An early example of his sensitivity was revealed in a letter the seven-year-old wrote to his father. Of Halloween, he said, "I got dressed up like a ghost and went all the way down the road. I didn't scare because you said not to scare anyone because they may have a weak heart."

The Kennedy parents divided their roles in an unusual way for their generation: Joe was the emotional center, the one the kids came to with their problems; Rose was focused on their education, always insisting that perfection was within their reach. When Jack came down with scarlet fever as a toddler and Rose had recently given birth to Kathleen, it was a frightened Joe who moved into the hospital to watch over the boy. "I have never experienced a family where the kids talk about and write about how much they loved, admired and respected their father as these kids did Joe Kennedy," says David Nasaw, an American history professor at the City University of New York, who has studied Joe Kennedy. "And he earned that. He adored them, and he was an extraordinary parent."

Joe always put the children first. "Don't hesitate to interrupt me, whether I am at a meeting, in conference, or visiting with friends, if you wish to consult me about my children," he told Alice Cahill Bastian, the children's nurse. Recalled Bastian, "He was always the first one up in the morning, and soon after, the house was filled with children's voices. The little ones had quietly crept down the hallway to enjoy a romp and reading the funnies with Daddy. This early morning visit was a highlight of their day and his."

When Joe was away on business, he kept in touch with his flock through relentless letter-writing, with telegrams for special occasions. He expected his children to do the same. Writing to 8-year-old Teddy, Joe at first chided him: "You and Bobby are the worst correspondents I have in the family." But he concluded: "Well, old boy, write me some letters and I want you to know that I miss seeing you a lot, for after all, you are my pal, aren't you?"

Frustrated with his silent son, Joe then wrote to Jean, who was twelve: "I wish you would get hold of that Teddy and tell him to send me some news. All he says is, 'I am racing. Get me the King's autograph. I will write soon.'" Another to Jean noted: "I certainly wish you could get that fat little brother of yours to write a little more frequently and tell me what he is doing." Over the years, his father would write Teddy about matters as serious as World War II and as frivolous as a tie he was sending him. He never failed to send treats. A regular customer of the renowned Toll House Restaurant in Whitman, south of Boston, Joe mailed boxes of Toll House cookies, brownies, and raspberry turnovers to his kids who were away at school.

But Joe's love came at a price. In the Kennedy household, it was not enough to be adorable; you had to show you had the brains and knowledge to keep up at the dinner table and prove that you could make something of yourself in the public arena. The intensity behind Joe's and Rose's grand ambitions showed up in their harsh questioning of their children. The Kennedy dining room had an adult table for the older children where politics, history, current events, and literature were digested along with Joe's favorite roast beef and strawberry shortcake. The parents quizzed the children and encouraged opinion.

Where is Siam? Who is the president of France? What are the national holidays?

When they were little, Teddy and Jean, the next-youngest sibling, would sit at the baby table in an alcove or breakfast room, sometimes with Rose or an assigned older brother or sister. But that grownup table had a lasting impact on all the children. In later years, Ted would tell his speechwriter that he spoke in half-sentences because it was the only way to be heard in his large family. "You don't understand—there were nine of us around the dinner table," Ted said. As a young boy, Ted learned an early lesson about that rectangular, well-polished dinner table: "If I wanted to contribute something worthwhile to the conversation, I would have to talk about a book I was reading or an interesting place I had visited."

Contribute something worthwhile. This was one of the many rules the Kennedy parents imposed upon their children. By the time Ted was growing up, Joe had made a fortune as a banker, shipyard builder, liquor distributor, real estate investor, and movie producer, pushing his way past obstacles in Boston, where Yankee bankers had shut out the Irish; New York, where the neophyte Kennedy mopped up profits on Wall Street; and even Hollywood, where his money opened the doors to studios as well as a movie star's heart. In 1928, he began a long affair with Gloria Swanson, handling her finances and scripts. He also gave her the starring role in *Queen Kelly,* which he produced.

Rose dealt with the pain of his infidelity by refusing to acknowledge it and by traveling to glamorous locales where she would engage in what is now called "retail therapy." By the time of Teddy's birth, the two parents were away from each other more often, and their estrangement may have been visible, at times, to the children. But their commitment to continuing their marriage was solid, as was their confidence in each other as a parent. Their money—which paid for Joe's affairs and Rose's extravagant vacations—allowed them greater freedom than most couples. And Joe hoped that his money would give his children freedom as well.

Determined that they would never be shackled by the need to earn a living, Joe set up million-dollar trust funds for each child and told them they should devote their lives to public service. And it was never too early to deliver that message. During World War II, he wrote to 8-year-old Teddy, "I hope when you grow up you will dedicate your life to trying to work out plans to make people happy instead of making them miserable, as war does today." His father's slogans included, "No losers in this family," "No sour pusses," and "No rich, idle bums."

The Kennedy children were expected to be cheerful. Tears, Joe told them, were worthless. Ted would later say of his father: "He wouldn't let any of his children feel sorry for himself. Yet he was quick to scold a child who tried to smile too readily, or to charm his way through life."

Charm played no role in Joe's own advancement; tales of his hardball business tactics reverberated through much of the country. But there was an element of romanticism in his belief that all those dubious business dealings would yield an upstanding, aristocratic life like the one bequeathed to his first great patron—and later nemesis— Franklin D. Roosevelt.

Like many self-made men, Joe craved the respect of the establishment he was challenging: he admired the WASP devotion to education and culture, and purposely directed his sons to go to Yankee-dominated Harvard—his own alma mater—rather than the many Catholic colleges that were striving to provide similar experiences to Irish Americans. Above all, he wanted to conquer that which still eluded his immigrant class: political power on the national stage. His father-in-law, Honey Fitz, had beaten the Anglo-Protestant establishment to become the first American-born Irish mayor of Boston. But Honey Fitz had simply mobilized the huge numbers of immigrant voters in a changing city. Joe had his eyes on Washington, which meant he needed the support and patronage of the same types of people who had looked down on his family.

An early and ardent financial supporter of Roosevelt, Joe was rewarded by being named the first head of the Securities and Exchange Commission, a position of enormous power on Wall Street, particularly since he occupied the office from 1934 to 1935, on the heels of the Great Depression. Then, in 1938, Roosevelt gave him the job of his dreams: he became the first Irish-American ambassador to the Court of St. James's. For a brief while, Joe started to entertain the unlikely notion that he could be the first Irish Catholic president of the United States.

In March 1938, the Kennedy family sailed to London on the USS *Washington* and settled into a 36-room Victorian estate overlooking Hyde Park at 14 Princes Gate, joining Joe, who had already been there for several weeks. Teddy was ecstatic about the mansion's lift, which he and Bobby nearly wore out, until their parents put a stop to it. To Rose, who was now befriended by lords and ladies, London was proof that she had finally taken her proper place in society. Though the winds of war were blowing, London danced on. There were parties and balls and luncheons, the opera, Ascot and Wimbledon — all in high fashion and in the best of company. The two oldest girls, Rosemary and Kathleen, made their debut during the 1938 social season, and a weekend at Windsor Castle with the king and queen would remain a highlight of Rose's life. In their stately tower rooms, Joe raised a glass to her and said: "Rose, this is a helluva long way from East Boston."

The Kennedys became instant media darlings. Weary of the talk of war and bored with stuffy King George VI and Queen Elizabeth, London embraced the energetic, photogenic family. The press followed the kids to the zoo, Kensington Gardens, Buckingham Palace, and Hyde Park. They were there when 7-year-old Teddy tried to take a picture with his camera upside down and when an elephant tried to snatch peanuts out of his hand. "The Kennedys were the royal family that England wanted to have," says Will Swift, who wrote about the family's London years.

Those were happy times for the Kennedys, a rare period when all eleven were together, at least for a while. Joe Sr. gave their nanny, Elizabeth Dunn, a movie camera and told her to record whatever she could: a frisky Teddy in short pants and knee socks, posing with the king and queen, goofing off with his father, sitting on his sisters' laps. Dunn also shot the family's travels around Europe and a costume party for which the two youngest Kennedys chose an American theme: Teddy dressed as a Pilgrim while Jean went as the Statue of Liberty.

What he remembers best about those years, Ted has said, is his sisters making their debut, receiving his first communion from Pope Pius

XII at the Vatican, and having his tonsils removed. (He didn't mind, he told his parents, because he thought he could have all the Coke and ice cream he wanted.) London gave Rose new opportunities to go on the road with regular shopping trips to Paris and holidays in Scotland. The girls were in convent school in England, Joe Jr. was just graduating with honors from Harvard, where Jack was enrolled, and Bobby and Teddy attended the Gibbs School in London.

Still, much of the time, only one—or neither—parent was in residence. While Rose remained in London during the winter of 1939, Joe went to Palm Beach for an extended vacation. When he returned to London, she left him in charge of Bobby and Teddy while she took a long trip to Italy, Greece, Turkey, Palestine, and Egypt. On September 3, 1939, Britain declared war on Germany. That first night, Teddy managed to rip the blackout curtain at 14 Princes Gate, precipitating a call from the air-raid police. Two weeks later, Joe sent his family home to their brick mansion in Bronxville, splitting them up among various ships in case of a German attack. Only Rosemary remained in school in Hertfordshire, where she was studying to be a Montessori teacher. She would return in the spring when she graduated. Joe stayed behind in the embassy, though he feared that Britain could not withstand the Nazi blitzkrieg. He wrote 8-year-old Teddy: "I can't get the King's autograph for you now, but I will try to get it before I go home."

The rise of Hitler and his assault on Britain were the events that ultimately killed Joe's political career. He badly misjudged both the Nazis' intentions and Britain's ability to withstand their attacks. Worse, he became a vocal critic of those who saw Hitler as a real threat and who advocated intervention. Further alienating Winston Churchill, Joe thought that Britain "would go down fighting" and "didn't stand a Chinaman's chance" if invaded. He clung to the notion that Hitler could somehow be appeased and that if America entered the war, "everything we hold dear would be gone." Joe was also widely considered to be unsympathetic to the plight of the Jews. "Well, they brought it on themselves," he told his aide Harvey Klemmer, who had visited Germany and reported back on the persecutions there.

Joe's views infuriated President Roosevelt, who thought his ambassador was dangerously misguided, and the president eventually cut him out of key discussions and communications. During the Blitz, Roosevelt complained to his assistant secretary of state that Kennedy was "a trouble-maker" and was "entirely out of hand and out of sympathy."

In October 1940, Joe returned to the United States and in December resigned his ambassadorship; by that point, he and Roosevelt viewed one another with mutual mistrust and antipathy. "I never want to see that son of a bitch again as long as I live," Roosevelt told his wife, Eleanor. Soon after, Roosevelt made a crucial speech affirming America's commitment to democracy and criticizing high-level American appeasers and defeatists who wanted to accommodate the Nazis, whom he called "a gang of outlaws that surrounds your community and on threat of extortion makes you pay tribute to save your own skins."

The summer of 1941, following those London months, was the last time the entire Kennedy clan was together. The years surrounding World War II would cost the family dearly: they marked the start of what later would be called "The Kennedy Curse."

In 1941, without telling the family, Joe had Rosemary, whom he feared was mildly retarded, lobotomized. The procedure was supposed to fix her mood swings and calm her down, and Joe believed he was doing the right thing. But the operation left her severely brain damaged, and at the age of twenty-three, Rosemary was confined to an institutional setting. She would spend most of her life at the St. Coletta School for Exceptional Children in Jefferson, Wisconsin, until her death in 2005.

In 1943, Jack narrowly escaped death when his PT boat was sunk in the South Pacific. A year later, Joe Jr. was killed when his Navy plane was shot down over the English Channel during a risky volunteer mission. It was August 1944, and most of the Kennedy family was at Hyannis Port, eagerly awaiting Joe Jr.'s arrival from England; he was coming home on leave. Rose, Joe Sr., Jack, Bobby, Teddy, Eunice, Pat, and Jean were there. But on August 12, priests arrived instead, bearing the news of young Joe's death.

In 1948, Kathleen, who had stayed in London and married the son of a duke, died in a plane crash over the French Alps. Her husband, Billy Hartington, had been killed in the war a month after Joe's death and just four months after their marriage. Kathleen, known as "Kick," was a bright, vivacious young woman, the outgoing leader of the Kennedy girls. Her marriage to a Protestant had alienated her from Rose, but she was especially close to Jack and Joe Jr., and was on her way to meet her father when her plane went down.

Teddy was eight when Rosemary disappeared from the home, twelve when Joe Jr. was killed, and sixteen when Kathleen died. When told of his sister's death, he left Milton Academy and took a train by himself to Hyannis Port. The house, scene of many of Teddy's happiest childhood memories, served as a comforting refuge; over the years, it also absorbed much collective and individual grief. During those difficult post-London war years, the Kennedy children were scattered at school or in the service. Surrounded by well-tended lawns and gardens and sweeping views of the ocean, the Hyannis Port house remained the one constant in their lives, particularly for Teddy, who spent many summers there with his Gargan cousins, Joey, Ann, and Mary Jo. Their parents had died when the three children were young; their mother, Agnes, was Rose's sister and best friend.

"For us younger children left at home, we were a little bit like the golden children of the war, and Teddy was the golden child of Joe and Rose at the time," recalls Mary Jo. "I think Uncle Joe made sure there was plenty going on in the house to take Aunt Rose's mind off things. Teddy was there with his smile, winning sailboat races and just being himself, giving joy and saying happy things at a time when his parents needed what he had to give."

After receiving news of Joe Jr.'s death, a shattered Joe Sr. went to the sunporch of the Hyannis Port house. "Children, your brother has been lost. He died flying a volunteer mission." His voice cracked, Ted said, "as tears came to his eyes he said in a muffled voice: 'I want you all to be particularly good to your Mother.'" Ted would later recall this heartbreaking moment as proof that his father really loved his mother.

Rose withdrew for awhile. She'd take her books, journal, and rosary beads down to her one-room hideaway at the water's edge. In some ways, she relied on her youngest child as a calming, cheery presence, an escape from sorrow. He easily took on that role.

His Cape Cod days were still filled with sailboat races, touch football, tennis, baseball, and basketball. Weekend nights, there were dances at the club or movies in Joe's basement studio where he also kept a sauna. Teenagers were in and out of the house, which rang with slamming doors, telephone calls, and lots of laughter. Because of his years as a movie producer in Hollywood, Joe would get the reels before they went to the theaters: John Wayne and Jimmy Stewart were Teddy's favorites.

Those summers, however, weren't just for movies, bike riding, and swimming. Joe, never one for idle pleasure, put Ted and Joey Gargan to work at a nearby farm and stables he owned in Osterville; Joe rode every morning. "They'd cut bridle paths through the woods. It was hard work, buggy and hot," remembers Mary Jo. The children also had to read the morning papers and listen to the radio so that they could discuss current events. Before they could go out, they had to read a book for at least an hour.

At Hyannis Port, Rose remained as decorous as if she were still in London society, dressing for dinner and insisting upon finger bowls. Weekend nights, she'd drive down to the club and peek in at the teenage dances. When the children came home, they'd find little notes pinned to their pillows. "Teddy, make sure you don't pump the girl's arm up and down when you dance." "Mary Jo, be sure to take off your lipstick before getting into bed."

After Jack came back from the war, decorated with a Purple Heart, he spent some time convalescing in Hyannis Port and injected more life into the house. Teddy reveled in his big brother's presence. He and Mary Jo would make up questions for Jack, whom they considered brilliant. "We'd say, 'What do you think about the economic situation in Czechoslovakia?' and Jack would talk for fifteen minutes about it," she says. They could never find a question that stumped him.

The summer of 1944, Jack took Teddy—whom he called "Eddie"

in private—to a naval base in Florida, where he smuggled him onto a PT boat at 4:30 A.M. He also introduced his little brother to some of his favorite writings, including the epic Civil War poem, "John Brown's Body," by Stephen Vincent Benet, which the two would read aloud. Jack, who was naturally introverted and spent hours reading alone, taught his brother about the Civil War, took him to battle sites, and tried to get him interested in more scholarly pursuits. "Jack told him never to be without a book in your hand," recalls Teddy's longtime friend John Culver. "For Jack, that was natural. For Ted it was acquired."

CHAPTER
2

When Ted was nine, Rose sent him to Portsmouth Priory, a Catholic boarding school along the shores of Narragansett Bay in Rhode Island where Bobby was also enrolled. Founded by a group of Benedictine monks, the school had a strict six-day week that included classes on Saturday. No matter that the school normally didn't take boys that young; Rose needed a place to put him for a few months while she traveled and spent time at the family's Palm Beach home.

It was a miserable time for Teddy, who was taunted both for being new and for being the baby in the school. "I went to classes, slept in my own little cubicle, learned something about geography, and was completely mystified by Latin," he would later tell an interviewer. Once, when another boy was pushing Teddy around, Bobby passed by but refused to step in, telling his kid brother, "You've got to learn to fight your own battles." Teddy, who never complained about other aspects of his childhood, would later concede that his school years were tough. "That was hard to take. I can't remember all those schools. I mean, at that age, you just go with the punches. Finally I got through schools where I spent some time learning and trying to find out where the dormitory is and the gym."

Teddy's childhood was in many ways very lonely, with his parents frequently on the road and his brothers and sisters back and forth from boarding school. Teddy had been in ten different schools by the time he was eleven, always the new boy, never able to put down roots. One of his closest friends would come to believe that shuttling from school to school gave Ted a special instinct for vulnerable people. "I think Ted probably did have a very sad childhood in spite of terrific parental support," says Culver, who met Kennedy when they were both in college. "I mean, to be away at school at that age is hard, and the thing that's amazing to me is how he's come through it, in terms of his personality. Part of it I think is reflected in his incredible empathy and sympathy and in the political positions he's taken."

At age eleven, when Teddy was upset about going to boarding school, Joe consoled him by offering some of his favorite butter crunch candy. But when Joe discovered the boy making off with two boxes of it, he exploded and sent him off without a bite. That was the Kennedy parenting philosophy: the love that gives also demands much in return.

Teddy finally found some stability at the Fessenden School, followed by four years at Milton Academy, both boarding schools outside Boston. Rose had wanted the boys in parochial schools, like the girls, but Joe insisted that they take their place with the children of Protestant powerbrokers, the better to ensure their success. Teddy's academic record was mediocre, and both parents were constantly on him about his spelling, his marks — and his girth.

Weight was a Kennedy family obsession, with the parents and their children often fretting in letters about their own and especially about that of the husky youngest Kennedy. When Teddy was going to play center on the Fessenden football team, his father wrote Jack: "I am still waiting to take a look at that one myself — he is too fat." Back when Teddy was seven years old, his sister Eunice had reported to her father: "Ted is getting bigger, better and fatter. [While] he weighs 89 and is only 15 pounds overweight, in fact he looks like two boys instead of one." Rose sent a telegram to her husband in 1940, when Teddy was eight: "Thinking of you. Teddy a little fatter, I am a little thinner." A few months later, she wrote again: "Teddy is really such a fatty." Joe once ended a letter to a lonely Teddy, who had complained about not getting enough food at school, on this sardonic note: "I am sorry to see that you are starving to death. I can't imagine that ever happening to you if there was anything at all to eat around, but then you can spare a few pounds."

But it was the boy's grades that most perturbed his parents. Rose didn't just write Teddy, chiding him about being "in the third fifth" of his class. She also wrote the headmaster at Fessenden to complain about his spelling and math. "Although I do not want him to lose the spontaneous quality of his letters, I do think he should practice the words he frequently misspells." She enclosed a word list for his teacher and sent such lists along every couple of weeks. The following summer, when Ted was eleven, she wrote the headmaster again, this time about numbers. "My only complaint about his work is that he still counts on his fingers. Will you please bring it to the attention of his arithmetic teacher in the fall?"

Joe—whose own grades had been mediocre—could be merciless too. He wrote Teddy: "You still spell 'no' 'know.' Skating is not 'scating,' " and so on. He didn't limit his critiques of Teddy merely to Teddy; he shared them with others. There were to be few secrets in the Kennedy family, at least not among parents and children. As Joe breezily reported to the others: "Teddy is the same as ever, quite self-sufficient and probably the worst speller Fessenden has ever seen."

Perhaps the toughest parental scolding was that which compared the siblings with one another. Joe wrote the 11-year-old Teddy: "You didn't pass in English or Geography and you only got 60 in Spelling and History. That is terrible . . . You wouldn't want to have people say that Joe [Jr.] and Jack Kennedy's brother was such a bad student, so get on your toes." The comparisons among the Kennedy brothers began at an early age for Ted and would become a lifelong challenge for him. Joe Jr. had been the charming, ambitious brother. Jack was the reflective intellectual. Bobby was serious and dogged. Teddy was the entertainer and more into sports than grades.

As parents, Joe and Rose had defined their jobs much like partners in a franchise. Their product: national leaders who would vastly expand the Kennedy name. As Rose once wrote: "A mother knows that hers is the influence which can make that little precious being to be a leader of men, an inspiration, a shining light in the world."

The couple worked with well-oiled efficiency to raise their children according to three guiding principles: "Family, Faith, Country." First of all, they were a unit. Despite the differences some family members had with each other, they were imbued with the importance of family—and of the Kennedy Family. It was all for one and one for all. Though they did allow a constellation of close friends and loyal retainers into the orbit, if you weren't a Kennedy, you just weren't a Kennedy.

Religious faith was also required. Rose ate fish every Friday, went to Mass twice on Sundays and often daily. She expected her children to follow suit and to go on annual religious retreats. The teenage Teddy, excited about a weekend of sailing races with his friends, meekly acquiesced when Rose sent him instead on a retreat in Lawrence, north of Boston. She once wrote Jack, who was campaigning for president, one line: "Dear Jack, This is a note to remind you of Church. Love, Mother."

As for country, Joe had always expected his children to enter public service and burnish the Kennedy name in the process. The boys would seek public office, the girls would do some sort of social justice work. As the children matured, Joe would take each one aside and speak to them about their plans. He would say, "What are you going to do with your life? Kennedys don't just sit around. They do something." Like his brothers before him, it was preordained that Ted would go into politics.

There were, at many points, tensions in the parental franchise, but Rose's commitment to her husband was almost as strong as her commitment to her church. Rose loved her children, but her husband came first. Whenever Joe would return from one of his trips, she'd be turned out in the latest fashion and would have the cook prepare his favorite meals—hearty New England fare like roast beef, roast potatoes, peas and carrots; or clams and lobsters and fresh corn, finished off with dessert of strawberry shortcake or chocolate cake and ice cream. Boston cream pie was the family favorite. When the inquisitive Eunice was ten, she asked her mother whom she loved the most, her children or her husband. "At first, she wouldn't answer, then finally after I plagued her for an hour, she said: 'I love Joe so much. I could never be happy without Joe.' "

She was protective of him, too. Rose once wrote Bobby and asked him not to telephone his father at the dinner hour: "If he gets too excited before dinner, as he did the other night when he talked to you about the labor legislation, it is not very good for his little tummy." She and Joe never had a fight, she once told her granddaughter Caroline, because "I just said 'Yes, dear,' and went to Paris." That was their contract: she would ignore his flagrant womanizing, and he would give her the freedom to travel whenever she liked and to spend whatever she pleased. At Christmas, it was his custom to bestow expensive jewelry on her. But unlike Joe, who expressed more affection for his children than his wife, Rose never stopped wishing he could be her romantic soul mate.

With nine children Rose had to run a tight ship, and she set household rules that few dared break for fear of a whack from her infamous wooden coat hanger. A perfectionist, Rose followed the child-rearing books to the letter. The children were to get up at the same time every day, take their meals at the same time, and go to bed at the same time. "Promptness is a compliment to the intelligent, a rebuke to the stupid," Rose would say. After lunch, they were required to nap or read quietly. On the beach, they all wore the same color bathing suit, the better to identify them, and the same color bathing caps in the ocean. She'd dole out candy one piece at a time—the better to save their teeth.

Dinner was always at 7:30, and the family would first congregate in the living room for cocktail hour, where Joe, in his Sulka lounge suit, might have a Scotch and water and the others a tomato juice. When the bell rang for dinner, Rose, always impeccably dressed, would lead the way into the dining room. At the end of the meal, she would lead the way out. When Jack became president, he jokingly told her that protocol demanded he be the first in and out of a room. After dinner, they sang Irish songs around the piano, or Irving Berlin or Cole Porter. Always, there was Joe's and Rose's special song: "Sweet Adeline," which had been her father's favorite. Rose would also read aloud or tell stories of growing up with Honey Fitz.

Rose was obsessed with learning. She would pin clippings from newspapers and magazines onto a bulletin board, so the children could bone up on the news of the day—and comment on it at the table. Like her father before her, Rose became famous for her field trips, in which she'd bundle everyone, including cousins, into the car and take them to Massachusetts historic sites such as Bunker Hill, the Old North Church, and Plymouth Rock. At Walden Pond, the kids didn't just swim and picnic; they also got a lesson on Thoreau.

She never stopped her quest for perfection. When Bobby was a teenager, she wrote him about a particularly bad report card, saying that he owed it to himself and to her to improve. "Remember, too, that it is a reflection on my brains as the boys in the family are supposed to get their intellect from their mother, and certainly I do not expect my own little pet to let me down."

Much later, after Teddy became a senator, Rose would write to chide him about his grammar. "I wish you would pay attention to this matter: Use 'whom' after a preposition. *For Whom the Bell Tolls.* The man to whom I wrote. If you listen to Jack's speeches, you will notice that he always uses this word correctly. It is the accusative case in Latin, objective case in English."

In 1972, when Teddy was forty years old, she scolded him about his language. "I noticed . . . you are quoted as using the word 'ass' in several expressions. I do not think you should use that word. I am sure you realize it really does not look very well in print." Still later, when Ted was a third-term senator and Rose was eighty-five, she wrote to him: "I watched you speak about drugs last Friday night . . . Please say, 'If I were president,' not 'If I was president.' The reason is the old what used to be known in Latin as condition contrary to fact. For instance, 'if I were he,' etc."

Teddy rarely recalled her remonstrations, perhaps believing them to be her way of showing love, and dwelt instead on the more tender moments he shared with her. As an adult, he recalled being a little boy in footsie pajamas and going into her room where she would read to him his favorites, such as *Peter Rabbit* or *Billy Whiskers.* When he was ten years old, sick with whooping cough and out of school for three months, he loved having his mother all to himself "as she nursed me back to health."

Teddy often disappointed Rose as a student. But instead of agreeing with Joe that their son simply wasn't studious, she attributed it to the younger generation's preference for the radio and comics. She wrote in her journal in 1942: "In the old days we played games, we read all the available stories, we made puzzles, we bought countless gadgets from the 5 & 10, blew bubbles." But by the time Teddy came along, things had changed and, in Rose's opinion, not for the better. "He sits comfortably in his bed next to his radio, requests a proper program and then by a mere turn of the wrist conjures up entertainment by the minute." *The Lone Ranger* was Teddy's favorite. Longing for the good old days, Rose recalled that Jack, while recovering from scarlet fever, had "books by the cartload" and that her older children had acquired a love of literature out of necessity. "This generation," she said of Teddy, "to my horror concentrates entirely on funny books, which they consider reading . . . A motley array of funny books with harsh-screaming colors."

Soon after he recuperated from whooping cough, Teddy shared a lower berth on the train with his mother en route to Palm Beach for the Christmas holidays. It was cold, and the boy was shivering under the single blanket while his mother said the rosary. At a stop in West Virginia, Rose dispatched him to get some food. As he was running back, the train started up. He wrote: "I can still see Mother, standing on the rear platform of the last car, calmly but firmly ordering: 'Mr. Conductor, tell them to stop this train. That's my son out there.' Of course, he did exactly as she asked. Everyone did."

It has been said that the Kennedys competed among themselves and against the world. Everything and anything could be turned into a contest. On road trips, the kids would divide into two teams and see who could spot the most animals. And on the fields of Hyannis Port, the play was always rough. The legendary Kennedy touch-football games often resulted in injuries.

They were even more competitive against outsiders. Neighbors in Hyannis Port still remember the baseball rivalry between the Kennedys, who called themselves The Barefoot Boys, and the neighborhood boys, who called themselves The Pansy Toes. "Jack was the pitcher, Bobby was first base and I think they had Teddy out in the field," says Terrill Griggs, who lived across the street. "You could tell Teddy revered his brothers. We would all gather around to watch. It was a riot, all very competitive." Each team had its own flag—a bare foot for the Kennedys and pansies on toes for the others—that they hoisted up on the pole. The Barefoot Boys would always put theirs above the Pansy Toes.

Even painting became a contest. Jack, home from World War II, challenged teenage Teddy, who'd never painted before, to compete in creating a picture of the family's Mediterranean-style Palm Beach house. "Then we all voted on which was the best. Teddy won," Ethel Kennedy would recall.

The Kennedy children were also expected to excel at the family's signature sport, sailing. Like politics, the ocean held a hypnotic lure, and sailing was as much a part of the Kennedy makeup as good teeth and strong jaw lines. They took lessons; the family owned boats. When there were only eight children, Joe named the family's boat *The Ten of Us*. When Teddy came along, he bought a smaller boat and named it *One More*. Once, when Teddy came in third in a race, his father was livid. "He said, 'We've got the best boat, we've got the best teacher, how come you're coming in third?' " recalls Mary Jo Gargan. Another time, Joe sent the teenage Ted to his room for goofing off and losing a race—Joe had been watching with binoculars.

At Milton, which was also Bobby's alma mater, Ted kept up the family's fierce competition in sports. There, he was remembered as a "vital and vibrant member" of his fifty-boy class and "an interested and enjoyable student" by Frank Millet, his English teacher and ninth-grade football coach. On the freshman team, Teddy started on both offense and defense and was a strong player. Teddy scored only one touchdown, but it was in the last game of his senior year against archrival Noble and Greenough.

He also had an active social life during his Milton years, writing his father that he went to the Totem Pole, "about the biggest dance place in the state for teen age people," where he had a wonderful time. He confided that he'd been to a girl's house for dinner and was "gradually getting to know more girls, which couldn't please me more." Once, playing hockey, he fell through the ice and thought it quite funny. His senior year, he was also a member of the "Boogies," an informal social club started by students who met after lunch in a dorm to listen to the *Bob and Ray* show on the radio.

His academic record was nothing to write home about, but he did anyway. "I have now dropped out of my Latin class, but I am tutoring and trying to keep up to the class . . ." Most of his letters to his parents dealt with sports, but he was also in the drama club, the debate club, and the glee club. His senior yearbook photo shows him with a wide grin displaying the famous Kennedy teeth, on the same page with two other somber young men. "Smilin' Ed" and "Big Ed" were his nicknames, and he came in a distant third in the "Class Politician" category. His senior year, the debate team won only two of its six debates—its first and last. The boys began the season by beating Roxbury Latin on the issue that national advertising "does more good than harm" and ended it by beating Noble and Greenough on the virtue of "the nationalization of industries."

Despite all the academic criticism that Ted received from Joe and Rose, he always remained deferential to his parents. Teddy took their comparisons to his older brothers as a normal part of growing up Kennedy. To him, family loyalty was paramount. He believed his parents' critical words were for their children's own good—a generous interpretation, since he often came out on the short end. After his father's death, he wrote: "His standards were the highest for each of his sons, but they were different standards for each one—standards which recognized our individual strengths and weaknesses. Often, he compared us to each other, but only in a way which raised each of our expectations for what we hoped to accomplish."

He had similar compliments for his mother's parenting skills. "Mother supplied the gentleness, support, and encouragement that made Dad's standards reachable." That Teddy never rebelled against his parents, who were often absent but always dominant, was remarkable. In fact, after his father's death in 1969, he wrote a letter to *Newsweek* magazine protesting what he called an "unnecessarily cruel" obituary. "I wish you could have devoted at least a line to the generosity, humor and heart my father had in such abundance."

Many family members have traced Ted's genial and forgiving personality to his maternal grandfather. During those years at Fessenden and Milton Academy, Ted grew especially close to Honey Fitz, who was the consummate constituent politician. Ted often spent Sundays with the old man, an affable and voluble character who would take his grandson on walking tours of Boston, explaining the importance of the Old North Church or the elegance of Louisburg Square. But he'd also take Teddy to the wharves where the immigrants landed, and introduce him around to his Irish and Italian pals. He knew everyone in the city and adored his hometown.

The similarities between grandfather and grandson were apparent to all: their social skills included a love of singing and practical jokes. "Teddy was more Honey Fitz than Joe Kennedy," says Bob Healy, who covered the 1960 presidential campaign for the *Boston Globe*. "Honey" was sweet and friendly, whereas Joe was more calculating. Like Honey Fitz, Teddy never met a stranger—a trait that would serve him well on the campaign trail.

But there were also signs in Ted's upbringing of some of the personal traits that would burden him in later years. He was unmindful of rules, and his behavior occasionally veered beyond careless to callous. Though his teachers at Fessenden remarked on his friendly personality, there were paddlings and notes home about demerits for minor offenses. While at Milton, Teddy borrowed the car of former Boston Police Commissioner Joseph Timilty, a close family friend. After it stalled out a few times, he simply abandoned it in Mattapan—though he did tell "the Commish" where it was. He also was nearly kicked out of church for misbehavior as an altar boy. The priest would later say that he would rather have had no one serve him than Teddy, and Ted would recall the rebuke as "a definite blow to my pride."

But despite his checkered school record, Ted showed initiative and promise as a deal-maker—something his father admired. Joe had instilled in his children both the value of a dollar and the virtue of frugality. Their allowances were meager, and they drove old cars. At Hyannis Port, Teddy sometimes cut the neighbors' grass to earn extra money. "The pay was usually better than at my house," he said.

At Milton Academy, Teddy's allowance was $1.50 a week, and Joe would not allow him to keep his bicycle on campus since few of his classmates did. While Ted was at Harvard, Joe heard that he had a "cow horn" on his car and warned against exerting "privilege that the ordinary fellow" didn't have. Always the pragmatic politician, Joe added that such excesses could land Teddy in the newspapers—his father's great fear, unless he himself had orchestrated positive publicity. It was okay, Joe told his son, to get "ahead of the masses" by hard work and good works, but not "by doing things that people could say, 'Who the Hell does he think he is?' "

Teddy took the penny-pinching lessons to heart. He often went to his father with business proposals, such as the time he and Joey Gargan wanted to rent a 44-foot boat for two weeks at $125 a week. Teddy had checked the rate out with several sources, and assured his father it was a good deal. He and Joey could work the $250 off in the summer for Joe, he said. He also pointed out that new boats were going for $1,300, and he reckoned that the Kennedys could get $1,000 for their old one. "Our boat is probably better and faster than a new one, but it is awfully hard trying to get someone to believe it," he concluded.

Joe could not hide his pride in Teddy's constant hustling. Back in 1944, when Teddy was twelve, his father had written to Joe Jr. that Teddy had gotten on board the train from Palm Beach to Boston with a box of sandwiches that "I am sure he planned to sell to the customers on the train because no human being—even with Teddy's appetite— could eat as much as there seemed to be in that box." And in a letter to Kathleen, he wrote about Teddy's business dealings at Fessenden. "Your youngest brother, Teddy, the merchant in the family, is as he says running a black market at Fessenden." When Teddy went into Boston for his catechism class, Joe explained, the boy would buy chocolate bars for a nickel each, then sell them for 10 to 15 cents to his hungry fellow students.

Teddy was revealing a good head for business and a natural ability to bargain. Behind the middling grades and his bluff good humor was a decent mind—one even the stern and over-achieving Kennedy parents were beginning to appreciate.

CHAPTER
3

IN FALL OF 1950, Ted followed his father and his brothers to Harvard, joining a class that included such future luminaries as novelist John Updike, attorney F. Lee Bailey, financial-services innovator Ned Johnson, writers Edward Hoagland, Christopher Lasch, and Richard Eder, as well as the heads of the Museum of Modern Art, the National Portrait Gallery, and several politicians, including Senator John Culver. As the youngest Kennedy, Ted was the most prominent among those nascent stars.

His main interest, however, was football. Teddy was a better athlete than Jack, who was sickly, or Bobby, who was smaller, and it thrilled old Joe, who had played baseball at Harvard, to go to the stadium and watch his youngest child perform on the gridiron. All the Kennedys were excited about Teddy playing this most manly of sports, and Ted was happy that, for once, the spotlight was on him.

Bobby, who was then in law school, reported back to his father that a family friend had attended a practice and talked to some of the players afterward. "They said he had no qualms about lowering his head and crashing in and that he has great potentialities and is one of the best ends they have. That is certainly good when his fellow players think that," Bobby wrote. Those players included three who would remain lifelong friends of his: Culver, Dick Clasby, and Claude Hooten, all of whom would later help kick-start his political career.

But his freshman year ended precipitously. That spring, Ted was in danger of flunking Spanish and needed to pass the final to be eligible for football the next year. He didn't like Spanish, and he wasn't good at it. A teammate took the test for him, but when he turned in the exam book, the teaching assistant recognized him as Bill Frate, not Ted Kennedy. Both boys were thrown out of school; they could return in two years if they exhibited good behavior. "Ted was a bright guy. He didn't have to cheat," recalls Ron Messer, who played freshman football with them. "It shouldn't have happened."

Burton Hersh, who went to Harvard with Teddy, recalls how the incident was interpreted in the Kennedy family. "Teddy didn't manage himself effectively. Afterward, his father said, 'Don't do this cheating thing, you're not clever enough.'" For Joe, whose affection for his youngest was mixed with concerns about his abilities, the cheating was proof less of bad character than bad judgment—and perhaps a lack of intelligence. In 1961, he would tell an interviewer that Teddy was the most attractive politically of the brothers, the best-looking and the best speaker—but not as smart.

For Ted, who was just starting to shine on his own, it was a devastating reminder of all the insecurities with which he had wrestled during his childhood. It seemed that he might never measure up. And for a while, at least, he would trade the rarefied environs of Harvard Yard for the metal bunks of the Army.

Arriving at Fort Dix, New Jersey, for basic training, he landed in the 39th infantry regiment, or Easy Company. Joseph Maguire, who was also from Massachusetts, was his sergeant and remembers having to get rid of reporters who showed up because he was the kid brother of Congressman John F. Kennedy. "He got no special treatment, he was a good soldier," says Maguire. "He was very athletic, he was a pleasant kid, very easy to get along with, never gave you any guff." Maguire remembers Teddy once telling him: "You know, you're the only one who ever told me what to do, except my mother."

At the time, Maguire administered a swimming test to his men. Teddy, who grew up on the water, was by far the best of the lot. "He swam down to the end of the pool and came back before the other guys got to one end. I never saw anything like it, and I tested thousands of guys. He probably could have been in the Olympics, he was that strong a swimmer." Maguire also remembers something else: on Sundays off, Teddy would pull up in late afternoon in a car driven by "a beautiful blond young lady. All the guys would be looking out the window at that."

It was during this time that his father wrote him a letter with more career advice that Teddy took to heart. Joe knew that Teddy would meet all sorts of people in the Army that he hadn't been exposed to in his privileged world. He saw that as a help to his son's future in politics. "I hope you will make up your mind to get to know as many different kinds of people as you can because that kind of education is more valuable than even a college education . . . All kinds of people are essential for one's development."

The Army, in its early stages of integration, offered Teddy a lens on the wider world. Joe Jr. and Jack had both been officers in the Navy, and naval officers were quite different from Army privates in terms of the company they kept. Bobby had enlisted in the Navy at age seventeen, but was ultimately assigned to an officers' training program at Harvard, so his military experience was also much different from his younger brother's.

Teddy was a grunt. After Fort Dix, he was sent to Fort Gordon in Georgia to train as a military policeman. In the Army, he lived with black people and the working class. To them, the Kennedy name didn't matter. If anything, it provoked a negative reaction in the barracks, where Teddy had to learn to hold his own, sometimes with his fists. Once, when he was dispatched to round up some black soldiers for a work detail, they refused to take orders from him and instead challenged him to a fight. The sergeant told them to take their problems outside, after hours. Teddy showed up at the appointed hour, but the men did not. Another time, a fellow soldier taunted Teddy with a dare that he could outrun him. Teddy, never one to turn down a bet, took him on. After a series of rigorous competitions, at which Ted held his own, the two men shook hands and became good friends. "I think he got to know more about 'the other America,' and how to get along with people across the cultural and class divide than either of his brothers had, at such a young age," says James Sterling Young, professor at the University of Virginia. The experience had a profound effect on Ted: back at Harvard, he would volunteer to coach basketball for inner-city youths in the South End of Boston.

While Teddy was in the Army, U.S. troops were fighting in Korea, but Joe used his connections to keep his youngest son away from any conflict. War had already robbed him of one son and nearly killed another. It was a move that made sense to Teddy's drill sergeant. "People like Ted, with his brother being a senator, they were kept away because it made it easier for the guys on the line. If the North Korean troops knew someone like him was around, they'd try to come after him," says Maguire. Ironically, a few months before the cheating incident, Joe had written Ted: "Keep after the books if only to keep the draft away from your door."

Private First Class Kennedy ended up in a NATO honor guard in Paris. It was a plush assignment, but for the privileged Teddy, even the trip across the ocean was a hardship. He wrote his parents that he had lost fifteen pounds in the thirteen-day voyage from New York. The trip seemed cursed from the beginning. The troops had boarded on a Tuesday morning and set sail in the early afternoon. But upon waking the next day, they found themselves back in New York because the ship had broken down. When they finally set sail again, Teddy was assigned a bunk five decks down — two decks below water level. Not only that, he had the top bunk, "which made it just that much hotter." He was one of 187 men out of 3,000 who were assigned to kitchen duty every other day for the entire trip. The seas became rough, and many of the men got sick. "Your ninth, however, was so busy washing the total of 25,000 trays during the voyage that he didn't have much time for anything else," he wrote his parents. Six days out, the ship broke down again. Finally, he arrived in France and began his job, along with French lessons.

Paris was Rose's favorite city. When feeling the stress of raising so many children, or faced with a husband who spent weeks away from home with other women, Rose would set sail for Paris, book herself into the Ritz, and shop on the Champs-Elysées. She and Joe both wrote Teddy detailed letters about the best places to eat and drink, including what dishes to order. At Maxim's, Rose told him to get a table in the highly coveted inside room. "So the best thing to do is call up there and ask for Albert (pronounced the French way) and tell him you are Ambassador Kennedy's son and he will fix you up." She also told him to drink the beer in Germany and the wine in France because they were the best. Joe was appalled and lectured her: "Rose, are you out of your mind?" He reminded her that all the children had pledged not to drink or smoke until they turned twenty-one; Joe had promised them $2,000 each if they abstained.

In Paris, Rose loved shopping for the latest designer fashions and made her pilgrimage to the Ritz several times during Teddy's years in France. During one visit, she offered to take him out to dinner. Teddy was looking forward to a feast: "a delicious prospect for a young private who had been living on mess hall food for what seemed like an eternity." But as they were preparing to leave the Ritz, Rose couldn't find her jewelry. She had never trusted the safe deposit boxes at hotels, and so she would hide her baubles in various corners of the room. On this particular night, however, she'd forgotten where she'd hidden the jewels. Fearing that they had been stolen, she refused to leave the room until they were located. She and Teddy spent an hour looking. "At long last, after missing our dinner reservation, we found the jewelry, pinned into the lining of the drapery," he recalled some years later. "I did not have my gourmet dinner but ordering room service with Mother was still a marvelous treat."

The next day, his mother gave him a ride to his post and Teddy said good-bye outside the gate: he didn't want his Army buddies seeing the limo she had hired. But as he was walking back inside, he heard Rose call: "Teddy, Teddy, you forgot your dancing shoes!" His friends teased him about it for months, and his mother never tired of hearing the story, even years later.

To Joe, she wrote that Teddy looked wonderful and seemed happy. His pudginess had left him. He was military-fit. A tall, handsome young man, he had no shortage of girlfriends. As Rose noted: "His girl, the nurse, is to come over this week and his girl from Texas has left, so he is lucky as usual." His sisters Pat and Jean went skiing with him in the Alps, and Jean wrote that Teddy had his skis on one shoulder and hers on another. "He may weigh 215," she said, "but it's all meat and muscles."

In 1952, while in the Army, Ted also traveled to Germany and Belgium. In Frankfurt, he wrote his parents about tossing the football around with a friend. "Several little fellows" wanted to play and within ten minutes, more than thirty people had assembled. Ted and his friend had trouble trying to explain the rules of the game. But he saw merit in the informal cultural exchange. "I really think that if the Army had some fellows go over to various places like this and started games of all sorts they would really do a lot of good and find some real interest," he wrote.

Discharged from the Army in the summer of 1953, Ted returned to Harvard determined to be a better student. "He was dead serious about his studies," recalls Claude Hooten, who played football and rugby with him. "He learned a lesson." Ted was an average student who was good at the subjects he loved, such as history and government, but not so adept at those that didn't hold his interest. Eager to prove his mettle at Harvard the second time around, he even earned an A-minus in Spanish, the course he had cheated on in his freshman year.

His great passion remained football, however, and he eventually returned to the team, a six-foot-two-inch, 200-pound end. His high point came senior year in a snowstorm, when he caught a short pass on Yale's seven yard line and scored—for Harvard's only touchdown. Harvard lost anyway, but Joe was deliriously happy, and Teddy got his varsity football letter. The proud father, who had attended every single game, home and away, even asked one of his connections at the Chicago Bears if his son could practice with them. "He put on the pads, took two or three hits and said he'd never been so frightened in his life," recalls Teddy's roommate Ted Carey. "He got out of there." Later, when he got a letter of interest from the Green Bay Packers, Teddy replied that he intended to go to law school.

His athleticism, love of a party, and family name made Teddy a big man on campus. Jack, by then a senator, came to some of the games and often brought their cousin, Mary Jo Gargan, who'd spent summers in Hyannis Port. On occasion, Jack would fix Teddy and his friends up with girls who worked at *Seventeen* magazine or elsewhere in New York. The girl on the right facing them, whoever it was, would be Clasby's date, the girl on the left Ted's. "We'd go to the Stork Club," Clasby recalls, "but we'd always stop to see Mary Jo at Manhattanville College on the way down to the city. Finally, I said, 'I like Mary Jo.' " The two were married in 1956.

Ted held court at a jocks' table in Winthrop House, where his brothers had also lived. Friends remember him as friendly and helpful, not one to grandstand or seek attention. "He had such a zest for life," says Claude Hooten. "We had so much fun." When Jack was in the hospital recovering from one of his frequent illnesses, Ted and Hooten would visit and sing "Bill Bailey" and "Heart of My Heart." One summer, they started a waterskiing school in Newport Beach, California; Joe lent them the money for the boat. They called it the Ho-Ke School, adapting both of their names, and their port of call was "Harvard." With Ted's business sense, they made money, paying Joe back with cash to spare. Another summer, Ted worked as a forest ranger in California. To Hooten, those were years when Teddy was beginning to come into his own. "He was good-looking and smart, he had such a great smile and was so sincere."

Since boyhood, Teddy had loved playing jokes. He and Dick Clasby were famous among their Harvard friends for their "mind-reading" card trick, with which they fooled so many brainiacs. Their secret: a system of verbal signals to each other that eventually narrowed the field down to the one card. "We had classmates thinking we were psychic," says Clasby.

On weekends, Teddy often took a bunch of friends to Hyannis Port for cookouts and touch football, and to dances with Wellesley girls. Teddy and Clasby would rate the girls they met: A through F. "He had a twinkle in his eye for pretty girls," says Clasby. As initiation into Pi Eta, a social club filled with jocks, both men had to come back from Radcliffe with bras: Ted, a size 42 and Clasby a checkered version. "We had girls at Radcliffe who were very good friends, so that was not a problem," Clasby says.

Like his brothers, Ted joined the Hasty Pudding Club and, as a senior, the Owl, a final club, one of several undergraduate clubs with membership limited to an elite few. (In 2006, he would resign from the Owl after news reports that the organization refused to admit women. The senator's membership came under scrutiny after he criticized Supreme Court nominee Samuel Alito Jr. for his membership in Concerned Alumni for Princeton, which opposed admitting women to the school.)

Ted, the good-sport loser in most battles with his big brothers, let his competitiveness shine at Harvard, both on and off the football field. Clasby, who earned nine varsity letters from Harvard and was an all-American football player, remembers Ted telling him that within five years, he'd beat him in the 100-yard dash. No chance, replied Clasby, who would later be named Harvard's greatest living athlete. Several years later, after they'd both graduated, they were skiing in New Hampshire. It was Clasby's first time on skis and it wasn't pretty. "I fell over trees, I broke the skis, I hurt my finger, I went down on my back," he says. Back at the lodge, Teddy saw his chance and challenged him to that 100-yard dash, then and there, and wouldn't take no for an answer. Clasby raced—uphill—with his ski boots on, one of them broken, and lost. He had to pay Teddy $10.

Ted's risk-taking extended to far more elaborate dares. At Winthrop House, he shared a small room with Carey, Carey in the top bunk, Kennedy the bottom. "We were as close as two peas in a pod," says Carey. One night, Carey was making too much noise, and Teddy remarked that he'd like to send him far away—perhaps to Egypt. But, he told Carey, you'd never go, even if I paid for the ticket.

The bet was on. It was a Monday, and the deal was that Carey had to leave by Friday. Ted would supply a one-way ticket. Carey swung into action. He went over to the Harvard student infirmary and got the necessary shots. He convinced the passport office that there had been a death in the family and he needed to get to Cairo, fast. Teddy, astonished, bought the plane ticket. "He didn't give in, he was a hard charger. He hated to lose a bet," says Carey, who believes the wager was $100.

Friday morning arrived, and there was Carey, with a towel on his head, and a packed bag in his hand. "I was trying to look like an Egyptian sheik." Pictures were taken, and Teddy and others drove Carey to Logan Airport. When Carey arrived at New York's Idlewild Airport, where he was to make the connection to Cairo, loudspeakers were paging him. It was Teddy on the phone, saying that the *Boston Globe* had gotten wind of the story and was going to break it.

"His brother Jack was a senator and his father had learned of it and he was wild," says Carey. "He controlled everything Ted did." But Carey wasn't ready to let his friend off the hook, not yet. He told Teddy he was headed for his connecting flight. Instead of flying to Cairo, however, he flew to Hartford, Connecticut, near his hometown of Westfield, Massachusetts, where he spent the weekend. As far as Teddy knew, his friend was bound for Egypt. "He was sweating bullets," Carey says.

There were other bets between the two. "I bet you can't hit a golf ball across the Charles River," Carey told him. Sure enough, Teddy did and Carey had to pony up the $5. Whenever he couldn't pay a bet, he'd shine Teddy's shoes for a week. More ambitiously, he once bet Teddy that he could outdo him in a speech assigned for their public speaking class. "All right, wise guy," said Teddy. "You're on." Each student had to give a 25-minute speech, and the professor would judge them. "I talked on the Yalta Conference," says Carey, who could not recall Ted's topic. Carey won, and Teddy had to pay up. "He went bananas about that. He didn't like to lose at anything."

During those Harvard years, Carey spent some time in Hyannis Port and sat at the table, wearing the required jacket and tie, listening to Rose, Joe, and Jack discuss politics. The house had only a modest liquor cabinet, and the boys weren't allowed to touch the hard stuff. "Teddy never drank much at Harvard, maybe a beer or so," says Carey. And every Wednesday night, Joe would call Teddy at Harvard. "You guys shut up!" Teddy would admonish, in an effort to hear his dad's words. Carey recalls a particularly hideous winter coat that Joe passed along to his son. "It was awful, a gray-green-mustard color," says Carey.

"Joe wouldn't wear it, but Teddy did. That coat probably weighed 30 pounds." Still, the dutiful son wore it only on weekdays, refusing to socialize in it on weekends.

On Wednesdays, the men would go to Bailey's Ice Cream shop in Harvard Square; Teddy said he had missed American ice cream while he was in the Army. Sometimes, Carey would have to pay. Teddy, like Jack before him, never seemed to have much money. It was a vestige of his privileged upbringing; someone else always carried the cash. He'd also borrow his roommate's shirts. One day, Carey realized he had no clean ones left. "Kennedy, what's going on? Where are my shirts?" he asked. They gathered up all the dirty ones and took them to the laundry. "All that stuff was always taken care of at his house," says Carey.

One summer, Carey worked construction in Alaska and brought back a secondhand wood-sided station wagon with a defective right door. Teddy borrowed the car for a date, and as he was turning a corner, the door popped open and out fell the young woman. "She didn't get hurt, but of course, it took the romance right out of things," says Carey. "He came back embarrassed." Ted, he said, was very popular with the girls, and had a special preference for those from Pine Manor Junior College, outside Boston. But he never had a serious girlfriend in college, preferring to play the field.

On the water, Teddy was also somewhat of a daredevil. One summer while at Harvard, he asked John Culver to be his first mate in the Nantucket Regatta. Culver, who was raised in Iowa, had never been on a sailboat. There's nothing to it, Teddy assured him as they drove to Hyannis Port. A storm was forecast for later that day, but Ted shrugged it off.

Culver wasn't as sanguine. "I'll never forget it. We went into the kitchen and the cook made us some salmon salad sandwiches. I had never heard of them before or since. I had two and a quart of milk." When Culver first laid eyes on the *Victura*—Jack's former boat, whose name means victory in Latin—he could not believe it. The 26-foot wooden sailboat seemed tiny against the huge waves. "The sky was nothing but black, and there was lightning," Culver says. "The two of us get in this boat and we shove off for Nantucket. He's at the tiller telling me what to do with the sails. He's yelling at me in this storm and I thought I was with some mad dog. The wind is unbelievable and of course I get deathly sick, losing my lunch." The two arrived at Nantucket at about 11:00 P.M. and slept in the boat, piling up some cushions in the three inches of water. The next morning, they went into town to recruit a third crew member.

Meanwhile, Joe Kennedy had arrived with some friends on his yacht to watch the race. Culver was thrilled and relieved to see the large, well-appointed vessel. "The plan was, when the race was over, we'd have a hot meal in the comfort of this large yacht," he says. The yacht would then tow the smaller sailboat back to Hyannis Port.

"We see the ambassador's boat and we come alongside it," Culver says. By this time, it was 4:00 P.M., and he and Ted had been aboard the *Victura* for twenty-four hours. "The ambassador has a megaphone and he yells down, 'Boys, I'm sorry to have to tell you this. The captain says conditions won't allow us to pull you back home.' I felt like one of those shipwrecked guys in World War II." Joe then lowered some hot clam chowder for the boys. Culver chuckles at the memory. "Ted claims to this day that I grabbed it, ripped the vacuum pack off and just guzzled it, and he didn't get any of it."

The young men sailed back to Hyannis Port and finally spied the lights of the Kennedy house. But the wind had completely died, and they had to hop off the boat "and push and kick it to shore" several hundred yards. "I could taste seaweed for a week," says Culver.

Culver and Clasby spent a lot of time with Teddy in Hyannis Port, and both remember not just the stream of Kennedys who came through at all times, but the way that Rose, in all the chaos, imposed her strong sense of religion on the family. Rose told her youngest son if he went to Mass seven straight Fridays, he was guaranteed to go to heaven. "So Ted and I went seven Fridays, and that was it," says Clasby. "That was the deal."

In the Kennedy family, Teddy said, you learned "the Glorious Mysteries" at an early age, along with sailing, tennis, and swimming. Through their mother's teachings, Ted learned the meaning of the rosary, the meditations of Cardinal Newman, and the Stations of the

Cross. The meditations were the cardinal's directives for contemplating Christian issues of faith, and the Stations of the Cross in Catholic churches depict the last hours of Jesus' life. It was faith that sustained Rose Kennedy through her devastating losses, and she passed that faith along to her children. "Through her we have learned to share the joy and bear the sorrow, the times to laugh and times to cry," Ted wrote upon her death. "She taught us early that the birds will sing when the storm is over, that the rose must know the thorn, that the valley makes the mountain tall."

Rose would also seek to instill religious values in her grandchildren. Kathleen Kennedy Townsend, Bobby's oldest child, described Rose's fervor in an essay after her death. One weekend, the young Kathleen stayed with Rose in her New York apartment. Rose had cooked Cream of Wheat cereal. "After I spilled my portion on the floor, she insisted that I eat it, noting that 'You have to eat six packs of dirt before you go to heaven,' " Kathleen said. Her brother Joe noted that Rose attended two Masses a day, always sitting in the pew on the left, three-quarters of the way up the aisle at St. Francis Xavier in Hyannis. Bobby Jr. said she paddled her own kids "for each grammatical or theological error." When Rose called them to say grace before meals, they'd shout, "Grace!" and then hide beneath the table to avoid a swat.

But the teachings stuck with Ted. Decades later, confronting his own children's battles with cancer, he would follow his mother's example of going alone to Mass and sitting silently in the pews, as if submitting himself to God's will. A lonely pilgrimage to church was a ritual in happy times as well. Every August, a group of Ted's friends, including Culver, would spend a sailing holiday with him in Hyannis Port, a special reunion that the men would cherish more and more as they entered their seventies.

But amid the fun and remembrances, Ted would always carve out time to attend Mass at St. Francis Xavier, by himself.

CHAPTER
4

POLITICS WAS IN Ted Kennedy's blood, and in his head. It was his grandfather's love, his father's ambition, his eldest brother's dream, his brother Jack's calling. Bobby, too, would surrender to it. Ted did so at any early age.

Clasby remembers that shortly after Ted returned to Harvard, he was scheduled to make a speech to the Boys and Girls Club of Boston on behalf of his family. He rehearsed in front of Clasby, who egged him on to do better. "Why don't you get up on the pool table and make the speech?" he asked. Teddy promptly climbed up and delivered it. "He kept practicing it, and it was very, very good," Clasby recalls. "If it wasn't his first political speech, it was close to it."

But politics was more than speech making, and Joe Kennedy wanted his sons to be world-class statesmen.

In 1956, Teddy graduated from Harvard and spent the summer exploring North Africa, as Jack and Bobby had. Kennedys didn't travel merely for fun, but with a purpose, experiencing the wider world. They took notes, wrote letters home about their experiences, and reported back to the dinner table. Rose was a travel fanatic and passed it on to Teddy. Her parents had taken her and her sister Agnes on a tour of Europe when she was eighteen. A few years later, she and Agnes took a train trip out west, riding donkeys in the Grand Canyon. At age sixty-seven, she would go skiing with Teddy in Mont Tremblant; since everyone else skied, she thought it was time she tried it, too. On her eightieth birthday, she would go to Ethiopia.

Teddy, always eager to emulate his brothers, recalled that by the time he was five, Joe Jr. had been to Russia, and by the time he was six, Jack had been to Poland. "I remember a lot of exciting talk about these and other places, and I guess I knew that when I was old enough I'd get my chance to travel on my own, too," he said.

For his trip to North Africa, Teddy obtained a press pass from the International News Service—Joe was a close friend of William Randolph Hearst, who owned the agency—and filed some stories from the field. Joe had set him up with notables, as he had Ted's brothers. Ted visited Morocco, Algiers, and Tunis, meeting the Moroccan ambassadors to Spain and the United States. He spent two days in the mountains with the Berbers, sleeping in tents. He followed a sultan to back villages and countryside "inhabited by the most rugged-looking individuals I have ever seen, all of whom are carrying about ten guns," he wrote to his father. He witnessed the incipient glimmer of nationalism in that part of the world and later claimed that he had influenced Jack, who made a speech in the Senate urging the French colonial powers to leave Algeria.

Ted had considered applying to Stanford Law School, but Joe wanted to keep his son back east. So in the fall of 1956, he enrolled in law school at the University of Virginia, Bobby's alma mater. At Virginia, Teddy pored over his books, writing to his father: "Am holding on down here on my 12-hour-a-day schedule." Good grades still didn't come easily to him, and despite his hard work he would end up just below the middle of his class.

The very first day of class, he met John Tunney, a top-notch student with a prodigious work ethic. "He'd gone to Harvard, I'd gone to Yale, but instantly I thought that this fellow was going to be one of my really great friends. He was very friendly, very outgoing. He had a warmth to him," recalls Tunney. Like Kennedy, Tunney was from a famous family. His father was the former heavyweight boxing champion Gene Tunney, whose fights with Jack Dempsey electrified the country in the 1920s. The younger Tunney and Teddy became inseparable, going to the law library before class and after. They'd break for dinner, then return to the library. "We were working ferociously hard," says Tunney. "I think the vast majority of us were scared to death we were going to get kicked out." At Thanksgiving, Teddy confessed that he didn't understand the tax material as well as he should; he was going to his father's New York office to consult with an accountant. He invited Tunney along, and both survived their exam.

Like Bobby before him, Ted was elected head of the Student Legal Forum, responsible for bringing illustrious speakers to the school. Because of the Kennedy name, he was able to recruit Senator Hubert Humphrey, labor leader Walter Reuther of the United Auto Workers — and his brother Bobby, among others.

At Virginia, Ted played hard, too. Once, he and Tunney were tossing the football around. "Now, you try to run by me, then I'll try to run by you," Ted said. Tunney, who thought they were playing touch, grabbed the ball and started running. "Teddy just tackled me and I went head over heels," he recalls. "I said, 'What the hell are you doing?' He said, 'We're playing tackle, didn't you realize it?' " No, Tunney replied indignantly, he did not.

"Are you afraid?" Teddy asked, half in jest. "You can throw it at me." The men spent the next half hour roughly tackling each other. Tunney, who was quite competitive himself, called it "a ritual by fire toward friendship." The two became roommates, renting a house a few miles from campus.

In the summer of 1958, after their second year in law school, the men attended the Hague Academy of International Law in the Netherlands, where they received academic credit for classes they took. Before classes started, they traveled in the south of France, Italy, and Spain, running with the bulls in Pamplona and attending bullfights. It was the perfect summer for two adventurous and privileged young men. "We were trying to live out our Ernest Hemingway fantasies," says Tunney. "We'd take a brandy now and then and talk about the great thoughts of western civilization."

The next summer, they decided to climb the Matterhorn. As a member of the Yale Mountaineering Club, Tunney had experience with ropes and belaying but Ted did not. They hired two guides and roped up with them, climbing out over a sheer rock face some 3,000 feet up. At one point, the guide in the lead climbed over an outcropping of rock; Teddy was to go next, followed by Tunney. Tunney was sitting on a narrow ledge, waiting his turn. "He called for Teddy to climb and I could tell very quickly he was in trouble because he was using too much physical strength and not enough in the way of skillful deployment of his body weight," says Tunney.

Tunney moved into a crevice and braced himself, while the guide pulled the rope tight in case Teddy were to fall. "Teddy falls and he swings out maybe three or four feet from the side of the mountain," says Tunney. "He was hanging there two or three minutes and he was obviously shaken up, but he gave no indication of panic at all, none." Pulled to safety, he perched next to Tunney on the ledge, withdrew some cheese and an orange from his pack, and talked about the tale he would tell when he got home. Tunney was impressed. "You learn a lot about a friend . . . when you see them in those kinds of conditions. He was a person of confident courage and he handled his situation just brilliantly and with aplomb. He could have been killed easily if he had panicked."

In Charlottesville, the two had their schedule down to a science: study, class, lunch, nap, study, walk, dinner, study. During dinner, they'd frequently have major disagreements on political issues. Tunney was then a Republican, much more conservative than the liberal Teddy. (Later, he would serve as a Democratic senator from California.) "We'd cover the entire waterfront with our discussions," says Tunney, who had no doubt that Teddy was bound for a political career. "It was just a question of when. I don't think either one of us thought it would be so early, but then his brother became president."

At the beginning of their second year in law school, Teddy asked Tunney if he wanted to enter the moot court competition with him. There would be five elimination rounds over a period of a year and a half. Sure, said Tunney, who "didn't think there was a chance we'd ever win the damn thing." But with his Milton Academy debate team skills and the few political speeches he'd made, Teddy turned out to be a skilled public speaker. After their first round, one of the judges told Tunney: "You know, you won this case because of Teddy Kennedy's speaking skills. You've got to improve your skills if you're going to move along in this competition." The men kept advancing through four rounds until the final arguments on Law Day of their third year.

The arguments took place in front of 400 graduates of the law school. The case raised the question of whether a corporate CEO was denied his freedom of speech rights by the Taft-Hartley Act that forbade him to make a political contribution. The three judges were the Lord Chancellor of England, Supreme Court Justice Stanley Reed, and federal appeals judge Clement F. Haynsworth (whose nomination to the Supreme Court both Ted and Tunney would later oppose). In the audience were Bobby and their sister Pat, who had come to cheer on their brother. When the winning team was announced, Teddy pounded his fist on the table in vindication. He and Tunney had beat fifty other teams, and it would remain the high point of his academic career.

"And of course, Teddy just loved the fact that he had won and Bobby had not," says Tunney. Just as important was a note Teddy got from Joe, who couldn't resist a family comparison: "You did a great job winning that event. Scholastically, it certainly fits with anything anybody has ever done before—including your father!" For once in Ted's life, he had done it all on his own, without his father's help. He had always understood the importance of winning, but he was only beginning to develop the famous work ethic that would later distinguish his career.

At Virginia, Ted and Tunney didn't just study. They had parties "that went down in the annals," as Tunney puts it. The two men lived on Barracks Road in Charlottesville, "just made for two young men who loved to speed because it had turns," says Tunney. "You could really pretend you were [race-car driver] Juan Fangio. We both got speeding tickets. But we never drank and got into a car."

Teddy's fast driving had long been noted by his friends: Ted Sorensen, JFK's speech writer, remembers riding back from Cape Cod to Boston with Teddy, then a Harvard student. "It was the first time in my young life that I realized when cars coming from the other direction blink their lights at you, it means there's a trooper up ahead and you ought to slow down," says Sorensen.

After one police chase while in law school, with speeds up to 90 mph, Teddy was charged with reckless driving and driving without a license, which he had left at home. The arrest seemed to revive Joe's doubts about his youngest son, erasing some of the good will generated by his moot court victory.

"If you're going to make the political columns," wrote his father, "let's stay out of the gossip columns." Joe, once again using his connections, managed to keep the arrest out of the news for several weeks. Then he released it just after he gave the wire services the news that Teddy was going to head Jack's 1958 Senate campaign. As so often happened with the Kennedys, the positive story had the effect of blunting the negative one.

CHAPTER
5

Joe and Rose soon decided that it was time to rein in their free spirit; he should have a wife. Jack had frustrated his parents by waiting well into his thirties and his Senate career before finally marrying the beautiful and elusive Jacqueline Bouvier. Bobby had married young, and his wife—the athletic, competitive Ethel—was already producing a large family. In this respect, at least, Joe and Rose wanted Ted to follow Bobby's example, not Jack's.

At the start of Ted's second year in law school, the family went to Manhattanville College in Purchase, New York, to dedicate a sports complex they had built in memory of Kathleen. There, Ted's sister Jean, a Manhattanville alumna, introduced him to Joan Bennett, a senior at the Catholic women's school. "I was not intimidated because I had never heard of the Kennedys before," recalls Joan, a sheltered young woman who had grown up in a comfortable Republican home. "No one had ever heard of the Kennedys outside Massachusetts. Jack was just a lowly junior senator."

Still, the big, handsome Ted made quite an impression on his own. "He was tall and he was gorgeous," Joan remembers. She was quiet, blond and blue-eyed; a self-described innocent. Ted was evidently impressed, too, asking her and her roommate to drive him to the airport so he could fly back to UVa. He called the next day, and every night after that.

Joan had almost missed that fateful meeting. She had skipped the gym dedication, where Ted delivered the keynote address, and was in her room studying. Her roommate returned and warned her that if she missed the reception for seniors that followed the ceremony, she'd get in trouble with the nuns. So she got up and went over—mostly, she says, to meet Cardinal Spellman, the head of the Catholic archdiocese of New York. Many of the Kennedy women, including Rose and Ethel, had attended Manhattanville. The school was run by nuns from the Order of the Sacred Heart, and the girls had to abide by strict curfews and other rules. Eunice, who was on the tennis team, was once sent back to her room to change clothes when she appeared on the court in shorts: she had to put on a skirt.

Joan and Ted's first real date was on the weekend after Thanksgiving. Thanksgiving in Hyannis Port was sacrosanct in the Kennedy family: you didn't dare make other plans. "It was a command performance for his father," says Joan. "Everyone had to be there." That Saturday after the celebration, Teddy and Pat left Hyannis Port for New York. He picked Joan up at her Bronxville home, and they met Pat for lunch at the St. Regis Hotel. Ted and Joan found they had some things in common: Teddy had spent his first several years in Bronxville, while his father worked on Wall Street. And Joan's grandfather had owned a house in Hyannis Port. Two of her grandfather's brothers had houses there, too. "So there was a Bennett compound before there was a Kennedy compound," Joan says. In 1930, her grandfather sold his house and bought property in New Hampshire.

The weekend visit to New York, with Pat along to chaperone, went well enough that Rose invited Joan to Hyannis Port, where so many Kennedy dates had been vetted. It was just the three of them— Ted, Joan, and Rose—and they ate every meal together each day. Joan, a gifted pianist, played for Rose, and Rose played some, too. Rose, Joan thought, approved of her. "I think she was thrilled that her son liked a nice, Catholic, Manhattanville girl." Over the winter, the couple went skiing with others, never spending a night alone. "You know, in the 1950s, girls didn't go anywhere without a chaperone," Joan says. "In those days it was much more formal." She and Ted were allowed little more than chaste kisses until their wedding night.

Joan spent a weekend at Charlottesville, and visited Ted at law school, and then Ted went up to the Bennett vacation home in New Hampshire. There were a dozen or so young people, and Joan's mother had bought easels and paints. The scenery was beautiful, and Ted, who hadn't painted much, proved himself to be pretty good with the brush.

In the late summer, Ted proposed to her on the beach at Hyannis Port, awkwardly mumbling: "What do you think about our getting married?" He also asked Joan's father, Harry Bennett, a wealthy advertising executive, for her hand in marriage. Tongue in cheek, Bennett replied: "Can you support my daughter in the manner to which she is accustomed?" (Joe Kennedy asked Joan a question, too: "Do you love my son?") But the truth was, the couple really didn't know each other very well. They had never discussed politics, the Kennedy family's great ambition. In fact, Joan says, there really were no deep talks at all.

Rose, from the Ritz in Paris, wrote a nice note upon hearing their news—but she got Joan's name wrong. "Dearest Connie," she wrote, "How delighted I was to hear on the telephone yesterday the wonderful news about your engagement to Teddy. I had hoped he would win you from the moment I first met you at the Cape." Joan would later reason that her mother-in-law mistakenly wrote "Connie" because she was thinking of actress Constance Bennett, who had a sister named Joan. (Constance Bennett, in fact, had married the ex-husband of actress Gloria Swanson, with whom Joe Kennedy had had a long affair.) If Joan thought that life as Rose's daughter-in-law would be easy, the mistaken name on the letter might have been good reason not to make that assumption.

As the wedding date approached, Joan told her father she was a bit nervous about it all. Harry Bennett spoke to Joe about delaying the wedding. But Joe was adamant: the wedding would go on. Ted and Joan were married November 29, 1958, by Cardinal Spellman at St. Joseph's Roman Catholic Church in Bronxville. Jack, the best man, wore a microphone because the Bennetts had hired a film crew to make a movie of the wedding. Later, watching the film, Joan would hear Jack whisper to his nervous brother that marriage didn't mean you had to be faithful. It was not the gift her father had planned, but it did serve as an early warning: like his father and Jack, Teddy would never bother living up to the fidelity part of the oath. During the reception, Rose found Ted and his two brothers watching the Army-Navy football game, and hurried them back to the party.

Nor was the honeymoon an auspicious start to the marriage. The first couple of nights were okay; Ted and Joan spent them at the Kennedys' house in Palm Beach. They stayed in Jack's bedroom, the only one on the ground floor, since he had so badly injured his back in the war. "You could walk right out to the pool and beach," Joan says. Joe had arranged for them to fly to Nassau, where they would stay with his old wartime friend, Lord Beaverbrook. "It wasn't very romantic, because we had to have breakfast, lunch and dinner with this old man," recalls Joan. "We had to eat what he liked to eat. I remember one day we had only a baked potato for lunch."

Then Lord Beaverbrook decided it would be romantic for Ted and Joan to stay on a small island he owned, all by themselves. He had his boatman take the couple over and drop them off. It was even worse than the manor. Bugs of all kinds, including mosquitoes and spiders, infested the tiny house. There was no air conditioning. It was hot as a furnace. "It was the most miserable day and a half of our lives," says Joan. "All we did was scratch ourselves. It was so awful, we just laughed. That was our honeymoon."

Three weeks before the wedding, Jack had won reelection to the Senate against an obscure candidate, Vincent Celeste, with an unprecedented 74 percent of the vote. It was Teddy's political baptism: Joe had tapped the 26-year-old to be chairman of the campaign. What Teddy lacked in experience he made up for in enthusiasm, crisscrossing the state in pursuit of votes, going to union halls and factory gates. Joe's plan had been to make this election the largest landslide in Massachusetts history, the better to position Jack for a 1960 presidential run.

Unlike his brothers, Teddy seemed to revel in the hand-shaking and backslapping of life on the campaign trail. "One of his abiding strengths was that he genuinely liked talking to people," says Gerard Doherty, who ran signature drives with Ted. "He'd talk to telephone poles if he could, whereas Bobby and Jack were a little more uncomfortable."

Teddy was only nominally in charge of the campaign. His main job, says Doherty, was to make sure the Kennedy organization had good field workers throughout the state. In those days, the candidates put out tabloids filled with their photos and positions. The papers would be given to campaign workers in each district, who would then distribute them to voters. Ted's task was to drop by the workers' homes and check in their garages; if he saw stacks of the papers sitting there, he'd know they weren't doing their job.

Together, Ted and Doherty would also go door to door and ask for votes. "Would you consider voting for John Kennedy? Will you sign a pledge of support for him?" Teddy was great at it. "He was the chief signature getter in the world," says Doherty. "Particularly if someone would give him a hard time, he'd spend a lot of time with them." If he had to sing in a bar, he'd sing. If he had to dance an Irish jig, he'd dance. And the workaholic Kennedys expected their staffers to exert themselves every bit as much as they did.

Jack had his own routine on the campaign trail, according to Doherty, and it was one that Teddy emulated. Jack insisted that they work very hard, but take from 3:00 to 5:00 P.M. off each day. Because of his bad back, Jack would find his way to a worker's home and ask if he could use their tub for a relaxing bath. In Jack's case, it was a medical necessity—easing his chronic back pain. But Teddy adopted it just to follow the rhythms of his adored big brother. "He'd recharge his motor and be ready again at 5:00," says Doherty.

Joe was impressed by his youngest son's flair on the trail and often remarked that he was the most natural politician in the family. Still, he was considered the kid brother, the understudy, the one who campaigned on behalf of others. It wasn't until the 1960 election that plans for Teddy, directed largely by his father, began to take shape. Alone with Jack after the victory party in 1958, Ted lifted a glass and said: "Here's to 1960, Mr. President—if you can make it." Without missing a beat, Jack replied: "And here's to 1962, *Senator* Kennedy, if *you* can make it."

Ted Carey helped out on Jack's 1960 campaign and remembers

Teddy talking about running for his brother's Senate seat, should Jack win the presidency. At the time, Teddy was twenty-eight, two years younger than the minimum age required to run for the office. "I said, 'Ted, you don't think you're going to be elected so young, do you?' " Carey recalls. "And he said something to the effect that, 'I can't escape the fact that I'm a Kennedy. I think I can win.' And you know, the crowds were there to see Ted Kennedy. The Kennedy mystique was already there."

After law school graduation in 1959, Ted and Joan moved to Boston, where he studied for the Massachusetts bar exam. But he soon told Joan she was a distraction to his studies and sent her to visit his father in the south of France. Joe was on the Riviera, where the family had often stayed. For ten days, Joan and Joe got to know each other.

"He was adorable," recalls Joan. Every night, the two would sit in lounge chairs overlooking the Mediterranean and listen to concerts on the BBC. Both of them loved classical music, and Ted was thrilled that the two got along so well. "He was such a sweetheart," Joan says. "He was a hugger, he'd even hug his sons." Manly handshakes, not warm hugs, were the norm between fathers and sons in the 1950s and 1960s. But until his father died, Teddy always kissed him on the cheek.

Still, Joan's relationship with her in-laws would remain a bit formal. Until she gave them grandchildren, she always opened her letters to them: "Dear Mr. and Mrs. Kennedy."

In August, after he'd taken the bar exam, Ted and Joan went on a real honeymoon to South America. He wrote to his parents from Chile and described a happy, active trip. He and Joan had flown to Argentina to get in a final week of skiing before starting up the coast. The locals had suggested they go by bus and boat through the lake and mountain district, which was gorgeous in the summer. But Ted was there during the South American winter. "Evidently only the hardier souls attack it in the winter," he wrote. "It takes three days in which I spent most of the time pushing a truck load of Chileans through various mountain passes of the Andes, being shouted at in Spanish. Our trip across the lakes was like being on the windward rail of the *Victura* on a sail to Nantucket in February."

Joan, he wrote, was really good on skis. Ted himself was even better, though. He raced against the Chilean national champion, losing by only three-fifths of a second. "The competition down here doesn't compare with that of the U.S.," he concluded. Deeming the trip a "great success," Ted informed his parents that he'd lost some more weight. "I am sure it is because I haven't seen a glass of milk for six weeks." He was, he noted, "ready for most anything in September," and was nervously awaiting the results of his bar exam. He soon learned that he had passed, but Joe had plans other than the law for his youngest. He was busy orchestrating Jack's 1960 presidential campaign, and what better way to prepare Teddy for the rigors of national politics than to give him a prominent role? So Ted was assigned the thirteen western states, which were predominantly Republican. "Teddy's role was that of young kid who would do anything to get his brother elected," recalls Bob Healy, who was covering the campaign for the *Boston Globe*. "He once got bitten by a dog putting stickers on car windows."

Tom Oliphant, who later would become a columnist for the *Globe*, was a teenager living in California when Ted made an appearance on his brother's behalf. "My best friend and I started canvassing, doing 'Dollars for Democrats.' You had a registration list and you went to every Democrat and you asked for a dollar," he says. But in northern San Diego County, there were few Democrats. "It was so right-wing that they didn't have anybody working that part of the county," recalls Oliphant. Because they raised some money, the teenagers got to attend a party in San Diego at which Ted and Bobby both appeared. "There wasn't any question about who the boss was," says Oliphant. "Teddy was considered the extreme baby brother. He had no clout." Just two years later, Oliphant would be amazed at the way Ted had morphed into a confident candidate himself.

In the 1960 campaign, Teddy's strategy was to find out where the crowds were, and work them. "Teddy was a good barroom vote getter," says Healy. In Wisconsin, Teddy promised folks at a bar that he'd go off a ski jump if they'd support his brother. Soaring off a 180-foot jump, he managed to land on his feet. "It was an incredible feat for a guy who had never jumped before," Healy recalls. Ted's and Joan's first child, Kara, was born during the campaign for the Wisconsin primary; he returned to Bronxville, where Joan had delivered the baby, and then flew back to Wisconsin for several days.

Soon, Joan herself got into the act, and they'd go "delegate hunting," appearing at Democratic events to elicit support from local party leaders. She'd watched her sisters-in-law in action and seen how it was done. Joan also campaigned with Rose, who, like her father Honey Fitz, was a natural on the trail. In West Virginia, Joan famously went into a coal mine with Jack, wearing a suit and heels. The miners were more attentive to Joan than to Jack. From then on, the campaign was more cautious about where it sent Joan. After the election, JFK would give his campaign workers silver cigarette boxes. On Joan's, he had engraved: "Joan Kennedy—Too Beautiful to Use."

Teddy's said, "And the last shall be first," from the Gospel of St. Matthew.

Jack, who sometimes chafed at the restraints of the political spotlight, lived vicariously through his youngest brother and his beautiful wife. Rose once recalled attending a charity ball with Jack and Ted. One of the entertainers was "a rather scantily clad woman" who sang and then danced with some of the men. "To my consternation, I suddenly saw Jack urging Teddy to get up and dance with this entertainer, which was all Teddy needed to proceed," Rose said. She was concerned that a photographer might put a picture in the paper, "and that was the one thing I thought the Kennedy family did not need at that moment, because Jack was preparing for the presidential candidacy." Jack, she noted, loved having Teddy do "what he could and should not do himself."

Later, Joe would write Teddy that "If you want to go to nightclubs, do not expect to go into politics."

In the 1960 election, the western states were considered friendly turf for Republican nominee Richard Nixon, but Teddy welcomed the challenge of promoting his brother. In Montana he came out of a rodeo gate riding a bucking bronco, holding on for five seconds before being tossed off. "I told him he'd get his picture in *Life* magazine and he got a whole halfpage spread," says Claude Hooten, Ted's Harvard friend. The other half of the page featured Nixon's running mate, Henry Cabot Lodge, with his sleeves rolled up, wearing a tie, on the beach.

Hooten and his wife lived with Ted and Joan and baby Kara briefly in San Francisco while on the campaign trail. But mostly, Hooten remembers the long days on the stump. They'd be up by 4:00 A.M., hit some outpost, do the college campuses, the plant gates, the teas. "He's the hardest working man I've ever known," says Hooten. The two lived on fast food, and weighed in at 207 (Ted) and 208 (Hooten). Though Hooten went on a diet and lost about 16 pounds, Ted did not.

During the nomination process, Wyoming had given JFK a boost with his victory in the state caucuses. Teddy hoped the delegates would repeat their feat and be the ones who officially handed his brother the majority of delegates from the floor. To that end, he'd flown into the western state seven times before the convention that summer. On the floor, he worked the Wyoming delegates hard. If they threw their weight fully behind his brother, he told their chairman, Wyoming could have the distinction of being the state that clinched the nomination for Jack Kennedy. Robert Shrum, Teddy's longtime political consultant, recounted what happened. "Teddy said, 'You can do it, you can be the people who do it.' And suddenly the chairman of the delegation grabs the microphone and says, 'Wyoming's what will make a majority.' And the convention went crazy." According to the *Philadelphia Inquirer*, Pat Kennedy "tossed her hat in the air, and Teddy Kennedy grabbed the Wyoming standard and waved it high." But in the general election, despite Ted's energetic efforts, Jack lost all but three of the western states that Ted had been assigned to oversee: New Mexico, Nevada, and Hawaii.

That night, November 8, the Kennedy family gathered at Hyannis Port, shuttling among the various houses in the compound owned by the younger generation. Jackie, who was eight months pregnant with John Jr., remained at Jack's and her house. The returns were razor-close, and at one point, Jack took a walk by himself on the beach that had sustained him through so many trials.

Rose went to bed late that night, believing that the tide was in

Jack's favor. In the wee hours, several of the Kennedy siblings retreated to the kitchen for a snack. Jack then left by the kitchen door, cutting across Bobby's yard to his own house for some sleep. The Secret Service had arrived and closed off the houses from the public; it appeared that Jack had won. The agents followed him closely to his house while a couple of his sisters called out: "Good night, Mr. President."

But it wasn't until later that morning that Jack was declared the winner. The family piled into a caravan of cars to go to the U.S. Armory in Hyannis, where he was to make his victory speech. Joe stayed on the porch, cherishing the moment. Having been such a big part of his son's success, he didn't want to share in the limelight. At the last minute, Jack realized what was going on, got out of the car, and insisted that Joe accompany the family.

Jack Kennedy had been elected the first Catholic president in the history of the United States. Soon, Bobby would become attorney general. And Ted was left to ponder his future.

CHAPTER
6

IT HAD BEEN the biggest test of his life, and by most measures he had failed.

Longing to be viewed as something besides someone's younger brother, Teddy had given everything he had to Jack's presidential campaign. In the period leading up to the Democratic National Convention, he found a way to shine, using his exceptional social skills and charm to line up support from delegates. But the task of translating that early support into election day results required a level of cold-blooded administrative discipline that eluded the youngest and breeziest Kennedy. When the votes were tallied, Jack Kennedy had lost all but three of the thirteen states that had been put under Teddy's command.

Teddy tried to take solace in the fact that most of those states had been Republican turf. But Jack, who managed to win the presidency with the slimmest popular vote margin in the twentieth century, was disappointed in Ted. Bobby, too, gave him a hard time about it. The *Denver Post* put the blame for Kennedy's loss in Colorado squarely on Teddy's broad but inexperienced shoulders. Not long after the election, the president-elect dispatched his kid brother to Africa, having him tag along with a couple of senators on a sixteen-nation fact-finding tour. A joke spread in political circles that JFK had exiled Teddy as penance for his election day performance.

"Can I come back," 28-year-old Ted wired his family in a post-election telegram, "if I promise to carry the Western States in 1964?"

The move was classic Teddy. One could almost see the faces of his brothers relaxing into smiles as they read the telegram. Growing up, Teddy had become expert in wielding his funny, fun-loving personality to paper over his failings. Even as he got older, he continued to lean heavily on that charm to get by. He still used them to break down Rose's stoical resistance by grabbing her from behind and saying, "How's my girl? Havin' any fun?" or using his baritone to belt out a comically overheated rendition of "Hooray for Hollywood." He would laugh broadly, and so would everyone else around. So it was no surprise that he would use humor to break the ice with his brothers and ease their disappointment.

But his telegram also masked a surprise: Ted Kennedy didn't really want to come home. At least not to Massachusetts.

Somewhere during the two years he spent on the campaign, making new friends and exploring the contours of the land clear across the country from the shores of Hyannis Port, Ted found himself with western sand in his shoes. Like a schoolboy showing his pal a secret path he'd discovered in the woods, Ted had delighted in whisking Joan around New Mexico, California, and Wyoming. In the natural beauty and wide open opportunity of these states, the young couple had glimpsed their future. They talked about how, after the campaign, they'd move there. He would practice law or maybe buy a newspaper to run, and, in a couple of years, launch a bid for office from his new perch.

As Ted became more serious about a move, New Mexico became the leading contender, given its gorgeous landscape and the fact that its two Democratic senators were getting old. It also helped that New Mexico was one of the three western states he'd helped his brother carry in the election. If his lifetime of unfavorable comparisons with his older brothers was only going to intensify now that one of them was about to become president and the other likely to become attorney general, Ted figured he'd have a better shot at being seen as his own man if he left the compound. As he once told an interviewer, "The disadvantage of my position is being constantly compared with two brothers of such superior ability."

Still, the 1960 campaign had helped Ted discover his natural political strengths—an ease with backslapping and a genuine love of people. These qualities were his inheritance from Honey Fitz every bit as much as Jack's intellectual curiosity and love of literature had been handed down to him by his mother. But there's a difference between being well-liked and being trusted with matters of consequence. Like Ted, Joan was prized in the family for her warm personality, but not taken all that seriously. So she had no trouble understanding what lay behind her husband's desire to find his destiny out west. "His main reason for wanting to move was a feeling that in a new state he would have to succeed or fail on his own," Joan would tell an interviewer in 1962. "Eventually, of course, we both decided that you can't run away from being the president's brother no matter where you go, and we came back to Massachusetts."

The realization was less gradual than that. Ted's wild west dreams were summarily shot down. "All I remember," Joan says, "is that Ted told me his father wanted him to run for the United States Senate." Specifically: the Senate seat from Massachusetts that Jack was vacating to become president. "We really wanted to go out west, but in those days, my late father-in-law said, 'You do this,' and you did that." Yet Joe's decision was grounded in sound political logic, according to Ted's sister Eunice. It would take too long for Ted to get known in a western state, and a place like California, which unlike Massachusetts had open-party registration, would put a Democrat like him at even more of a disadvantage.

Ted did not resist or complain to Joan about the old man's interference. Even though his father had ridden him hard as a child, there was no mistaking the deepening bond between them. Ted both recognized and appreciated the patriarch's willingness to put his thumb on the scale in Ted's favor. If his inclination to go west was motivated by a desire to measure up, Ted was willing to trust his father's judgment on how he might best do that. Now he embraced the opportunity to prove that Joe's faith in him had not been misplaced.

This sequence of events fit a wider pattern in the youngest Kennedy's life. He had repeatedly contemplated stepping off the path set by his brothers only to stay, time and again, faithfully on the Kennedy course—following one brother or another to Milton Academy, to Harvard University, and to the University of Virginia Law School. Now he would try the same with the United States Senate.

His brothers had different ideas this time. Though Jack had once joked about Teddy succeeding him in the Senate, he and Bobby, and especially their advisers, worried that Ted wasn't ready for it. It would be another two years before he even reached the minimum age for senators set by the Constitution. (That wouldn't prohibit him from running, though, because by the time a new election for JFK's Senate seat could be held in 1962, Ted would have turned 30.) Moreover, his brothers feared that, win or lose, his campaign would reflect poorly on the new president. But Jack agreed with their father that if Teddy was serious about running for office, he'd be foolish to throw his hat in any ring outside of Massachusetts.

The president-elect arranged for Ted to tag along on the African trip so he could burnish the foreign policy portion of his resume. But Jack told his brother that as soon as he returned he should begin getting himself better known around Massachusetts. "I'll hear whether you are really making a mark up there," he told Teddy. Jack and Bobby and their advisers thought Ted might be smarter to seek a lower-profile position in his first bid for office—state attorney general, congressman, or even governor. But each of those positions had problems. Jack's old congressional seat was occupied by the popular and effective Thomas "Tip" O'Neill, the attorney general position wasn't considered prestigious enough, and the governorship in Massachusetts at the time had very little power but lots of responsibility for presiding over the state's corrupt political system. Joe was adamant that Ted should aim high and seize the opportunity for the Senate while he had a clear shot.

A fawning 1957 *Saturday Evening Post* profile of the Kennedy family, which the patriarch had ginned up long before Jack's presidential ambitions were taken seriously outside of Massachusetts, predicted the future for his sons. "Fervent admirers of the Kennedys profess to see in their rise to national prominence the flowering of another great political family, such as the Adamses, the Lodges and the La Follettes," the article gushed. "They confidently look forward to the day when Jack will be in the White House, Bobby will serve in the Cabinet as Attorney General, and Teddy will be the senator from Massachusetts." After reading that passage, anyone who knew Joe well would have come to two inescapable conclusions. First, the "fervent admirers" making the bold prediction was, in fact, code for Joe himself. Second, the old man was going to do everything in his power to make that prediction come true. Clearly, he was seeing something in his youngest boy that others were overlooking. He told author Bela Kornitzer that Ted was "really the man to watch. Teddy is by far the best speaker in the family and the best-looking, too . . . I would like to see Ted in public life."

Upon his return from Africa, Ted followed Jack's advice, taking the copious notes he had jammed into several brown spiral notebooks during his tour and converting them into a speech he delivered around the state to every Kiwanis Club, PTA, and Temple Brotherhood that would lend him a microphone. While the decision on whether to run for the Senate in 1962 remained unsettled, Jack agreed to keep his brother's options open. He saw to it that his old college roommate, a non-threatening former mayor of Gloucester named Ben Smith, was appointed to warm the Senate seat for the two years until a new election could be held. If Ted decided to run in 1962, Smith could be counted on to step aside and offer his full backing.

Meanwhile, the patriarch put the wheels in motion for Ted's eventual campaign. Not long after Jack's inaugural, Ted took a job as an assistant district attorney in Boston under Suffolk County DA Garrett Byrne. Byrne's son, in turn, took a job in Washington under U.S. Attorney General Robert Kennedy. The annual salary for assistant district attorneys at the time was $5,000, but in a gesture of goodwill made possible by the million-dollar trust fund his father had given him, Ted accepted the job for just $1 a year. Fellow prosecutor Newman Flanagan recalls that because staffers were required to pay $50 annually into the pension system, the joke around the office was that the job cost Ted 49 bucks a year.

Despite being low man in office seniority, Ted found attention shadowing him wherever he went. He was, after all, the charismatic new president's handsome brother. At 6'2", he shared that famous Kennedy toothy smile, but he enjoyed facial features that were more angular than Jack's and more proportional than Bobby's. A subsequent *Saturday Evening Post* article by Stewart Alsop described Ted as "decidedly better-looking than his brothers, with the precisely balanced features of the old Arrow-collar ads." (In a prescient aside, Alsop continued, "There may come a time when he will have to worry about jowls, but there is still now on his rounded cheeks the blush and bloom of youth.")

The talk was rampant that it wouldn't be long before Ted would be topping some ballot in Massachusetts. On the eighth floor of the court building, there was a small room where two older matrons cared for the children of witnesses appearing in court. That's where Flanagan and Kennedy would chat over coffee most mornings. When they did, the matrons couldn't help but dote on Teddy, whom they adored. In February 1961, a run-of-the-mill driving-under-the-influence case drew a flock of lawyers to the spectators' gallery. The crowd was there to watch Ted Kennedy's first trial as a prosecutor.

Around the DA's office, Kennedy quickly earned a reputation as a hard worker who took his job seriously and made friends easily— someone who was comfortable with his celebrity. He worked just as hard after he left the office, keeping up with the responsibilities that continued to accrue to him as his father's grooming plan took shape. He was named president of the Joseph P. Kennedy Jr. Memorial Foundation and chairman of the 1961 Cancer Crusade. He took periodic fact-finding tours to Latin America and other foreign lands. And he toured the state with Francis X. Morrissey, a municipal judge from Charlestown and longtime errand man for Joe, who now helped Teddy make the acquaintance of every county commissioner and municipal clerk from Pembroke to Pittsfield. Teddy kept his father informed every step of the way.

"Dear Dad," he wrote, "Frankie [Morrissey] is keeping me on the go day and night. I think that the reaction has been quite good except for a few cynical old pros. I have found some old Irish stories that Grandpa use to tell which have really helped out during the octave of St. Patrick's Day. Love, Ted." After a trip through western Massachusetts, he attached a note to a clipped newspaper article about him. "Dear Dad, this fellow Abe Michelson is probably the most influential political writer in the Western part of the state. He gave me a few digs the last time around but this story isn't too bad. Love, Ted."

If Ted still harbored a desire to step out of the long shadow cast by his brothers, he showed no signs of that in public. He often began those set speeches to Kiwanis Clubs and the like with a joke about two brothers who go fishing together, one of whom scores a big catch and the other nothing. The next day the unlucky brother borrows his brother's pole and tackle and goes fishing alone, but again comes up empty. Disgusted, he gets ready to leave when a fish jumps out of the lake and asks, "Where's your brother?"

On the family front, Ted and Joan did make a break from the Kennedys in February 1961, but it was a far more modest one than moving to New Mexico or California. Instead of buying a summer home adjacent to the family's Hyannis Port compound, they bought a gray-shingled, four-bedroom place on a bluff on Squaw Island, about a mile away. They both loved being around the extended family but cherished the extra bit of breathing room allowed by their one-mile buffer. That summer, however, the president and the first lady rented singer Morton Downey's house across the street from Ted and Joan's place, after the Secret Service determined Jack's house in the compound could not be adequately secured. Because Downey's house had no access to the beach, Jack would cut through Ted and Joan's living room whenever he wanted to take a dip. Joan would voice mock offense, saying, "Jack Kennedy, where are your manners?" To which he would reply, "Joansie, I don't have to ask permission because I'm your brother-in-law. And also I'm the president of the United States."

Their close proximity also allowed Joan to bond with Jackie Kennedy. When Bobby's athletic wife, Ethel, and the Kennedy sisters were playing touch football with the men at the compound, Jackie and Joan would steal away—Jackie painting, Joan playing her classical piano.

The Kennedys had trouble understanding why anyone would opt for alone time and artsy pursuits when there was so much fun to be had competing with the clan. "They think we're weird," Jackie told Joan.

Meanwhile, Ted kept plugging along with his unofficial Senate campaign, trying to line up support. But he was doing it without the muscle of his brothers' machine. The advisers around Jack and Bobby looked at untested Ted and they saw only trouble. He could lose the election and puncture the bubble of Kennedy invincibility in Massachusetts. He could win and sully the image of JFK, from inspiring leader for a new generation to greedy agent of a dynastic power grab for his family. And if he were to win, he would have to beat Edward McCormack, the popular state attorney general and certain candidate for Senate. McCormack happened to be the favorite nephew of the childless U.S. Speaker of the House, John McCormack, whose support President Kennedy needed to get his ambitious agenda through Congress.

Presidential adviser Ted Sorensen says Jack was particularly sensitive about the nepotism charge—that it wasn't enough to have his brother Bobby as attorney general, now he needed his kid brother in the Senate? Jack also knew that his old college roommate Ben Smith had taken to the Senate seat he was warming and was planning an ambitious barnstorming tour around Massachusetts in the hopes of building support for his own run in 1962, if the Kennedys gave their assent. In the end, according to Sorensen, JFK accepted the inevitability of Ted's Senate run. The president was already opposing his father on too many fronts in his new administration. And, on family matters at least, even the president answered to a higher authority.

Yet Bobby remained skeptical. In the summer of 1961, Ted wrote to inform his father that Eddie McCormack had told a mutual friend he doubted Ted was going to run for the seat. That's because at a luncheon in Washington, Bobby had publicly showered McCormack with praise. "When I heard this, I ran down brother Bob and he said, 'What's so bad about that?'—he would say some nice things about me too," Ted wrote. "So you can see what I am up against here, Dad."

Most seasoned pols in Massachusetts were staying on the sidelines

in order to avoid offending either one of the state's two most powerful political families. Ted turned again to Morrissey, his father's sup-
plicant, who in turn sought help from a young state representative
from Charlestown by the name of Gerard Doherty. In the fall of 1961,
Doherty organized a lunch for Kennedy with a group of young state
lawmakers at Boston's swankiest restaurant, Locke-Ober, to try to line
up more support. Most of the lawmakers had never eaten at Locke-
Ober, so they watched for cues from each other when it came time
to order. All of them dutifully ordered club sandwiches, which were
comfortably priced at $1.85. Then the waiter came to Billy Bulger, a
recently elected state representative from South Boston. He turned
heads by ordering Lobster Savannah, which at $10 was the most ex-
pensive item on the menu. In between bites of his sandwich, Doherty
went around the table, asking each lawmaker how many delegates he
thought he could deliver for Kennedy. When it was his time to speak,
Bulger hemmed, "I can't be with you, Ted. The McCormacks are my
neighbors." Doherty could see the frustration in Kennedy's eyes, so
he tried to salvage the situation, asking Bulger if they could at least
keep talking about the possibility of his support. Just then the bill arrived. Ted—who at this point, according to Doherty, was required to
go through his sister Eunice for money for the race—took one look at
the total and cracked to Doherty, "I don't know whether we should try
to persuade him. I don't think we can afford to feed him."

A few days before Christmas 1961, Joe Kennedy fainted on a golf
course in Palm Beach, Florida. He was driven in his golf cart back to
his winter estate and, when his condition worsened, whisked to the
hospital. It turned out to be a massive stroke. Ted rushed from Boston to Florida, bringing a vascular specialist with him. His brothers
came as well, but it was Ted who stayed at his father's bedside for three
straight nights. A priest was brought in to administer last rites. When
it became clear the patriarch would survive, but in an incapacitated
state, robbed of much of his mobility and most of his ability to speak,
the news was crushing to his children. As demanding as their father
had been with them—Ted once compared him to a blowtorch—and as
unscrupulous as he had been in other facets of his life, for his children

he had been both a rainmaker and a source of incredible love. That was especially true of Teddy. Now he had lost the benefit of his father's sure hand just when he needed it most.

With Ted's strongest ally silenced, many people expected him to drop his Senate plans. The Kennedy advisers in Washington certainly hoped he would. Yet inexperienced, undistinguished, untested Teddy chose to soldier on. Instead of making a name for himself in a new state as he had once hoped, he would cut his political teeth running for his brother's old seat, working out of his brother's old Beacon Hill apartment, and seeking the reflection of his brother's glow with the winking campaign slogan of "He Can Do More for Massachusetts."

CHAPTER
7

ON MARCH 11, 1962, Ted had his national coming out, appearing on NBC's *Meet the Press*. Confronted with the claim that his family was seeking too much power in Washington, he relied once again on his sense of humor. "If you are talking about too many Kennedys," he said, "you should have talked to my mother and father at the time they were getting started." Three days later, in a news conference at his Beacon Hill home, Ted officially announced his candidacy, continuing to wield his wit to brush back criticism. "I am aware that my brother is the president and my other brother attorney general," he said, stressing that neither would campaign for him in Massachusetts. His sisters, he said, would "come for a visit and we won't keep them in a closet all the time."

The president did act early on to try to solve one of the most problematic aspects of Ted's candidacy. He sent Ted to meet with Tip O'Neill, who was close to the McCormacks, and asked him to deliver a message to the speaker. "I don't want to run against Eddie," Ted told O'Neill. "It's not good for the party. It's not good for the relationship in Washington. And we understand Eddie owes $100,000. We'll take care of his expenses. My father will see that he gets a good client. Anything that he's interested in, he can have—an ambassadorship or something of that nature." O'Neill said he took that message back to Speaker John McCormack. "John talked to Eddie and I talked to Eddie, and Eddie made the decision that he was going to run anyway."

Family and friends say Eddie McCormack, and especially his wife, felt he had earned the right to run for Senate, and did not want to step aside for someone whose only evident credential was his bloodline. In fact, the imbalance in experience would become the cornerstone of McCormack's campaign pitch. One of his pamphlets, called "The Qualified Candidate," listed in the left-hand column twenty-six of his credentials—the various posts he had held in government, from Boston City Council president to attorney general, and the accumulated achievements and accolades of his tenure. In the right-hand column, he listed Ted Kennedy's credentials, which consisted of just one entry—"Brother of the President"—and a whole lot of white space. In an effort to draw the support of the legions of Irish Catholic voters in Massachusetts who had President Kennedy's picture hanging on their kitchen walls, McCormack began pushing the slogan, "I back Jack, but Teddy isn't ready."

The most strident opposition to Kennedy's candidacy came from the intellectual community. Harvard Law School professor Mark De Wolfe Howe emerged as Teddy's most vocal critic, declaring him a "fledgling in everything except ambition." Kennedy also drew scorn and ridicule from liberal-leaning national media. Influential *New York Times* columnist James Reston wrote, "One Kennedy is a triumph, two Kennedys at the same time are a miracle, but three could easily be regarded by many voters as an invasion." A Chicago satirist cracked, "If Teddy wins, Laos won't be the only country with three princes."

Massachusetts liberals favored McCormack largely because of his civil rights record, which was surprisingly progressive considering he was the son of South Boston neighborhood powerbroker Edward "Knocko" McCormack. Burly, round-faced Knocko kept a chalkboard in his Southie bar listing the names of people he had personally banished, at times using ethnic slurs to describe the reason for their banishment, such as "Brought a Guinea to the bar." But Eddie had taken more of his cues on social issues from his uncle, the speaker, who was beloved in the Jewish community for his early support of Israel. (Many in the Jewish community distrusted Joe Kennedy Sr. for his resignation to Nazi aggression during his period as ambassador to England.) As attorney general, Eddie McCormack had created a groundbreaking state civil rights division and ended the practice of forcing defendants who had not yet posted bail to be kept in courtroom cages. In 1962, the same year he ran for Senate, he persuaded nearly two dozen attorneys general to sign on to an amicus brief favoring legal counsel for indigent defendants, which he submitted to the United States Supreme Court in the landmark *Gideon v. Wainwright* case. Among McCormack's eager campaign volunteers were future liberal standouts Michael Dukakis and Barney Frank.

The rejection of the youngest Kennedy by liberal intellectuals in Massachusetts was troubling for two reasons. Many of them had been enthusiastic supporters of Jack's, and many of them knew Teddy's secret. Chatter about how Ted had been kicked out of Harvard for cheating, proof in many minds of his inferior character and ability, finally forced JFK to intercede. The president summoned the *Boston Globe*'s top political writer, Bob Healy, to the White House, where he negotiated how the cheating news would be released. Healy resisted pressure to bury the revelation in a profile in the features section and insisted it be a page one story. But he and his *Globe* bosses did agree to blunt the impact of the revelation, using the softball headline of "Ted Kennedy Tells About Harvard Examination Incident." The article did not mention his transgression until the fifth paragraph and never once used the word "cheating." At the height of the negotiations, President Kennedy remarked, "Jesus, we're having more fucking trouble with this than we did with the Bay of Pigs." To which his adviser McGeorge Bundy, a former Harvard dean, replied, "Yes, and with just about the same results."

A few minutes before 7 o'clock one morning in March 1962, Gerard Doherty arrived at the Parker House in Boston. The fact that Doherty, a 33-year-old state lawmaker largely unknown outside his home base of

Charlestown, was emerging as Ted Kennedy's primary political adviser was evidence of the shaky state of the campaign. But Doherty, whose thick brownline glasses magnified his eyes, was exactly the kind of operative the Kennedys prized: ambitious but loyal, street-tough yet book smart. Although he had made it to Harvard and become fluent in Russian, he stayed rooted to his native world of struggling Irish Catholic laborers. He fit the part so well that he even looked something like a young Joe Kennedy Sr., albeit with a much fuller head of hair.

In preparation for the Democratic state convention in June that would endorse one of the candidates for Senate, Doherty had invited the delegates from Boston to a breakfast meeting. But when he stepped into the room a few minutes before it was scheduled to begin, he was the only soul there; no one had come to see Ted, probably because the McCormacks had just about locked up the Boston delegation for Eddie. Doherty hustled outside where he found Ted getting out of a cab.

"Teddy, I screwed up," Doherty said, thinking fast. "I thought it was at 7 o'clock, but it's 8:15. Why don't you go for a walk."

After Ted left, Doherty phoned anyone he could think of from Charlestown and pleaded with them to come and fill the room. After he delivered the talk, Kennedy smiled to Doherty, "That was terrific! What a great reception."

Doherty needed to do whatever he could to pump up Teddy's sagging confidence. Though Kennedy had an easy way with people, his first stretch on the campaign trail had been marked by stiffness and uncertainty. He was not deaf to the withering criticism that had been leveled at him. In fact, he seemed to know he was overreaching, like a teenager with a fake ID straining to appear older while standing at the liquor store counter. He sometimes performed with the hesitancy of a man who believed most of what his critics had to say about him.

With Ted's brothers and their advisers largely out of reach, and his father incapacitated, Doherty looked around for other family members who could serve as advocates. Ted's brother-in-law Steve Smith, Jean's husband, had inherited from Joe oversight of the family business operations. But because he had also taken over the patriarch's responsibilities as family fixer—the man who could make problems of all sizes simply go away—Smith was careful to maintain a low profile. Both Doherty and Ted were surprised to find a disarmingly effective surrogate closer to home: Joan.

Innocent, sheltered Joan Bennett had simply not been prepared for the hard-driving Kennedy culture. She and Ted hadn't had the chance to get to know each other that well before their wedding day and had spent more time apart than together ever since. She had just delivered their second child, Teddy Jr., who joined young Kara. But it was already clear that she didn't have the constitution to meet Ted's ambition to have a huge family, matching the nearly one-a-year output that Ethel Kennedy was delivering to Bobby. Even though Joan had developed more of a bond with Jackie Kennedy, given their shared interest in the arts and aversion to contact sports, there was distance there as well. Although Jackie outshone her in elegance and international élan, Joan was prettier in a wholesome blond kind of way—so much so that Jack Kennedy nicknamed her "The Dish." Yet Joan lacked the toughness and wariness that girded the first lady's polished presentation. Joan's naivete—she would reveal to a journalist such private matters as Jackie's fondness for wigs and the bad back that prevented Jack from lifting his kids—caused consternation within the family.

But Ted's feeling of being on his own in 1962 provided an opportunity for Joan to prove her value as a partner in politics. "Let's show them, Joansie," he told her. And she responded with aplomb, displaying stamina and charm all along the trail. Doherty, who was hoping to see Ted outgrow his initial stiffness in front of crowds, noticed how quickly voters warmed up to unpretentious, candid Joan. So he put her in heavy rotation. She focused mostly on outreach to women, who, judging from some of Ted's comments during the campaign, were not a group he took as seriously as he should have. Asked about how he decided what his speeches would include, he told *Esquire* magazine, "You can't give women too much. They get confused. Besides, if they've seen you on TV, they can't think anything bad about you."

Regardless, Joan relished the chance to be in common cause with her husband. "It was just us kids," Joan says now. "And it was one of the happiest years of my life."

The early stretch of the campaign was nothing if not rocky, with the pushback remaining strong from the academic community. At one Harvard function, Ted was called out by a classmate who barked, "You're an insult to our class, running for this." Kennedy replied calmly, "Well, that certainly is a point of view." Although he was shaken by the criticism, Ted in time learned to float above it and keep plugging away. Ted's driver, a hard-edged South Boston native named Jack Crimmins, encouraged Kennedy to ignore the eggheads. About one, Crimmins cracked, "That professor is as soft as a sneaker full of shit."

But others in the campaign knew they needed to draw at least some of the support from intellectuals that JFK had enjoyed. Ted's pal John Culver was charged with lining up academic support. Although the tall, broad-shouldered Culver had been a star on the gridiron, he was also an intellectual force, and was on track to graduate from Harvard Law School that spring. He dragooned five academics and packed them behind a table in a television studio, having them talk before the cameras about why they supported Ted Kennedy. "I was trying to give the impression," Culver says, "that there were five of these outstanding academics testifying to this, and the other academic crowd was being held back outside only because of the strength of the door." The academics who had signed on—such as Harvard's Sam Beer and MIT's Bob Wood—did so in exchange for Kennedy's commitment to help them reform the state Democratic Party, which at the time was drenched in graft.

A few days before Easter, Doherty handed Ted an exhaustive town-by-town analysis he had prepared showing his strengths and weaknesses with delegates across the state. Soon Doherty and a few other advisers to Teddy were called to the White House to explain the findings in more detail. They met in the Oval Office with the president and some of his top advisers who had strong Massachusetts connections. These included Kenny O'Donnell and Larry O'Brien, who had been the biggest opponents to Ted's run and who were still refusing to return the campaign's calls. The president grilled Doherty for quite some time, drilling down into ward politics with a specificity that impressed his aides. The president's special assistant Arthur

Schlesinger Jr. described the meeting in his journal later that night. "It was the first time in some time that I had seen JFK at work as a politician, and it was most enjoyable." After the president was reassured about Doherty's nose for counting delegates, he moved the discussion to how to strengthen his brother's position. "In effect," Schlesinger wrote, "the President was calling for a discreet mobilization of the resources of the federal government to put over Teddy's nomination."

Just then, there was a loud noise coming from outside. British Prime Minister Harold Macmillan had arrived by helicopter on the White House lawn. As President Kennedy stood up to leave the room, he turned to his advisers and said, "I want everyone to know that it's very important to me—and to everybody in this room—that my brother does well." The next day, Bobby Kennedy grilled Doherty some more. Sharing the president's satisfaction with Doherty's handle on Massachusetts politics, Bobby then told him, "Okay, you're in charge." He gave Doherty his home, office, and car telephone numbers, and told him to call him if he wasn't getting the support he needed.

"That meeting," Doherty says, "was the turning point." While Jack and Bobby continued to keep their distance from the race in public, the Kennedy machinery kicked into gear to support Teddy. Larry O'Brien devised a campaign manual, gathering the latest in polling and research on ethnic voting trends to map out a strategy. And Steve Smith now had the flexibility to ensure that the campaign had whatever financial resources it needed to dominate the race.

Ted's crew roared into the state Democratic convention in Springfield that June, from which either Kennedy or McCormack would emerge with the endorsement of the party. The McCormack camp complained that the Kennedys were muscling delegates, threatening to hold up postmaster and other federal appointments to those who refused to back Teddy. Knocko McCormack gnashed his teeth. "It's pressure, pressure, pressure, post office, post office, post office," he grumbled. In truth, given the power of the presidency, and the Kennedys' infamous reputation for score settling, just the implied threat of payback was enough to get many delegates to line up behind Teddy. Logistically, the Kennedy camp left nothing to chance, even bringing in their own telephone switchboard to ensure smooth contact throughout the convention.

Sumner Kaplan, a Brookline lawmaker who was running McCormack's campaign, soon realized how outmatched his camp was organizationally. "When we knew we were going down the tubes, Knocko had the idea of disrupting the convention," he says. "He was going to cut the switches on all the lights. We had to stop him. You never knew what he was going to do."

Kennedy won the convention's endorsement easily. While McCormack left the convention determined to fight on to the primary election that fall, he was now clearly the underdog. And that wasn't just because of the muscular machinery behind Ted. Something else had changed during his many months on the trail: Ted was evolving into a very good campaigner. Doherty noticed how he had learned to relax and be himself as he pressed the flesh, channeling his inner Honey Fitz. He demonstrated sharp political instincts, reaching down manholes and climbing up telephone poles to shake hands with workmen on the job. He could go all day and night, sometimes making up to forty stops a day, crisscrossing the state to shake hands at plant gates and speak before groups ranging from the Melrose Catholic Women's Club to the Italo-American Club of Dedham to the Wilbraham-Hampden Regional High School student body. And he could roll with the punches. At one stop at the Charlestown Navy Yard, a union worker confronted him, "Teddy, I hear you've never worked a day in your life." Kennedy smiled as he waited for the other shoe to drop. "Well, let me tell you, you haven't missed a thing," the worker quipped.

If campaign aides sent him to the wrong stop or got him there at the wrong time, Kennedy's temper would flare up and the expletives would fly. But his anger would fade just as quickly. And he refused to allow aides to speak ill about each other in his presence.

One day, his advance man, Charles Tretter, found himself running late for an event in the factory city of Brockton. As he hurried down the street to meet Kennedy, he expected yet another lecture on tardiness. So he was taken aback by Kennedy's choice of greeting. "Where did you get those shoes?" he asked.

Thinking Kennedy was admiring his loafers, Tretter proudly responded that he had bought them in Rome two years earlier.

"Don't you understand," Kennedy replied, "we're in Brockton—the shoe capital—and someone is going to notice those shoes?"

He sent Tretter home to change.

This attention to detail, combined with his relentlessness on the trail, turned Ted into a much more formidable candidate. Burton Hersh, a Harvard classmate who would write two books about Ted, says his rabid work ethic could be traced back to his standing in the family. "If you have a sense of inferiority," Hersh says, "if you think you're not that smart, you work harder." Although he was indefatigable on the trail, Ted still adhered to Jack's practice of taking a restorative soak in the tub in the afternoon, a request that forced one aide or another to go scrambling to find someone willing to turn over their bathroom to Kennedy.

Ted's adventurousness grew with his confidence level. One day, he was shaking hands at Kelly's Landing in South Boston with John Culver and another aide named Ed Moss at his side. Pointing across the street, Moss told Ted where Knocko lived. "Let's go over and say hello," Ted said. They walked down a driveway to get to Knocko's back yard, where they found him hammering together lawn signs for his son. Ted extended his hand, but Knocko refused to shake it. He glanced up at his neighbors who were watching the scene from their three-decker back porches. "The neighbors will see me," Knocko said. Then he pointed to the signs he was hammering together. "Every time I drive a nail, it's right in your butt."

Still, there were limits to Kennedy's growth. All summer long, McCormack pushed hard for a debate with Kennedy. He rented an empty office next to Ted's on Tremont Street and posted a sign chronicling the number of days Kennedy had refused to debate. Steve Smith still felt Teddy wasn't ready. Finally, toward the end of the summer, Smith told Doherty to say yes. The Kennedy camp surprised McCormack by insisting the first debate be held at South Boston High School, the epicenter of the McCormack family base. It was a strategic calculation on the Kennedys' part. If Teddy failed in his

performance, they could blame it on having to debate in hostile territory.

The scene in the South Boston auditorium was raucous. McCormack, down in the polls, decided this was his last chance and came
out swinging. The hope among the McCormack camp, Kaplan says,
was that "Teddy wouldn't be able to take the pressure and he might
blow up."

McCormack wore his white-blond hair slicked back and his per-
manently crooked smile, which gave him something of a shifty look.
He wasted no time in ridiculing Kennedy for his lack of qualifications
and dismissing his travels on "fact-finding missions" to foreign lands
as little more than a rich kid's getaways where Teddy's inexperience
brought embarrassment to those around him. "The office of United
States senator should be merited, and not inherited," the Speaker of
the House's nephew thundered.

Kennedy, shaky at times, tried to stick to his rehearsed answers
and not take McCormack's bait. His speechwriter, Milton Gwirtzman, had prepared a line for him in anticipation of McCormack's flavor of attack. Kennedy delivered it in his closing statement, with his
voice cracking: "We should not have any talk about personalities or
families."

But that just fired McCormack up more for his closing. "I ask,
since the question of families and of names has been injected, if his
name was Edward Moore, with his qualifications," McCormack repeatedly jabbed his finger at Kennedy, who was now seated, "with your
qualifications, Teddy. If it was Edward Moore, your candidacy would
be a joke."

There were big laughs from the blood-smelling crowd, followed
by applause.

"But nobody's laughing because his name is not Edward Moore.
It's Edward Moore Kennedy!"

The veins bulged on Kennedy's neck, but he contained his rage.
When the debate ended, he turned away and walked off the stage
without shaking McCormack's hand. As he walked with Doherty, he
muttered, "I'd like to get that guy and punch him in the nose!"

Fortunately, for Kennedy's sake, he wasn't the only one fuming.

Kaplan, McCormack's campaign manager, walked into the crowd to chat with his mother. "All I can remember," he says, "is my mother blasting me. She didn't talk to me for about three months because of the way we dealt with poor Teddy."

Immediately after the debate, the Kennedy camp worried that McCormack might have delivered fatal blows. Teddy, though, seemed less concerned with politics than family pride. He was incensed because he felt McCormack had insulted the man he had been named after, Eddie Moore, who had been his father's most loyal assistant. Gwirtzman was struck by how Teddy's first move when he returned to his place was to call Eddie Moore's widow to apologize for any pain the incident may have caused her. It reflected the premium he placed on the feelings of others, even at times when he would have been forgiven for being focused on himself.

Meanwhile, Kaplan and McCormack left the debate in the same car. The driver turned on talk radio, and one caller after another, many of them older women, expressed the same indignation with McCormack's behavior that Kaplan's mother had. They had been repulsed by McCormack's jabbing finger and the piling-on of laughter and cheering in the crowd. The whole scene had helped transform Teddy's image from pampered playboy brother to someone as sympathetic as a toddler separated from his parents in a department store. At the time, Rose Kennedy was one of the most highly respected women in Massachusetts, especially among older women, and they felt McCormack had no right to bludgeon her fine young son.

"Turn it off," McCormack said finally. "The race is over."

He was right. On primary day, the president and first lady caused a scene by interrupting their Newport vacation to helicopter into Boston and cast their votes for Teddy. The Speaker drew no notice when he returned to town to do the same for Eddie. Kennedy won by more than two to one, even beating McCormack in Knocko's home ward. So few were the towns that McCormack won that, in later years, every time he drove his sons to prep school in western Massachusetts, when they passed the sign for the tiny town of Otis, McCormack would shout with a laugh, "We carried Otis!"

In the general election, Kennedy faced yet another political scion,

Republican George Lodge. If the charge that Kennedy was trading on his family name had rung hollow when leveled by the nephew of the Speaker of the House, Lodge knew better than to attempt it. After all, he was the 35-year-old heir to a Massachusetts political family that had passed down this particular Senate seat like a cherished gold pocket watch. Both his great grandfather and his father had held the seat he was now vying for, and their hold on it was seriously threatened only by the extended Kennedy clan. In 1916, Henry Cabot Lodge Sr. held onto the seat after a bitter campaign waged by Honey Fitz. But the Kennedys would gain the upper hand in later years, with JFK taking the seat from Henry Cabot Lodge Jr. in 1952 and defeating him again when Lodge ran as Nixon's vice presidential candidate in 1960. In a reflection of just how much this 1962 Senate race turned out to be a battle of dynastic power, even the fringe independent candidate, H. Stuart Hughes, couldn't call out Teddy for relying on his family connections to get to the upper echelon of government. Hughes's grandfather, Charles Evans Hughes, had served as Chief Justice of the United States and been the Republican presidential nominee in 1916.

Ted Kennedy beat George Lodge by a wide margin. Ted, who had longed to escape the smothering shadows cast by his brothers, was now headed to live and work in Washington, where there were no bigger names than Jack and Bobby.

CHAPTER

8

THERE WAS A pause in the conversation, and Ted Kennedy didn't know what to do. So he said something he was quickly made to regret.

It was January 1963, and the freshman senator had begun making courtesy calls to the hidebound leaders of the ultimate old men's club. The men who ran the Senate, many of them conservative southerners, expected the president's kid brother to breeze into their exclusive chamber with the swagger of entitlement. They were determined to put him in his place.

Kennedy's old Harvard football teammate John Culver had followed him to Washington to serve as his legislative assistant. Heading into a meeting with Senator Richard Russell of Georgia, Kennedy told Culver that his brother Jack had prepped him on what to say: "Tell him that even though the president didn't always vote with him, there was no one in the Senate for whom he had greater respect." As Kennedy stepped inside Russell's office, Culver waited outside the door. About ten minutes later, Kennedy emerged from the office and he and Culver silently walked out into the corridor. After they were out of earshot of Russell's office, Kennedy burst out laughing. "I told Russell what Jack suggested and then I didn't really know what to say next," Ted explained, "so I said, 'you and I have one thing in common, senator. We both came to the Senate in our early thirties.'"

But Russell had not taken kindly to the ad-libbed comparison.

"That's right, son," Russell told him, in the slow cadence of an elder's lecture. "But, of course, I'd been governor first." Recounting the exchange for Culver, Kennedy laughed that he had gotten the message loud and clear.

Other courtesy calls were far more successful. Surprisingly, Ted immediately hit it off with Mississippi Senator James O. Eastland, the powerful Judiciary Committee chairman and a segregationist from the bottom of his feet to the top of his head. It didn't take them long during their first meeting to begin sharing laughs and pops of Eastland's drink of choice, Chivas Regal scotch. Because Judiciary would be his highest-profile committee assignment, Kennedy concluded that Eastland was someone whose favor he needed to cultivate. So rather than argue racial politics with him, he politely listened as Eastland told him he'd put him on the immigration subcommittee because "you got a lot of Italians up there" in Massachusetts, and assured him he could do what he wanted with civil rights on the constitutional rights subcommittee because "We don't kill the bills in subcommittee, we kill them in full committee."

Kennedy generally followed Jack's advice to keep a low profile during his first year in the Senate, declining national media in favor of interviews with the Massachusetts press, and building up his constituent services operation. The idea was to prove to Massachusetts voters and Senate leaders alike that Ted Kennedy knew what his place was, and what his priorities should be. The Senate leaders who expected Ted to be a spoiled and demanding newcomer were delighted when he turned out to be the model of deference, charming his elders with warmth and self-effacing humor. Growing up the youngest of nine had prepared him well for an institution that runs on seniority.

And while he hadn't flaunted his status as brother of the president, he had taken to the arrangement. The many people in the federal bureaucracy who owed their appointments to Jack or Bobby were eager to ease Ted's transition to Washington, returning his calls a lot more promptly than those from other freshman lawmakers. And because Jack enjoyed Ted's company, he often had him come to the White House for cigars and laughs after hours.

This was a marked contrast from Ted's earlier life, when he saw Jack as a revered but more detached figure—his godfather more than his friend. Once, when fellow senator George McGovern asked Ted about his childhood memories of Jack, Ted told him, "Well, you know, George, interestingly enough, I didn't know him very well." Ted told McGovern that even when he and Jack were both in Hyannis Port in their earlier years, Jack would spend most of the time in his room, reading and nursing his ailing back. But their relationship had begun to change when Ted worked on Jack's campaigns in 1958 and 1960, and truly deepened during Ted's freshman year as a senator, when a more robust relationship served both the president and his kid brother well. As much as Bobby functioned as Jack's most trusted adviser when it came to the business of governing, Arthur Schlesinger Jr. once pointed out, Ted was the brother who got the call when the president wanted a break from the pressures of the presidency. "At the end of a long day [Bobby] was often too demanding, too involved with issues. Teddy made the President laugh. Bobby was his conscience."

As a senator, Ted demonstrated a new maturity in his willingness to take his time and play by the rules. He seemed to be moving beyond the clownish behavior of his past, when he would do things like drive at incredibly high speeds in his car while being pursued by a police cruiser during law school or diving fully clothed into Bobby's swimming pool during a crowded party a few years later. Yet there were still a few flashes of recklessness. He had, after all, grown up in a privileged existence, where fixers were always available to clean up messes, pick up tabs, and make problems go away. So it was no surprise that he would occasionally crack under the heightened scrutiny that came with his status as a U.S. senator and brother of the president. Just a month after taking office, during a ski trip with Joan in Stowe, Vermont, Ted had a run-in with a newspaper photographer who snapped a shot of him. Ted grabbed the man's camera and theatrically opened the back of it to expose the film to light before returning the camera to him.

There were weightier matters on which he was called to account. In September of 1963, Ted was in Belgrade to speak before the 59-nation Interparliamentary Union Conference. He was photographed chatting over lunch with Madame Ngo Dinh Nhu, the erratic, quick-tempered sister-in-law of President Ngo Dinh Diem of South Vietnam. Madame Nhu bent Ted's ear, telling him that the Buddhist monks that her brother-in-law was accused of mistreating were in fact Communist spies. Madame Nhu had previously accused President Kennedy of appeasing U.S. politicians in setting his Vietnam policies. So the public perception that Ted was giving her a sympathetic audience and wading unwisely into dangerous diplomatic waters was enough to prompt a volley of confidential cables between Secretary of State Dean Rusk and the head of the U.S. embassy in Belgrade, with the goal of keeping Teddy in line. Eric Kocher, the chargé d'affaires, took Ted for a walk outside the embassy, to get away from listening devices, and delivered word that his discussions with Madame Nhu "were causing unpleasant and embarrassing attention in the United States." Ted got the message.

Yet the Belgrade trip also showcased his more serious side, and foreshadowed how out in front he was willing to be in the area of civil rights. "We are determined to clean our hands of racial prejudice so we can go before the world with deeds to match our words," he said in his address to the conference, backing its draft resolution on ending racial discrimination. In another preview of the way he would frame the issue in personal terms, he said, "Neither I, nor the president of the United States, would hold the positions we do if America had not taken down the sign that said, 'Irish Need Not Apply.' " At a news conference around the same time, he was even more pointed. "There has to be an understanding by the whites," he said, "that the day of the billy club and the whip and the others are gone by."

By the fall of 1963, Ted Kennedy had been in office for less than a year, but already was showing signs that he was developing a plan for becoming a successful senator. He knew how to use his emotional intelligence to read people and build alliances. He was aware of his own intellectual deficiencies and was determined to compensate for them through hard work, balanced between a few important, high-profile issues and laserlike attention to the less glamorous but vital constituent service side of his job. He didn't flaunt his brother's celebrity, yet managed to convert the reflected glow into political currency that he could cash in when he needed it later.

This emergent Ted was on display on October 19, when he shared the dais with President Kennedy for a black-tie fundraiser that drew more than 7,000 supporters to Boston's Commonwealth Armory. Actually, in an echo of his younger days, Ted was seated at the head table in an annex to the cavernous main hall—an arrangement he mined for big laughs. "I come from a large family and I am accustomed as the youngest to sit at the end table," Ted said, "but he didn't have to put me in the other room!" Later, he cracked, "This is the first time since my election that my brother has allowed me to appear on the same program with him. I think it's because I sold more tickets to this dinner than he did."

It was all a put-on. If anything, the laugh-packed dinner was a public display of how genuinely Jack and Ted enjoyed each other's company, and how much their once lopsided relationship had begun to mature. It was also a public recognition by the president that the Massachusetts Democratic Party was now his kid brother's to run. The president laughed heartily when Ted told him on stage, "If he thinks he's running again, he's going to be running on my coattails in Massachusetts, and he's going to have to treat me better." In fact, following through on the pledge to reform the state party that he had made to the few liberal academics who had supported him in 1962, Ted had already installed his own people to run the party apparatus, beginning with his old campaign manager, Gerard Doherty, as state chairman.

When it was his turn to speak, the president told the crowd, "My last campaign, I suppose, may be coming up very shortly. But Teddy is around and, therefore, these dinners can go indefinitely!" Then he dusted off a joke he had told before about Teddy. "He's been around Washington a while and he's tired of being called the younger brother of the president and a Kennedy. He's thinking of changing his name and going out on his own." Jack said he asked him what name he had in mind. "Oh, just an ordinary everyday name," Teddy told him. "Roosevelt."

Ted Kennedy was presiding over the Senate, sitting at the upper level of the two-tiered dais, staring out at the hundred members' hand-carved mahogany desks arranged in a semicircle atop the chamber's royal blue carpet. It was an august spot, but in fact not much was happening in the chamber on this afternoon of November 22, 1963, so the largely thankless procedural task of presiding over routine business was assigned to its more junior members. Ted was using the time to catch up on signing a backlog of correspondence, pausing periodically to recognize one colleague or another who wished to be heard.

A little before 2:00 P.M., a press aide came running onto the Senate floor and toward the rostrum. It was a violation of Senate protocol, but it was clear from the panicked look on the aide's face that the violation was warranted.

"The most horrible thing has happened!" cried the aide, Richard Riedel. "It's terrible, terrible."

"What is it?" Kennedy asked nervously.

"Your brother. Your brother the president. He's been shot."

"How do you know?"

When Riedel told him he had seen the urgent bulletin on the wire service ticker, Ted gathered his papers and raced out of the chamber. He needed to talk to Bobby. He stepped into the office Vice President Lyndon Johnson kept at the Senate, and picked up the phone, but the line was dead. He headed for his office in the Old Senate Office Building where, after some struggle, he finally got through to the White House. He learned that Bobby was at his home in Virginia, but he couldn't get through.

Worried about Joan—it wasn't clear if his brother's shooting was part of some kind of wider plot—he decided to head to their home in Georgetown. He told an aide to fetch his car but found that another staffer had borrowed it. His speechwriter Milt Gwirtzman was in the office and volunteered to drive Ted home. Gwirtzman—a Harvard classmate, who had heavy glasses, thick hair, and a gravelly voice—retrieved his black 1960 Mercedes 150, and Ted hopped in. In the backseat was Ted's old college pal Claude Hooten. The avuncular Texan had come to Washington to attend Ted and Joan's fifth wedding anniversary party at their home that night and then head with Ted to the Harvard-Yale game. Gwirtzman raced his Mercedes down Pennsylvania Avenue, blowing so many red lights that Ted cautioned him to be careful of the oncoming cars. Upon arrival at Ted's rented brick Georgetown house on 28th Street, the maid informed him that Joan was at the hairdresser's. Gwirtzman headed off to fetch her, while Ted tried again to reach Bobby, but found the lines in his house were also dead. As it turned out, the phone company's circuits were overloaded. So he and Hooten each took a side of 28th Street, knocking on doors and trying to find a live phone line. Ted was the first to find one, though the maid refused to let him in, telling him, according to Hooten, that the lady of the house "said don't let nobody in unless she's home."

Hooten, who now joined Ted at the front door, implored her, saying, "He's the brother of the president!"

"He sure do look like the president," the maid said, and ushered them in.

At last, Ted was able to reach Bobby, but he had only hideous news to report. "He's dead," Bobby said. "You'd better call your mother and our sisters."

His choice of possessives in this time of crisis was telling. *Our* sisters, but *your* mother. He didn't even mention their father, no doubt because of Joe's incapacitated state, though informing him would prove to be the most fraught task of all.

Of all the Kennedy brothers, Ted may have been the only one who never clashed with, or tired of, either parent. While Jack recognized he would have never made it to the White House without his father's orchestration and intercession, there had always been a palpable tension over control and respect in their relationship. Bobby had once adored his father, embracing his more conservative politics early in his career as a legal attack dog for his father's pal, the red-baiting Senator Joe McCarthy. But by the time he had become attorney general, his politics had shifted and he had openly defied the old man in significant ways, most notably in his zealous pursuit of the mob, which included some of his father's former associates. As for their mother, Bobby by this point may have been fatigued enough by her demands and detachment to want to subcontract out the responsibility for helping her through the tragedy.

Teddy, meanwhile, would remain the dutiful, grateful son to the end with both of his parents, someone willing to overlook their obvious faults and focus exclusively on their many gifts as he authored an idealized version of Kennedy family history. If Rose's needling notes signed "Mrs. Joseph P. Kennedy" drove some of her children crazy, Teddy would let her missives roll right off his back. He preferred to concentrate on her positive attributes, particularly the deep faith in God that she had instilled in him. When she wrote to correct his grammar or his mispronunciation of the word *nuclear* or to chide Joan into getting him the correct collar and tie when he wore formal wear, he would simply laugh off her admonishments. Occasionally, he would needle her back, but only in the most loving way, such as the time he came across one of her early report cards and called her out for having had trouble in geometry, "which you have obviously been careful to conceal from your children." (Rose wrote back: "Never had any trouble! Your record must have been incorrect. Always 'A' in everything.")

Now it was Ted's job to break the news about Jack's death to his parents. Yet as soon as he hung up with Bobby, the neighbor's phone line that he was borrowing went dead. Eventually, he reconnected with Gwirtzman, hopping back in his Mercedes and speeding to the White House. Once again, Ted was silent during the whole ride. He did not mention the news he had heard from Bobby; Gwirtzman did not mention that he had heard the same news over the radio before Ted got back in the car. From the White House, Ted reached his mother on the phone, but she, too, had already heard that Jack was dead. She became focused on how to deliver the shattering news to her husband without further compromising his ailing health. She told Ted to fly to Hyannis Port and tell him in person.

While Bobby was responding to the crisis by demanding answers from those in the highest levels of the federal bureaucracy, Teddy made do with his own lower-profile associates. He called Eddie Martin, his former campaign spokesman, who was now again working at the *Boston Herald*. He asked Martin what he was hearing about the arrest of Lee Harvey Oswald, saying his mother had conveyed her doubts that they had gotten the right guy. A while later, he called Martin back, asking him to check on space at the cemetery in Brookline where the family owned a plot. (He would subsequently call to tell Martin to disregard his earlier request, since Jackie Kennedy had insisted that JFK be treated not like some Boston pol but rather as a national figure for the ages, with his body interred in Arlington National Cemetery.)

Until Ted arrived with his sister Eunice at the Hyannis Port compound, their mother had instructed the staff to do whatever they had to in order to keep the news from her husband. Soon after their arrival, the family decided they should delay breaking the news longer, until their father's physician could be there with them. So at the time of the family's most crushing grief, everyone was engaged in an elaborate charade—which included tearing out television cords to pretend that the TV sets were broken and prevent the old man from watching his regular diet of news programs. The patriarch became increasingly suspicious, until Ted finally told him, "There's been a bad accident. The president has been hurt very badly. As a matter of fact, he died." Ted then dropped to his knees and buried his face in his father's hands. Tears streamed down the old man's cheeks.

The family feared that the trauma might cause the patriarch to slip away. But the next morning he surprised them by insisting that his nurse, Rita Dallas, bring him downstairs in his wheelchair. His father gestured to Teddy that he wanted to go for a ride. Ted lifted his father into the front seat of the car, then opened the rear door to let Dallas in. They headed first to his favorite spot, the Hyannis airport, so he could see the family airplane, the *Caroline*. Once there, Teddy explained that the plane was out, but the captain would return with it later in the afternoon. "I thought maybe I'd go down to Washington late tonight, if it's okay, and come right back," Ted said. While he had been in Hyannis the previous night, friends had descended on his house in Georgetown. Joan, who was crumbling under news of the assassination, had turned the anniversary party she had planned into a mercy meal, instructing the caterers to make the food go farther by converting the entrees into hors d'oeuvres for the many more friends and family who now somberly filled their house.

Ted proceeded to drive along the back roads of the Cape for several hours, talking with his father about the weather and other innocuous matters unrelated to the assassination. Finally, he turned to his father and said, "Dad, I'm lost. You'll have to help me find my way home." Dallas, a quick-witted, no-nonsense woman who had been widowed young, had fit in well with the Kennedy family by refusing to be overly awed by its celebrity. But she had already developed a fondness for big-hearted Teddy, and the way his arrival at the staid compound would immediately light up both his parents. In this darkest of times, she knew Teddy would be key to helping prevent the ailing patriarch from mental withdrawal. Now, sitting in the back seat of the car, she wondered if Teddy had truly gotten lost, or if he was faking it in the hope of engaging his father and making it clear how much his family still relied on him. If it had been a plan, the plan worked. The old man smiled for the first time since hearing the devastating news about Jack, and proceeded to use his good arm to point out all the lefts and rights it took to help Teddy get back to the compound.

For Teddy, the next few days and weeks were a blur of events and obligations, of being strong for others—parents, extended family, the nation—and sublimating his own pain as he grieved on stage. True to form, he tried to use humor to ease the pain of others, and maybe even his own. On the morning of the president's funeral, he and Bobby tried to distract Jackie by recounting how Ted's tuxedo had arrived without pants, and how they had to scramble to borrow the trousers Jack had worn to his inaugural, but how Teddy's much wider waistline had demanded on-the-fly alterations.

Shortly after the funeral, the family reconvened at the compound for a somber Thanksgiving. One night that weekend, Ted stayed up all night, drinking and swapping ribald stories with friends about the good times with Jack. The next morning, his children's governess quit in a huff, telling Rita Dallas how horrified she'd been by Ted's behavior. Dallas believed the woman couldn't grasp the concept of an Irish wake. But it was more than that. A man who had spent most of his life drawing laughs in his role as the baby brother must have known that, on some level, the laughter had already ended.

So much more would be expected of him now.

The following spring, Ted made a nine-country tour of Europe to raise money for the Kennedy Library that the family was hoping to see built on the Harvard University campus in Cambridge. The most poignant stop on the tour was Ireland, where Jack had visited not long before his death. During his visit to the family homeland, President Kennedy had vowed, in accordance with an old Irish song, "to come back in the springtime." Now, it was spring, but it was Ted who had arrived in his brother's place. At every stop, he was mobbed by adoring throngs, who strained and stretched to touch him, as though they were touching a part of the slain president.

During a talk on May 29, Ted told the crowd, "Today is a day of joy and sadness for me. Joy because I am in Ireland on a beautiful spring day. Sadness because today is the president's birthday," he said. "My brother will not be able to come back and enjoy any more spring days."

CHAPTER
9

ON APRIL 9, 1964, Ted Kennedy rose to deliver his first major speech in the Senate. The civil rights bill that his brother had filed the previous spring had come up for debate. Despite Lyndon Johnson's commitment to harnessing the national sorrow for Jack Kennedy into getting the bill through Congress, many of those same old conservative southerners whom Ted had charmed with his deference were determined to block it. This was no time for deference. "My brother was the first president of the United States to state publicly that segregation was morally wrong," Ted told his colleagues, as Joan watched from the gallery. "His heart and soul are in this bill. If his life and death had a meaning it was that we should not hate but love one another, we should use our powers not to create conditions of oppression that lead to violence, but conditions of freedom that lead to peace."

Powerful words, delivered powerfully. Although Ted had avoided speechmaking in the Senate, he now impressed his colleagues with his oratorical skills. (This came in contrast to the problems he had with garbled syntax when he wasn't reading from a script—problems for which he would eventually seek help from a speech therapist.)

More than two months and much filibustering later, the Senate was poised on June 19 to break the impasse and pass the civil rights law, which would ban racial discrimination in employment as well as public accommodations, such as restaurants and hotels. It was a year to the day since JFK had sent the bill to Congress. Ted expected the vote to happen by early afternoon, after which he would fly to Massachusetts where he would be formally nominated by the state Democratic party for his first full term as senator.

Joan, who had recently suffered her second miscarriage, was already at the convention, which was taking place at the Coliseum at the West Springfield Fairgrounds. To get her mind off the loss, Ted had encouraged Joan to attend a high-end antique sale in Newport, Rhode Island, and buy expensive furniture for their house. She did, staying with Jackie Kennedy's mother, before driving to Springfield. In some ways, Ted was showing in his own marriage reflections of his parents' relationship. Although Ted enjoyed a warm relationship with his mother, his model for masculine behavior and what it meant to be a husband was his father. And as much as Joe valued his cultured wife as an essential extension of his own image, he was a man whose idea of emotional investment in his marriage was bankrolling European trips for Rose to buy expensive clothing. Now more than five years into their own marriage, Ted and Joan still didn't know each other all that well. While many political spouses dreaded the grind of election years, it was telling that Joan was looking forward to her husband's upcoming reelection campaign. She had felt closest to Ted during the 1962 run, when she had been freed from her role as the wife and mother at home, and when face time with her husband was guaranteed in posted daily campaign schedules.

In a break during the Senate floor vote on the civil rights bill, Ted returned to his office to celebrate the birthday of one of his staffers. Another aide, Ed Moss, updated arrangements for the trip to Springfield. Moss, who had a quick wit, a round face, and a 6'3" linebacker's build, was a favorite around the office. He had met Ted years earlier at a golf tournament in Pittsfield, Massachusetts, where he had been working for the telephone company. Through his work on Ted's campaign and now in his Senate office, serving as Ted's administrative aide, travel secretary, logistics coordinator, and bodyguard, the pair had become good friends.

Whenever Ted appeared at an event where there was a band, Moss would head straight for the piano player to request "Sweet Adeline"—Honey Fitz's signature campaign song, which Ted had watched his grandfather sing at every stop. Wherever he was in the crowd, Ted would crane his neck to make eye contact with Moss and smile.

"You should make some kind of a spectacular entrance to the convention," Moss told Ted in between bites of birthday cake.

"What do you want me to do," Ted asked with a smile, "crack up the airplane?"

"Nope, just parachute out of it into the convention."

Back in the Senate chamber, debate dragged on. The civil rights bill didn't pass until 7:40 P.M. Kennedy and Moss then boarded a twin-engine private plane along with Ted's Senate colleague, Birch Bayh of Indiana, and his wife, Marvella. Kennedy and Bayh had joined the Senate at the same time, meeting for the first time in front of the Senate elevators in January 1963. Although much was made of the fact that Kennedy was just thirty years old when he entered the Senate, Bayh was only thirty-four. They had quickly bonded as personable, fresh-faced youngsters trying to find their way in an old men's club. Their wives hit it off as well, so they often went out socially, making an attractive, exciting foursome new to the Washington scene. Kennedy had asked Bayh to join him at the Massachusetts convention and deliver the keynote address.

As the afternoon had worn on, weather conditions had deteriorated dramatically. Ted had asked Howard Baird, captain of the *Caroline,* to fly him to Springfield, but Baird refused, citing the severe fog and weather warnings. Baird did fly Bobby from Washington to Hyannis earlier in the day. Later that evening, over dinner at the Candlelight Motel with his crew and Joe's nurse Rita Dallas, Baird complained about what he felt was Ted's reckless decision to go ahead with the flight. "It's bad weather," he said. "The fog is really rolling in." Because Ted felt he simply had to get to Springfield, Moss had arranged for another plane and another experienced pilot, 48-year-old Edwin Zimney.

It was a bumpy ride. Birch and Marvella Bayh were seated in the rear of the Aero Commander 680, facing forward. Ted was in a rear-facing seat, with his back to the cockpit. Moss was in the copilot seat.

Late in the flight, Birch watched as Ted, himself an experienced pilot, got up to talk to Zimney, and then kept nervously craning his head toward the cockpit, keeping an eye on the instrument panel.

Just before 10:45 P.M., the pilot called the control tower at Barnes Airport in Westfield, where the plane was scheduled to land. "We are over the Z marker," he reported. Straight ahead and a little over five miles away was the newly extended 9,000-foot runway at Barnes Airport.

That was the last contact the pilot had with the control tower. The dense fog forced him to attempt an instrument landing.

Birch Bayh looked out his window and saw a dark line. He assumed it was another thunderstorm. He heard a loud crack, and figured it was lightning. In fact, the plane had hit the top of a 65-foot tree about 3 miles shy of the runway. The plane continued gliding along a row of treetops, turning the descent into a frightening toboggan ride. Birch assumed they would all die, and was comforted only by the fleeting thought that at least he and Marvella had recently updated their will to take care of their son, Evan.

A short time later, the big-bellied plane crashed in an apple orchard, with both wings sheared off, its nose smashed into the trunk of a tree. The top of the engine had been ripped off and twisted under the plane. The steering wheel was bent 180 degrees and hanging outside of the plane. Birch briefly lost consciousness but was jolted awake by his wife's screaming.

On impact, the window nearest them popped open. He crawled out of it, then helped his wife get out. He screamed for Kennedy, but got no reaction. It was too dark and foggy to see inside the cabin. He walked around to the front of the plane, and peered in. Both the pilot and Ed Moss appeared to be dead. He and Marvella decided to run for help. But as they walked away from the plane, Birch smelled fumes. He worried the wrecked plane might burst into flames.

"I've got to go back and make another try for Ted," he told his wife.

"No," she protested, "it'll blow up on you."

"All the more reason to go get Ted."

"Then I'm going with you."

As they approached the plane this time, Birch noticed a small ray of light coming from inside the cabin—an emergency light. It was faint, but enough to illuminate Ted's cuff link. He reached in through the window, grabbed Ted's arm, and pulled him out. Ted couldn't move from the waist down, so Birch carried his body like one of the sacks of feed he had grown up lugging around his grandfather's Indiana farm. When he was a safe distance away from the plane, he laid Ted down in some weeds. Marvella asked, "Is there anything we can do for you, Ted?"

"Well," he replied, "you can get this weed out of my face."

When word of the accident made it to the convention floor, it caused confusion and turmoil. Someone offered a moment of silent prayer. Joan was whisked out of the hall and to Cooley Dickinson Hospital in Northampton to see Ted, who had arrived at the hospital in shock and badly injured. The convention was then abruptly disbanded. The pilot was dead at the scene, but Moss was still clinging to life. Ted was transported in one ambulance, Moss in another, along with Birch and Marvella. From the front seat, Birch could hear Moss's haunting death rattle. The father of three young girls, Moss survived for six more hours. A state police cruiser rushed his wife from their home in Andover to the hospital in Northampton, where she was able to see her unconscious husband before he died.

At the hospital, Birch grabbed a phone and called Bobby, telling him there'd been a terrible accident.

"He isn't dead, is he?" Bobby asked.

"No, we've been told by the doctor that he had a serious back injury."

Just seven months after JFK's assassination, which had shaken the nation and triggered a period of deep soul-searching within Bobby, he simply couldn't take another blow. He tracked down Captain Baird at the Candlelight Motel, asking for an emergency flight. Baird checked with Flight Control at Hyannis Airport and received clearance to fly Bobby to Boston, but said he would have to drive to Northampton because the airport near the hospital was still closed because of the fog.

When Bobby arrived at the hospital, a reporter friend asked him, "Is it ever going to end for you people?" Somberly, Bobby responded, "I was just thinking out there—if my mother hadn't had any more children after her first four she would have nothing now. My brothers Joe and Jack are dead and Kathleen is dead and Rosemary is in a nursing home. She would be left with nothing if she had only had four. I guess the only reason we've survived is that there are too many of us. There are more of us than there is trouble."

Doctors initially feared a spinal cord injury, but Ted was fortunate that the injuries were limited to three fractured vertebrae in his lower back, a collapsed lung, and two fractured ribs. It would be a long time before he walked again. After a few weeks, he was moved to New England Baptist Hospital in Boston. Staffers from his Washington office set up shop in nearby rooms, keeping his Senate operations going from the hospital. Ted's father was worried enough that he made a rare trip out in public, accompanied by Rita Dallas, to see his son in the hospital. He was in the room when doctors delivered their recommendation that Ted undergo complicated lumbar fusion surgery. Old Joe had an immediate and violent reaction, summoning what little ability he had to speak.

"Naaaaa, naaaaa!" he barked, shaking his head vigorously. Ted's doctors circled around the patriarch, worried that he might be suffering some kind of attack. There were confused looks all around. Finally, Dallas sensed what might be happening.

"Do you want to discuss your son's operation, Mr. Kennedy?" she asked. "Is that it?"

The patriarch fell back in his chair and said, "Yaaa."

Teddy then asked his father a few additional yes-or-no questions, and determined that he was dead set against his youngest son undergoing the complicated surgery. "Dad," Ted told him, finally, "you've never been wrong yet, so I'll do it your way." Dallas later learned from Rose Kennedy why her husband had been so opposed. When Jack had undergone risky spinal surgery in 1954, a urinary tract infection—complicated by his adrenal insufficiency and suppressed immunity—sent him into a coma. He came so close to dying that a priest was called in to administer last rites. The patriarch wasn't going to take that chance again.

Instead, Ted was confined for months to a Stryker frame bed, in which he could be kept completely flat so his vertebrae could fuse back together, but be flipped around, rotisserie style, to prevent fluid from collecting in his lungs. The arrangement certainly complicated his bid for reelection. But it provided another opportunity for Joan to prove her usefulness. She began gamely filling in for her husband, showing up at campaign events, delivering cute stories and updates on Ted's condition before reading the texts of his speeches. The crowds bathed her in support. White-haired ladies would press religious medallions into her hands and tell her they were praying for Teddy. And the media ate it up. The *Boston Globe* called her "the beauteous blonde," the *Boston Traveler,* "the blonde vision with the wide Alice-in-Wonderland look." After her talks, she'd head straight for the hospital to update Ted on what had happened.

There, she'd often find her husband lying in the prone position, facing the floor, dictating a letter to one of his staffers. One aide, Charles Tretter, barely had the strength to watch whenever orderlies moved Ted around in his Stryker frame. "I never got over my stomach turning with anxiety when they would strap him in and turn him. Every time, there was a risk that something could happen, and I would get a flip in my stomach."

Mixed in with all the supportive mail were occasional letters of instruction from his mother, who suggested he use the time in the hospital to work on his writing and speaking. "When you are lying in bed, you can read a paragraph and then try to rewrite it or resay it," Rose wrote her son. "Then notice the difference between succinct, dramatic impressions of the author and your (verbose) discursive, dull recital of the same events."

Unexpectedly, there was a major upside to Ted's long convalescence, besides the remedial writing help from his mother. It provided a time away from the spotlight that had been trained on him since childhood. He was allowed to grow. Respected academics began coming in weekly to give him bedside tutorials across a wide range of topics. John

Kenneth Galbraith briefed him on economics. Jerrold Zacharias and Jerome Wiesner of MIT talked to him about math and science. Even his blistering critic from the 1962 campaign, Mark De Wolfe Howe, who gave him a tutorial on the legal underpinnings of civil rights law, had to admit that the kid had learned a lot during his short time in Washington.

When George Lodge, his Republican opponent from 1962, showed up for a visit, he noticed a towering stack of books near Ted's bed. Joan quipped, "Teddy's reading all the books he should have read in college."

Through these months, a new seriousness and sense of purpose developed in Ted. Jack had been cut down in his prime, joining their older siblings in an early grave. He himself had barely escaped death in a crash that had killed two others. Life was too precious to waste coasting and clowning around. During one bedside talk with Gerard Doherty, his manager from the 1962 campaign, Kennedy asked how his firefighter father had survived financially when Doherty endured a long battle with tuberculosis during college. Ted knew that Doherty had had to leave Harvard for two years while he stayed in a sanatorium. How had his father afforded that?

"Harvard helped a little bit," Doherty told him, "but my father was a string saver, and he saved a lot of string." Ted also asked about a former neighbor of Doherty's who was working on his staff and who also had health problems. In Ted, Doherty detected a growing appreciation for the economics of healthcare: If medical crises test even wealthy people like the Kennedys, how do ordinary people cope?

When Jack had been laid up after his back operation in the mid-1950s, he filled the time working on *Profiles in Courage*, his book about senators who had risked popularity to take a righteous stand. The book won him the Pulitzer Prize (despite its contested authorship) and helped develop his national following. During his hospital stay, Ted also chose to work on a book, but one that would do him absolutely no political good. *The Fruitful Bough* was a collection of mostly gauzy tribute essays about his father. His brothers had been exceedingly careful to limit their public associations with their father, for fear of reminding voters of the patriarch's controversial past involving his dealings with unsavory characters as a businessman and his accommodationist approach to Nazi aggression as an ambassador. But Teddy, whether because of his special bond with the old man or just because he generally valued loyalty and relationships over calculation, never seemed the least bit concerned about that.

One day during the summer, the White House called Ted's staff to inform them that President Lyndon Johnson planned to visit the senator at New England Baptist Hospital that evening, on his way back from a speech in New Hampshire. As the clock ticked past midnight, Ted and his aide Eddie Martin worried that an after-hours visit from the president would cause too much commotion in the hospital. So Martin phoned Air Force One, while it was in the air, and delivered the message. "The senator really appreciates your interest, but it's late and we would like to have you understand that it's a hospital and there are patients there, and you know, the disturbance, I'm sure, is apt to bother them."

LBJ was having none of it. "You tell Ted Kennedy that I'll be there," he bellowed into the phone. "And don't worry about the patients. They all can sleep later in the morning!"

The president showed up with his entourage after 1:00 A.M. and spent twenty boisterous minutes with Ted in his fifth-floor hospital room, sharing stories and laughs. As Johnson prepared to leave, he bent over and kissed Ted on the cheek.

There were all sorts of complications surrounding Ted and LBJ, but their actual relationship was surprisingly uncomplicated. Simply put, the two men liked one another. Johnson in particular seemed to enjoy Ted's company, seeing him as a different kind of Kennedy. He didn't have to worry about being overshadowed by him, as he had been by Jack. He didn't have to worry about being belittled by him, as he had been by Bobby. In Ted, LBJ found a fun-loving, non-threatening Kennedy who shared his love of people and his respect for the customs and seniority rules of the Senate that Johnson had once run.

Remarkably, Ted was able to maintain strong relationships with both LBJ and Bobby, even as the dealings between the two of them became increasingly poisonous. The roots of the feud dated at least to the 1960 Democratic National Convention, when Bobby had vociferously opposed the idea of having Johnson run as Jack's vice president. Even though it became clear on election night that Jack almost certainly would have lost the election without Johnson's help in carrying Texas, Bobby worked to marginalize Johnson once they took office. The animus between them was intense: The JFK assassination had shaken Bobby to his core, unleashing a period of deep searching and uncertainty. But in cold political terms, its effects were unmistakable. Not only had it stripped Bobby of the reins of power, but it put them firmly in the hands of someone he personally disliked and had publicly disrespected. There would be payback.

Still, leading up to the 1964 Democratic National Convention, Bobby, who had remained attorney general, held out hope that Johnson would name him as his running mate. Johnson had, after all, made clear his intention of carrying out the Kennedy legacy. What better way to ensure that than to keep a Kennedy on the ticket? But there was no way Johnson was going to allow himself to be overshadowed again. When Bobby refused to take his name out of the running for vice president, Johnson went so far as to announce that no one from the cabinet would be considered for that office.

Ted's loyalty, of course, remained with his brother. But he was also practical. While it was clear to everyone whose side he would fall on in matters of consequence, Ted made it equally clear that he didn't have to adopt his brother's personal distaste for LBJ. As much as possible, he tried to keep the relationships separate. He knew that the new president personalized everything, and if he could remain on good terms with the Johnson White House, it would be to the benefit of his constituents and his career. Ted was like a guy who loves his sister and likes his brother-in-law, and struggles to keep things friendly even as they head into an increasingly acrimonious divorce.

Just a few weeks before his plane crash, Ted had sent his brother a detailed analysis he had one of his aides prepare, outlining Bobby's best political options in light of the VP slot being closed off. Pros and cons were spelled out for the two offices Bobby was contemplating most seriously: governor of Massachusetts and senator from New York. The governorship, which he could win easily, would make best use of his executive skills, the memo said. But as Ted had realized when he had considered running for the job, it was a constitutionally weak office. The U.S. Senate seat offered a higher national profile, but it would be harder for him to win because, well, he wasn't from New York and the "carpetbagger" label might be particularly stinging because it would be so true.

In late August 1964, Bobby hastily joined the Senate race in New York. Accordingly, he had to give up his position as a Massachusetts delegate to the Democratic National Convention. He handed it over to Joan, who was still drawing rave reviews for her performance as the public face of Teddy's reelection campaign. From his hospital bed, Ted saw the convention on television, relying on an elaborate system of mirrors to watch when he was lying face down in his Stryker frame. LBJ insisted on moving a planned tribute to JFK, which would be introduced by Bobby, to the final night of the convention. That would avoid any drumbeat from misty-eyed delegates for Johnson to reconsider and name Bobby as his running mate. When at last Bobby stepped onto the stage to introduce the tribute, waves of applause cascaded over the convention floor. For twenty-two minutes, the cheers continued, interrupted only by Bobby's pleas to the pols running the convention to help bring order, "Mr. Speakah, Mr. Chairman," he said, smiling wanly, bathing in the warmth for him and for Jack's unfinished legacy.

Through the fall, Teddy continued his recovery at New England Baptist. Late on the December night before his scheduled release from the hospital, he slipped out of the hospital with Eddie Martin and headed northwest to Andover, so he could pay his respects at the grave of his former aide and friend, Ed Moss. Gingerly, he walked with his cane up an icy hill to the gravesite. Afterward he went to the Moss house to visit with Ed's widow and three young daughters. The girls delighted in showing him the German shepherd guard dog they had gotten after the crash and named Teddy. Kennedy, who still had great difficulty walking and had been ordered to wear a back brace, wasn't exactly thrilled when, while sitting in an armchair in the Moss living room, Teddy the dog welcomed Teddy the senator by jumping into his lap.

The girls, who ranged in age from five to eleven at the time of the crash, were still too young to comprehend all they had lost. The gifts they had gotten for their father for Father's Day had remained under their parents' bed before finally being packed away. In the six months since the accident, the girls had seen the cardinal visit their home (their mother had to teach them how to bend before him and kiss his ring), and they had seen their mother go back to work. If Katie Moss harbored any anger toward Kennedy for his need to go ahead with the flight despite the weather warnings, she never shared it with her daughters. In fact, she would talk little about the accident to her daughters or to anyone else. She didn't want people coming forward to ask her for a favor from the senator, or to bad-mouth him — depending on their politics.

Ted, however, would make a tradition of sending the girls gift baskets every Christmas, usually containing the most popular toys, such as stuffed animals with transistor radios inside them.

On Election Day, a month and a half before his release from the hospital, Teddy had walloped his Republican opponent, grabbing three-quarters of the vote. Bobby had also won his Senate seat, though by a much slimmer margin, and after having to suffer the indignity of calling in LBJ to campaign for him.

At a joint news conference on the terrace outside Ted's hospital room, Bobby stood in a suit next to Ted lying in his pajamas in bed. When Ted ribbed his brother about his narrow margin of victory, Bobby quipped, "He's getting awful fresh since he's been in bed and his wife won the campaign for him."

A photographer told Bobby, "Step back a little. You're casting a shadow on Ted." Teddy shot back, "It'll be the same in Washington."

CHAPTER
10

IN THE SUMMER of 1965, Ted invited Birch and Marvella Bayh to the Hyannis Port compound. He was still wearing the back brace, but his recovery had gone well. Birch joined Ted on his sailboat. Bobby got in his own sailboat, and they began an impromptu race. "The swells were high," Bayh recalls. "We were bumping around. I got so sick I thought I was going to die." At one point, the spinnaker on Bobby's boat came off and floated in the ocean. Ted sailed right on by. He won the race. Back on shore, Bobby was furious that Ted hadn't stopped to pick up his spinnaker. "We were in a race," Ted replied, laughing, "and I wasn't going to stop for anything."

The relationship between the two brothers had always been like that, fierce competition leavened with teasing and laughs. Their personalities reflected their appearances — Bobby's sharp and taut, Teddy's softer and rounder. There was never any doubt, though, that Bobby, six years Teddy's senior and always more serious and intense, was firmly in charge. Yet Bobby's arrival in the Senate in January 1965 injected new questions into the relationship. Bobby was still the senior brother and the uncontested head of the family. But in terms of Senate seniority, his younger brother outranked him. Ted had spent his first two years getting acclimated to the institution, being solicitous of his elders and building the relationships that would lay the groundwork for a more robust role. The fact that he had spent the last half of the previous year enrolled in a sort of bedside graduate school spoke to how determined he was to leave his mark as a senator. On some level, the groundwork that Ted had laid was threatened by Bobby's arrival.

It didn't help that Bobby's temperament was wholly incompatible with the Senate. A natural executive, ruthless when he needed to be, Bobby had already accomplished much in government. Still recovering from the soul-crushing assassination of his brother, he was restless to get more done. But the shift from being the president's most influential adviser to being only one of a hundred senators represented a dramatic step-down in power. Bobby could barely conceal his impatience with, and sometimes contempt for, the grinding tedium of lawmaking. To many members of the old guard, he entered the Senate like the entitled, headline-grabbing upstart they had initially feared Teddy would be.

As for his sense of Teddy as a senator, Bobby's opinion sometimes seemed rooted in memories of the chubby baby brother who liked to clown around at the compound. Burton Hersh, Ted's biographer, recalls one conversation he had with Bobby in his Senate office during this period. Ted had just delivered a speech, and Hersh told Bobby, who had not been present at the speech, that he thought Ted had done an excellent job. "Robert Kennedy looked at me a moment, those opaque, rather baleful eyes narrowing beneath their slanting folds. 'Well,' he said finally, 'I wonder who wrote it for him.' "

Bobby brought with him to the Senate a cadre of high-achieving, Ivy-educated staffers. Like Bobby and unlike Teddy, many of these aides saw the Senate as a way station to something bigger, an opportunity to cherry-pick national issues that they could carry out from the executive branch when Bobby inevitably assumed control of the White House. Many of them looked down on Ted and his staff.

On visits with his father at the compound, Teddy would quip, "I was okay in the Senate until Bobby came in and upset everything."

In reality, Ted didn't complain too much. As fiercely competitive as the Kennedy siblings were raised to be, they were taught always to close ranks and join in the fight against outside opponents. Moreover, the new arrangement, coming not long after the loss of Jack, allowed for a maturation of the relationship between Teddy and Bobby. Before long, the older brother began to see the younger brother as an astute politician who had lessons to share about how things got done in the Senate. The younger brother began to appreciate his elevated status in his big brother's eyes, and glimpse how the new arrangement could be a plus for both of them. Bobby had essentially set up a shadow government to LBJ's from his Senate office. With the cameras pointed squarely at Bobby, Ted could step out of his shell in the Senate and push through his own ambitious agenda without fear of being seen as an upstart or publicity hound.

The first step for Ted was remaking his staff. Ed Moss had died, and his pals and former aides John Culver and John Tunney had moved on to their own congressional seats. A few others on the staff were seen as loyal and competent but incapable of leading a dramatic upgrade of the office, so Ted asked around for the best talent. He found what he was looking for in 29-year-old David Burke. A former aide to the commerce secretary, Burke was a sharp University of Chicago–trained economist who looked the part—wiry, with horn-rimmed glasses and a serious face. But he was also the tough son of a cop whose accent signaled his Boston Irish Catholic roots. He knew how to read a situation and how to throw a punch.

Ted told Burke to put together a collection of young talent that would rival the legendary staff of New York's Republican Senator Jacob Javits and the emerging collection of go-getters working for Bobby. Burke did just that, scouting for highfliers with Harvard Law Review stints and Phi Beta Kappa honors on their resumes. His pitch to them? Come to Washington to help Senator Kennedy make history. More than a few asked "which Kennedy?" but Burke had little trouble spotting those who would be a good fit for this particular Kennedy's office.

In 1965, in the days of murders and marches in Selma, voting rights became an enormous issue, the natural extension of the landmark civil rights legislation passed the year before. Ted and Burke sounded out prominent civil rights leaders on their priorities, and kept hearing the same refrain: "Poll tax, poll tax, poll tax." Since the days of Jim Crow, the poll tax had been a cynical and noxiously effective device used to deny blacks the right to vote. But LBJ and Nick Katzenbach, Bobby's former assistant who had succeeded him as attorney general, had opposed adding an amendment to the voting rights bill to eliminate the poll tax. They worried that it might cost the overall bill key swing supporters and feared that if the amendment were found to be unconstitutional, it could jeopardize the entire package, or at least keep it tied up in the courts for years.

Ted decided to take up the cause against the poll tax. As a member of the Judiciary Committee, he was the logical Kennedy to lead the fight, so Bobby deferred to him in the same way that Teddy was deferring to Bobby in many other matters such as foreign policy and nuclear proliferation. After seeking out, and then soaking up, the best expert advice on the matter, Ted put to use everything he had learned about the Senate during his first two years.

Following intense research and tutoring by academics from Harvard and Howard universities, including his new ally Mark De Wolfe Howe, he entered the debate thoroughly prepared for any argument the amendment's opponents would make on the floor. Yet he remained unfailingly polite throughout, declining to move in for the kill even when an opponent showed himself to be clearly out of his depth.

For Ted, the cause showcased a new determination mixed with his usual deference. Despite being engaged in a seemingly hopeless fight against a popular liberal president and powerful conservative senators, he managed to make it a surprisingly close vote. The amendment lost, 49–45. But his performance won him wide praise outside the Senate and a new reputation as a force to be reckoned with. Full victory came the following year, when the Supreme Court ruled the poll tax unconstitutional.

Around the same time, he took up another cause that was just as rife with political danger: immigration reform. Since the 1920s, immigrants had been allowed into the United States under an absurdly lopsided quota system that heavily favored Northern Europeans. If you were an Asian, good luck getting through, but if you were Irish or English, it was seldom a problem. As a senator, Jack Kennedy had tried unsuccessfully to reform the quota system. Now Ted picked up the mantle, this time with the support of the Johnson administration. Ted framed immigration reform as a simple matter of fairness, echoing his approach to civil rights, when he had reminded people of how disadvantaged the Kennedy clan would have been had the nation never taken down the "Irish Need Not Apply" signs.

But many of those European natives who had benefited from the current system and whose family immigration journeys were fresher and less complete than the Kennedys' saw danger in this reform. In a small preview of a divide that would become much more pronounced during Boston's school busing wars a decade later, Ted staked out progressive policy that created distance between him and many of the working-class Irish who had always been the Kennedys' bread-and-butter supporters.

Burke recalls walking through an underground tunnel into an arena where Ted was to deliver a speech. A young compact guy with a thick Irish brogue came up and angrily confronted Kennedy for having sold out the Irish. "You know what I'm going to do?" the man yelled, "I'm going to get up on the stage, and I'm going to yell you down." He didn't get the chance. As they passed a men's room, Burke hip-checked the guy through the door and into a stall, and stayed with him in the bathroom until Ted was safely on stage.

Ted was showing he knew how to get things done in the Senate, and the keys to his success were some of the same skills he had learned growing up with so many older brothers and sisters ahead of him. He had a knack for when to jump into the fray, and when to hang back. Exhibit A was his handling of the immigration bill and, in particular, the unapologetically racist Judiciary Committee Chairman James O. Eastland. As journalist Meg Greenfield observed at the time:

When, on occasion, Eastland denounces him as a fomenter of racial violence and a veritable menace to the Republic, Kennedy lets it pass, knowing both the southerner's need to make his remarks for the record and their profound irrelevance to what goes on in committee. Eastland, for instance, in an unprecedented bit of graciousness, permitted Kennedy to take over his own subcommittee for the period of time required to hold friendly hearings on the immigration bill, which Eastland fervently opposed. Kennedy thus became Senate manager of the bill, which he shepherded through committee and the floor with scrupulous tact, at all times willing to indulge the Southern Senators' fulminations against it—so long as they would leave it alone. As a result, the southerners conspicuously failed to try to amend it during the four days it was on the floor.

The immigration reform bill easily passed the Senate in September of 1965 and was signed into law by President Johnson a few weeks later.

Late in 1965, on the heels of his biggest successes in the Senate, Kennedy committed the biggest political blunder of his young career. It came in the form of one Francis X. Morrissey. An old political hand with slicked-back black hair and apple cheeks resting on either corner of his easy smile, Morrissey had squired Ted around the state leading up to his 1962 election. One of a dozen children from a poor Charlestown family, Morrissey had worked in service to the Kennedy family for decades, as a small-time operative and full-time errand man for Joe. As his detractors liked to joke, in forty years, he never let Joe Kennedy's coat hit the ground.

He had worked in Jack's congressional and Senate offices, but Jack and some of his aides had distrusted him, concluding with some justification that Joe had installed him to extend his control over his son by serving as the patriarch's eyes and ears. In the late 1950s, Joe had orchestrated Morrissey's appointment as a municipal judge in Boston. But even the relatively uncomplicated docket of municipal court had proved tricky for Morrissey. For his unfailingly tentative performance on the bench, he earned the nickname "I'll-Take-That-Under-Advisement" Morrissey. His undistinguished tenure could not have come as a surprise, considering that he had twice failed the bar and had procured, under dubious circumstances, a quickie law degree from a diploma mill in Georgia. Yet now he wanted a promotion to the federal bench.

In fact, he'd been angling for the promotion since JFK's election. In 1961, under pressure from their father, Jack and Bobby had tested the waters for a Morrissey federal judgeship. The pushback from the legal community was so swift and forceful that President Kennedy wisely tabled the matter. Still, Morrissey's lobbying with the surviving Kennedy brothers continued apace, and, unlike many of Joe's other coat-holders, he continued to be a faithful visitor to the compound long after the stroke had incapacitated the patriarch. So his backing from the head of the family was undiminished.

In September 1964, in one of his final private letters to President Johnson before vacating his post as attorney general, Bobby had written, "I want to express to you my appreciation for your statement that, at an appropriate time, you would give sympathetic consideration to Frank Morrissey for appointment to the United States District Court for the District of Massachusetts." He went on to lay it on thick about Morrissey's experience, character, and judicial temperament.

Now, one year later, it was apparently the time. And Teddy, as the senator from Massachusetts, where Morrissey would sit on the federal bench, would be the point person. Remarkably, the sharpened political skills Ted had shown in his work on voting rights and immigration reform seemed to desert him when it came to the Morrissey matter, as he allowed himself to be played by the pols around him. When Ted approached the president, LBJ agreed to submit the Morrissey nomination to the Senate as a favor to him and his father, even inviting Ted to the Oval Office so they could call Joe and deliver the good news together. LBJ had always had a more accommodating relationship with Joe than with Jack or Bobby, so Ted might be forgiven for failing to look for the calculation behind the president's cooperative spirit. It seems clear now that LBJ, as much as he may have liked Teddy, saw in Morrissey the opportunity to embarrass his nemesis, Bobby. If he was so inclined, he knew he could leak a copy of the letter in which the righteous, corruption-fighting former attorney general had extolled the manifestly unqualified Morrissey's fitness for the federal bench.

For added insurance, around the same time that LBJ was celebrating the planned nomination with Ted and Joe, he was directing FBI director J. Edgar Hoover to dig up enough dirt on Morrissey to sink it.

On September 26, 1965, President Johnson was vacationing in Texas. His press aide Joseph Laitin issued an agenda for that day's press briefing with a single item: The nomination of Francis X. Morrissey to the federal district court of Massachusetts. "For the past seven years, Mr. Morrissey has been a judge of the Municipal Court of Boston," Laitin explained, "and for several years served as a secretary to the late President Kennedy before he was president. He served at various times for Congressman Kennedy and Senator Kennedy."

Kennedy aides recall that Morrissey was impressed with himself to be garnering such high-level attention. But savvier students of Washington politics saw it for what it was: a setup to draw heightened attention to an otherwise routine judicial nomination, the likes of which happen all the time and seldom with this kind of major announcement. The frequent mentions of the Kennedy name succeeded in branding it a Kennedy—rather than a Johnson—appointment.

The reaction from the legal community was pointed. The American Bar Association came out against the nomination. Charles Wyzanski, one of the top jurists in Massachusetts, expressed his horror at the prospect of a Morrissey promotion. When Ted met with Senate Minority Leader Everett Dirksen to shore up his support by explaining the circumstances behind Morrissey's failed attempts to pass the bar, Dirksen replied, "Your story does not fall on unfriendly ears. As a young man, I took the bar on more than one occasion in order to successfully pass it." Ted left the meeting reassured.

Before long, though, Dirksen turned into Morrissey's most relentless and indignant critic. Despite all the opposition, Ted remained firmly behind Morrissey. No doubt he was doing it partly out of loyalty to his father. But Ted also took offense at the class dimensions he detected behind the criticisms of Morrissey. If the guy had grown up wealthy rather than poor, he surely could have procured a degree from a prestigious law school rather than the lesser one that he had to attend part-time while continuing to provide for his family. And it wasn't lost on Ted that many of the loudest critics of Morrissey came from the same intellectual crowd that had been so appalled by Ted's lack of fitness when he first ran for office.

Regardless, the Morrissey nomination quickened its course down the drain. Bob Healy, the *Globe* writer who had gingerly broken the news of Ted's expulsion from Harvard, uncovered material that made for a withering indictment of Morrissey's lack of candor over his credentials and lack of readiness for the federal bench. The *Globe* was handed the Pulitzer Prize for its coverage, and Ted was handed an embarrassing defeat.

In late October, lacking the votes, Bobby persuaded Ted to give up on the nomination. While Ted still felt he might be able to twist enough arms to help Morrissey squeak by, his brother told him bluntly that the fight to keep the nomination alive wouldn't be worth the political favors he'd have to repay for the next decade. Morrissey may have been a loyal servant to their father, but it wasn't worth sacrificing so much of the Kennedy agenda to get him through.

There were other struggles during this period, especially on the home front. While Joan had proved herself to be a crucial stand-in for her husband during the 1964 campaign, when she could use her sweet, girl-next-door personality to further his political goals, now she was asked to resume the role of Kennedy wife. And in this area, she had trouble competing. Joan idolized her mother-in-law, showing appreciation rather than offense at Rose's chiding correspondence, replying with innocent notes to the woman she addressed as Gramma K. But she could not match the matriarch in so many of the ways in which Rose had fortified the family—as a prodigious producer of offspring, and as a strong-willed person who always knew how to play her public role perfectly, even if that meant blinding herself to her husband's adultery.

Between young Teddy's birth in 1961 and Patrick's birth in 1967, Joan suffered two miscarriages. And by the middle of the decade, she was well aware of Ted's extramarital affairs, which had been whispered about around Washington for some time. She didn't know what to do, so she sought advice from Jackie, a woman she knew had extensive experience in coping with a cheating husband.

Jackie, who as a widow had become close to Ted, told Joan, "He adores you. He thinks you're a wonderful wife and you're smart and you're talented and you're a wonderful mother. His mother and father adore you, and the whole family loves you. You're just the perfect wife. But he just has this addiction."

Jackie was telling her it wasn't her fault. Infidelity was part of the male Kennedy inheritance. Joan believed her. But as a vulnerable soul, and the daughter of an alcoholic mother, she eventually would find support only in a bottle. And the distance between her and Ted would grow.

In another reflection of his father's behavior, Ted maintained strong, warm relations with his children even as he cheated on their mother. Whenever he was on the road, no matter where he might be, he would stop to call home at night to talk with his kids. He'd make animal noises or pretend to be one character or another—always leaving his children laughing as they hung up the phone. As busy as life became, he was faithful in remembering the birthdays of each of his many nieces and nephews.

Like Joan, Ted also came to rely on drink for release during this period, though aides noticed that the senator was careful to keep his drinking in check and to curb any skirt-chasing when David Burke was around. In addition to becoming Ted's chief aide and consigliere, Burke also served as something of a moral tuning fork. "He wouldn't do any shenanigans if David was around," Milton Gwirtzman says. "David had a strong moral sense."

Because Ted was developing a remarkable ability to compartmentalize his life, his personal issues didn't seem to affect his work. Every night he'd pore over the materials his aides had stuffed into his bulging briefcase—"the bag"—earlier in the day. At meetings, he'd often impress aides and colleagues by being the most prepared person sitting at the table.

It was yet more evidence of his determination to put in the hard

work as compensation for his shortcomings, and prove once and for all
that the kid brother could finally measure up.

In the fall of 1965, around the same time of the Morrissey debacle, Ted
made his first trip to Vietnam. The American public was still firmly in
support of the war effort, and Kennedy was no different. It was, after
all, a war still closely associated with his brother's administration.

He made the trip in connection with the subcommittee on refugees that he chaired. Accordingly, the treatment of the many souls being displaced by the war was his prime area of interest once his plane
touched down. Still, like most lawmakers who had taken similar fact-
finding trips to Vietnam before him, Kennedy was given the full dog-
and-pony show by the military and diplomatic corps, and reassured
that the war was going well.

Publicly at least, he showed no signs of any disbelief. "I support our
fundamental commitment in Vietnam . . . I don't have reservations,"
he said. True to form, when he returned, he opted to work backdoor
channels with Secretary of State Dean Rusk to try to improve conditions for refugees, rather than pick a headline-grabbing fight with the
Johnson administration.

If he had been played by LBJ during the Morrissey nomination,
Ted chose not to see it, taking the president at his word when he had
pledged his support for Morrissey. That was probably for the best, since
Ted was able to rebound quickly, working with the Johnson administration to push through lasting legislation. He successfully advocated
the creation of a National Teacher Corps, which awarded scholarships
to those who promised to spend two years teaching in poor rural and
urban neighborhoods. And a visit he made to a new health clinic at a
Boston housing project led to his first legislation in the area he was to
become most passionate about: health care.

In the summer of 1966 he toured the clinic at the Columbia Point
housing project in Boston, which two Tufts University Medical School
doctors had created on the model of the type of full-scale local clinics
that had been opened in developing countries. The idea was to improve

health through prevention and maintenance, by bringing comprehensive medical care to where the people were, rather than forcing them to seek it out. Touring with Kennedy, Burke saw how the potential of the place immediately registered in the senator's eyes, right down to the rocking chairs that were available in waiting rooms for mothers to use while nursing their babies. Within months, Kennedy had secured funding for the creation of some thirty similar health clinics in low-income areas across the nation, a roster that would eventually grow to 850.

On the issue of civil rights, Kennedy continued his pattern of remarkably candid talk about the sins of his race and the need to do better. The same summer he toured the health clinic, he traveled to Jackson, Mississippi, to address the Southern Christian Leadership Conference. "My state, as the other states in the North, has very difficult and dangerous problems in the field of civil rights," Ted said. "I cannot come here to Mississippi and say that our hands are clean. We have done too little. We started quite late. The Negro in Boston, to our shame, goes to a segregated school, holds an inferior job, and lives in one of the worst parts of the city." It was an approach that established his bona fides with civil rights leaders, black voters, and white liberals, even as it created additional distance between him and some of his white constituents who were more conservative when it came to matters of race, particularly those in the working class who would be asked to bear the brunt of racial remediation. Still, there was a limit to how far Kennedy would go. He was still on record as opposing the mandated busing of school children to address racial imbalance.

By 1967, Ted's grasp of the workings of the Senate had matured to the point where he felt confident in taking on some of its most powerful members. And he soon would do so over the issue of redistricting. The Supreme Court had ruled that the constitutionality of legislative districts could be challenged in court if they encompassed populations that differed significantly in size. The constitutional guarantee of "one man, one vote" was by definition unattainable if, for example, one congressman was asked to represent the interests of 100,000 constituents, and another, the interests of one million. The creation of districts of varying size had, for years, given disproportionate representation to rural residents. Their representatives in Congress were determined to keep things that way.

Everett Dirksen, the Republican minority leader from Illinois, joined forces with some of the most powerful elders in the Senate and their counterparts in the House to push legislation to delay redistricting and maintain the system of districts of varying size. Somehow, Ted found himself leading the fight against Dirksen's bill assisted by Jim Flug, one of those best-and-brightest Harvard men that Burke had recruited in his effort to upgrade the office staff.

Adopting the kind of bipartisan approach that would become the hallmark of his Senate work in years to come, Ted teamed up with freshman Republican Senator Howard Baker, who had earlier spoken out strongly against unequal districts in his home state of Tennessee. It was a tough position for Baker to take, pitting him against not just the leadership of his party but also the leadership of his family. His father-in-law was none other than Everett Dirksen.

The fight took on many twists and turns, but this time it was Ted who ultimately outmaneuvered and outfoxed the old men who ran the ultimate old men's club. He enlisted support from organized labor and editorial writers from across the country. In the end, he won, preserving the integrity of "one man, one vote."

As with the poll tax, Ted had taken the lead and Bobby had played a supporting role. It was an arrangement that would have been unthinkable just a few years earlier, but which now spoke to the manner in which Ted had emerged as a force in his own right. It also spoke to the genuine closeness with which he and Bobby were now operating. Because they served on only one committee together, they learned how to carve out their own areas of emphasis. As impatient as Bobby was with the slow pace and elaborate niceties of the Senate, he increasingly came to appreciate Ted's mastery of the workings of the institution. Not that there wasn't still some rivalry between the brothers, but for the most part that was expressed through humor. During a string of speeches on the West Coast, Bobby joked about the telegram he had received from Washington. "Lyndon is in Manila. Hubert [Humphrey] is out campaigning. Congress has gone home. Have seized power. Teddy."

In his own speeches afterward, Ted would recount Bobby's joke and then add, "Everyone here knows that if I ever did seize power the last person I'd notify is my brother."

CHAPTER
11

EVERYTHING CHANGED IN 1968, and it all started with Vietnam.

So much was different about the war since Ted's visit to Vietnam in 1965, when he had done little to dispute the rosy predictions given to him and other members of Congress by the administration and the Pentagon. Still, even as the antiwar effort intensified and public support for the administration's policies softened, and even as Bobby's opposition to the war came into fuller view, Ted strained to avoid a full break with the president.

In March of 1967, Bobby had given a speech in the Senate in which he called for a unilateral suspension of American bombing of North Vietnam, in direct opposition to the Johnson administration's policies in Vietnam. Perhaps mindful of his own responsibility for a military commitment that had been expanded on his brother's watch, Bobby at that time continued to argue against a U.S. withdrawal from Vietnam "until we have fulfilled our commitments." (Instead he argued for a gradual withdrawal of U.S. troops and their replacement by an international peacekeeping force.) Yet by the early part of 1968, Bobby was saying the war was hopeless.

Even as he continued to move closer to Bobby's position, Ted remained a few paces back. He knew the war had the potential to rip apart not just the Democratic Party but the nation as a whole. And, in the same way that he tried to bridge the chasm between Bobby and

LBJ, he focused on problems at the edges of the war rather than the war itself—the treatment of refugees, civilian casualties, medical care, and the draft.

On the first day of 1968, Ted was back in Vietnam. This time, he had no interest in a whitewashed dog-and-pony show. Instead, David Burke had prepared for the trip like a high-profile campaign event. In late 1967, he had dispatched four intrepid lawyers to act as advance men and scope out the spots and people who could show Kennedy the true state of the war. Their movements around Vietnam did not go unnoticed in the Johnson administration. A confidential telegram sent in December to Nick Katzenbach, who had moved from attorney general to undersecretary of state, reported that the "Kennedy advance team has been extremely active visiting countryside, have been closemouthed about conclusions but several thrusts evident . . . rules of engagement, control of air strikes and artillery, selection of targets, coordination of supporting arms, etc. Special effort made in visiting hospitals to obtain estimates of proportion of casualties."

Upon landing, Ted toured refugee camps and hospitals, met with weary relief workers and hardened war reporters. During one stop at a military base, the captain had his men put on the standard show by firing a shell into the distance. Kennedy was disturbed. "Where did that shell go?" he asked the captain. When the captain responded that it went down into a certain Vietcong sector, Ted shot back, "How do you know it didn't hit somebody?" The captain said they knew they were directing the fire into an unsettled area of Vietcong fighters. Kennedy wasn't buying it. Furious, he told the captain they had seen people in the area as they had helicoptered over it on their way to the base.

Burke looked at his boss and saw his refusal to accept the numbing indifference to the human condition that accompanied war, and he felt proud.

The trip confirmed in Kennedy's mind that the war was going badly, causing unacceptably high casualties, and was not going to turn around. He returned to the States and spoke out against the war in his starkest terms yet, though still pulling some punches. In a speech before the World Affairs Council, he said, "Continued optimism cannot be justified." He said that during the trip, "I found that the kind of war we are fighting in Vietnam will not gain our long-range objectives, that the pattern of destruction we are creating can only make a workable political future more difficult."

For weeks, the silence from the Johnson administration was deafening. LBJ, haunted by his nosedive in popularity thanks to Vietnam and convinced that Bobby was plotting to do him in, was clearly not eager to be told by Bobby's brother how poorly things were going in Southeast Asia. Finally, in the last week of January, Ted received word that the president wanted to see him.

Burke and Ted prepared their presentation for Johnson and then sat with him in the Oval Office. As Ted began his remarks about the failure of the United States to win over hearts and minds of the Vietnamese, Johnson cut him off.

"Now wait a minute, Teddy," the president drawled. "There's no need to rush on this. There was something I wanted to ask you first, and then we can get down to what you wanted to say."

"Yes, sir."

"Teddy," Johnson said, pausing for effect. "Do you want a Fresca?"

"Um, no thank you, Mr. President," Ted stammered.

As Ted tried once more to deliver his report, Johnson again interrupted and turned to Burke. "Dave, would you like a Fresca?"

"No thank you, Mr. President."

"Well, I'm going to have a Fresca," the leader of the free world announced. Then he turned to look at his butler, who was holding a silver beverage tray. "I'll ask you again, Dave, are you going to have a Fresca with your president? We'd enjoy it."

Burke caved. "Yes, Mr. President, I'll have a Fresca."

Johnson smiled. "Good, good. Now that's good." He turned to his butler. "Dave and I will have a Fresca." He waited several beats before adding, "Teddy doesn't want one."

As the butler left the room, one of Johnson's dogs came bounding into the room and leaped onto Burke's lap. So in between sipping his Fresca, Burke sat in the Oval Office dutifully petting a dog. He couldn't have looked more like an 8-year-old boy if he tried, which was precisely what LBJ had in mind. Ted tried to suppress a laugh as he glanced at Burke.

From there, Ted tried resuming his remarks, but it was clear to both him and Burke that Johnson had absolutely no interest in anything he had to report. Their command performance in the Oval Office had been just one more exercise in Johnson proving who was top dog.

Johnson used to tell Burke, "I like Teddy. He's good." Burke understood it was the president's way of conveying how much he didn't like Bobby without having to actually say that. But he also could tell that Ted's intensifying opposition to Vietnam and Bobby's intensifying challenge to Johnson were combining to overpower the natural warmth that had long existed between the youngest Kennedy and the man who had succeeded his brother as president.

As the election year of 1968 dawned, with the once robust support for LBJ becoming as weak as tea from a reused bag, most of Bobby's advisers and supporters urged him to run. It would be the only way, they argued, to stop an unwinnable war. Only then could the nation truly have a shot at eradicating urban and rural poverty at home, a cause that had touched Bobby's soul during his period of deep introspection that followed his brother's assassination.

But amid all the egging on for Bobby to run, Ted was a consistent voice of opposition. If it was partly motivated by a fear that he might lose another brother to a madman's bullet, Ted didn't let on. Instead, he framed his opposition solely in cold political terms: Bobby could not take down a sitting president, even one as weakened by war as LBJ. And just by trying he would divide the party, ensure the election of a Republican, and perhaps cost him his chance for the presidency in 1972.

Ted was perceptive enough to see the hazards of his brother being seduced by the drumbeat for him to run. He was determined that Bobby not get caught up in the hopes of all the ambitious people around him who may have had their own reasons for wanting him to run. With Jack's campaigns, Bobby had played the role of the ruthlessly clear-eyed adviser, the guy who could see through the smoke to distinguish between those who would be true supporters no matter what happened, and those whose squishy encouragement would fade at the first sign of pressure. To the best of his abilities, Ted tried to play that same role for Bobby this time around, even if he lacked his brother's capacity for ruthlessness. When people around Bobby would talk about the supporters who would be sure to line up behind him, Ted would push back, trying to divine what their self-interest might be and determine how many delegates they might actually be able to bring along.

One day in the Senate gym, he ran into George McGovern, his liberal colleague from South Dakota who was quietly encouraging Bobby to run. "You know, George, I am not for this," Ted told him. "And unless there are a lot of people willing to come out and endorse him if he decides to go, I don't think the thing would go anywhere." When he asked McGovern point-blank if he'd be willing to endorse Bobby, McGovern equivocated, saying he couldn't afford to come out publicly for Bobby and endanger either his own reelection campaign or his relations with the Democrats from neighboring states who were also interested in running.

"Well, shit," Ted shot back, "don't keep telling him to run then! If even you are not going to endorse him, don't tell him to run."

Eventually, Ted's appeal to Bobby's inner political calculus won. As determined as Bobby was to bring down Johnson, he had to agree that his brother was probably right. To the indignation of many of his antiwar supporters, he declined to enter the race. But the decision was in no way settled. As the New Hampshire primary approached, Bobby and a few advisers talked more seriously about his jumping in. Then on March 12, Minnesota Senator Eugene McCarthy, a peace candidate whom LBJ had once considered a fringe challenger at best, pulled down 42 percent of the New Hampshire primary vote. Suddenly, Johnson's vulnerabilities were laid bare.

Bobby's advisers immediately ratcheted up their campaign to get him to enter the race. It became clear to Ted that there would be no holding Bobby back now. So Ted flew to meet with McCarthy. Since McCarthy had assumed the risk of taking on an incumbent president from his own party when that appeared to be a futile task, Ted felt the man at least deserved the courtesy of a face-to-face meeting from the Kennedy family to be informed of Bobby's intentions. Frank Mankie-wicz, one of Bobby's top aides at the time, says Ted's decision to make the trip says a lot about the two Kennedy brothers and their markedly different operating systems. "That was pure Ted Kennedy—go by the rules," he says. "Bob didn't even know the rules."

On a visit to the compound, Bobby told his father he was going to run, as Joe's nurse Rita Dallas watched from the hall. The patriarch dropped his head on his chest. "It's going to be all right," Bobby said reassuringly. "It's going to be all right." It was unclear whether the old man's resignation sprang from a fear for his son's safety or for his son's electoral prospects. Of course, Joe's incapacitated state prevented him from playing the pivotal role behind the scenes that he had during Jack's 1960 campaign.

Four days after McCarthy's stunning performance in New Hamp-shire, Bobby announced he was in the race. Once that decision was made, Teddy threw everything he had into getting his brother the nomination. Ted and Burke headed out on a tour to line up support from big-city mayors and labor leaders. With just about Bobby's entire Senate staff decamping for the campaign, and much of Ted's as well, Ted instructed his aide Jim Flug to handle operations for both Sen-ate staffs. He also dispatched Gerard Doherty to Indiana, where he was tasked with hurriedly qualifying Bobby's name for the ballot in the first state primary the new presidential candidate would enter.

The fact that Doherty, who knew nothing about Indiana, would be running operations in such a critical state was an indication of how rushed and improvised the whole Bobby-for-president operation was turning out to be. It also didn't help that campaign staffers who briefed Doherty on his assignment could give him the names of only three people on the ground in Indiana he could turn to for help.

The slapdash nature of the campaign was not lost on longtime po-litical observers, and few were as astute as Cardinal Richard Cushing, the Boston prelate who had long ago forged a backdoor alliance with Joe Kennedy that proved beneficial to both their enterprises. "The family is divided," the cardinal told LBJ adviser Eugene Rostow, according to a summary of the meeting that was swiftly forwarded to the president. "Ted Kennedy is not entirely behind this campaign. Their organization is not nearly so good as in 1960 . . . Bobby had made many enemies for President Kennedy and the cardinal said he didn't think those enemies had forgotten."

Yet whatever his reservations may have been, it was clear to everyone how hard Ted was working on his brother's behalf. He was forever on the go, and though he and Bobby were seldom in the same city during the frenetic primary months—a consequence of the rush to build operations in a host of states, almost overnight—they usually talked on the phone at least once a day. If Ted never reached the same position of authority that Bobby had in advising Jack, he had grown into the role of his brother's trusted confidant. And there now appeared to be more affection between the two brothers than there had been between Jack and Bobby.

Indiana remained the first big prize. It also happened to be the home state of Ted's close friend from the Senate and fellow plane crash survivor, Birch Bayh. But since he was involved in his own tough reelection fight, Bayh felt forced to back the state's Democratic governor, Roger Branigin, who was running a native-son campaign for president as a stand-in for Johnson. Branigin was doing everything he could to complicate the effort to certify enough signatures to get Bobby on the Indiana ballot. In a heated conversation, he told Ted that he'd "deserted all his natural friends, including Birch Bayh." As for the Kennedy campaign's efforts in his state, Branigin said, "You probably can buy the state, and I'll just call it 'Kennedy' instead of 'Indiana.' You bought West Virginia and you can buy this one."

In reality, Bayh cared little for Branigin, so he quietly instructed his aides to do whatever they could to help Bobby and Ted through back-channel means.

On the last day of March, Ted was in Indianapolis, having supper at a hotel with Doherty. They kept their eyes on the television set as LBJ addressed the nation, announcing a reduction in the bombing campaign in North Vietnam. Then, buried at the end of the address, was LBJ's shocker: "I shall not seek, and I will not accept, the nomination of my party for another term as your president." With Election Day just seven months away, an already uncertain race instantly became chaotic, as Vice President Hubert Humphrey quickly jumped into the fray.

The chaos would never recede.

On the afternoon of April 4, Doherty was preparing for Bobby's arrival in Indianapolis when he received a phone call from Richard Lugar, then the city's mayor. "Martin Luther King has been shot," Lugar told Doherty. "We understand that Robert Kennedy is going to speak tonight. We want you to call it off."

Doherty said he would talk to Bobby when his plane landed, which he did. "No, we're going to go ahead with it," Bobby told him.

That set the stage for one of the most quietly powerful political speeches in the modern age. As he headed toward the stage to speak to a packed stadium in an Indianapolis ghetto, Bobby asked an aide, "Do they know?" Told that most had not heard about the assassination, he stepped on stage. With his scrawny body standing behind a microphone, he pushed back the sweep of hair that perennially descended below his eyes, and began. "I have some very sad news for all of you, and I think sad news for all of our fellow citizens, and people who love peace all over the world," he said. "And that is that Martin Luther King was shot and was killed tonight in Memphis, Tennessee."

Over gasps and screams, he continued, in an understated but mesmerizing way. "For those of you who are black and are tempted to be filled with hatred and mistrust of the injustice of such an act, against all white people, I would only say that I can also feel in my own heart the same kind of feeling. I had a member of my family killed, but he was killed by a white man." Never once referring to the prepared text he held rolled up in his hand, Bobby kept the shaken crowd rapt as he recited verse from his favorite poet, Aeschylus. "In our sleep, pain which cannot forget falls drop by drop upon the heart until, in our own despair, against our will, comes wisdom through the awful grace of God."

Unlike many other big cities across the country, there was no rioting in Indianapolis that night.

On the last day of April, Bobby Kennedy won the Indiana primary.

He followed that up with a win in Nebraska before losing to McCarthy in Oregon. The focus then shifted to the biggest prize, California, a must-win for Bobby and a place where his campaign organization was struggling because of infighting.

On the primary night of June 4, David Burke stood in the packed California Hall near San Francisco's City Hall, watching Ted deliver a speech over the shouts of campaign workers ecstatic over Bobby's make-or-break victory in that state. Surveying the crowd, Burke was in no mood to celebrate. It was a volatile scene. The characteristic late-60s protest placards, the people drinking out of paper bags, the absence of personal security for his boss—all this made Burke determined to get Ted out of the auditorium as soon as he stepped off the stage.

They were in San Francisco, 400 miles away from Bobby and the real primary night celebration, because Bobby's close friend and aide John Seigenthaler wanted a big name on hand to thank the Northern California campaign workers who had made the Golden State victory possible. And besides Bobby, Ted was the biggest name in the campaign. After the speech was over, Burke whisked Ted out of the hall and back to the Fairmont hotel. As they walked into their suite, an aide picked up the phone to order some drinks and ham and cheese sandwiches while Ted sat down and flicked on the television to watch Bobby's victory speech.

"Be quiet, be quiet!" someone was yelling on the television, straining to rise above the pandemonium. "Everyone be quiet!"

Burke looked up, and Ted turned to him. "What the hell's going on?" the senator said. "Dave, what's going on?"

"I don't know," Burke replied, trying to suppress his panic.

"We'd better go there," Ted said.

Realizing that Bobby had been shot, Burke rushed out of the room, his mind racing. They were on the twelfth floor, but instead of waiting for the elevator he sprinted down the fire stairs. In the lobby, he hurried over to the woman at the American Airlines counter, adrenaline pumping, and told her she needed to get them to Los Angeles immediately. She flashed him a look that said, "Who are you and what are you doing here?" He realized there were two worlds of people coexisting in that lobby, those who had heard the news, and those who hadn't. He told her, "Senator Kennedy has been shot."

A California congressman standing nearby heard the exchange, and also knew the awful news coming out of Los Angeles. He approached Burke. "Maybe I can help you guys get down to LA," he said. "Let me call the National Guard. And if I get you something," he added, "the condition is I'm coming with you." That last demand struck Burke as the definition of low class, a politician whose offer to help in a crisis seemed less motivated by genuine concern than by a desire to insinuate himself into some kind of photo op. But the key at this point was getting his boss to his brother's side, so Burke voiced no complaint.

He went back to the room and heard that Bobby had been taken to a hospital. No one knew what kind of condition he was in. A few minutes later the congressman called to tell Burke there would be a state trooper in the lobby in fifteen minutes, and the National Guard had a plane ready to fly them to LA. By the time Burke returned to the lobby, this time with Ted at his side, the place was a sea of commotion. Everyone knew now. Burke feared for Ted's safety, worrying that the gunman who had shot down Bobby might be part of a network determined to take out both remaining Kennedy brothers on the same dreadful night.

As the trooper escorted them and Seigenthaler toward the cruiser, Burke pulled him aside. "If anyone else tries to get into that car, you stop them."

"Yes, sir," the trooper replied.

As the cruiser pulled away from the hotel, Burke dreaded the news that lay ahead. But at least he had the satisfaction of looking out the back window and seeing the opportunistic congressman left behind on the curb.

The bumpy, rumbling plane ride to Los Angeles seemed to Burke to last an eternity. It was made even longer by the fact that easygoing, chatty, backslapping Teddy Kennedy barely said a word for the whole flight.

The next day, after it became clear that Bobby could not be saved, his spokesman Frank Mankiewicz was walking out of Bobby's hospital room when he spied a figure standing in the adjoining, darkened bathroom, leaning on the sink. It was Ted. "I have never, ever, nor do I expect ever, to see a face more in grief," Mankiewicz recalls. "It was beyond grief and agony."

Jim Flug had been watching Bobby's victory speech on television back in Washington. As soon as the shooting happened, he raced over to the campaign headquarters. Because just about every campaign official with any kind of seniority was in California, he took it upon himself to field the hundreds of calls that began to flood the office. All through the night and the next day, he ran the office's old-fashioned switchboard. The frenetic work would keep him preoccupied, staving off the feeling of profound powerlessness that would wash over all of Bobby's supporters.

When Bobby died, Flug's attention shifted to funeral arrangements. Given Bobby's international stature, they would essentially be planning a state funeral without the usual resources of the state, although the Johnson administration did offer assistance. Flug and another aide were flown on a military plane to New York to meet with Kennedy brother-in-law Steve Smith, who would oversee funeral plans. There, they summoned all the people who had been personal secretaries to any of the Kennedys, from every era, having them flip through their Rolodexes and pore over their address books and help decide who would be invited to the funeral at St. Patrick's Cathedral. "We had one or two people there from each generation," Flug recalls, "who could give us an up or down vote."

Once they had settled on the list, they sent color-coded Western Union telegrams that would function as people's tickets to the funeral Mass. "You are invited to attend a requiem Mass in memory of Robert Francis Kennedy at St. Patrick's Cathedral in New York City on Saturday, June 8, 1968, at 10:00 A.M," the telegram read. "You are welcome to travel on the funeral train from New York to Washington. . . . This telegram will admit only the person or persons to whom it is addressed and must be retained and presented for identification whenever it is requested. The Kennedy Family."

Meanwhile, Ted's old speechwriter Milt Gwirtzman was at work on writing the eulogy Ted would deliver. Gwirtzman had been in California working on Bobby's campaign and had recently married a fellow campaign staffer. They had delayed their honeymoon until after the California primary. Now, grieving like the rest of the staff and the nation, Gwirtzman sat down to write with two messages foremost in his mind. The first was from a column he had read a while back by Tom Wicker of the *New York Times*, who lamented the way an assassin's bullet had artificially inflated John Kennedy's reputation. The second was the only instruction Ted had given Gwirtzman about what he wanted in the eulogy: "Make it about love."

Ted had flown to New York from California, sitting next to his brother's coffin, on an Air Force jet, trying to console campaign aides. But to one confidant, he allowed his grief to take the form of pure anger. "I'm going to show them what they've done," he said, "what Bobby meant to this country, what they lost."

He joined the family for a brief service at the cathedral after the arrival of the coffin, but then returned on his own later that night, sitting in a pew for several hours, fingering rosary beads.

For much of the night before the funeral, Ted drove around and around New York with John Culver. The grief was unspeakable, so the old friends didn't speak much. By now, Culver knew that as garrulous as Ted could be in happy times, in grief he turned inward and grew quiet. As he watched Ted stay strong, Culver couldn't help but marvel at all his friend had endured. The early deaths of Joe and Kathleen, and the effective loss of Rosemary after her botched lobotomy. The incapacitating stroke of Joe Sr. The assassination of Jack. The plane crash that cost the life of his friend and very nearly his own. And now the assassination of Bobby. "The enormity of this series of tragedies, any one of which would have put most of us out of commission," Culver says. "But Ted has all of them. And he has to be strong for everybody."

The next morning, as Ted rose to deliver the eulogy, he remained strong. Yet when he neared the end of the tribute, where Gwirtzman had tried to get at the essence of Bobby while focusing on love and guarding against reputation inflation, Ted's voice did crack. And it was in those cracks that he allowed a nation stricken by the madness and relentless loss of the 1960s, and the fear of what might be next, to grieve with him at Mass.

"My brother need not be idealized or enlarged in death beyond what he was in life," Ted said, looking down, "but be remembered simply as a good and decent man who saw wrong and tried to right it, saw suffering and tried to heal it, saw war and tried to stop it. Those of us who loved him and who take him to his rest today pray that what he was to us and what he wished for others will someday come to pass for all the world."

The whole world was watching, but Teddy was all alone. Jack's assassination had devastated him, but at least he'd had Bobby to turn to. Bobby's assassination was more crushing. They had helped each other weather the tragedy of Jack's murder. Moreover, for Ted, Bobby's assassination removed the last buffer. Just as Bobby had done after Jack was gunned down, Ted now felt the obligation to lead the family, caring not only for his own children while trying to salvage his own strained marriage but taking care of the children and widows of his slain brothers, a towering task in and of itself, considering that Ethel was pregnant with hers and Bobby's eleventh child.

More than that, the baby brother felt the responsibility to honor both Jack and Bobby by picking up their fallen standard. "There was this crushing drive and desire," John Culver says, "to fulfill their agendas, and be worthy of his brothers' initiatives, and at the same time continue his own. And he had to be the father figure for all these children. It was extraordinary that he was able to just put one foot in front of the other."

Still, much more was asked of him.

Even before Bobby had been buried, supporters and party leaders began pressuring Ted to take his place, for the unity of the nation.

A week after the funeral, he appeared on television with his mother to offer thanks for all the expressions of sympathy the family had received. "Each of us," Ted said, "will have to decide in a private way, in our own hearts, and in our consciences, what we shall do in the course of this summer, and in future summers, and I know we shall choose wisely." Rose, from whom Ted had inherited his forward-looking disposition, also seemed determined to convey strength. "We shall honor [Bobby] not with useless mourning and vain regrets for the past, but with firm and indomitable resolutions for the future," she said.

In fact, the family was reeling. Rita Dallas was struck by how much more broken Rose Kennedy appeared to be after Bobby's assassination, compared with JFK's. "With Jack, it was the death of the president," she says. "With Bobby, it was a son. She just bent under it." So did the rest of the family. "Everybody fell apart," she says. "Even now, I get chills just remembering that day."

No doubt that was partly the result of the cumulative effect of having lost three Kennedy sons in their prime, all in violent ways. But it also appears to have been the result of the central role Bobby played in the management of the family. For many years, and in particular following his father's stroke, he had been the executive of the family, the one the rest of the clan turned to for direction, particularly in a crisis. Even when Jack was president, Bobby was the one who had inherited from his father oversight of the family. While brother-in-law Steve Smith was charged with overseeing family finances, there was always an actual Kennedy man firmly in charge.

Now, as the last brother, Teddy was expected to fill that role. Yet everyone knew that wasn't his strength. Teddy was the one who brought joy and laughter—not order—to the family, as he belted out songs while sitting with his mother at the piano, arms around her, or cracked jokes as he pushed his father in his wheelchair. Through the sheer buoyancy of his personality, he had been able to light up his parents' house as soon as he crossed its threshold. Even in his grief, he continued to try to lift his parents' spirits by turning on the charm, Dallas says. "But when he wasn't with Mr. and Mrs. Kennedy, he'd get very solemn, very downcast, very alone. He would walk around the compound a lost soul."

He spent much of the time at sea, literally and figuratively. Sailing day and night, sometimes with a close friend like John Tunney but more often entirely alone, he found some comfort in the endless expanse of the ocean. He could escape the burning obligation he carried to be strong for everyone around him and finally be honest with himself about how dark and lonely he felt. He once drove from Hyannis Port to Washington, but when he arrived in front of his Senate office building, he could not find the strength to get out of the car. So he turned the car around and drove back.

"It was like a gruesome nightmare replayed," Tunney says. "There was only darkness, terrible feelings of emotional anxiety and depression." Knowing the pressure that Ted was feeling to step into his brother's place, regardless of the risks, Tunney told him, "You've just got to get away. You can't think about this. You must not allow yourself ever to think of yourself as being next in line for this terrible treatment."

Yet so many people were arguing for him to step forward. Going into the Democratic National Convention in Chicago just two months after the assassination, Chicago Mayor Richard Daley and other party power brokers pushed Ted to agree to be drafted as the Democratic presidential nominee. If not that, then at least as the vice presidential nominee. They decided the divided Democrats were doomed to lose the presidency under presumptive nominee Hubert Humphrey. Only a Kennedy could unite them.

The idea that the kid brother whose candidacy for the Senate was widely seen as a joke just six years earlier would now be seen as the best prospect to become leader of the free world was testament to the power of tragedy to transform someone. It also spoke to the desperation of the times, of a shaken public that was frightened by not knowing when the madness of the 1960s might end, grasping for a connection to the hope-filled days when a Kennedy last occupied the White House.

Ted's closest friends and advisers—Tunney, Culver, and Burke—thought it would be crazy for him to even consider a presidential run, given how worried they were about his mental state. His exposure to so much tragedy, so much violent death, had thickened his scar tissue, but the obligation he felt to be strong in public prevented him from dealing with his grief.

"If you were going to be silly, you would have succumbed to the people who were trying to draft you," Burke says now. "But it's a terrible thing. You've haven't prepared to run for president, you haven't given it a moment's thought. You don't have any issues. You're emotionally in trouble." Burke also worried for Ted's life if he were to run, that he would be a target for another madman looking to finish off the family name. But that fear remained unspoken. While sending strong signals that he wasn't interested, Ted declined to issue a categorical refusal. So people read into his words what they wanted. When he came out of seclusion on August 21 to speak before the Worcester Chamber of Commerce, he vowed that he would not leave political life. "There's no safety in hiding," he said.

Maybe he was too depressed to think clearly. Maybe some part of him—the angry part that had shown itself during the flight from California with Bobby's body—wanted to leave open the option of taking power to show the haters and the killers that the Kennedys would not be cowed. Or maybe he didn't want to close off any option that would allow him to carry on the legacy of his brothers and ease the burden that strained his shoulders.

He was careful to keep his distance from all the jockeying, staying at the compound or out at sea. While he kept Burke close by, he sent Steve Smith to Chicago to meet with Mayor Daley and other party heavyweights. Smith's instructions were to be discreet as he heard people out, but in no way to look as though he was trying to garner support for a draft-Teddy movement. On Sunday, August 25, the day before the convention was to begin, Daley told Smith he still wanted Ted and would postpone the decision about which candidate would get the endorsement of Illinois' 118 delegates. "I'm going to hold off for forty-eight hours," Daley said, "to see if something develops." Smith once again told Daley that Ted had no interest in being drafted.

By Tuesday afternoon, Smith was sitting in a hotel room across from peace candidate Eugene McCarthy, in a meeting arranged

by Kennedy-turned-McCarthy adviser Richard Goodwin. Smith repeated the same line about Ted's lack of interest in being drafted. But
McCarthy said point blank that he didn't have enough votes to beat
Humphrey and he offered to throw his support behind Ted. Smith said
he would have to check back with Ted. Later that night, the CBS News
reporter who had long been covering the McCarthy campaign broadcast a story saying Smith had gone to McCarthy soliciting his support
for Ted Kennedy. Smith was livid and demanded that Goodwin call for
a retraction.

Smith had been in contact with Ted several times throughout the
evening, as Ted wrestled with what to do. But the mess caused by the
CBS News report, which succeeded in making Ted look calculating
and craven, forced him to act once and for all. He called Humphrey
to let him know he would refuse any draft and then instructed John
Culver to deliver a letter to the convention chairman, telling him it
should be read to the delegates in the event Ted's name was offered for
nomination. "I am deeply grateful to those who have expressed their
confidence in me and their interest in placing my name before this
convention. But I respectfully request that the nomination be with-
drawn."

Culver says Ted knew that even if he were able to win, it would only
be as a stand-in for his brothers and not on his own merits. Not only
was he in no shape to assume the presidency, he didn't want the job on
those terms. But would he have wanted the job under other circumstances? Deep in his heart, did he ever want to be president? Culver
isn't sure. Ted's reluctance to quash the draft movement, Culver says,
had less to do with a genuine interest in the job than with his sense of
duty—to keep the country together, to end the war that was tearing
it apart, and to honor his brothers by carrying out their agendas. "He
didn't want to leave on the ground any of those issues that meant so
much to Jack and Bobby," Culver says.

What was abundantly clear, however, was that in less than six years
as a senator, Ted had found his place. After a lifetime of coming up
short in comparisons to his brothers, he had already proved himself
to be a more effective legislator than either Jack or Bobby. If he could

honor their legacies without changing offices, Culver says, that would have been his preference.

Besides, no one could have foreseen how his presidential prospects would forever be changed just one year later. "He felt understandably that he was thirty-six years old," Culver says, "and that ring would come around again."

PART TWO

THE TRIALS AND TRIBULATIONS

"I recognize my own shortcomings—
the faults in the conduct of my private life.
I realize that I alone am responsible for them,
and I am the one who must confront them."

—Edward M. Kennedy, October 25, 1991

CHAPTER
12

ON A HOT, humid Friday afternoon, a plane carrying Senator Edward M. Kennedy banked low over the Atlantic Ocean and touched down on the small, rural island of Martha's Vineyard. It was July 18, 1969, the opening day of the annual Edgartown regatta, and the town—a quiet, windswept port most of the year—was at its most alive as the midsummer weekend approached. Sailors and spectators streamed along its narrow streets, between rows of elegant, white clapboard mansions built by long dead sea captains. Its harbor foamed and glittered with the busy back-and-forth of countless boats.

Ted had come to the Vineyard to sail in the races, a family tradition, and to attend a party that night for a group of young women who had worked on Bobby's campaign for president. By all accounts, the 37-year-old senator was weary. It had been just over a year since Bobby was killed, since the youngest Kennedy had stood up in St. Patrick's Cathedral and delivered his brother's eulogy.

For Ted the last thirteen months had been shadowed by grief, a pining both physical and psychological for the brother who had been his confidant and trusted Senate colleague. But the period had also been marked by mounting pressure. He had replaced Bobby in the spotlight, and he was the subject of unrelenting speculation in Washington and the press about his presidential aspirations for 1972.

Almost 80 percent of voters believed he would be the Democratic nominee for president one day, according to one poll. The new president, Richard Nixon, was already fixated on him as a threat, tracking his TV airtime and his every move. The feeling of momentum was almost palpable; it was as though he were wearing the clothes of Jack and Bobby, fulfilling their destiny, which was now his own. "There was all this rising, boiling feeling about this meteor getting ready to take off," recalled Robert Bates, one of Kennedy's top aides of that period. "Everybody wanted to be connected with Ted."

It seemed sometimes like there was no escape. At a raucous St. Patrick's Day party that spring, held at the home of a lobbyist friend of the senator's, congressmen Tip O'Neill and Ed Boland serenaded Kennedy with an old JFK campaign song. "It's Kennedy," they belted out as other guests joined in. Ted looked embarrassed, said a reporter who was there, and swiftly retreated to the bar to get a drink. "Whatever his own wishes," columnist David Broder would write later in the *Washington Post*, "he has known that, with every passing day, the choice was being taken out of his hands and being forced on him by politicians and pundits."

The senator spoke little of the pressure. But it was clear he was conflicted. Two weeks after he had turned down an appeal from Democratic leaders at the 1968 convention, knowing he was in no shape for the task at hand, his friend Lester Hyman had visited and found him still adrift, prone to bouts of brooding silence. "He would be doing fine, then he would stop, stare out the window," Hyman said. "Ted didn't do that." At times he tried recklessly to slip his burdens. His heavy drinking on a flight back to Washington from Alaska, where he had gone for a hearing on Eskimo education in the spring of 1969, became legend among reporters who were there, who did not report the incident but privately described his raucous talk and unsteady gait as he wandered the aisles of the plane.

But Kennedy had also taken on more responsibility in the Senate, seeking and winning the role of majority whip—the number-two post in his party's leadership—in a step seen as boosting his resume for the White House. He had not shied away from making bold statements and had spoken out sharply against the war in Vietnam after the bloody battle known as Hamburger Hill made headlines that May.

Some friends saw him steeling himself to his duty. "I thought he was willing himself to go through everything he had to go through, to do what had to be done, because he was the last surviving son," says Charles Tretter, who remained on Ted's staff.

At home, his three children were frightened by the talk of his running for president. So were the thirteen fatherless nieces and nephews also in need of his guidance. He had two aging parents who had been nearly destroyed by the violent, untimely deaths of his siblings, and a fragile, beautiful wife, whose drinking was increasingly out of control. At the same time, he felt the longing gaze of Democrats around the country, who looked to him for leadership and hope. So on this bright July day as his plane approached the Vineyard, a humpbacked island off the coast of his treasured Cape Cod, Kennedy looked forward to time on the water, where he had always sought refuge from his inner conflicts. He would be out of the Washington spotlight, riding the roll of the waves on board a familiar family yacht. Some of his tension seeped away as he strode to meet his driver.

Jack Crimmins, sixty-three, had chauffeured Kennedy for nine years on nights and weekends when the senator was in Massachusetts. He had brought Kennedy's car, a black Oldsmobile, over to the Vineyard on the ferry from Cape Cod, and he had also brought a stockpile of liquor for the weekend: three and a half gallons of vodka; four fifths of Scotch; a couple of cases of beer; a couple bottles of rum. After a stop for fried clams, Crimmins and Kennedy headed for Chappaquiddick, a smaller, sparsely populated island separated from Edgartown by a narrow, saltwater channel. They made the quick trip across, which lasted just about a minute, on board the simple, bargelike ferry that breezed back and forth across the channel. Then they were on their way again, down the island's main road, through a landscape of sandy marsh and dense scrub pine and oak.

Ted wanted a swim before his race, so Crimmins took him to the house where the party for the young women who had worked on Bobby's campaign would be held. It was a small, gray-shingled, yellow-shuttered cottage three miles down the paved road from the ferry. There the senator changed into a bathing suit. Then Crimmins drove him to East Beach: a half mile back up the paved road toward the ferry, slowing at the sharp, L-shaped curve, then a deliberate right turn onto sandy Dike Road. A mile down the dirt road, the woods fell away, and the narrow, wooden Dike Bridge came into view. Crimmins eased the Oldsmobile onto the rail-less, one-lane span and steered carefully across, above the swirling tidal flow of the saltwater inlet known as Poucha Pond. Beyond the bridge were rolling dunes and crashing surf. As Crimmins waited in the torpid afternoon, Ted dove below the ocean's surface.

His next trip to the wooden bridge, ten or twelve hours later, would change the life of Edward Kennedy forever.

It is hard to imagine a more unlikely place for such a drama to unfold. Just a handful of families lived year-round on Chappaquiddick. The tiny island had no bars or restaurants, no traffic lights, no crime to speak of. Remote and untouched by major development, it was a place sought out for its silence and seclusion. The party that Friday night had been planned by Joey Gargan, the cousin who had grown up with Ted and worked on all the family campaigns. He had rented the modest cottage that week for his family, but when his mother-in-law took ill, it became the venue for a cookout with the former campaign workers.

It was not the first reunion of Bobby's former staffers. The six young women who gathered that weekend on the Vineyard—sisters Nance and Maryellen Lyons; Rosemary "Cricket" Keough; Mary Jo Kopechne; Esther Newberg and Susan Tannenbaum—had come together several times already to reminisce about their days in the "boiler room" of the brief campaign. The Kennedys had hosted one such affair at Hyannis Port the previous summer; another had been held that spring in Washington. "It was almost like war veterans getting together," says one family friend. The women were not close friends of Ted, but he appreciated their loyalty and didn't want to disappoint them by skipping the party, the friend says. There was value, too, in keeping the team together, in case he decided to run for president in 1972.

Hardworking and highly trusted, the women invited to the Chappaquiddick party had never had an experience like the boiler room of 1968. It was a buzzing nerve center, housed in a windowless room for secrecy, and named for "the intensity of the heat and noise" found within it, according to K. Dun Gifford, who ran the operation and later became an aide to Ted. Inside, each woman was responsible for tracking the allegiances of delegates in several states and for helping to secure their support. "They were the best of the best," Gifford says of his team. "They could call people up, talk, get information, make stuff happen. . . . It was fun, and so exciting. When another [delegate] was going to pledge, we would all start cheering." The boiler room workers were chosen for their clear heads and their willingness to devote long hours to a difficult, sensitive job, Gargan said later. "They knew all our secrets," he said. "They were girls who had, basically, to have no personal lives, no personal problems."

Serious-minded and "notorious" for rarely drinking alcohol, according to friends, Mary Jo Kopechne had volunteered for John F. Kennedy's campaign as a college student. She worked for Robert Kennedy in his Senate office from 1965 to 1968, where she was known for her "convent school" demeanor. She cheered for the Boston Red Sox and took special pride in the success of Carl Yastrzemski, because of their shared Polish heritage. At Bobby's last senatorial Christmas party, she spent time talking with the youngest Kennedy children while her colleagues chatted up big-name guests like former Defense Secretary Robert McNamara. After Bobby's death, Kopechne had joined the George McGovern campaign, invited by Frank Mankiewicz, who had worked for both candidates. When McGovern faltered, Kopechne took a job with a Washington consulting firm, setting up campaigns for other candidates. At the time of the party on Chappaquiddick, her father said later, the 28-year-old had just finished work on the mayoral election in Jersey City, New Jersey. "Politics was her life," said Joseph Kopechne.

The Kennedys, especially, inspired her loyalty, and Bobby's death had been crushing. She had known him well, once staying up all night at his Virginia home to type a landmark speech on Vietnam. Long after Kopechne encouraged a constituent who wanted an island in Long Island Sound to be turned over for use by the mentally disabled, the senator still teased her about it, asking if she'd "given away any islands that morning." After Robert Kennedy was killed, Kopechne told a former teacher, she felt unable to return to Capitol Hill. "I just feel Bobby's presence everywhere," Kopechne said, according to her teacher. "I can't go back because it will never be the same again."

To be with friends and former colleagues who felt the same way was comforting, and the "boiler room girls" began their Vineyard weekend in jovial good spirits. Friday morning the group of friends crossed the Dike Bridge to swim at East Beach on Chappaquiddick. Then they took a chartered boat from Edgartown to watch the sailing races. After the regatta, the men convened first at the cottage. Ted soaked in the bathtub to ease his aching back while Gargan started dinner preparations, baking frozen hors d'oeuvres, some cheese and some sausage, and tending to the grill in the fading light outside the shingled summer house. The mood was easygoing; the liquor bottles sat on a table by the door. Ted asked Crimmins to mix him a rum and Coke, and teased his chauffeur about the level in the bottle, jokingly demanding, "Who's been drinking all the rum?"

Tretter, who was also along for the party, headed back to town to pick up ice and cigarettes. A fifth guest was Paul Markham, a Kennedy friend and former U.S. attorney. A sixth man, Ray LaRosa, who worked as a gofer for Gargan, took a rented car to pick up the six young women at their Edgartown hotel. It was, in some ways, an unlikely gathering: A 37-year-old senator—famous, moneyed, and the hottest presidential prospect in the country—snacking on cheap hors d'oeuvres at a tiny house in the middle of nowhere with a group that included his cantankerous, 63-year-old chauffeur, three lawyers, and six 20-something women.

But it was also a typically Camelot-style affair. During Jack's presidency, there had been almost a sense of glamour about the idea of middle-aged married men, high on power, socializing with younger unmarried women, while their wives stayed home—forgotten women, as one such spouse, Katharine Graham, would later write. Sometimes the younger women went along because it was the only way for a generation of women to further their own careers in the political world.

And the women who came to a cottage on the remote island of Chappaquiddick to socialize with Ted and his friends were unusually accomplished and ambitious. They had postponed marriage and children in favor of careers. The daughters of doctors and civic activists, they had studied government at private colleges including Wheaton and Regis. Nance Lyons had previously worked in public relations; her sister Maryellen had been recognized as a "woman doer" by the Democratic National Committee.

The steaks cooked slowly on the small grill as the guests milled back and forth between the cramped, humid cottage and the mosquito-plagued front yard. Conversation, by some accounts, was stilted. Tretter would later say that Kennedy "was not having a hell of a good time" as he labored to be a good host. Stories were told, and Bobby Kennedy "was a presence," Tretter said. Seeking to lighten the mood, Tretter and Keough drove back to Edgartown to borrow a radio from the inn where Kennedy had a room, and when they returned, some people danced. The party guests would later insist that the drinking was moderate.

According to Crimmins, it was 11:15 P.M. when Ted approached him and asked for the car keys. The senator said he was tired and wanted to return to his hotel and sleep. He said he was going to drive Kopechne back to Edgartown, too, because she'd had too much sun and wasn't feeling well. Kennedy's request was unusual. The senator rarely drove himself anywhere, in Washington or in Massachusetts. And with only two cars at the cottage, the departure of the Oldsmobile would leave behind ten guests, most of them planning to return to hotel rooms in Edgartown, who would have to squeeze into one car to get back to the ferry. Later, Crimmins would be asked why he didn't drive them to the boat. "He asked me for the keys," the chauffeur told a judge. "It was his automobile and I gave them to him. I didn't question him."

The pair's departure caused hardly a ripple, according to the other guests. Kopechne told no one she was ill, or that she was leaving, her friends said. She left behind her purse and the key to her hotel room. The only hint that anybody may have wondered where she was going—and suspected that it wasn't home to bed—came months later in a courtroom, and then only in the nuance of a single phrase, when her friend Esther Newberg was asked about Kopechne's exit from the party. "I caught them—" Newberg began, before starting over with a less suggestive choice of words: "They were leaving through a screen door," she corrected herself.

As the screen door clicked shut behind them and the car pulled onto the pavement, Ted Kennedy's career was only minutes from derailment. All the responsibility that had cascaded down upon him—the duty to honor his dead brothers and make good on their dreams and promises, and all of the potential in his own swiftly rising career—was about to come down to one decision, to be made in the darkness at the edge of a vast ocean.

The car approached the L-shaped intersection, where the paved road cut sharply left, toward the ferry, and the hard-to-see right turn led down the dirt road to the bridge. For decades, people who know Chappaquiddick, and the starkness of that intersection, have struggled to imagine how Kennedy could have turned right if he meant to go to the ferry, on the main road he had already traveled several times that day. But Kennedy's story has not changed: He was confused. He thought the ferry was the other way. And so he turned to the right.

Traveling at 20 miles per hour, it would have taken less than two minutes for the Oldsmobile to cover the length of sandy Dike Road. The black sedan rolled between shadowy thickets of stunted island trees, at least one of its windows open to the salty breeze, heading quickly, too quickly, for the bridge ahead. There were no lights or signs to alert a nighttime driver to the Dike Bridge, which sat at an odd angle to the road, forcing drivers to adjust their course. By the time Ted knew what was happening, it was too late to react. The front tires of the Oldsmobile lifted up, over the stacked planks that were the only barrier along the right edge of the bridge.

For an instant, then, the black sedan was in flight, poised between land and water. The car somersaulted through the air, hurtling through a strange, unstoppable transition where an easy summer weekend became tragedy, an unwanted milestone known by one word: Chappaquiddick.

The car hit the water and sank, settling upside down in the pond.

The next thing Ted knew was that he was going to die. "There was complete blackness," he remembered later. "Water seemed to rush in from every point, from the windshield, from underneath me, above me. It almost seemed like you couldn't hold the water back, even with your hands." Conscious of Kopechne struggling beside him, he lifted the driver's door handle and pressed. Nothing happened. He drew what he believed was his last breath. "I can remember the last sensation of being completely out of air and inhaling what must have been a half lung full of water and assuming that I was going to drown," Kennedy would recall in court. He thought how "no one was going to be looking for us that night until the next morning and that I wasn't going to get out of that car alive."

And then, somehow, he did. "I can remember coming up to the last energy of just pushing, pressing, and coming up to the surface. . . . I have no idea in the world how I got out of that car." Swept away by the swift-moving tide under the bridge, calling out Kopechne's name as he drifted, Kennedy said he recovered his footing some 30 feet away. He waded back to the car through waist-deep water, gasping and coughing, guided by the glow of the headlights underwater.

Back at the car but unable to stand in the current, he grasped the metal undercarriage to hold himself steady, then dove below the surface, trying to get inside the car to reach Kopechne. Failing, he tried again, seven or eight times in all, according to his testimony. But he was by this time winded and exhausted, unable to hold his breath for more than a few seconds. Finally, he let himself float away from the car. He crawled onto shore and lay on the grass, coughing up water. Then he staggered up the bank and started back down Dike Road, "walking, trotting, jogging, stumbling, as fast as I possibly could."

It would have been a dark walk, dogged by panic and mosquitoes and slowed by powdery sand. There was a crescent moon that night, but trees cocooned the road. He passed houses but did not stop for help, later saying that he saw no lights. Back at the cottage, spent and soaking wet, Ted collapsed in the backseat of the rental car outside. He sent LaRosa to find his two closest friends at the party, Gargan and

Markham, both lawyers. They came out of the house and got into the car. "The senator said to me, 'The car has gone off the bridge down by the beach and Mary Jo is in it,' " Gargan said later. "With that I backed up the car and went just as fast as I could toward the bridge."

There was no phone in the cottage. But there were other houses clustered nearby, and a few hundred feet away, a volunteer fire station with an alarm. The three men never paused, though, as they raced to the pond. Later, in court, Gargan tried to explain why. "I felt there was only one thing to do and that was to get into the car and as quickly as possible, because I knew if I did not there wasn't a chance in the world of saving Mary Jo," he said. "When we failed in that . . . I didn't think that there was anything more that could be done."

At the bridge, Gargan and Markham said, they stripped off their clothes and dove into the water, but the current kept them from Ko-pechne. As the water swept past them, they clutched at the wheels of the car and tried to open its doors or push through one of its windows. Nothing got them any closer to the young woman inside. When they gave up and headed back up the dirt road—again passing but not stop-ping at several houses—Ted broke down, according to his friends. "He was sobbing and almost on the verge of breaking down crying," said Markham. "He said, 'This couldn't have happened, I don't know how it happened.' "

"Well, it did happen and it has happened," Markham replied.

"What am I going to do, what can I do?" Ted asked.

It had been two hours since the car went into the pond. Gargan drove to the ferry landing, where the conversation continued, steps away from a working pay phone at the water's edge. The night was still, the narrow channel smooth as glass. Just what the men said then, and what kind of plan was hatched, would be the subject of speculation for decades. In the weeks, months, and years that followed, all kinds of theories would surface: that Kennedy wanted to tell the police that Kopechne was driving; that she was alone in the car; that he asked his cousin Joe to take the rap.

Ted would deny every story. But a few months later in his court-room testimony, he acknowledged the powerful, almost dreamlike longing that came over him that night, to somehow find a way to make the problem go away. He thought about the phone calls he would have to make, to Mary Jo's mother, to his wife and his own parents. And somewhere in the man who had already borne so much, the will to do the right thing bent and buckled. "I just wondered how all of this could possibly have happened," Kennedy said. "I also had sort of a thought and a wish and desire and the hope that suddenly this whole accident would disappear." Maybe, he thought, Kopechne had escaped from the car. Maybe she had swum free and made her way back to the cottage.

Meanwhile, Gargan and Markham kept talking, insisting, they would testify, that the accident must be reported. But Gargan also urged Kennedy to protect himself by calling his trusted assistant Dave Burke and the family lawyer, Burke Marshall. No one knows exactly what Ted heard or understood. Soon afterward, he would be diagnosed with a concussion. But when the senator stood and gave his orders, they were simple and direct: "You take care of the girls; I will take care of the accident."

With that, he dove into the water and started swimming to Edgartown.

Weakened by his ordeal, Ted felt, for the second time that night, like he might drown as he crossed the channel. When he finally struggled onto land in Edgartown, he leaned against a tree to rest. Then he continued up the street to his hotel, the Shiretown Inn, a pair of shingled houses a few steps from the harbor, connected by two outdoor walkways like a spider's web.

Shaking with chill, he went to his room, took off his clothes and collapsed on the bed, conscious of throbbing pain in his head, back, and neck. Confused, after a while, about how much time had passed, Ted said he dressed and went out to the walkway, spotted a man standing below, and asked him the time. It was 2:25 A.M. The senator went back to his room. He did not go to the police, as he had told his friends he would. In the morning, when Gargan and Markham arrived at his hotel and demanded to know why he had not reported the accident, Kennedy tried to describe the denial he had cultivated in the hours before dawn.

He told them how he "willed that Mary Jo still lived . . . was hopeful even as that night went on . . . that somehow when they arrived in the morning that they were going to say that Mary Jo was still alive." He told them "how I somehow believed that when the sun came up and it was a new morning that what had happened the night before would not have happened." He confessed that he "just couldn't gain the strength within me, the moral strength to call Mrs. Kopechne at two in the morning and tell her that her daughter was dead."

But now the sun was up, and the mess he'd left behind on Chappaquiddick was not a bad dream. The nightmare, it turned out, was just beginning. The symbols and shadows of that night, and the crucial failure of his moral strength, would be etched forever into the private, personal identity of Ted Kennedy and into the public perception of the man.

For the moment, though, it was time to start the cleanup.

CHAPTER

13

ON SATURDAY MORNING, in the harsh light of day, Ted could no longer dodge reality. He finally resolved to go to the police, more than nine hours after driving off the bridge. First, though, escorted by Gargan and Markham, he took the ferry back to the Chappaquiddick landing to use the pay phone there, where he would have more privacy. He started calling family members and lawyers, every minute adding weight to the moral case against him.

Steve Ewing, then a 17-year-old deckhand on the Chappaquiddick ferry, took Kennedy across the channel, noticing the senator "like you would notice any movie star–type person." He watched as Kennedy huddled near the pay phone with his aides. "You could tell something was building," Ewing says. "There was a little bit of tension." The teenager used a phone on the other side of the channel to call his dad, a reporter for the New Bedford, Massachusetts, *Standard-Times*. "Something's going on down here," the young man told his father.

Meanwhile, three miles away at the Dike Bridge, the car in the water had already been discovered. Two boys fishing on the bridge that morning had spotted the submerged Oldsmobile. They went to the nearest house, 100 feet from the bridge, and asked the woman there to call police. Edgartown Police Chief Dominick Arena responded to the scene. He, too, stopped at the house by the bridge, borrowed a bathing suit there, and swam out to the car. The current was strong, and he could not get inside. So he sat on top of the metal undercarriage, the cold water rushing past him, and waited for the fire department diver who had been summoned.

There was no reason for Arena to think that the accident would be momentous. A former state police officer, he had taken the job on the Vineyard two years earlier and had seen little excitement, besides the drunken escapades of some winter-weary islanders during the long, gray season he called "funny February and mad March." But as he perched there in the water, chilled by the soaking T-shirt clinging to his chest, the tall, good-natured lawman was swept by an ominous feeling. "Something told me it was more than just a car in the water," he remembers. "Sitting there, I had this feeling there was someone in that car."

The chief called out the license plate number to one of his men onshore. Within minutes, the officer had an answer from back at the station. He yelled the news to the chief across the water: The car was registered to Edward Kennedy. "Another family tragedy," Arena thought. He continued waiting on the car as diver John Farrar disappeared below the water. Wearing a wetsuit, breathing from a tank of air, Farrar peered through the open window on the driver's side. He saw nothing there. As his eyes adjusted slowly to the darkness, he made his way around to the back of the car.

There he saw what Arena had been dreading: Two feet, close together, visible through the rear window. Farrar moved to the open right rear window, where he could now make out a woman's body. Her head was cocked back, her face pressed into the footwell on the floor of the car. Her hands tightly gripped the edge of the backseat.

Still, Farrar could not be sure if she was alive or dead. He pushed himself through the open window and reached out his hand. His fingers touched her cold, hard thigh, and he knew then that she was dead. Farrar tied a safety line around the woman's neck, to prevent the body from being lost to the current, and pulled the body with him, out of the car and up to the surface. Mary Jo was free, but it was far too late to save her.

To Arena, the girl who emerged from the water looked surprisingly tidy for all her suffering. She was blond and well-groomed, dressed in a white, long-sleeved blouse, dark pants, and sandals. "If you'll forgive me," he told reporters later, "if she hadn't been wringing wet, it were as if she were about to go to work or to a party, because everything was in place." Arena and Farrar placed the body in a boat, and firemen pulled the boat to shore. Somebody covered the body with a blanket.

Then the chief returned to the house by the bridge and called his office. Kennedy had been spotted at the ferry landing, and Arena wanted someone to go there and find him.

No need, his secretary said: The senator is here.

Ted got on the phone, and Arena broke the bad news. "I'm sorry," the chief told him. "Your car was in an accident over here and the young lady is dead."

"I know," Kennedy said.

The police chief paused. "Was anybody else in the car?" he asked.

"Yes," Kennedy answered.

"Are they in the water?" asked Arena.

The senator said no. Arena asked if they could talk. Ted agreed.

The police chief, a Massachusetts native, was only two years older than Ted. He says he was not in awe of Kennedy, but when he got back to the station, the balance of power between them seemed uncertain. Arena's hair was wet; he was still wearing borrowed swim trunks. Kennedy, with Markham by his side, was somber, clean-shaven, and well dressed, talking on the phone in Arena's office.

Ted hung up the phone and shook Arena's hand. Then he dropped a bombshell that the chief had not seen coming.

"I was the driver," Kennedy said.

Arena was momentarily struck speechless. "I was taken aback," he recalls. Somehow, he had not imagined that the senator might be at fault.

"What would you like for me to do?" Ted asked then. "We must do what is right or we will both be criticized for it."

Arena recovered. "The first thing we will have to do is have a statement from you about what happened," he said.

He led Kennedy and Markham down the hall to the selectmen's office and let them in, giving them "a little privacy" to prepare the statement. The tiny police station was beginning to fill with reporters who had heard about the accident involving Kennedy's car. One of the first on the scene was the *New York Times*'s James Reston, who happened to be on vacation on the Vineyard.

The news was ricocheting fast. When Arena told Walter Steele, the special prosecutor for the Vineyard, about Kennedy's accident, the response was incredulous: "That's impossible," Steele said, according to Arena. "They," meaning the Kennedys, "don't drive anywhere." Bob Carroll, then the chairman of the Edgartown Board of Selectmen, also got a phone call from Arena.

"He said, 'Jesus, Bob, we've got a problem,' " Carroll remembers.

Edgartown at the time was still a conservative bastion. But Carroll was a lifelong Democrat, like his butcher father before him. He had grown up with few advantages, in a house where the rent was "$4 a week and hard to come by," but he had become a success. A year earlier, the selectman had purchased the premier hotel property in town, on a point by the lighthouse overlooking Chappaquiddick.

Carroll's first impulse was to protect the senator, "to get him off the island before the press got here," he says. The police did little to stand in the way of that plan. Arena typed up the brief, handwritten statement that Ted had dictated to Markham. Just 230 words, it made no mention of the party or the rescue attempts by Gargan and Markham. It left out Kopechne's last name, because Kennedy could not spell it. And it bluntly brushed aside the ten-hour delay in reporting the crash. "When I fully realized what had happened this morning," Ted wrote, "I immediately contacted the police."

In spite of the obvious gaps in Kennedy's story, Arena asked no follow-up questions. The chief did ask the senator for his driver's license, and Ted was unable to produce it. He thought he may have left it in Washington. By noon on Saturday, barely two hours after he appeared to make his report, Ted was on his way to the Martha's Vineyard airport, escorted by an inspector from the Registry of Motor Vehicles who was investigating the accident. Carroll provided his private plane, a seven-seat Comanche, and his services as pilot, and flew Kennedy across Nantucket Sound to Cape Cod. The senator was "pretty quiet" on the short flight to Hyannis, says Carroll. Before Ted left the plane, Carroll volunteered his further assistance.

"I said when they got out, 'It's my town, Senator—call me,'" Carroll remembers.

Alerted by Ted's phone calls from the island, his family and advisers were already assembling, bent on controlling the damage to his career. Before the weekend was out, a crack team of allies had gathered at the family compound on Cape Cod, including some of the era's top lawyers, legislators, speechwriters, and strategists: Richard Goodwin and Ted Sorensen; Milton Gwirtzman, David Burke, and Burke Marshall; brother-in-law Stephen Smith; and his close pals John Culver and John Tunney, both now congressmen.

The idea was to manage the crisis, minimize it, in the hopes that the last brother could preserve some part of his power and potential. But from the first discussions, said K. Dun Gifford and others, there was an understanding that the world had changed forever. "You just knew it would never be the same again, you knew that right away," says Gifford. "It didn't mean he couldn't have a life in public service, but it wouldn't be a charmed life. It was going to be different."

Gifford, who had worked closely with Kopechne in the boiler room of Bobby's campaign, was sent to escort her body from the Vineyard to Pennsylvania, where she had been born and would be buried, and to help her parents make the funeral arrangements. Gifford denies the allegation, made repeatedly over the years, that he rushed the body off the island to avoid an autopsy. Kennedy "was totally on the high road, and that made it easier to go through that week of dreadful things," says Gifford. "It was his and my decision to do what needs to be done and do it right."

Ted had called Kopechne's parents Saturday morning, but he shared few details of the accident. They did not learn until later that he was driving the car. Ted called them again on Sunday from Hyannis Port, but "he was so broken up I could hardly understand him," Mary Jo's father, Joseph Kopechne, told a reporter. On Sunday, after a rough flight in thunderstorms and fog, Gifford delivered the young woman's body to a funeral home in Plymouth, Pennsylvania. There, he acted more like a brother than a former boss, advising the staff on what kind of clothes and hairstyle Kopechne favored and requesting that her makeup be toned down. Among the flowers placed around the coffin was a bouquet of white and yellow daisies sent by "Senator and Mrs. Kennedy."

Gifford faced his grimmest task when Kopechne's parents arrived to bury their only child, and he found himself "helping them get past the fact that it really was their daughter in the casket." Later, he faced a mob of reporters who crowded him against the wall of the funeral home. Not trusting his own judgment, Gifford called Ted for guidance. "He said, 'Just do what you're doing, and tell them the truth,' and he made me feel I could do it," Gifford says. "I just kept saying [to the press] that I wasn't there [at the party]. When they asked about the drinking, I said that wasn't what I talked about with the senator."

Wilfred Rock, the pilot who flew Gifford to the Vineyard on the morning after the accident, remembers the fateful words spoken by the Kennedy aide as Rock steered his Cessna five-seater over the Dike Bridge for a view of the car in the water.

"He looked down and said, 'There goes the presidency,' " the former pilot remembers.

Back on Martha's Vineyard, Chief Arena also felt his back against the wall. Markham had asked him not to release Kennedy's statement until he could speak to the senator's lawyer, Burke Marshall. But by Saturday afternoon, the crowd of reporters outside the police station was clamoring for information, and the phones were jammed with calls from international media. Arena gave in at about 3 P.M. and read the statement.

At the same time, the story was becoming more complicated. That afternoon, Arena heard for the first time about the party that had preceded the crash. There were apparently witnesses he should be talking to, but he had no idea who they were or where they could be found. In fact, they were fast on their way off the island; Gifford had

seen Kopechne's five grieving friends onto an afternoon ferry back to Cape Cod.

Clearly, Kennedy's statement was marked by some major omissions. But the facts it did contain were also now in question. Before the Oldsmobile had even been pulled from the water, a respected deputy sheriff named Huck Look, a resident of Chappaquiddick, had come forward with a story that directly contradicted Kennedy's account. Coming home late that Friday night after working a security shift at the Edgartown Yacht Club, Look said, he had seen a car like Kennedy's at the L-shaped intersection, with a man and woman inside and a similar license plate number, at about 12:45 A.M.—an hour and a half after Kennedy said the accident happened, and 45 minutes after the last scheduled ferry.

The car passed him at the sharp curve on Chappaquiddick Road, Look said, and then pulled into a dirt road known as Cemetery Lane, as if the driver was lost. Intending to offer assistance, Look pulled his car over, got out and approached the dark-colored sedan. Before he got close, the driver backed quickly out of Cemetery Lane and sped down Dike Road toward the beach.

The account, by a witness whose reliability seemed unassailable, fueled deep suspicions about Ted's story. It cast serious doubt on his claim that he and Kopechne had been trying to make the last ferry, and with that basic fact in question, everything else he had said seemed suddenly shaky.

Arena had plenty of questions. But he also felt pressure to act. The medical examiner had declared the cause of Kopechne's death as drowning and saw no need for an autopsy. The district attorney had not stepped into the case. There were no surviving witnesses to the senator's driving, and it was too late to determine if he had been drinking.

A test of Kopechne's blood alcohol level found it was .09 at the time of her death. The young woman had not been legally drunk under Massachusetts law, but she had been close; legislation was then pending to reduce the legal limit from .15 to .10 percent. To reach .09, Kopechne might have consumed three to five drinks, each containing an ounce of alcohol, in her last hour of life, or more drinks over a longer period of time, the superviser of the state police lab said.

The police chief began preparing the only charge he felt he could reasonably make against Kennedy: leaving the scene of an accident, a misdemeanor punishable by no less than two months in prison—and a more serious offense, under state law, than reckless driving. To step the charge up to manslaughter, also called negligent homicide, authorities would have to prove that Ted showed "reckless disregard" for human life. Arena says he simply could not see making the case. "You don't have 150-foot skid marks," he says. "And the fact is it occurred on a dark road with a bend in it, with no lights, no rails, and the bridge at an angle. Why he turned down the road; what he was doing with her—all of that is not my concern."

"I will always be convinced that what happened was an accident," Arena adds. "What happened afterward is what he had to live with."

In that Monday morning's papers, though, Arena sounded too easily satisfied. He said he was "firmly convinced that the senator told me the correct story" and told reporters that Kennedy "impresses me as a senator and as a man who would tell the truth." He acknowledged that he had not asked Kennedy if he had been drinking.

Others close to the episode had their own views. John Farrar, the fire department diver who had removed Kopechne's body from the car, believes she might have lived longer than most people thought possible, breathing from an air pocket inside the Oldsmobile.

"She was floating, and I had to pull her down," Farrar says, describing the condition of Kopechne's body, which led him to believe she did not drown but suffocated. She might have survived, Farrar has long maintained, if Kennedy had called for help immediately. Farrar says his theory brought him years of grief, including anonymous phone calls that threatened him and his family. "It was grim," he says. "It was tough for my wife."

The public's obsession with the accident was becoming clear. Officials had to cover "the death car," as the *Boston Globe* described it, with a tarpaulin after vandals stole the gas cap, the gas pedal, and bits of shattered windshield. Someone hung a sign on the car warning that vandals would be prosecuted.

The same appetite for fragments of the tragedy could be felt at Arena's press conference on Tuesday, where he was grilled by thirty at times hostile newsmen in the drably furnished parish hall of a downtown church where two prints of Jesus gazed down kindly from the walls. About 22 miles across Nantucket Sound, at the Kennedy compound in Hyannis Port, the advisers gathered there were not satisfied, either. Behind closed doors, some at Hyannis Port were concerned by the senator's dazed, emotional condition, weaknesses that made more sense after a family doctor diagnosed a concussion. One of those present, lawyer Burke Marshall, later said he believed that Ted "had a blockage, that a lot of his mind wasn't accepting what was happening to him. . . . The Kennedys have a way of seeming fine, going forward without interruption under stress . . . but inside a great deal is blocked off. That night, in that situation, I think [Kennedy] might have very well functioned so that the people with him . . . would think that he knew exactly what he was doing," said Marshall.

Whatever his private unrest, Ted pulled himself together for Kopechne's funeral on Tuesday. He flew to Pennsylvania with Joan and Ethel and a pack of other supporters including Culver and Tunney, David Hackett and Jack's old friend LeMoyne Billings. As his entourage approached St. Vincent's Church in Plymouth, an old coal mining town dominated by Czech and Polish Democrats, the mood inside the car was somber. But for some in the crowd, the young senator still warranted a rock star reception. Girls swarmed close and squealed, "I saw him! I saw him!" newspapers reported. "This is the biggest thing to hit this town since 1960," police officer Larry Karnes said, referring to the year that John F. Kennedy campaigned there. The town's mayor, Edward Burns, helped control the crowd outside the church. He drove a car adorned with "Kennedy in '72" signs.

Just before the funeral Mass, Kennedy met briefly with Gwen and Joseph Kopechne in the rectory next to the red brick church. The shades inside were drawn for privacy. Gwen Kopechne leaned heavily on Dun Gifford, one hand held over her mouth, as they slowly made their way to the rectory door. Later, Joseph Kopechne told reporters Kennedy had said he wished that he had died instead.

The day was hot and muggy, and some 500 mourners crowded into the church. A lone bell tolled as the Kopechnes and Kennedys entered through a rear door. Afterward, a 22-car procession wound its way uphill to a mountainside gravesite. The family sat under a faded green canopy; Ted stood nearby, wearing a neck brace.

Reporters were waiting on the Cape when his plane landed later that day, but Ted declined to speak to them, saying the time was not right. But patience with the senator's silence was eroding fast. Frank Mankiewicz, the former press secretary for Robert Kennedy, says he felt a growing restlessness as he consulted by phone with the team in Hyannis Port. "My advice in all situations is to tell the truth, tell it all, and tell it now, and as it dragged on, I was troubled by it," he says. "I said, Jesus, why don't they say something, because it was getting worse by the day." Mankiewicz was right: the commentary was growing merciless. A *Newsweek* story made the claim that Kennedy's "closest associates" had been "powerfully concerned with his indulgent drinking habits, his daredevil driving, and his ever-ready eye for a pretty face" in the months leading up to Chappaquiddick.

Ted himself was still trapped inside his mind in that dark night on the island. Devastated by his responsibility for the accident, he was weighing the wisdom of leaving the Senate. During a long walk on the beach, his trusted aide David Burke urged him to stay in the game, reminding him that he would never escape scrutiny, but would be giving up his best chance to make a difference. "He was seriously considering leaving, and Dave was explaining to him that . . . there was nowhere he could go that he could do anywhere near what he's doing now," says Milton Gwirtzman, another top aide who counseled Ted that week.

On Wednesday, Arena met in secret with Steele, the Vineyard prosecutor, and Robert Clark Jr., a former judge and Kennedy attorney. They convened at Steele's out-of-the-way Vineyard cottage, to avoid reporters who were already convinced that Kennedy was getting special treatment. Clark said that Kennedy wanted to plead guilty to the charge of leaving the scene of an accident. Arrangements were made for a hearing Friday morning.

The clamor had reached a fever pitch on Martha's Vineyard, where the number of reporters had swelled and the bar at the Harborside Inn had started staying open until 1:00 A.M. But Arena had canceled his daily press conferences, scolded by higher-ups who said he was talking too much. For lack of other news, journalists had been reduced to stunts. One TV crew paid a man $10 to swim across the channel from Chappaquiddick to Edgartown, to test if the crossing could be made as Kennedy had claimed. (It could.)

Medical examiner Dr. Donald Mills, who had determined Kopechne's cause of death, told reporters he would have ordered an autopsy if he had known at the time that Kennedy was driving, "just to have avoided all this awful hue and cry about nothing," and "to make sure the senator's name was cleared." The furor was not helped by officials who made contradictory statements about the investigation and the possibility of further charges. Arena and Steele told reporters that state police had taken charge of interviewing the party guests, but the lieutenant they named as the investigator then denied having anything to do with the case.

Writing in the *Washington Post* on Thursday, columnists Rowland Evans and Robert Novak concluded the accident would knock Kennedy out of presidential contention for 1972, partly because of "the sudden freeing of anti-Kennedy sentiment bottled up since the assassination of Robert F. Kennedy." Above all, the consensus was that the last living brother must speak. "Whether this glee of anti-Kennedy forces turns out to be premature depends, in the short run, on whether the present silence is broken by a full and satisfactory explanation of events," Evans and Novak wrote. The break in the silence was coming, but few would find it satisfactory.

❧

Nantucket Sound was choppy and shrouded in fog Friday morning— less than perfect conditions for a sail, but fitting weather for a trip to a court hearing. Ted crossed from Hyannis Port to Martha's Vineyard on board the family yacht *Marlin,* accompanied by Joan and Steve Smith. His other escorts, a pair of Secret Service men, had been assigned by President Nixon because of the hate mail the case had generated.

Ted entered the tiny brick courthouse in Edgartown under an umbrella. Stepping into the courtroom was like stepping back in time; built in 1858, the room was still outfitted with the same narrow, wooden benches and cracked, horsehair-stuffed leather cushions that had met jurors and defendants for more than a century. Judge James Boyle, his mustache snow white above his black robe, presided from the massive wooden bench. Ted sat with his head down while Joan, wearing a stylish black and white plaid coatdress, watched from her assigned seat in the jury box.

The 9:00 A.M. hearing began when Clerk Thomas Teller stood to read the charge against Ted. "This complaint alleges that Edward M. Kennedy of Boston, Mass. . . . did operate a certain motor vehicle upon a public way in said Edgartown and did go away after knowingly causing injury to Mary Jo Kopechne without stopping and making known his name, residence, and the number of his motor vehicle. How do you plead, guilty or not guilty?"

The senator spoke, but his voice could barely be heard. The clerk asked him to repeat his answer.

"Guilty," he said in a louder voice. The packed courtroom stirred.

As Ted sat with his hands clasped before him, Arena described the discovery of the car, the recovery of Kopechne's body, and the delay in the reporting of the accident. An investigation had "produced no evidence of negligence on the part of the defendant," Arena said, but "there appears there were opportunities for the defendant to have made himself known to the proper authorities immediately after the accident."

Richard McCarron, the lawyer representing the senator, asked for a suspended sentence, asserting that imprisonment "of this defendant would not be the proper course. I believe his character is well known to the court," McCarron said. "His reputation is well known to the world." Judge Boyle consented to a suspended two-month sentence, given Kennedy's "unblemished" record. "It is my understanding that he has already been and will continue to be punished far beyond anything this court can impose," said the judge.

After the hearing, which lasted less than ten minutes, Arena and Steele faced the horde of reporters outside. Some, shut out by the limited space in the courtroom, had climbed trees and onto porches for a better view. The two men announced that they were satisfied and their investigation was closed, "unless something comes up," said Arena. He still regrets the words he chose to finish his thought: "We will cross that bridge when we come to it."

With his guilty plea behind him, Ted flew back to the Cape to prepare for an even more public reckoning. That Friday night, his advisers had decided, he would appear on national television to explain the events on Chappaquiddick and to ask the Massachusetts voters if he should stay in the Senate. The timing and content of his speech had been fought over for days by the assembled wise men at the Kennedy compound. The lawyers had insisted that Ted say nothing until his court date was over, while other advisers had railed against the delay, citing mounting damage to his reputation. "I watched things get worse and worse in terms of his position because he wasn't saying anything," Gwirtzman recalls. "But the lawyers were saying, 'You cannot say anything until next Friday' . . . and Tunney was saying if we wait until Friday we're dead."

It was Gwirtzman's idea to appeal to the voters for guidance, he says. Believing they would urge Ted to stay, he was willing to gamble on the base, "the people who know you," because of their long, emotional ties to the Kennedy family, he says. "It was a relationship that had all kinds of layers in it," says Gwirtzman. "It was very strong."

As badly as his brothers' deaths had hurt Edward Kennedy, they had also bruised the voters who clung to him now. In Massachusetts, reaction to the speech would be shaped not just by the news of the accident, Gwirtzman guessed, but also by "the grief they had and what he meant to them, what he meant to the Catholics as the last surviving son." It was a strategy with no guarantee of success. "They could have all come back saying, 'Get out,'" Gwirtzman acknowledges.

The major Boston television stations cut away from their regular programming at 7:30 P.M. Ted was waiting in the library of his parents' house at Hyannis Port, surrounded by books, dressed in a dark blue suit. A crew from WHDH-TV was on hand to produce the national broadcast; the Kennedy family would not be billed for the airtime. The rules had been clearly established in advance: no reporters; no questions to follow the statement.

He began with an attempt to explain his week of silence. "Prior to my appearance in court," Ted said, "it would have been improper for me to comment on these matters. But tonight I am free to tell you what happened and say what it means to me." His manner was calm and coherent, but muted, seeming at times almost mechanical. He looked into the camera for long stretches, and sometimes glanced down at his notes, but his demeanor seemed distant—that of a polished, practiced speaker, speaking well but feeling little. He described the cookout that he had "helped sponsor for a devoted group of Kennedy campaign secretaries," and he spoke of Kopechne's dedication. "For this reason, and because she was such a gentle, kind, and idealistic person," he said, "all of us tried to help her feel that she still had a home with the Kennedy family."

Then he addressed the rumors directly. "There is no truth, no truth whatever, to the widely circulated suspicions of immoral conduct that have been leveled at my behavior and hers regarding that evening," he said. "There has never been a private relationship between us of any kind." He denied driving drunk, and he described his attempts to rescue Kopechne. For the first time, he explained how Gargan and Markham had also tried to help.

As for his failure to report the accident promptly, he frankly acknowledged his failing, but added no new insight to defend his actions. "My conduct and conversation during the next several hours, to the extent that I can remember them, make no sense to me at all," he said, adding that he was just as dismayed and baffled by his behavior as everyone else. He noted that his doctors had diagnosed shock and a concussion, but said he did not "seek to escape responsibility for my actions by placing the blame either in the physical, emotional trauma brought on by the accident or on anyone else. I regard as indefensible the fact that I did not report the accident to the police immediately," he said.

Kennedy went on to describe the "scrambled" and "irrational" thoughts that consumed him that night, such as wondering whether Kopechne might still be alive, and "whether some awful curse did actually hang over all the Kennedys."

"I was overcome, I'm frank to say," he said, "by a jumble of emotions, grief, fear, doubt, exhaustion, panic, confusion, and shock." Finally, Ted appealed to his audience to tell him what he should do next. He said he believed he should not continue in office if "the citizens should lack confidence in their senator's character or ability, with or without justification." Yet he also carefully reserved the right to ignore their advice. "You and I share many memories — some of them have been glorious, some have been very sad. . . . And so I ask you tonight, people of Massachusetts, to think this through with me," he said. "In facing this decision, I seek your advice and opinion. In making it, I seek your prayers. For this is a decision that I will have finally to make on my own."

He might have ended there. Instead, he went on to echo his brother Jack's book, *Profiles in Courage,* without attribution: "The stories of past courage cannot supply courage itself. For this, each man must look into his own soul," he said. "I pray that I can have the courage to make the right decision."

When it was over, after just thirteen minutes, WHDH-TV returned to an episode of *The Wild, Wild West* already in progress. On NBC, John Chancellor led a post-speech critique. In South Boston, the last light of dusk still lingered outside the Car Stop Café, a blue-collar watering hole. At the bar, between two large, color photographs of John F. Kennedy hanging on the wall, patrons watched Ted deliver his address with a mix of cynicism and regret. When the senator said he wasn't driving drunk, one woman could not contain herself. "Oh, the big liar!" she exclaimed. "Shhhh!" someone scolded, annoyed. When Ted's voice trembled near the end, a man in a booth pretended to play a sad violin.

"Too bad it happened," someone else said. "He might have been president."

At the *Boston Globe,* the phone calls started coming in two-to-one in favor of Kennedy. "I think they should give the guy a break," said one caller, Donald Glover of Woburn. "He has enough trouble in his life." "I just think he's a very honorable man and God bless him," said Mrs. Frank Gustin of Dorchester. "We trust you," said Senator Thomas J. McIntyre, a Democrat from New Hampshire. "Stay with us." "It was a straightforward story," said Senator Edmund Muskie, the Maine Democrat. "I believe it." Even Gwen Kopechne granted her approval, soon after the speech, in a handwritten statement passed to the reporters waiting outside her house. "I am satisfied with the senator's statement," she wrote, "and do hope he decides to stay in the Senate." It looked like Gwirtzman's gamble had paid off.

On Sunday, Ted went to church, where a crowd of well-wishers surrounded him. Western Union delivered more than 10,000 telegrams to the compound over the weekend; an aide said they urged Ted not to resign by a 100-to-1 margin. A certain hometown pride factored into voters' calculations. "A blow to Ted Kennedy shocked the sustaining mythology of public life," Christopher Lydon would write in the *New York Times.* "Mr. Kennedy's retirement or ultimate defeat would poison the faith that Massachusetts, for all its faults, is still the most fertile political ground in America."

By midweek, aides had confirmed to reporters that Ted would return to the Senate and would seek reelection in 1970. On the Cape, Ted went fishing on the *Marlin,* where he was seen teaching some of the Kennedy children how to cast.

But if Massachusetts had decided to accept his transgression, Ted faced a tougher crowd in Washington and around the country. A national Gallup poll conducted just after his televised speech found a sharp drop in the number of people with "extremely favorable" attitudes toward him as a person: 34 percent, compared with 49 percent just four months earlier. Unsatisfied by his vague explanations and emotional appeals, many political pundits shook their heads and threw up their hands. "Pro-Kennedy Democrats who had optimistically suspended judgment before Kennedy's Friday night television appearance are now deeply saddened and deeply critical, sensing that he

has said his last word," Evans and Novak wrote in the *Washington Post.* They acknowledged "valid reasons for not definitely writing off Kennedy nationally, even for 1972. There remains a hard and intensely loyal national cadre of Kennedyites, some of whom have political futures of their own inseparably tied to his future. As one Kennedy backer told us, 'Charisma is in very very short supply.' "

Another Gallup poll suggested as much. After the accident and the televised speech, respondents gave Kennedy 36 percent of the vote in a three-man race against Nixon and George Wallace—3 points more than in the same poll three months earlier. But as the commentators saw it, charisma would not be enough. As long as he failed to answer the lingering questions, wrote Evans and Novak, his political future would be forever clouded.

CHAPTER
14

KENNEDY RETURNED TO the Senate on July 31, his every step scrutinized by a sea of trailing reporters. As television crews waited in his Virginia driveway for him to be driven to work, a maid emerged from the house with coffee and Toll House cookies. When Ted arrived at the Senate, in a blue convertible driven by his friend Claude Hooten, the press stood four or five deep on the steps.

"I'm glad to be back," the senator said when the microphones were pushed before him. When he made it to the Senate floor, Majority Leader Mike Mansfield pulled him close.

"Come in, Ted," said Mansfield, the Montana Democrat. "You're right back where you belong."

"Thanks a million, Mike," Kennedy said at the end of the daily press briefing.

Senator Hugh Scott, a Pennsylvania Republican, came by to shake hands. Senator Alan Cranston of California patted Kennedy's elbow. The scene was one of a return to normalcy, the political prodigy reclaiming his rightful place. But Chappaquiddick had changed everything. Asked repeatedly that day about his plans, Kennedy made it clear to reporters that he would not run for president in 1972. The accident remained a front-page story. That same day, back in Massachusetts, District Attorney Edmund Dinis announced he would ask for an inquest into Kopechne's death.

Kennedy was back, but Chappaquiddick was not finished.

Throughout the dog days of August, with little happening in Washington, the steady drumbeat of coverage of the accident continued. On August 5, Kennedy canceled a work trip to Europe to ensure he would be available for the inquest. Two days later, an assistant district attorney from Massachusetts, Armand Fernandes, was in Pennsylvania asking authorities there to exhume Kopechne's body for an autopsy—an ultimately unsuccessful request opposed by her parents. On August 8, Judge Boyle set the date of the inquest for early September. A week later, in an interview with the *Boston Globe*, Kennedy said he could live with himself in the wake of the accident. "I feel the tragedy of the girl's death. That's on my mind. That's what I will always have to live with," he said. "But what I don't have to live with are the whispers and innuendoes and falsehoods, because these have no basis in fact."

Three days later, in an interview in the *New York Post*, Gwen Kopechne said she found the circumstances of her daughter's death "confusing," especially the account of the deputy sheriff who saw a car at 12:45 A.M., after Kennedy said the accident had occurred, and the revelation by the senator that he had sought help from Markham and Gargan after the crash.

"Why wasn't help called for my daughter by Gargan and Markham?" Kopechne asked. "I can understand shock but I don't see where they went into shock. Gargan and Markham are my puzzle."

On Martha's Vineyard, August had become a strange new kind of tourist season, as hundreds of visitors flocked to the now infamous Dike Bridge. They ripped off splinters of wood for souvenirs, and their cars jammed the line for the Chappaquiddick ferry, increasing wait times and irritating natives and summer residents who resented the invasion. Dr. Edward Self, a surgeon and the president of the Chappaquiddick residents' association, told a reporter that the extra traffic was "a nuisance and hardship" that discouraged "repair people and contractors" from taking jobs on the island. He said he planned to ask Edgartown selectmen to restrict the use of the ferry to passengers with "legitimate business" on the island.

The tragedy was taking a more serious toll on the Kennedy family. On August 28, with her husband and two of her three children away from home on a camping trip to Nantucket, Joan Kennedy suffered her third miscarriage. Her pregnancy, still in the early stages, had been kept quiet until after the accident on Chappaquiddick, when it was disclosed to explain her absence from the party. Because of her previous miscarriages, her doctor had advised her to stay in bed. She had done so while pregnant two years earlier and successfully delivered hers and Ted's third child, Patrick Joseph Kennedy. But when her husband asked her to go with him to Kopechne's funeral, and to his court appearance in Edgartown three days later, she felt obliged to play the part of the dutiful wife. "So I stood next to Ted," she says. "Only back then, it was sort of more of a big deal. . . . If a dutiful wife was standing next to you it meant that she was forgiving you."

Underneath her composed public demeanor in the Pennsylvania church and Massachusetts courtroom, Joan felt deeply, painfully divided. "I felt like—I felt like it was choosing politics over our baby," she says. Later, after the pregnancy was over, she wondered what might have happened "if I hadn't gone down on this bumpy little plane to the middle of Pennsylvania." It was one of many questions, impossible to answer, that drove her to drink more after Chappaquiddick.

As the summer waned, Kennedy's lawyers were busy trying to shape the rules of the inquest more to their liking. Judge Boyle had declared that the hearings would be open to the public and the press; the senator's team argued that publicity would "taint" the proceedings. His lawyers also sought the right to cross-examine witnesses, a trial practice not allowed within the confines of the rarely used inquest mechanism. On September 2, as the lawyers dug in, the judge postponed the inquest one day before it was to begin. In Edgartown, crews pulled down the scaffolding that had been erected across from the courthouse, intended for visiting cameramen, and hundreds of reporters checked out of their hotel rooms and made plans to travel home.

In Washington, Ted tried to anchor himself in his work. The press had "essentially decided that he could not run for president," says his former aide Bob Bates, and so, in a way, his focus was clearer than it had been the previous spring, when a possible run for the White House had been a constant distraction. "There was a redirecting of ambitions. . . . He had to figure out which way to go," recalls Bates. "And I think he felt the weight of that and threw himself into his work, and it allowed him to become a more serious legislator." He began to adopt health care as one of his signature issues, supporting a vigorous campaign by the country's union leaders for a national health insurance program. Late that fall, he gave a speech at Boston University calling for all children to have health care by 1971.

With his father crippled by a stroke and his brothers gone, Kennedy had already become the head of the family. But his role as patriarch came into stark relief that fall, when his father slipped into a coma and died on November 18, 1969, with Ted and his sisters praying by his side. Only a day or two earlier, for the first time, the senior Kennedy had failed to recognize and respond to Teddy's voice. Joseph Kennedy was eighty-one years old. He had shaped his sons' ambitions and had suffered cruelly when those ambitions turned tragic. He had outlived three of his four sons. He had lived to see the youngest touted as the Democrats' best hope for president—and then he had lived long enough to see those last hopes dashed.

Just four months before his father's death, on his return from Chappaquiddick, Ted had come to his father's bedside at Hyannis Port to tell him what had happened. "Dad, I'm in some trouble," he said. "There's been an accident, and you're going to hear all sorts of things about me from now on. Terrible things. But, Dad, I want you to know that they're not true. It was an accident." Joseph Kennedy took his son's hand, Joe's nurse Rita Dallas recalled, and held it to his chest.

Now, his father's death made Edward Kennedy the last man standing. There was no father figure left to defer to, even symbolically. The decisions and the duties would be his and his alone. The night before his father's funeral, the youngest Kennedy dragged a sleeping bag into the room where his father's body lay and spent the night underneath his casket.

The Chappaquiddick inquest was finally held in early January 1970. Kennedy's lawyers had prevailed, and the four days of testimony were closed to the public and the press. His lawyers had another reason to be pleased: a sympathetic state police investigator had secretly briefed them on the case and assured them there was no new evidence, the investigator, Bernard Flynn, admitted years later.

Together again on the island for the first time since the accident, the guests from the Chappaquiddick party were called to the stand one by one. Kennedy went first, followed by his friends. The five women did not testify until the final day. Forty photographers trailed the "boiler room girls" as they walked single file down Edgartown's quaint Main Street, crunching over ridges of old snow in their high boots and short wool coats.

Barred from the proceedings, 100 reporters loitered in the cold outside the courthouse, behind police barricades, watching witnesses go in and out and hoping for leaks, of which there were few. Unable to tell the public what was going on, and uncertain when the transcript of the testimony would be released, reporters barred from the court-room wondered how the lack of coverage might affect the outcome. "It can help prosecutors to have another set of eyes and ears to pick up contradictions," recalls Stephen Kurkjian, the *Boston Globe* reporter. "Or some neighbor reads about it and says, 'That's not what I recall.' To have that daily coverage, that incremental building of the story, is essential in getting at the truth, and we didn't have that."

As spring began, Kennedy was still a muted presence in the Senate. His legislative aide, Carey Parker, convinced him to try to lower the voting age to eighteen—the same as the draft—and Kennedy cospon-sored legislation, but he let others take the lead in advocating for the successful change. Another Kennedy aide, James Flug, spearheaded a fight against President Nixon's weak Supreme Court nominee, G. Harrold Carswell, who had been found to have endorsed "prin-ciples of white supremacy" two decades earlier. "When it started, no one thought it was winnable," Flug said of the fight against the flawed nominee. "No one was jumping up to lead it."

Kennedy did his part on the Senate floor, insisting that Nixon should not have free reign to choose a judge who would be "unworthy of respect." Nixon was furious. His previous nominee, Clement Haynsworth, the man who had favorably judged Ted's moot court performance a decade earlier, had also been recently rejected. The battle over Carswell, decided by a narrow, 51–45 vote, was important in protecting recent gains in civil rights. It was also a formative lesson for Democrats in how to dig in their heels. "It was a learning experience for the younger members of the Senate and their staffs, on how to run a fight like this — how to investigate and what to do with what you found," Flug says. "There hadn't been a lot of that."

Ted, meanwhile, was preparing for a fight in Massachusetts, as he stepped up campaigning for his Senate race. But the omens were favorable. The questions he was asked at a series of town hall meetings around the state were friendly, and he was warmly received at St. Patrick's Day parades in Lawrence and South Boston — encouraging signs that Chappaquiddick would not prove a stumbling block, at least in his home state. The voters "need to see me, to be convinced that I'm reliable and mature," Kennedy told the *New York Times*. "You can't counter the Chappaquiddick thing directly. The answer has to be implicit in what you are, what you stand for and how they see you."

But in making his first spate of public appearances since his second brother was assassinated, Ted was also facing graver fears about his own safety. When firecrackers popped at the parade in Lawrence, "Kennedy's smile froze immediately," his classmate Burton Hersh recalled. "I saw his legs buckle and his entire body flinch as he fought the impulse to flatten himself against the asphalt. I remember how ashen he went, how clouded his eyes looked until he recovered himself." Death threats arrived at Kennedy's office roughly twice a week — three times as many as any other senator and more than anyone else in government except the president and vice president. Secret Service agents followed him everywhere. The threat was so much a part of daily life that some aides made jokes about it. "The Secret Service protection reminded us of the threats, and it was not very comfortable," Bates says. "We used to joke that we were going to get a sign with an arrow pointing to him. I guess that was our way of coping." Joan

Kennedy confided her fears in an interview with *Ladies' Home Journal*. "What's left of the Kennedys? Besides Ted, only women and children. You don't seriously think we want Ted to be president, do you?"

That April, the final legal chapters in the Chappaquiddick saga played out their strangely inconclusive conclusion. A grand jury on Martha's Vineyard opened its own investigation of Kennedy's accident and closed it two days later, after hearing less than twenty minutes of testimony from four minor witnesses who had not appeared at the inquest. Jury members voted to issue no indictment in Kopechne's death. They made their decision without the benefit of the still-impounded inquest transcript, including the testimony from Kennedy himself and the ten other party guests, which the judge told them would not be admitted without a ruling from the state supreme court. Later, some jury members would claim that the judge and district attorney had discouraged them from mounting their own full-fledged hearing of the evidence.

Within days of their decision, Judge Boyle authorized the release of the 764-page inquest transcript—including his own stunning conclusion that Kennedy's negligence had contributed to Kopechne's death. Based on the testimony at the inquest, including the fact that Kopechne told no one she was leaving and left her purse at the party, "I infer that Kennedy and Kopechne did not intend to return to Edgartown at that time; that Kennedy did not intend to drive to the ferry slip and his turn onto Dyke [sic] Road was intentional," Boyle wrote in his report. Furthermore, the judge wrote, because the bridge was a traffic hazard to be approached with caution, and because Kennedy had been driven over it earlier in the day, the senator "would at least be negligent and, possibly, reckless" when he approached it, as he had testified, at 20 miles per hour.

"I believe it probable that Kennedy knew of the hazard that lay ahead of him on Dyke [sic] Road but that, for some reason not apparent from the testimony, he failed to exercise due care as he approached the bridge," the judge wrote. "I, therefore, find there is probable cause to believe that Edward M. Kennedy operated his motor vehicle negligently . . . and that such operation appears to have contributed to the death of Mary Jo Kopechne."

FAMILY LIFE

LEFT: Edward Moore "Teddy" Kennedy as a baby in Hyannis Port, 1932. (*Courtesy of the John F. Kennedy Presidential Library*)

ABOVE: A family portrait in Bronxville, New York, 1938. L-R (*seated*) Eunice, Jean, Teddy, Joe Sr., Patricia, Kathleen; (*standing*) Rosemary, Bobby, Jack, Rose, Joe Jr. (*AP/Wide World Photos*)

LEFT: Teddy and his sister Jean take time out to photograph the changing of the guard at Buckingham Palace. (*AP/Wide World Photos*)

ABOVE: Hanging with big brother Joe in 1939. (*Courtesy of the John F. Kennedy Presidential Library*)

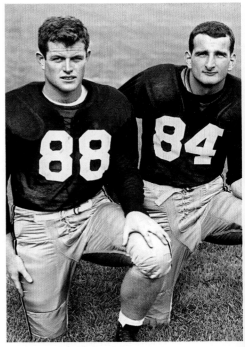

ABOVE: Conquering a palm tree at the Kennedy estate in Palm Beach, 1941. (*Hulton Archive/ Getty Images*)

ABOVE: Harvard football teammates Ted Kennedy (*left*) and Bob Morrison in 1955. (*Paul J. Maguire/The Boston Globe*)

ABOVE: Newlyweds Joan and Ted exit the Church of St. Joseph in Bronxville, New York, on November 29, 1958. (*Jacob Harris/AP/Wide World Photos*)

RIGHT: Kara has a kiss for daddy and Ted Jr. cuddles with mom in November 1962. (*Jack O'Connell/The Boston Globe*)

LEFT: Recently widowed Jackie gets support from her youngest brother-in-law during a benefit at Boston's Symphony Hall, 1965. (*Frank Curtin/AP/ Wide World Photos*)

LEFT: Rose and Ted summering on Cape Cod, July 1972. (*Phil Preston/ The Boston Globe*)

ABOVE: The senator gears up for a roller coaster ride with son Patrick and niece Rory at Riverside Park in Massachusetts, July 1976. (*Joe Dennehy/The Boston Globe*)

ABOVE: At St. Christopher's Church in the Dorchester section of Boston, the Kennedy clan pauses for a photo before heading off to the dedication of the John F. Kennedy Presidential Library and Museum, October 1979. (*George Rizer/The Boston Globe*)

ABOVE: Ted Jr. and Patrick (in suit and tie) help their father hand out holiday gifts at a party for children and families in the Roxbury section of Boston, December 1985. (*George Rizer/The Boston Globe*)

ABOVE: Uncle Ted escorts Caroline into the Cape Cod church where she married Edwin Schlossberg on July 19, 1986. (*George Rizer/The Boston Globe*)

ABOVE: Kara Kennedy's wedding day on the Cape in September 1990, with new husband, Michael Allen, on her arm and supportive parents, Joan and Ted, by her side. (*Mark Wilson/The Boston Globe*)

ABOVE: John F. Kennedy Jr.'s somber cousins and beloved uncle oversee the transport of recovered remains near the scene of his tragic plane crash off Cape Cod in July 1999. (*David L. Ryan/The Boston Globe*)

ABOVE: Beaming newlyweds Ted and Vicki hold hands during an interview at the Kennedy compound in Hyannis Port, September 1992. (*John Tlumacki/The Boston Globe*)

LEFT: Edward Kennedy III is embraced by his dad, Ted Jr., and admired by his grandfather, the original Teddy, in July 1998. (*Suzanne Kreiter/The Boston Globe*)

BELOW: Diagnosed with a brain tumor in May of 2008, the senator leaves Massachusetts General Hospital with a thumbs up and niece Caroline looking over his shoulder. (*George Rizer/The Boston Globe*)

ABOVE AND RIGHT: Mere hours after leaving the hospital, Ted and Vicki go for a sail aboard the *Mya* and stroll with their dogs, Splash and Sunny, in Hyannis Port. (*Matthew J. Lee/The Boston Globe*)

POLITICAL LIFE

LEFT: In March of 1958, times were good for Senator John F. Kennedy and his kid brother, Teddy. (*UPI/Bettman/Corbis*)

BELOW: Making his first Senate run in 1962, Ted marches in Boston's St. Patrick's Day parade. (*Paul J. Connell/ The Boston Globe*)

LEFT: He faces stiff opposition from Edward McCormack, who comes ready to debate in August 1962, but Ted triumphs anyway. (*Samuel B. Hammat/The Boston Globe*)

ABOVE: Senator Ted jokes with President Jack during a spirited New England salute to the popular Commander in Chief, October 1963. (*Edmund Kelley/The Boston Globe*)

ABOVE: With Bobby to her right and Ted to her left, grieving widow Jacqueline Kennedy leads JFK's stately funeral procession on November 25, 1963. (*Paul J. Connell/The Boston Globe*)

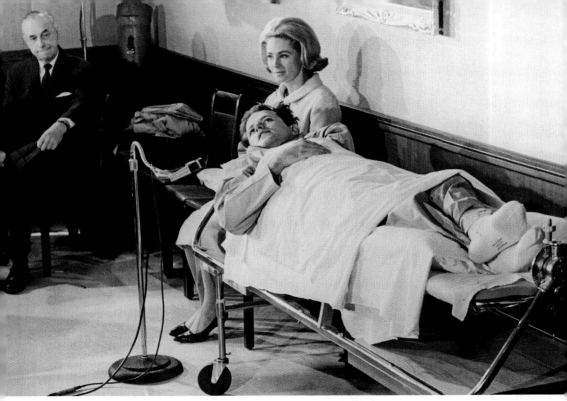

ABOVE: Ted takes questions from reporters, and Joan looks on as he recovers from back injuries suffered in a plane crash in 1964. (*Edmund Kelley/The Boston Globe*)

ABOVE: Migrant workers show the Massachusetts senator a few things about farming America in 1967. (*AP/Wide World Photos*)

RIGHT: The brothers Kennedy arrive at Boston's Logan Airport for a campaign rally in 1966. (*Frank O'Brien/The Boston Globe*)

BELOW: Ted visits a civilian hospital in Da Nang during a 1968 trip to Vietnam. (*AP/Wide World Photos*)

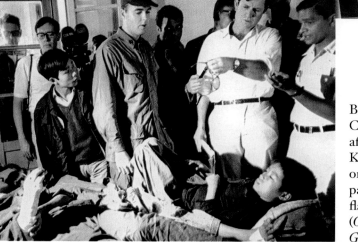

BELOW: Exiting St. Patrick's Cathedral in New York after the funeral of Robert Kennedy, the youngest and only surviving brother leads pallbearers carrying another flag-draped Kennedy casket. (*Ollie Noonan Jr./The Boston Globe*)

ABOVE: At water's edge, the car driven by Senator Edward M. Kennedy, which plunged off a bridge in July of 1969, killing passenger Mary Jo Kopechne. (*UPI/Bettmann/Corbis*)

LEFT: The senator and his dutiful wife, Joan, on their way from a Cape Cod airport to the Kopechne funeral in Pennsylvania. (*Joe Dennehy/The Boston Globe*)

BELOW: Antibusing demonstrators jeer the senator at Boston's City Hall Plaza, September 1974. (*Ulrike Welsch/The Boston Globe*)

LEFT: Championing the need for national health care reform at a conference in August 1978. (*William Ryerson/The Boston Globe*)

RIGHT: Winning smiles from the National Organization for Women at a 1979 fundraiser for ratification of the Equal Rights Amendment. (*Dennis Cook/AP/Wide World Photos*)

LEFT: In a career-defining moment, Ted delivers his passionate "dream shall never die" speech at the 1980 Democratic National Convention. (*AP/Wide World Photos*)

RIGHT: He keeps his distance from Jimmy Carter after Carter's nomination acceptance. (*Stan Grossfeld/The Boston Globe*)

LEFT: Supreme Court nominee Robert Bork gets a boost from Gerald Ford and Bob Dole during Senate confirmation hearings in 1987 but is ultimately defeated by a fierce campaign led by Kennedy. (*Charles Tasnadi/AP/ Wide World Photos*)

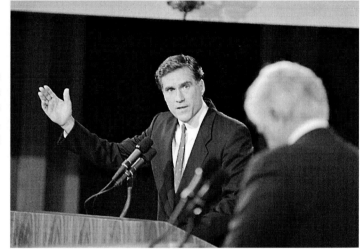

RIGHT: Mitt Romney mounts a serious challenge that in the end falls short of taking Ted's Senate seat in 1994. (*Jim Davis/The Boston Globe*)

BELOW: Senators Christopher Dodd, Joe Lieberman, and Ted Kennedy work their cell phones during a tour of hurricane-ravaged New Orleans, September 2005. (*Paul Sancya/AP/Wide World Photos*)

ABOVE: On Capitol Hill, Republican Senator Orrin Hatch makes a habit of meeting Ted halfway, and the two are unlikely friends as well as productive colleagues. (*Doug Mills/The New York Times*)

BELOW: Surprising fans and doctors, Ted journeys to the 2008 Democratic National Convention in Denver, where he basks in applause and delivers yet another stemwinder. (*Yoon S. Byun/The Boston Globe*)

The judge's report was startling, after months in which most observers had come to expect no further consequences for Kennedy. And
in fact, it soon became clear, there would be no consequences. Under
the odd, archaic rules of the inquest, Judge Boyle was not required to
take legal action based on his findings, released just days before he retired from the bench. The district attorney and the attorney general
made no move to take action, either.

In truth, there was not much more to do. The charge the judge
seemed to advocate, reckless driving, was part of the same section of
the statute to which Kennedy had already pleaded guilty and carried
no greater penalty. Kennedy, nonetheless, rejected the findings as "not
justified."

In a separate finding a few weeks later, the Registry of Motor Vehicles also judged that Kennedy had been driving too fast and was
at "serious fault" in the accident. The agency revoked his driver's license, already suspended, for six more months. During the summer,
a $141,000 settlement was reached with Mary Jo Kopechne's parents
after they hired an expert to project her lifetime earnings. Kennedy's
insurance company paid $50,000, the limit under state law; he pro-
vided the rest of the money himself.

In the fall, he found out what Massachusetts voters made of it all.
They reelected him over his poorly financed Republican rival, Josiah
Spaulding, by a margin of almost 500,000 votes. Spaulding never made
Chappaquiddick an issue in the race, and Kennedy won 63 percent of
the vote. It was less than the 71 percent he had received in 1964. But it
was more than enough.

✺

The young senator had weathered his disgrace. But in January 1971,
Ted suffered a loss of standing when his colleagues chose Senator Robert Byrd of West Virginia to replace him as whip.

Ted was bitter about this setback, believing that some Democrats
who had pledged their support to him had then defected to Byrd's
camp. Later, though, he would see his ouster as a lucky break that led
him to embrace committee work and excel at it. He became the chairman of the Senate's subcommittee on health, and he fought hard to

increase funding for cancer research. He proposed spending $1.2 billion over three years, four times as much as President Nixon had called for. By the end of the year, Kennedy's plan was approved—and Ted had secured even more money for it, $1.5 billion.

He was also deeply concerned with the war in Vietnam, but he pursued the issue in his own way, sometimes opening himself to criticism. When groups of senators collaborated to draft joint letters about the war, Kennedy sometimes declined to join in, preferring his own, more in-depth problem-solving efforts. Some legislators "would use prisoners of war to make political points," recalls Dale de Haan, a former aide who worked with Kennedy on foreign policy. "He had more of a long-term interest, in finding out their names and who they were, their conditions. Because he was an independent person, he wouldn't necessarily go along with their letters—but he produced the goods, a list of names and a lot of information." When American prisoners of war captured in Vietnam were finally handed over to U.S. officials in 1973, Kennedy staff members were there to observe.

Ted advocated for the protection of civilians against new forms of guerrilla warfare, and for the elimination of incendiary weapons and the use of starvation as a weapon, as had been seen in the recent Nigerian civil war. He successfully pushed for the creation of a new relief force within the United Nations, to respond to human and natural disasters. "It was something senators didn't get too involved in, but he knew his stuff backward and forward," says de Haan. Ted was also working for the poor at home, pushing through a bill that guaranteed federal support for programs to feed the elderly. He introduced legislation, eventually adopted, that improved funding for schools on Indian reservations.

Battling for the least powerful, the senator may have felt energized by a return to the simple lessons of his childhood, "the sense that to whom much is given, much is expected," says Paul Kirk, his longtime friend and colleague. "His commitment may have been reinforced [by the tragedies he weathered], where some of us would have been discouraged," says Kirk. "In the face of adversity, if you have the right upbringing, sometimes strengths emerge." His fellow legislators noticed

Kennedy's hard work. Senator Edward Brooke, his Republican colleague from Massachusetts—whose constituents had split 50–50 on
whether Brooke should call for Kennedy's impeachment after Chappaquiddick (Brooke stayed silent)—saw the younger man maturing in
the aftermath of the accident. "He just went about his business and
didn't let it overcome him, and I began to see a change in him," recalls
Brooke, who was not close to Kennedy. "I saw a very serious young
man, a man who had been hurt and who was sorry, and I saw him rise
above it and go on with his life. You had to respect that—he was standing up like a man."

It would have been understandable if he avoided any step that
might raise talk of Chappaquiddick. But Ted also inserted himself into
a fight where the memory of the accident was sure to be invoked: the
protection of Cape Cod's natural beauty. Ted had loved the peninsula
and its islands all his life, and it had fostered in him a deep desire to preserve the coastal environment. In the early 1970s, such action seemed
urgently needed on Nantucket and Martha's Vineyard. Second-home
development was booming on the long-unspoiled islands—a change
some residents blamed on Kennedy himself and the spotlight he had
brought there with his crash on Chappaquiddick.

A study in 1971 concluded that by 1990, the rural environment of
Martha's Vineyard could be destroyed by developers, to the economic
disadvantage of the island.

"There is not one inch of available land on the island that is not
being eyed by developers today," Massachusetts Governor Francis
Sargent observed. Ted knew his intervention would be badly received,
given the islands' Republican landscape and his recent history there.
Regardless, he leaped into the fray in the spring of 1972, after months
of research, by filing the Nantucket Sound Islands Trust bill. The legislation proposed dividing the islands into four categories of land,
including "forever wild," where any further development would be
banned.

"The legislation will not make these islands into a federal preserve," Kennedy said on the floor of the Senate. "To do so would ignore
their fragility, would chill their liveliness, and would in fact accelerate

their destruction. Instead, the legislation seeks to harness and channel extensive local efforts . . . which hold great promise of securing a guarantee against the islands' ultimate and fast approaching ruin."

The reaction was immediate. The *Boston Globe* called the proposal "a legislative bomb . . . dropped on the islands" while islanders, outraged at the prospect of federal meddling in their affairs, denounced it as "inhumane" and "arrogant." Citizens' groups formed; Kennedy met with constituents. In an unusually collaborative process, the federal legislation was amended to reflect local concerns. At the same time, Governor Sargent had joined the debate and was developing similar state legislation. In the end, facing inescapable pressure to accept protections, the islands took it on themselves to act. In 1973, all six towns on Martha's Vineyard adopted their first comprehensive zoning regulations, using Kennedy's plan and the maps he had developed as their model. The state added to the new restrictions by establishing a regional commission to regulate large development on the island. Without the senator's first aggressive steps, the changes might have come too late, says Ronald Rappaport, now the attorney for five of the Vineyard's six towns.

"The character has been preserved, and the island is the way it is today, because of him," Rappaport says. "I call him the father of zoning."

Ted had made it clear, when he returned to the Senate two weeks after his accident on Chappaquiddick, that he would not run for president in 1972. By 1971, that pledge seemed long forgotten. Not by the senator, who reminded the press of it often. But by almost everyone else in Washington—pundits, political junkies, columnists—who speculated relentlessly and breathlessly about his intentions as spring turned to summer and summer to fall. Almost anything he did was seen as evidence that he would run: A cross-country trip to survey the state of health care. A speech that recalled his brother's presidency and declared that it was "time to rekindle that spirit." A pair of gold cufflinks, engraved "JFK," glimpsed on his shirtsleeves. "Short of self-immolation, nothing he can say will convince me he is not a candidate," wrote the editor of the Republican National Committee publication *Monday,* John D. Lofton Jr.

Ted had acknowledged in a *New York Times* interview in May that he would like to be president one day. "That's where the power is," he said. He admitted he thought he could win the nomination. But the timing "feels wrong in my gut," he said. He needed "breathing time," to build up his experience and care for his children, nieces, and nephews. He did not mention Chappaquiddick, but it hung in the air. Meanwhile, his Senate work was fun and satisfying. His defeat as whip had freed him to pursue his own passions, he acknowledged to another interviewer, while his decision not to run allowed him to speak his mind. Weekly, and increasingly harshly, he lashed out at President Nixon. Threatened by his potential candidacy, Nixon lashed back sharply. Ted called Nixon's list of possible Supreme Court nominees "one of the greatest insults to the Supreme Court in its history." A White House spokesman accused Kennedy of having "childish tantrums." At a breakfast meeting in September with families of soldiers missing in Vietnam, Ted called Nixon's trip to China "a smokescreen."

"While he is over there in Peking, your husbands and sons are rotting," said Kennedy. Nixon had previously declined an invitation to speak at the meeting, but he showed up unexpectedly that evening to respond to Ted's criticism.

The Watergate scandal broke in the spring of 1972, and Ted pushed for a government investigation. His staff started tracking the money involved in the break-ins as reporters sniffed out the same story. Staffers traced phone records that connected Donald Segretti, a key figure in the dirty tricks surrounding the scandal, to the president. Ted knew he was making Nixon nervous. That was part of the purpose. But as the Senate moved to a full investigation of Watergate, majority leader Mike Mansfield asked Ted to step aside and let someone else take charge. In the midst of endless speculation about a Kennedy presidential candidacy, Democrats did not want the probe to be seen as a political hit job, led by Nixon's archrival.

Ted had done little to encourage the campaign talk. He had voiced support for Democratic candidate George McGovern, praising the South Dakota senator's opposition to the war. But union leaders preferred Kennedy and insisted he should run. The head of the AFL-CIO asked him to consider accepting a draft at the convention. That did not happen, but McGovern did try to recruit Kennedy as his running mate. Frank Mankiewicz, then McGovern's press secretary, says the specter of Chappaquiddick loomed large. But Kennedy's resurgent popularity seemed larger. "We all were afraid of [Chappaquiddick], but we thought he would be a terrific addition to the ticket," says Mankiewicz. "He was my number one choice, but because I knew him, I didn't think we would get him. . . . He had pretty much taken himself out of the race. I had the feeling he didn't want to raise those issues."

McGovern chose Kennedy's brother-in-law, Sargent Shriver, as his running mate instead. Kennedy spoke on McGovern's behalf at the convention. He had said, after all, that he would serve out his term in the Senate. Keeping his commitment was made easier by his growing influence in his position and his deepening enjoyment of it. "Unlike either of his brothers, he loved the Senate and he took to it like a duck to water," says Mankiewicz. "By 1972 and 1976, he had an alternate route."

CHAPTER
15

RELIEVED, AT LEAST for a time, of the pressure to aim for the White House, Ted was beginning to find some peace in his life. But in 1973, after Nixon's reelection, he would again be punched in the gut by a family tragedy, this one involving his oldest son.

Edward Kennedy Jr., known as Teddy, was twelve years old that fall, a tow-headed boy with a mischievous streak and an ingrained concern for others. When he traveled with his father, he bought gifts for siblings or cousins left behind. Asked to choose a bicycle or a telescope for a birthday present, he chose the telescope. At eight, Teddy had written to his father, demanding emancipation from the senator's oversight of his schoolwork: "You are not ascing [sic] me questions about the five papers. You are not creting [correcting] my homework. It is a free world." The senator loved it. He called it "the Teddy rebellion" and hung it in his office.

Like his siblings, Kara, thirteen, and Patrick, six, Teddy was close to his father. The senator had never barred the children from briefings in the library at their gray-shingled, tree-shaded home in Virginia, recalls Melody Miller, a longtime senior aide. Sometimes he asked for their opinions. When he had to stay late at the Capitol for a vote, Ted would have the children brought over for a picnic on the grounds. As they ate, he would ask about their day and explain what he was working on.

November 1973 brought the tenth anniversary of John F. Kennedy's assassination, with countless mournful tributes. And then it brought devastating news about young Teddy. A sore bruise on the boy's right leg, X-rayed at the urging of his worried governess, was found to be cancer, and doctors believed it had spread. The leg would have to be amputated above the knee.

The senator "was as devastated as any parent would be," Miller recalls. "It was horrendous to contemplate. He convened a group of cancer experts, including some doctors on his Senate staff, and they all went to the house and talked about how to proceed. And we had to be careful not to let anything leak out, because the senator had yet to tell Teddy." Like his father, Joe, who was fascinated with the possibilities of modern medicine and always aggressively sought out the latest cures—sometimes to the family's detriment—Ted demanded that doctors pursue every option for his son. Meanwhile, he tried to keep the boy's life as normal as possible.

Of course, for all the secrecy, the boy knew something was wrong. He and his young friend Teddy Tunney, the son of his godfather Senator John Tunney, agreed that he had a right to know what was happening and felt it was unfair of the grownups not to tell him. Ted finally broke the bad news to young Teddy the day before the surgery was scheduled. Both of them cried. Teddy wanted to know if he would still be able to go camping and sailing. He wanted to know what would happen to his amputated leg, and he asked if it could be donated to research.

Joan Kennedy, traveling in Europe, took the news hard, and "broke down" when she heard it, the senator told a reporter. She hurried home. On Saturday morning, November 16, 1973, the couple escorted Teddy to the operating room at Georgetown University Hospital. Then Senator Kennedy went to Holy Trinity Church, where he walked his niece, Robert's daughter Kathleen, down the aisle at her wedding to David Townsend. "The last song was 'When Irish Eyes Are Smiling,' and everyone was half crying," Miller remembers. "Then the senator went back to the hospital."

Emerging from his surgery with a temporary prosthesis already attached, Teddy Jr. wasted no time in putting it to use. He stood up the next day, worked out on the parallel bars a few days after that, and took his first walk, afraid but uncomplaining, two weeks later. As he recovered, some 30,000 get-well cards and gifts arrived for him from around the world, including a mechanical mongoose from a man in Akron, Ohio, and a dozen red roses ordered by a well-wisher in Italy. Teddy chose a few favorites—the mongoose topped the list—and the rest were sent to other hospitalized children.

The news about his cancer was better than expected. It had turned out to be a rare type, chondrosarcoma, which attacks the cartilage rather than the bone. Slower to spread than bone cancer, this disease was also less lethal. Seven of ten people diagnosed with it survived at least a decade. Within six months, Teddy would ski again and travel to Russia with his father. But a recurrence of the cancer could not be ruled out, at least not until five years had passed. In March of 1974, Ted called a summit of cancer specialists at his home in Virginia—doctors flew in from California, Boston, and New York—for a four-hour discussion of further treatment options. They decided on an aggressive schedule of chemotherapy treatments, a cutting-edge regimen not yet available to the public. The boy would be injected with massive doses of the harsh anticancer drug methotrexate, along with an antidote to offset the harmful effects, every three or four weeks for two years.

The drugs caused crushing nausea and forced Teddy to spend a weekend each month at Children's Hospital in Boston. His father was often there overnight, holding Teddy's head as he vomited, and the senator learned how to inject the antidote at home so his son could leave the hospital earlier. But Teddy Jr. never lamented his misfortune, the longtime Kennedy family nurse Luella Hennessey Donovan told the *Boston Herald*. "The Kennedys have the ability to put the past in the background," she said. "They're always facing the now. . . . What happened in the past, especially if it's unpleasant, is never brought up in their discussions. It's a long-established trait, and Teddy has acquired it." Still, the threat to his child shook the senator badly. "It was very rough," Ted said later. "Very, very rough. He's a courageous boy, but it is very tough, the whole thing. Starting with the process of telling a child that he is about to lose a leg." Joan Kennedy struggled harder to move forward. Although Teddy's progress was encouraging, the doctors made no promises about his long-term survival. "They couldn't give Ted and me a good prognosis, or a prognosis at all because they just didn't know," she says. She held herself together through the immediate crisis, lavishing time and attention on her son. But as his treatment dragged on, she drank more. In June, she was hospitalized for "emotional strain," spending three weeks at a Connecticut sanatorium. After a brief reemergence, she returned to the hospital for another week. In September, she checked into another private clinic in California.

The senator, attentive to her fragile state, stepped up his support of Teddy and the other children, according to a family friend. He called in a priest at one point to attempt counseling. When the couple had an evening event to attend, Kennedy would call home often during the day to assess her condition, and make excuses if she was unable to leave the house. "You never heard an unkind word about Joan," the friend says. "It was just matter of fact—'She can't make it.'" Joan had been vulnerable from the beginning, with a history of alcoholism in her family and long-standing feelings of inferiority to the Kennedy family. Although she was well-liked within the clan, admired for her beauty and musical talents and her sweet, unassuming nature, unathletic Joan was always insecure about her standing. She failed to keep up on the tennis court; she failed to bear as many children as her sister-in-law Ethel. She had not followed politics until she met her husband.

Joan pushed herself, and she had successes. Starting in the 1960s, she set aside her shyness to win respect as an asset on the campaign trail, and in the early 1970s, she rededicated herself to her music, overcoming a crippling fear of performing in public to play the piano with orchestras in Philadelphia and Washington. She showed courage in acknowledging her inner turmoil and seeking help from a psychiatrist, despite the stigma then attached to mental heath care.

But the senator's own failings played a crucial part in his wife's unraveling. As the decade wore on and tales of her husband's womanizing spread, Joan's feelings of inadequacy took over. "Of course they hurt my feelings," she says of the stories she read about Ted's affairs. "They went to the core of my self-esteem. . . . I began thinking, well, maybe I'm just not attractive enough or attractive anymore, or whatever, and it was awfully easy to then say, 'Well, after all, you know, if that's the way it is, I might as well have a drink.' "

As his wife battled her own demons, shifting more responsibility for their three children onto the senator, Ted was also surrogate father to thirteen nieces and nephews, the role he had first stepped into when he stood by Ethel Kennedy as she gave birth, six months after Bobby's assassination, to her last child, Rory. The job was not an easy one, but Ted accepted it unquestioningly. It was what his own father would have expected.

Once, according to a family story, after President John F. Kennedy impatiently shooed his daughter, Caroline, out of a meeting in Hyannis Port, Joseph Kennedy took the president aside. "Just remember," his father told him. "The most important thing you will ever do is raise these children." That lesson had lodged with the last brother, who was now the last father. "It was his Irish heritage, his faith, his father's example," says Miller. "It was second nature to him. It was absolutely natural. But it was a huge responsibility."

Bobby had been the first to step up to the task. After Jack was assassinated in 1963, Bobby sought to rally the family's spirits and strengthen their bonds by rounding up the clan for annual white-water rafting expeditions in the western United States. It worked, at least for the teenaged Kennedys. They found the daredevil dynamism of RFK—Daddy to his own kids, Uncle Bobby to the rest—captivating as he led them down the biggest rivers and through the fiercest rapids. As always with the Kennedys, a spirit of competition-bordering-on-combat reigned: from their side-by-side rafts, the adults and the kids waged exuberant water fights all the way down the river.

The Kennedys had always felt most like a family when they were breaking a sweat. Whether it was touch football, tennis, or skiing, tackling a physical challenge somehow made the other challenges seem manageable. But after Bobby's assassination, the family learned that overcoming the death of their leader was a much harder task than conquering any river.

It fell to Ted to try to recapture the old solidarity. So, in the summer of 1969, with the wounds from Bobby's loss still raw, Ted organized another rafting trip, this time to Utah's Green River. By gathering the family again, he hoped, in the words of Christopher Kennedy Lawford, the son of Patricia Kennedy and Peter Lawford, to "prove that despite Dallas and Los Angeles the family would go on."

But the trip was a disaster. The adults were mired in grief and gloom; they "floated along with their daiquiris and Pouilly-Fuissé and didn't want to be bothered," Lawford recalled. "They were angry and not in the mood to indulge the high jinks of the younger generation." So grim was the mood that when the youngsters tried to rekindle the tradition of a water fight, the adults refused to join in and demanded that they stop. And when the kids kept it up, the irritated grownups sent a guide to make their point by forcefully tossing Robert F. Kennedy Jr. and David Kennedy into the river. "The glory and happiness of the early days were gone," Lawford recalled of the trip. "Uncle Teddy was left to pick up the pieces and be harshly judged for his humanity. The older generation was wounded badly, and their wounds were showing."

Most ominous for Ted's future as family leader, "The mistrust and estrangement from our parents' generation was solidified—hard and fast," wrote Lawford. In the years that followed, the next generation of Kennedys would challenge their Uncle Teddy in ways he had never been challenged—with everything from drug addiction and car accidents to charges of rape. They would add incalculably to the weight upon his shoulders, and they, along with his sick son and wife, would factor into his decisions not to run for president.

Ted was an imperfect role model, to be sure. The older children, advancing through adolescence in the turbulent 1970s, understood his stature in government, but they also knew about Chappaquiddick and his reputation for partying as hard as he worked. By nature, he was comfortable providing the needed love, but he was less well-prepared to cover for the loss of a father's discipline. Still, the senator threw himself into the task of surrogate dad. Somehow reengineering his hectic work schedule, he made sure to be present at First Communions, confirmations, and graduations. He showed up for dinner every week or two with Ethel Kennedy's brood, asked the children about their grades in school, and gently but firmly requested explanations for their Cs or Ds. He never failed to call them on their birthdays. It was Ted who took Joe II, Bobby's eldest son, on a trip to Spain in 1968, away from reminders of his father's murder.

But as hard as he tried to fill the void, he could not erase the pain of a lost father. He could not take away the memory of violence, seared into the children's psyches, or shade them from the spotlight it would train on them for life. As the consequences of their shared history grew clearer, many of Ted's nephews ran wild, caught up in what Lawford, speaking of himself but in words that also applied to several of his cousins, described as a "relentless quest for girls, drugs, and trouble."

As early as the summer of 1970, Bobby Jr. and his cousin Bobby Shriver, both sixteen, were charged with marijuana possession on Cape Cod. The senator flew in from Washington to escort his nephews to court. The case against the boys was continued without a finding of guilt or innocence. There was talk that the police had gone after the young Kennedys. That perception may have fueled tensions between the privileged teenagers and the authorities, and contributed to another incident in Hyannis the following summer, when Bobby Jr., then seventeen, was accused of spitting ice cream at a policeman after the officer asked him if he had been drinking. The young Kennedy, who had attracted police attention because his car was blocking traffic on a busy street, appeared alone in court, without a lawyer, to plead no contest to a charge of loitering. He wore sandals and "patched dungarees," the *New York Times* reported, and did not have the cash to pay his fine of $50.

When the boys were in trouble, Senator Kennedy was called in. His appeals to his nephews to behave were not without power. Lawford admitted it was "very important to me to get his approval." He put in words what many of his cousins felt. "Teddy was mythic in my life. He was the link between the future and the past. His spirit and position were daily reminders of all that was great about our family. His energy and enthusiasm were boundless, but like most members of my family he had very little capacity for disappointment or things not going his way. Of everything he was, and all he represented, the biggest part of him was his heart."

Ted was not the authority figure his father had been, the all-powerful judge and arbiter of discipline. His was a gentler, more collaborative style. When his nephews spiraled out of control, Ted would sometimes call their sister Kathleen at the Putney School in Vermont to talk about ways to straighten out her brothers. He believed, like his father and brothers before him, in the positive effects of family togetherness and group activity. During summers in Hyannis Port, Uncle Ted was "the center of our lives," recalls Kerry Kennedy, the seventh child of Robert and Ethel. "He took us sailing and taught us how to sail, and he told us stories, about politics, American history, our family. He was always very curious about what we were doing." Above all, she says, his effect was to keep them grounded while at the same time reminding them of the family's public achievements. "He gave us a sense of continuity," she says. "That sense of a role model, someone I could depend on, was very, very important."

To Ted, it must have seemed the calls for help would never end. Ethel Kennedy struggled to control her sons. Bobby Jr. left home for several months in 1972—and when the 18-year-old finally called and asked for money to get home, his mother told him to get a job. Ted had also remained a confidant of Jackie Kennedy after the deaths of his brothers, which had made her deeply fearful for herself and her children. When she fled the spotlight for a new life overseas with Greek billionaire Aristotle Onassis, Jackie even called on Ted to help negotiate their prenuptial agreement, according to one of her biographers. (Ted denied he was involved.)

Then, in the summer of 1973, in an almost unthinkable echo of Chappaquiddick, another Kennedy was at the wheel in another tragic car crash off the coast of Massachusetts. This time, the driver was Joseph Kennedy II. When the Jeep he was driving skidded and flipped on a Nantucket road on an August afternoon, the crash injured his younger brother David and five young women passengers. One, Pamela Kelley, eighteen, the daughter of a Cape bartender, was paralyzed. Young Joe was cited for negligent driving. According to some friends, David's later cocaine addiction began with the painkillers he took after the accident.

David was one of the nephews whom Ted worried about most. At twelve, he had accompanied his father, Bobby, on his final campaign trip. He had watched on television, alone in a hotel room where he was supposed to be sleeping, the chaos of the assassination. He struggled with drug addiction for much of the 1970s, and he would die of an overdose in 1984, at age twenty-eight, alone in a hotel room in Florida, where he had gone to visit his grandmother Rose.

When the family problems seemed overwhelming, the senator reverted to the model most familiar from his childhood. In the mid-1970s, he began to organize family outings that helped steep the younger generation in an appreciation of history and nature, while also sending them a message: we are an unbreakable unit. "He [took] us on all these history trips: Bunker Hill, Valley Forge, Harper's Ferry, Philadelphia, Richmond: all the historic sites," recalls Caroline Kennedy. Her uncle saw it as "a way for the kids to learn about history, to share his love of history, to get to know each other, and to spend some time together."

He recruited an old family friend, Don Dowd, to plan an educational camping trip every summer. Ted's pal John Culver says the idea of the trips was "to get these children who had no father the experience they might not otherwise get."

"I think that came very naturally to him out of his love and loyalty that he felt to the family generally, and certainly his relationship with his brothers, where the children needed attention," Culver says. "I think being the last of nine almost made him more sympathetic and empathetic." Usually Dowd drove the Winnebago loaded with Kennedy's children and nieces and nephews, but sometimes Ted took the wheel. By day, they hiked or swam or rode canoes across a lake; by night, they built bonfires and Ted led them in song or told them stories. They visited Massachusetts museums and historic sites: the Clark Art Institute in Williamstown; Herman Melville's home in Pittsfield. One year they took in a Linda Ronstadt concert at Tanglewood. Ronstadt's manager invited Ted to say hello to her after the concert and was startled when nearly twenty nieces and nephews accompanied him backstage.

One day in the mid-1970s, Ted took the kids for a tour of Old Sturbridge Village. Attired in Bermuda shorts, he presided over a picnic, then exhorted the youngsters to take part in foot races. Larry Morrison, who was then director of communications for the village, recalled that when one of the youngsters broke a rule, Kennedy gave him an instant time out, saying: "Sit down, I will be back to you in a minute, young man."

But on many excursions, Ted also carved out time to take the youngsters, singly or in pairs, for walks in the woods so they could talk privately. "He got close to the kids on those trips," says Dowd. "He made sure he had different areas to talk to them, especially Bobby's kids. He would talk to all of them, from Caroline down. He knew his role. He knew that basically they turned to him now." He never missed a chance to serve as the ceremonial patriarch. In the fall of 1978, for instance, he presided at a joint birthday party for Caroline and John F. Kennedy Jr., who turned twenty-one and eighteen that November. During the celebration at a Manhattan restaurant, the room quieted when the senator ascended partway up a staircase and raised a glass to toast his niece and nephew. It should be their father doing this, he acknowledged, but his tone was joyful, not somber. He went on to talk about the happy years they had ahead of them.

Ted may also have relied on the nieces and nephews to bolster his sense of himself as a responsible family figure. To many on the outside, the Kennedys seemed to be fraying. The antics of the teenaged kids only added to a sense of chaos in which Ted's own problems—Chappaquiddick, heavy drinking, a decaying marriage—played a part. He needed to reach out to the younger generation as much as they needed him. "I think that he's been great, but I also think it makes him feel like he's needed and wanted and loved, like we all want to feel," Joan says of Ted's exertions as surrogate father. He knew parental love was no guarantee against trouble. His daughter, Kara, feeling the strain of her brother's and mother's illnesses, struggled through her own rebellious stage in the 1970s and would sometimes run away from home. His son Patrick would suffer a drug problem of his own. Chris Lawford, living in Boston, was charged with heroin possession. David Kennedy reported being mugged at a New York hotel frequented by drug dealers, then sought treatment for a life-threatening cardiac infection often caused by drug abuse. In time, many members of the family's younger generation would emerge from the shadows and thrive. But for some, carrying burdens thrust upon them by a badly broken family, it would be a long, hard passage.

And part of Ted Kennedy could foresee how long it would take. Those closest to him are convinced that is the main reason he decided to forgo running for president in 1976. At the end of September 1974, Kennedy, then forty-two, returned to Boston to announce his "firm, final, and unconditional" decision not to pursue the presidency in '76. Instead, he would run for reelection to the Senate. His wife beamed at his side, looking tanned and healthy on the heels of her most recent hospitalization, as he spoke to a packed room at the Parker House Hotel in downtown Boston.

His personal safety was not the main reason, he said, despite the death threats against him. Neither was Chappaquiddick. He was making his decision now, he said, "to ease the apprehensions in my family" about his possible candidacy and "to clarify the situation within my party."

Once upon a time, Kennedy would have sat with a roomful of advisers to hash over every pro and con. But he was older now. His father and brothers were dead. Many of the old advisers had moved on. This time, he made the decision alone. And the decision was harder than he had made it appear. "That's where the power is to do what you want to do," he said of the presidency. "And the way we were brought up, you know, my father told us we should make things happen. . . . That was true of Jack, but less true of Bobby and least of me. A lot of things happened to me."

Concern for his family drove his decision. "I can see the impacts on other people. I see the fallout with Bobby's children. They've had troubles they just wouldn't have had if he was around," Ted said.

Paul Kirk, his longtime friend and colleague, saw up close Ted's need to embrace his fragile family. "I believe it was much more his obligations, his worries about his own children, having watched what their cousins went through," he says. "It's so searing, parental love and fear. It's a powerful thing."

CHAPTER
16

IN 1977, NEWLY elected President Jimmy Carter took office. The Democrats were back in command of the White House, and in many ways it would make Kennedy's job easier. But Ted's relationship with the new president did not have an auspicious beginning.

Like most of his colleagues, Ted did not know Carter, a Washington outsider who prided himself on that status and had used it skillfully to his advantage. The former Georgia governor had done little to build their relationship. Carter had not included Kennedy on his list of vice presidential prospects, and the candidate's overheard remark that he was glad he didn't have to "kiss [Kennedy's] ass" had been widely reported. Asked, before the election, if he had "complete confidence" in Carter, Ted hedged. "Well, I have confidence in him," he said. He was just as lackluster when pressed on his plans to help Carter campaign, telling a reporter, "I suppose I'll be glad to help him in some way."

He did send two aides to work on Carter's campaign, but he also pushed the candidate hard on health care, at one point publicly lamenting that Carter kept his plans intentionally vague. Ted was given little to do at the Democratic National Convention in July, and he left New York early. When party leaders surged onstage to close the convention's final night, the senator was missing from the celebration, already on his way to the airport. His aide Paul Kirk told reporters that the call to invite Kennedy onstage had come too late, giving the senator the impression that his presence was not "that important" to the event planners. A few weeks later in Boston, during a lunchtime speech before a meeting of gas dealers, Ted joked about his limited role in New York. "I want to tell you how pleased I am to address your national convention," he said. "I didn't get a chance to speak much at the last national convention." His candid comments to a reporter that day revealed a sense of disaffection, with hints of regret and bitterness at finding himself outside the inner circle. "I don't know the man," he said of Carter. "I guess he's looking over his shoulder at me, although God knows why at this point."

Increasingly, what mattered most to Ted was establishing a national health insurance system. His experience with Teddy's cancer, spending hours in hospitals and talking with other parents, had given him a more intimate understanding of his own privilege as a consumer. He had learned more about the average family's struggles with medical bills, and the painful choices some were forced to make between paying the mortgage and buying medications. He knew his son had been treated with experimental medicines that most families could not even dream of affording. "He became really aware of how the majority of Americans could not cope financially with this type of illness," says Melody Miller. "It really energized him in terms of health insurance." Hundreds of parents had written to him of their children's battles with cancer. His staff replied with what they called "courage letters," urging them to focus on the good and keep on going. Many parents called to say the letters helped them through.

Kennedy redoubled his push for national health care and helped draft successful legislation that started up health maintenance organizations, to be known as HMOs, seen as a way to make health care more affordable. He obtained increased research funding and broadened access for poor women and children with the Women, Infants, and Children Nutrition Program, known as WIC. He had hammered away at Presidents Nixon and Ford on the need for broader health care legislation. He had traveled the country, from New Mexico reservations to Florida migrant camps, to better understand the medical problems faced by the poor. Now, with a Democrat back at the helm of the country, Kennedy was becoming impatient. In published editorials and speeches around the country, Ted described the struggles of his sick constituents, some of whom faced handing over their life savings or forgoing treatment altogether. He tried to frame health care as a basic human right. "He saw it as his job to speak for the voiceless," says Dr. Lawrence Horowitz, a staff member who worked closely with Kennedy on health care legislation. "He always said the very people who railed against his proposal for national health insurance would then walk down to the capitol physician's office and get what they needed, and they wouldn't get a bill. He used to say, if it's good enough for senators and congressmen, it's good enough for everyone—and he meant it."

Kennedy had a plan, the Health Security Act, that would make health insurance a universal government benefit. The proposal was controversial, and, critics charged, too costly. Carter had endorsed its basic principles, but he was focused on balancing the budget. As his administration approached its half-year mark, he made no move to action. Ted was helping the president work to stem violence in northern Ireland and develop new diplomatic policy with China. But he did not see Carter returning any favors. In May 1977, in a speech before the United Auto Workers national convention in Los Angeles, Ted aired his frustration. "One hundred and sixteen days after the inauguration, President Carter and his administration have made commendable progress in most areas," he said. "But health care has been left behind."

Ted reminded his audience of Carter's statements just a year earlier, as a candidate for president, when he called the health care system a "catastrophe" and "made clear that the years of frustration and discontent were over." Now, Ted said, "health reform is in danger of becoming the missing promise in the administration's plans." It was a bold attack. But it did not do much to advance the cause.

In the Senate, the sweep of Ted's work was increasingly confident and ambitious, and it showed no loss of humanity. He widened his long-standing interest in foreign affairs, studying conflicts in Africa and the Middle East. Back in 1974, he had led a Senate fight to block further funding of the war in Vietnam, but he also found time to visit Portugal, and to convince Congress to spend $50 million to help the leaders of that country's recent revolution fend off Communism. Unlike many senators and presidents "who had to be the smartest guy in the room," Kennedy "had none of these hang-ups," says Robert Hunter, who advised him on foreign affairs in the 1970s. "He knew he wasn't the smartest guy in the room on these issues, but he hired good people and he listened to them." Ted read constantly when he traveled and never suffered jet lag. He got upset if there was too much time between flights, and sometimes insisted on leaving the airport for a quick museum visit. "He always operated as if tomorrow was going to be his last day," Hunter says.

In 1978, he ascended to a new seat of power, becoming chairman of the Senate Judiciary Committee. President Carter was intent on making human rights the cornerstone of American foreign policy, and Ted himself began using his legal perch to assume a high profile on the issue, speaking out against the atrocities committed by death squads in El Salvador and the mistreatment of Soviet Jews. On a trip to Moscow, Ted met with Jewish dissidents who had been denied exit visas, and took up their cause personally with Soviet leader Leonid Brezhnev, whom he had known since the 1960s. And Ted's success in persuading Brezhnev to allow one dissident couple to leave for humanitarian reasons was hailed as an international triumph.

By the fall of 1978, Boris and Natalya Katz had been struggling to get out of the Soviet Union for four years. They lived in a one-room apartment on the outskirts of Moscow, eking out an uneasy existence as a pair of refuseniks, dissident Soviet Jews who were not allowed to leave the country. Several years earlier, the Katzes had decided that they no longer wanted to live where anti-Semitism was openly practiced, where Jews were routinely denied access to the better jobs and universities. And they chafed under the restrictions of Communist rule. "What bothered me was the total lack of freedom," Boris recalls. "There was no notion of saying what you think. We didn't want our children to grow up in a country where people are afraid of the truth."

So from 1974 onward, every six months, like clockwork, the young couple applied for an exit visa. Every six months they were rejected. Natalya lost her job, a common fate for those who even hinted at dissatisfaction with the Soviet system. Boris was allowed to keep his job at a mechanical engineering research institute, but it was located 50 miles from Moscow.

Then Jessica was born on October 3, 1977. The birth of their first child intensified their determination to get out of the Soviet Union. When Jessica was about three months old, she mysteriously stopped gaining weight. Soviet doctors were stymied as she grew weaker and weaker. She lost weight and became critically ill. Other parents told the Katzes that their own children had died after showing similar symptoms. "It was very horrible," said Natalya.

Boris's mother and two brothers had made it to the United States several years earlier. They contacted American doctors, who speculated that Jessica was suffering from malabsorption syndrome. It is a broad term that refers to the inability to absorb certain nutrients adequately into the bloodstream, often caused by the failure of the body to produce the enzymes needed to digest certain foods. Supportive tourists from the West began smuggling Pregestimil, a baby formula unavailable in the Soviet Union, to the Katzes. Jessica began to get a bit better, but the Katzes did not know how long their clandestine supply line would last, and they desperately wanted the baby to be seen by Western doctors.

Soviet authorities, though, unwilling to lose face by acknowledging that perhaps the West had superior medical care, stiffened their resolve against letting the Katzes emigrate. Boris and Natalya grew so desperate that they took a dangerous step: They began protesting in the heart of Red Square. Risking arrest and imprisonment, they held placards that read "Let us go." Police broke up their protests each time. Once, when the couple tried to protest outside KGB headquarters, with baby Jessica in a carriage and Natalya pregnant with another child, they were beaten up by what Boris calls "hired goons." But pressure on Soviet authorities was building from the outside. The case became an international cause célèbre, and the media dubbed Jessica "the littlest refusenik." There were petitions and marches in the West demanding that the Soviet Union "Let Jessica Go!"

Back in Boston, meanwhile, Boris's mother, Clara, though she could barely speak English, was steadfastly pressing their cause. Letters about the case poured into Ted's office. He decided to use an upcoming trip to Moscow to press for their release with Brezhnev, who was trying to cultivate a friendly relationship with Ted, perhaps assuming that he would one day be president.

But the Katzes didn't know that, and it was hard to keep their spirits up as the months dragged by. Boris grew convinced that he and his family would soon be exiled to Siberia. Then one night the telephone rang in their apartment. On the other end of the line was Alexander Lerner, a fellow refusenik. "Somebody wants to meet with you," Lerner said mysteriously. He refused to say who. Boris took the subway train to his friend's neighborhood on the outskirts of Moscow and knocked on the door of the apartment. When it opened, Boris saw famed Soviet dissident Andrei Sakharov, his wife, Yelena Bonner, and about ten others. "Senator Kennedy will be here shortly," Lerner told him. "He asked to arrange a meeting with you."

At midnight, the door opened and Ted came in. KGB officials, who had accompanied him to the apartment in half a dozen cars, tried to enter as well. Kennedy turned to them and asked them to leave. They reluctantly did so. He began moving through the room, shaking hands. When he was introduced to Boris, Ted stopped. "I need to talk to you privately," the senator told him. They went into the kitchen, where Ted told Boris that he had just come from meeting with Brezhnev in the Kremlin, and that the Soviet leader had agreed to let the Katzes emigrate. "It's embarrassing to admit now that I did not believe him," Katz says. "There had been so much suffering."

When the Katzes stepped off a plane at Boston's Logan Airport on November 28, 1978, Senator Kennedy was waiting there for them. Only then, in the crowded tumult of that scene, did Boris Katz get a sense of Kennedy's political importance. In the years to come, as the

Katzes built new lives in the United States, they would sometimes go to Kennedy's campaign events, where he would invariably spot them and inquire about Jessica. "That girl is always in my heart," he would say. The feeling is mutual. "He saved my life," Jessica says simply, as her parents nod in agreement. Adds Boris, "A miracle occurred, thanks to Senator Kennedy."

The late 1970s gave Ted some of his most longed-for victories in the Senate. In 1975, he had kicked off a year's-long battle to reform the federal criminal code. Ultimately, the legislation he pushed to passage would do away with parole for federal prisoners, ensuring they would serve their full sentences. It would overhaul sentencing guidelines, creating narrower, more predictable ranges, to send a clearer message to criminals about the punishment they could expect. "A mandatory minimum sentence is not based on a vindictive desire to punish," he wrote in an opinion piece in the *New York Times*. "It arises out of the belief that certainty of punishment is the most effective deterrent to criminal conduct." Getting a deal on the new guidelines would take months of painstaking negotiation with Republican colleagues. Kenneth Feinberg, a former assistant U.S. Attorney who worked with Ted on the sentencing guidelines, says he was tenacious and practical, a consummate legislator. "'The perfect is the enemy of the good' was his philosophy," says Feinberg. "He'd say, 'I'll yield on capital punishment if you yield on other things.' His view was, let's get a package, and we can improve it later."

Beginning in 1976, Kennedy also spent years advancing the Foreign Intelligence Surveillance Act, known as FISA, which regulates the use of electronic surveillance for national security. And he dug in deep on efforts to reform the tax code, spurred by controversy over tax shelters used to benefit the oil and gas industries. Paul McDaniel, then a professor at Boston College Law School, was called in to bring Ted up to speed on tax law. Through the summer, McDaniel spent long weekends tutoring the senator at his Virginia home, where he found a conscientious student willing to spend hours on the subject. "About the only thing he would let interrupt him was if one of his children or one of his nieces or nephews needed help, in which case the study session would end immediately and resume when he was finished," says McDaniel.

When the legislation came up for debate, the process was grueling, and compromise after compromise was called for. After Kennedy proposed an amendment denying tax deductions for any type of airfare except coach class, Senator Lloyd Bentsen, the Texas Democrat, stopped by to express his regrets. "I've been working all my life to afford first class, and I'm going to have to vote against this one," Bentsen said, according to McDaniel. On another front, after years of effort by Ted and his Judiciary Committee counsel, the future Supreme Court Justice Stephen Breyer, Congress passed legislation to deregulate the airline industry, which would drive down fares with increased competition.

⚔

As the tenth anniversary of Chappaquiddick approached, it brought a spate of reassessments of the tragedy and its effects on Kennedy's career. He had seen how the issue could explode back into headlines the previous year, after a speech in Alabama where he criticized former President Nixon for his role in Watergate. Senator Barry Goldwater lashed back, condemning such "unctuous righteousness" from "the last person in the country to lecture us on such matters. Until all the facts involving the Chappaquiddick tragedy are made known, the American people can do without moralizing from the Massachusetts Democrat," Goldwater had said. Afterward, a Kennedy aide said he planned to send a copy of the massive Chappaquiddick inquest transcript to Goldwater's office.

The core question had not changed in a decade: should Kennedy's judgment on that single summer night bar him from the office for which he had once seemed destined? The voters did not think so, according to a *Time* magazine poll in August 1978. A vast majority of those surveyed, 79 percent, said Chappaquiddick should not be a factor when considering Kennedy as a possible presidential candidate.

But behind the numbers, it was clear that many people had neither forgotten nor forgiven Ted. Mary Jo Kopechne's parents, Gwen and Joseph, who had initially been strongly supportive of Ted, seemed to give way to some doubts, telling the *New York Times* that Kennedy had "grown up in the last few years." But they pointedly suggested that if Kennedy ran for president, they would have to see who else was running before they decided whether to vote for him.

In an attempt to put the Chappaquiddick incident behind him, Ted finally agreed to sit down with reporters of the *Boston Globe* in October 1974. For both Ted and the reporters, it turned out to be a disappointing two-hour interview. At the outset, Kennedy had urged the reporters to "feel completely free" to ask whatever they wanted. But by the end, the senator looked exhausted, resting his head on his desk and using his arm as a pillow as he rehashed his five-year-old inquest testimony. Ted again dismissed the testimony of the deputy sheriff, Huck Look, who claimed he had seen Kennedy's car at 12:45 A.M. He again denied driving drunk and rejected Judge Boyle's conclusions that Kennedy had been deceitful in his testimony and reckless in his driving as "erroneous and mistaken." He again expressed regret for his failure to call for help for Mary Jo Kopechne. "I could have and perhaps should have seen the red light that was at the fire station and either sounded some alarm which I should—evidently could have—which I did not," he said. "I could have used the telephone to alert people on the Chappaquiddick side. I could have gotten the ferry. In retrospect all of these things could have been done."

But he stopped short of accepting full responsibility, leaving the question of his mental state that night ambiguous. "You were in control enough to have done those things?" the reporters asked him. "It was strictly a state of mind. It was strictly a state of mind," Kennedy said, obliquely.

The stories that followed in the *Globe* raised other questions. They quoted an anonymous source who claimed that Gargan, Kennedy's cousin, had agreed to take the fall after the wreck, but that plan was abandoned. They quoted Gwen Kopechne describing her continuing frustration with the lack of answers. "Sometimes I'd like to scream a lot but I'm trying to hold it back," she said. "It would be nice if somebody would speak up." No one did. The men and women who were present at the party slammed doors and hung up on the reporters who approached them. Told that the Kopechnes had questions about his conduct that night, Gargan responded, "I don't care about that."

Ted reacted angrily to the series that appeared in the *Globe* that October. In a long letter to the editor, he criticized the paper for its "cursory treatment" of a study he paid for, examining conditions at the bridge, that he said had "disposed of the issue of negligent driving." The *Globe* responded with an editorial in defense of its work. "Until Senator Kennedy or someone else is willing to discuss the gaps in the story . . . or until the senator is no longer in the public eye, the tragedy at Chappaquiddick Island will be a proper subject of attention and concern," it said.

On the tenth anniversary of the accident, members of a group calling itself the Mary Jo Kopechne Memorial Society staged a brief ceremony at the Dike Bridge on Chappaquiddick. A small crowd gathered there above the water, mostly reporters marking the occasion and vacationers who happened by on their way to East Beach. The main purpose of the gathering was to keep Kopechne's memory alive, said Frank Fusco, the founder of the group. The other goal, he said, was to foster hope—"the hope that someday we can persuade Senator Kennedy to come forth and reveal exactly what took place here ten years ago."

CHAPTER
17

ON OCTOBER 12, 1979, CBS correspondent Roger Mudd asked Senator Edward M. Kennedy why he wanted to be the next president of the United States. He was preparing to announce his candidacy in a matter of days. With the cameras rolling, Kennedy said this:

"Well, I'm—were I to make the announcement, and to run, the reasons I would run is because I have a great belief in this country. That it is—there's more natural resources than any nation in the world; the greatest education population in the world; the greatest technology of any country in the world; the greatest capacity for innovation in the world; and the greatest political system in the world.

"And yet I see at the current time that most of the industrial nations of the world are exceeding us in terms of productivity and are doing better than us in terms of meeting the problems of inflation; that they're dealing with their problems of energy and their problems of unemployment. It just seems to me that this nation can cope and deal with its problems in a way that it has in the past.

"We're facing complex issues and problems in this nation at this time and that we have faced similar challenges at other times. And the energies and resourcefulness of this nation, I think, should be focused on these problems in a way that brings a sense of restoration in this country by its people in dealing with the problems that we face: primarily the issues on the economy, the problems of inflation, and the problems of energy.

"And I would basically feel that—that it's imperative for this country to either move forward; that it can't stand still or otherwise it moves backward. And that leadership for this nation can galvanize a—a—an effort with a team to try and deal with these problems that we're facing in our nation, and can be effective in trying to cope with the problems that we'd face. And I think that'd be the real challenge in—in the 1980s. I think it's a watershed period in our country, from a variety of different points, primarily from an energy point of view and from an economic point of view."

He spoke from a strange, bloodless remove. His failure to answer the question clearly astonished friend and foe alike—not the least of whom the man who asked it.

"It revealed that he really hadn't gone to the mountain and figured out why," says Mudd.

And yet Kennedy, who had passed up chances to run in 1968, when Democrats tried to entice him to replace Bobby, and 1972, when the nomination was his for the asking, and 1976, the post-Watergate year when a Democratic victory was almost assured, was finally preparing to make a run in 1980, when there were extra obstacles to overcome.

Not only was the Democratic Party increasingly unpopular, but Ted would have to defeat an incumbent president, Carter, even to earn the right to take on the Republicans. By 1979, however, the seams of the Carter presidency were coming apart. As of June, only 28 percent of voters viewed him favorably as the nation suffered from double-digit inflation, double-digit interest rates, and long gasoline lines.

Ted, who had repeatedly disappointed his supporters by failing to run for president, felt responsible for the mess by not having taken on Carter four years earlier. Now, he was convinced that a Carter reelection campaign would end in disaster for the Democratic Party. But as his muddled answer to Mudd showed, there was little evidence he had fully thought out the question of why to run. People who had known

Ted for years saw signs of the same ambivalence that he had harbored about the presidency throughout his career. "He never called me up at two in the morning and said, 'What do you think?' " says David Burke, his first chief of staff and the tough, discreet confidant who later ran CBS News. "It is my opinion that he didn't want to run. . . . It would not have bothered him if it went away nicely."

Vice President Walter Mondale tried to talk Ted out of getting into the race. He didn't think the time was right, and he felt it would be unfair to Carter. "There was a lot of anger that he shouldn't be running," recalls Mondale. "The president didn't deserve this." Ted, meanwhile, was still mouthing the mantra he had repeated for months: he expected the president to be renominated and reelected, and he intended to support him. But speculation about a Kennedy challenge was so rife that Carter told a group of congressmen at a White House dinner in early June that if Kennedy ran, he'd "whip his ass."

Carter's weakness became more exposed when he retreated to Camp David in July. Legions of thinkers, politicians, and businesspeople ventured to Maryland's Catoctin Mountains to give the president advice about how to reignite the American spirit. In a televised address on July 15, Carter delivered what became known as "the malaise speech," though he never used the word malaise. Carter told the American people that they suffered from a crisis of confidence: "We can see this crisis in the growing doubt about the meaning of our own lives and in the loss of a unity of purpose for our nation. The erosion of our confidence in the future is threatening to destroy the social and the political fabric of America."

The speech gave Carter an initial boost in the polls, but then backfired. Carter's standing dropped again when three days later he fired four of his cabinet secretaries, heightening the sense of disarray. A Gallup poll taken in the middle of August showed Kennedy ahead of Carter among Democrats, 55 percent to 28 percent.

Ted thought the speech was a failure because Carter chose to bemoan the state of the country rather than infuse it with hope. Ted convened meetings with his inner circle at Hyannis Port to take their soundings on his prospects for a challenge. His longtime counselor

Paul Kirk remembers one Hyannis Port conclave in July with Joan, Steve Smith, speechwriter Carey Parker, and Eddie Martin, a veteran Kennedy confidant, among others. Kirk, who was in line to become the fledgling campaign's national political director, was alone among the group in questioning the wisdom of Ted's challenging Carter. "I said, 'I'm not sure this is a good idea, running against an incumbent president of your own party,' " he recalls.

The same group met again in late summer. By then, the pressure from all sides made the campaign inevitable. Many leading Democrats, including New York's Senator Daniel Moynihan and Governor Hugh Carey, were pushing Ted to do it, and even Joan—who was still often apart from him, she in Boston and he in Washington—signed on. Their three children were now older and all healthy, with the youngest, Patrick, getting into his teen years. They, too, were on board.

Whatever his state of ambivalence, Ted had never seemed to doubt that he would, at some point, have to run for the presidency. After all, everyone told him so. Perhaps, many friends believe, he simply wanted to stop the noise in his ears. "It was an event that had to occur," says Burke. "It was expected of him to run. People were saying, 'When are you going to do it? When are you going to do it? Why not now?' He could never escape 'When are you going to do it?' He may have succumbed or reached the point when he decided to get it done."

Despite the lingering questions about Chappaquiddick, Ted and his advisers did not consider it a major impediment to his candidacy. They believed the issue would eventually recede behind a roster of pressing national concerns. A Lou Harris poll taken in June indicated that a mere 23 percent of voters would refuse to vote for Kennedy because of Chappaquiddick. "It was understood that this was an element of [Kennedy's] story," recalls Kirk, adding that "a judgment was made that, yes, it was going to be an issue, but the issues facing the country were more important." And Kennedy still carried the best brand name in politics. Ted's aide Rick Stearns describes the feelings of many that September by saying, "The Carter campaign will be like the French army in World War II, an obstacle but not a deterrent." Kennedy, his inner circle believed, would cruise to the nomination.

Almost thirty years later, many former Kennedy and Carter aides would remain convinced that Carter could have ended the challenge before it began by cutting a deal with Ted on a national health insurance plan. Back in December of 1978, the Democrats held what they called a "mid-term convention" in Memphis, and Ted delivered a stemwinder of a speech calling health care "the great unfinished business on the agenda of the Democratic Party." He also took issue with Carter's tentative leadership: "Sometimes," he declared, "a party must sail against the wind. We cannot afford to drift or lie at anchor. We cannot heed the call of those who say it is time to furl the sail."

Hamilton Jordan, the brash and boyish political operative who came out of nowhere to lead Carter's 1976 campaign and then became his White House chief of staff, listened to the speech and then told Carter's pollster Patrick Caddell that Kennedy was clearly laying the groundwork to challenge Carter: "The son of a bitch is going to run." Others in the Carter camp felt that Kennedy was merely allowing speculation of a primary challenge to build in order to gain leverage with Carter on health care. But Carter never budged, in part because health care wasn't his highest priority and in part because the economy was falling into recession. By 1979, Carter felt it would be irresponsible to spend an estimated $60 billion a year on national health insurance. The price was simply too high.

Carl Wagner, who would serve as Kennedy's national field director for the campaign, remains adamant that the Carter forces missed a key opportunity to neutralize a political enemy. "If Carter had said, 'Let's do it,' there would have been no race," he says. Carter's domestic policy adviser Stuart Eisenstadt agrees. He spent hours negotiating with Ted and his aide Larry Horowitz in the senator's Capitol hideaway office over a health insurance package. "We were down to the real short strokes," recalls Eisenstadt. "We had a construct."

But Carter's economic and political teams killed the deal, says

Eisenstadt. Jordan didn't want Kennedy in the race, but he felt that Kennedy would find another reason to run against Carter even if the White House gave him his health plan. Carter apparently agreed. "Once they had the challenge, the president's attitude was, 'I wasn't going to kiss his ass to keep him from running,'" recalls Caddell. "Carter didn't want to look afraid."

Caddell had worked for Ted in the 1970s and had remained on good terms with many people in the Kennedy camp. He called Bob Shrum, Carl Wagner, and Gerry Doherty, among others, in an effort to bridge the gap between the two sides. He could not pull it off. Ultimately, the two camps failed to get beyond a rivalry that dated back to Carter's ascent as a national figure. Carter and his people felt that Ted had never accepted the legitimacy of the Carter presidency. Ted's people countered that Carter had arrived in Washington, along with loyalists like Jordan and press secretary Jody Powell, with a chip on his shoulder and hostility toward the Washington establishment.

Three days after the Mudd interviews aired, with negative reviews echoing throughout the political world, Ted and his swollen press entourage arrived in two planes in Boston on a bright fall day for the announcement of his candidacy. Both Jack and Bobby had announced their candidacies in the same place—the magisterial Senate Caucus Room in the Russell Senate Office Building on Capitol Hill. Not Ted. He and his staff decided to make the announcement at Faneuil Hall, Boston's historic gem where John and Sam Adams talked revolution. This, too, was a kind of revolt.

Kennedy spoke with vigor about how disastrous he felt the Carter presidency had been. "For months we have been sinking into crisis. Yet we hear no clear summons from the center of power. Aims are not set. Yet the means of realizing them are neglected. Conflicts in direction confuse our purpose. Government falters. Fear spreads that our leaders have resigned themselves to defeat. This country is not prepared to sound retreat. It is ready to advance. It is willing to make a stand. And so am I."

The crowd—including a vivacious 89-year-old Rose, a supportive Joan, and the rest of the clan—loved it. How could he possibly lose?

But while others were expecting a romp, Ted himself was more skeptical. "I've got 45 percent," he reasoned to a reporter at a time when he was polling much higher. "The last 6 percent comes hard."

That turned out to be an understatement. The 1980 Democratic contest would prove to be memorable for a lot of reasons. It would become one of the ugliest in memory, and it would create hard feelings on both sides that never would heal.

For Ted, it would start and end badly. Almost as soon as the applause ended at Faneuil Hall, Democratic loyalists and outsiders alike found themselves shocked by the sorry state of his early campaign, especially given his vaunted name and the large numbers of Jack's and Bobby's supporters who had been waiting for decades to make another run. The whole effort felt like a drive-by operation. He was late, and low on money and organization. There weren't many Kennedy people on the ground in contested states.

Ted and his staff decided to make their first stand against Carter not in Kennedy's next-door New Hampshire, but in the state that had defined Carter's own miraculous campaign-from-nowhere in 1976: Iowa. Before Jimmy Carter, few candidates had even bothered to contest the arcane caucuses of Iowa, but Ted's staff felt it would be a good place to deliver an initial blow. "Step one was, let's really make Iowa the big deal," recalls Bill Carrick, a key Kennedy strategist in the 1980 race. "We'll throw everything in there. That became the number one imperative of the campaign."

Caddell, for one, felt the president was vulnerable to the Kennedy challenge, perhaps even in Iowa. The pollster conducted in-depth interviews with people across the country that November and December. "We asked people, 'Okay, the election is over. Teddy is now president, how would he do?' " he recalls. "A lot of people said he'd be fantastic. I brought these results to the president. He locked them in his safe and said, 'No one is ever to see this.' "

But Hamilton Jordan felt confident from the start that the president could beat Kennedy, especially in Iowa. Carter's political organization there dated back six years, and much of it was still intact. A Carter win in the caucuses, Jordan figured, would create momentum that could be followed up with back-breaking victories in Kennedy's own backyard of New England. Ted's team, for its part, was confident enough to think that he could win in Iowa and New Hampshire, and then surprise Carter in his native South.

In late November, Ted made a shakedown cruise into the South. Accompanied by Carrick, a native South Carolinian, he made stops in Nashville and Charleston. South Carolina was then a caucus state that had heavy African American participation, and Ted's staff reasoned that his lifelong advocacy of civil rights—at the expense of some political support among working-class whites in Massachusetts—would be remembered. But Carter's election had been a point of pride among many in the region, a symbol of the ascendancy of a New South that was beginning to assert its power across the whole nation. And while African-American voters liked and respected Kennedy, they also saw Carter as a major figure in racial reconciliation, one who had taken on his white friends and Georgia neighbors to support the black cause.

"The Carter people, after they came to their senses and decided they might be challenged by Kennedy, started working African-American leadership pretty hard," recalls Carrick. "John Lewis [the iconic figure in the civil rights movement, and later a Georgia congressman] ended up with Carter. A lot of black judges did, too. The Carter people really focused on shoring up their African-American support."

Meanwhile, Ted's brother-in-law and campaign chairman Steve Smith, along with Kirk, started hiring good people like Paul Tully, a veteran political organizer, and Rick Stearns, a delegate counting whiz, sometimes at lavish salaries. But little work was done to chart a detailed campaign blueprint. Smith did charter a campaign plane, a big Boeing 727, at a cost of $5,000 a day. It was dubbed "Air Malaise," a smirking reference to Carter, but the joke was on the cash-strapped Kennedy campaign: The plane was gone by late January. The grass-roots energy that helped convince Ted he could beat Carter—emblemized by the Draft Kennedy movements that had sprung up in chaotic profusion even before he announced—was proving impossible to harness. "No one could capture it," says Carrick about their energy. "Everybody wanted him to run. It was crazy. But there was no centralized campaign authority capturing names of donors, workers—no framework to fall back on."

The disorder extended to Ted's own syntax, something he had struggled with since childhood. A charismatic campaigner in small groups, and often an electric speaker before large audiences, he struggled to articulate his views when standing in front of a microphone before the medium-sized groups that made up most of the primary election crowds. Edward Fouhy, a veteran TV producer who covered Kennedy for multiple networks, says bluntly, "He couldn't articulate an English sentence. He was hopeless on the stump. . . . How bad was it? The standards at NBC [where Fouhy worked] required that someone take down, word for word, what the speaker says in any sound bite we're going to use on the evening news. The guy who did that took down something Kennedy said and then brought me what he'd written. You couldn't make any sense of this."

Ted's verbal gaffes in Iowa were frequent and often hilarious. He talked about "fam families" and the need to support the Wabash Railroad, which had gone out of business ages ago. He was also unprepared for the extent to which candidates were expected to talk meaningfully about their personal lives. Back in 1976, Carter had won a lot of support, and some ridicule, for opening up about his born-again religious beliefs, his upbringing on a peanut farm in tiny Plains, Georgia, and his eccentric relatives. He even confessed "lust" in his heart for women other than his wife. The Kennedys, however, had been raised to keep their interior lives to themselves; Joe and Rose had taught their children basic Yankee reticence. To pour one's heart out would be unthinkable among the Kennedys, particularly the Kennedy men. Roger Mudd, for one, had pressed Ted about why he couldn't open up, and in a mumble a lot of men could understand, he said that it just wasn't him.

This sense of detachment hurt him in front of a camera. Recalls one reporter, "He was a rollicking man who didn't rollick when the film was rolling." After a poor performance on a Sunday morning show, a reporter who had been traveling with him on a New York City subway remembers telling Ted he had been awful. Couldn't he open up a bit? Ted turned on him and said, "What do you want me to do? Lay out my intestines on a table?"

Meanwhile, as the Iowa campaign began in earnest, the nightly news was increasingly dominated not by the poor state of the nation's economy, which had driven Ted to run, but by foreign policy, which gave Carter a chance to look measured and presidential. On November 4, 1979, while Ted and his staff had been preparing their Faneuil Hall announcement, America was blindsided by the news that the staff of the U.S. embassy in Tehran, Iran, had been taken hostage by militant students. Both campaigns were confident that the hostages would be released in a matter of days. But the crisis dragged on and completely changed the Iowa equation. People sat riveted in front of their television sets every night, following news from the embassy. Kennedy couldn't get airtime. Iowans, like most Americans, rallied around their president in a time of crisis.

Then, to further scramble the international situation, the Soviet Union invaded Afghanistan on Christmas Day. Carter now had a strong argument that he needed to be in the White House instead of on the campaign trail, and so he pursued a Rose Garden strategy. Every day, the president would be seen delivering sober messages with the backdrop of the White House while Ted jousted with voters in crowded settings such as restaurants and high school gymnasiums. On December 28, Carter announced that the need to monitor the two overseas crises would prevent him from participating in a debate with Kennedy that had been set for January 7.

This was a huge blow to Ted, who had counted on that opportunity to confront his rival face-to-face. Kennedy complained that Carter was ducking him, but Iowans were predisposed to give Carter the benefit of the doubt, recalls David Yepsen, the political columnist for the *Des Moines Register*. "This guy's a peanut farmer," he says of Carter. "There's a cultural affinity. The Democrats were unhappy with Carter, but they weren't willing to desert him." When Carter imposed a partial grain embargo of corn, wheat, and soybeans against the Soviet Union on January 4 in response to its invasion of Afghanistan, many Iowa farmers grumbled, but most went along with the move.

Ted opposed the embargo, hoping to peel away some of Carter's support, but it was too little, too late. Back in the late spring of 1979, when he was still pondering a run, Ted had told the *Globe*'s Tom Oliphant about his admiration for George Norris, a Nebraska senator who had carried the flag of the progressive movement in the 1930s. Oliphant assumed that if Kennedy decided to run, he would bring a Norris-like message into his fight, especially in a place like Iowa where Democrats had a strong progressive tradition. He didn't. Instead, he launched his campaign with a listless theme about leadership. It was a cautious message that lacked passion and specificity. "Our mistake was thinking we were at 65 percent, so why would we take tough positions?" says Shrum, who wrote many of Kennedy's speeches and was on the plane with him throughout the whole campaign.

"Ted Kennedy is the worst politician I've ever met, bar none, at saying nothing," he adds. "The message was about leadership, but not a lot of content. It was a classic front-runner speech. It wasn't him. There was no meat on it."

Without a strong message, Ted was in trouble in Iowa, because the Carter campaign had a giant phone bank that could reach almost every Democratic household in the state. And the message the campaign heard from voters was that "the character issue"—read Chappaquiddick—was on people's minds. The Kennedy campaign built a workable organization in an astonishingly short time (two months) but it made a crucial mistake: it assumed only about 65,000 people would venture out to the caucuses. In the end, about 110,000 people came out. "We massively underestimated the turnout, and that was an organizational flaw," says Carrick. "Rural participation went way up that year. We didn't have the organizational capacity to handle [a contest involving] 110,000 people."

Kennedy lost the caucuses by a whopping 59–31 percent. He had seen it coming. After lunch with senior campaign staff at his McLean, Virginia, home on caucus day, he had told Bob Shrum, one arm imitating a crashing plane, "This baby's going down."

Watching the results in Washington, a joyful Hamilton Jordan was convinced the race was already over. "Kennedy will get out," he declared.

It never happened. Two days later, Ted met with eight of his top advisers in his Senate office in Washington, where they watched Carter's State of the Union address. Afterward, he polled them whether or not he should stay in the race. There was a 4–4 tie. Ted broke it by telling them he was staying in: "Let's get ready and go."

CHAPTER
18

His campaign was in trouble, but, freed of the expectation that he would win, Ted seemed to regain his vigor—and his sense of humor. During the run-up to the New York primary, for example, Kennedy flew to Syracuse expecting to get the endorsement of Congressman James Hanley. Before he spoke to reporters, Hanley privately told Kennedy how much he admired him, yet when standing on the rainy airport tarmac, Hanley couldn't deliver the endorsement. (The fact that Carter was leading by a significant margin in some polls may have had something to do with it.) Standing before the microphones, Hanley twisted himself into a verbal pretzel to avoid endorsing Kennedy. The Kennedy contingent there, meanwhile, was first dumbfounded and then irritated at these contortions. They saw it as a long trip for nothing.

Except for Ted. He saw the plumb ludicrousness of the situation. At one point, with a grin, he shouted, "Do the right thing, Jim." Hanley responded that he wanted to keep his choice private, prompting Kennedy to put his arm around him and say, "You can tell these guys, Jim. They won't tell anybody." Hanley never did come out with an endorsement, but Ted had already put it past him as they flew out of Syracuse.

After the drubbing in Iowa, Ted put aside his failed message of "leadership" and returned to his core beliefs. He began to speak his mind. On January 28, he went after Carter in a strong speech that he delivered at Georgetown University. First he criticized the president's foreign policy, charging that Carter had missed early warnings about Afghanistan and been caught by surprise when the Soviets invaded. "It is less than a year since the Vienna summit when President Carter kissed President Brezhnev on the cheek," said Kennedy. "We cannot afford a foreign policy based on the pangs of unrequited love." Ted drew clear distinctions between himself and Carter on Iran as well. He said he opposed sanctions because they would drive the country's fanatical leader, Ayatollah Ruhollah Khomeini, toward the Soviet Union. He excoriated Carter for the hostage crisis, then in its eighty-sixth day, maintaining it should never have happened. Had the United States steered the deposed leader of Iran, Reza Shah Pahlavi, to another country for medical treatment, Ted thundered, the embassy would never have been taken.

Ted had a point about the shah, but so did Carter. No other country but Egypt was willing to take in the shah, a longtime supporter of the United States. Carter had concluded that a far more important U.S. ally, Egyptian President Anwar Sadat, could risk serious internal unrest for hosting the deposed Iranian monarch. This obliged Carter to allow the shah to come to the United States for medical treatment, as a last resort. Carter then leaned on Panamanian strongman Omar Torrijos to accept the shah, which he did temporarily. Ultimately, the shah did indeed end up in Egypt, where he died of cancer.

Kennedy laid out other stark differences with Carter in the speech at Georgetown. He opposed Carter's plan to deregulate oil in the face of huge spikes in its price and called instead for gasoline rationing and at least six months of wage and price controls. He wanted universal health care. He opposed Carter's reinstatement of draft registration for men between the ages of eighteen and twenty-one. It went on.

"I have only just begun to fight," Ted declared.

What Kennedy did at Georgetown was to lay out a platform for the progressive wing of the Democratic Party, an ambitious agenda that made him the undisputed standard-bearer for liberals, a role he never would relinquish. "It really rallied people to his side, particularly blue-collar Catholic voters," says Carrick. "Voters rally to more specific messages. They identify with them, with their hopes and aspirations."

Jordan and Powell watched coverage of the speech on the evening news, and bristled at Ted's criticism of their boss. Powell, a shrewd Georgian separated at the hip from Jordan, was characteristically pithy in his reaction: "Bullshit," he said. "He's against our grain embargo, against the boycott of the Olympics, and against draft registration. Sailing against the wind? The only time Ted Kennedy sails against the wind is when he can't figure out which way it's blowing."

And none of Kennedy's proud words seemed to matter much in the next round of contests. He proceeded to lose the Maine caucuses on February 10, the New Hampshire primary on February 26, and the Vermont primary on March 4. Carter's strategists had believed that if the president could humiliate Kennedy by winning all three states in his northern backyard, he might drop out. But Ted wouldn't go away. He was starting to have fun, to find his voice, and to remind people — and himself — why he was in politics.

In March he took the battle to Illinois with its huge trove of delegates. But he soon found himself trapped in a local political feud involving Mayor Jane Byrne, who had first promised to support Carter, then switched to Ted. The problem was that virtually no one in the Chicago machine built by Ted's longtime supporter Mayor Daley liked her anymore. She had been elected as an insurgent after her predecessor, Michael Bilandic, who had taken over after Daley's death, failed to get the snow plowed on time. But Byrne quickly lost support from the constituencies who helped elect her because her record of reform turned out to be spotty. She also had a firecracker temper and used it on many Daley loyalists. This situation left Ted with the endorsement of an unpopular mayor with whom he had committed to walk in Chicago's St. Patrick's Day parade the day before the primary.

The parade was a disaster for both Kennedy and Byrne, who received boos, jeers, and worse as they walked along Chicago's State Street. Ted tried, literally, to distance himself from Byrne, by falling back and then darting to one side and the other like a hummingbird. He plunged into the crowds, but sometimes was faced with new anger over Chappaquiddick, with people yelling "Where's Mary Jo?"

If ever there was proof that the Kennedy team had misjudged the impact of Chappaquiddick, it was Illinois. The issue bit harder there than in any other state. Catholics in the Midwest were less likely to be of Irish extraction and lacked the sense of commonality that many of their East Coast brethren felt toward Ted. They were less inclined to give him the benefit of the doubt. "Catholics west of the Susquehanna River in Pennsylvania hated Kennedy and Catholics east of it liked him," says Caddell, who saw this distinction consistently in his polling data throughout the campaign.

Through an arcane set of state party rules, the winner in each of Illinois's congressional districts took all of its delegates. When the counting was done, Carter had won 155 out of 169 delegates. If Iowa was a mortal blow to Kennedy, Illinois was the exclamation point that followed. So when Kennedy still refused to drop out, Carter's people went from irritated to furious. After his latest drubbing, Ted's mathematical chances of winning the nomination were almost zero. Still, he limped into another large state, New York, on March 25. It turned out to be his wildest sleigh ride of the election year. He and his campaign were both running on empty. But a bright spot quickly appeared in the form of a boffo television spot that his new advertising consultant, David Sawyer, put together.

On screen was Carroll O'Connor, the actor who played Archie Bunker, the iconic blue-collar worker from Queens in the hit TV show *All in the Family.* O'Connor called Carter perhaps the most Republican president since Hoover, and a man who could give America a depression that would make would make Hoover's look good.

Then another unexpected boost came via the United Nations. On March 1, the U.N. Security Council voted to reprimand Israel for building settlements on the occupied West Bank of the Jordan River, concluding they had no legal validity. Instead of abstaining, which the United States often did on anti-Israel votes, Carter's U.N. ambassador Donald McHenry voted yes. It was a principled but unpopular stand against Israel's settlements, which would loom as an obstacle to Mideast peace for three more decades. The outrage among much of

New York's large Jewish community was instant. Many Jewish leaders started campaigning hard against Carter. He then lost the respect he had earned from those who supported the U.N. vote by reversing himself, claiming there had been a communications failure with McHenry. The ambassador, however, insisted he had voted based on the instructions he received from the Carter administration. So Carter got nothing out of the U.N. vote. Still, a Harris poll released the day before the primary suggested that the president was poised once again to whip Kennedy by eighteen points.

Paul Kirk checked into the Parker House hotel in Boston, scene of countless political births and deaths, in anticipation of a withdrawal press conference there the next day. Bob Shrum started writing the speech, which began, "First of all, I love New York anyway . . ." But Caddell's numbers told a completely different story. In his poll, Carter trailed Kennedy by double digits and was dropping fast—and it wasn't just because of the U.N. vote. By March, five months after the embassy takeover, Carter's Rose Garden strategy was fraying. The American people had tired of his remaining in the White House to monitor Iran and Afghanistan. Voters' attention had shifted from Kennedy to Carter, and a growing number of people were underwhelmed by what they saw. For one thing, he had repeatedly refused to debate Kennedy. (There would be no debate at all in the primary elections.) Catholics in New York were much more forgiving of Kennedy on Chappaquiddick than those in Illinois. "New York and Carter were a bad match," says Carrick, adding that "Carter looked like he was winning, and then people woke up and said, 'Oh my God, he's winning.' "

Kennedy beat Carter in New York by almost twenty points. Ted's campaign team was stunned. There would be no withdrawal statement. Staffers called it "the miracle." Kennedy had desperately needed a big, splashy win, and New York gave it to him. "It meant we lived to fight another day," says Kirk. "It put a little puff in our sails."

Shrum was at Steve Smith's home on the Upper East Side of Manhattan early in the evening, girding himself for another defeat, but then went back to Kennedy's headquarters at the Halloran House hotel, a far from luxurious establishment on Lexington Avenue, and found a crowd of supporters ready to celebrate a big win. Ted turned to him and said, "Can you believe this?" The tide seemed to be turning against Carter elsewhere as well. Lost in all the attention given to Ted's New York win was another one in neighboring Connecticut. It meant that Carter could not claim that his loss in New York was simply an aberration.

Suddenly, the Pennsylvania primary on April 22 loomed as a major challenge to both camps. Carter needed to stop his slide. And Pennsylvania was not looking good. According to Caddell's polls, the president was down almost eighteen points to Ted with only a few weeks remaining until the primary. "That's when I pulled the trigger on the character issue," recalls Caddell, referring to an ad campaign that Carter would run on Chappaquiddick. Looking back on it, Caddell remembers arriving at the decision in this way: "Yes, it would do irreparable damage if we do that to him. He'll never forgive us. But we'd have lost Pennsylvania by twenty points or more. Even with the delegate lead, what happens if we lose all the [remaining] primaries? I knew what the damage would be. It worked."

So Pennsylvania voters saw a series of television spots featuring average people who looked into the camera and said, "I don't trust him" and "I don't believe him." The ad blitz succeeded in driving down Ted's support, and he ended up scratching out only a tiny victory. The coda to the primary season occurred on June 3, with the three big states of California, Ohio, and New Jersey in play. By now, Kennedy's team had come together. The young and talented Ron Brown, who would later become Bill Clinton's Secretary of Commerce, ran California for Kennedy. Paul Tully ran Ohio, and John Sasso, an emerging political talent who had played a key role for Ted in Iowa, oversaw New Jersey. Kennedy victories in all three states would help legitimize his promise to keep fighting all the way to the August convention in New York, but Ted's aides believed he only had a chance in two of them, California and New Jersey.

Ted himself questioned whether he should be spending more time in Ohio. Carter, after all, was so worried about his standing there that he emerged from the White House to campaign in the state. But the polls didn't look good, Ted's aides told him, so don't waste time there. In retrospect, says Shrum, "He was right. We were wrong." Kennedy won in California and by a large margin in New Jersey. He lost a close race in Ohio, which turned out to be a major consolation for Carter, allowing the president to claim a bounce heading into the convention. The primaries were over and Carter had won enough delegates to be renominated. But still Ted refused to concede.

⚘

From June 3 to the convention in August, Ted Kennedy juggled principle and petulance. He believed he was standing up for constituencies that were being given short shrift by the Carter wing of the Democratic Party. One such constituency was homosexuals: Ted became the first presidential candidate to attend a gay fund-raiser, according to David Mixner, a prominent member of the California LGBT (Lesbian Gay Bisexual Transgender) community who helped organize the event. The fund-raiser was held at the Hollywood Hills home of Clyde Cairns and John Carlson, an openly gay couple, and everybody who was anybody in the LGBT community was there. Ted learned while on his way that it had been closed to the press. He promptly stopped his campaign caravan and asked reporters to accompany him. His desire to attend the all-gay event and to advertise his presence there showed the boldness he was willing to exhibit at the end of the 1980 campaign. He was determined to break new ground, to take his party in a more radical direction.

But he still had to persuade Carter's own delegates to abandon the president. Many Democrats were infuriated that Kennedy would go to such lengths to destroy a chief executive of his own party. But Ted hoped to persuade the delegates, even those committed to voting for Carter, that the president would be a weak opponent against the Republican standard-bearer, Ronald Reagan, and that he, Kennedy, represented the Democrats' only chance for victory. On June 25, Jordan wrote an "eyes only" memo to Carter addressing the problems facing the president. The picture he painted in unvarnished language was grim. "The Kennedy challenge hurt us very badly, not only within the

Democratic Party but with the electorate as a whole," he wrote. He added that serious speculation about a Kennedy challenge had begun the previous June, effectively making the campaign a yearlong struggle. "As a result," he continued, "the American people today are sick of the process and tired of the candidates."

He went on: "Kennedy's sustained and exaggerated attacks on your record and his unrealistic promises have alienated key groups in the Democratic Party by obscuring the solid record we have. . . . The Kennedy attacks, reinforced by the media's natural tendency to see everything in the context of the campaign, have made you seem more like the manipulative politician bent on reelection at all costs than the man and the President that you are." Jordan ended as follows: "For all of the reasons presented here, we have come out of this primary year and the unsuccessful Kennedy challenge not enhanced or strengthened by the contest, but damaged severely."

One place where Kennedy could flex his muscles was over the Democratic platform. Negotiations between the Carter and Kennedy camps over the platform began in June and went nowhere fast. By the last day of the negotiating period, hardly any progress had been made, recalls Carl Wagner, Kennedy's convention manager. He then instructed Susan Estrich, a Kennedy Judiciary Committee aide who joined the campaign, to file about 200 minority reports—positions that ran against the planks written by the Carter-dominated platform committee. If they all came up for debate, the convention would be tied up for days. The White House called Wagner the next day, he recalls, and new negotiations began in earnest. The number of minority reports shriveled as the summer went on.

The signature fight at the convention was over the rule that bound delegates to vote for the presidential candidate with whom they had been aligned in the primaries and caucuses. If allowed to stand, the rule would guarantee Carter's renomination. Ted, whose forces called it "the robot rule," wanted the delegates to vote to free themselves to bolt to another candidate. This vote became, in effect, the contest for the nomination. Should Kennedy persuade the delegates to overturn the "robot rule," all bets were off. It would be a new race, and Madison

Square Garden was teeming with Carter delegates who would happily switch to Kennedy given the chance: Ted's dominance of the later
primaries, plus Carter's continued decline in the polls, had left many
Democrats open to a change of nominee. So Carter needed to win the
rules fight as much as Kennedy did.

First came a debate over what day the rules vote would take place.
Jordan was adamant that it occur on Monday, August 11, the first night
of the convention. His fear was that if the vote were held after Kennedy spoke on Tuesday, issuing a passionate exhortation to his troops,
Carter could face a runaway convention. If Ted did not agree to a Monday night vote on the rules change, Jordan said, he would prevent Kennedy from speaking at any time. The issue of when and whether Ted
would speak had been brewing for a long time. At one point, Jordan
had vowed to block any Kennedy speech until Ted endorsed Carter.
In return, Wagner had threatened to distribute a thousand "cricket"
noisemakers among his delegates in the hall and have them make a
racket together when the president delivered his acceptance speech
on Thursday night. "Have you ever heard the sound of 1,000 crickets
chirping together?" he asked a Carter operative.

Eventually, Paul Kirk spent two days with Jordan holed up in a
room at the Waldorf-Astoria hotel, negotiating over the platform and
the schedule for the vote on the rules change. They finally arrived at an
agreement acceptable to both sides.

Kennedy ended up getting much of what he wanted on the platform, but Carter prevailed on the Monday night vote. And, as expected, Carter beat him on the all-important rules change, 1,936–1,390.
Some, but not nearly enough, of Carter's delegates abandoned him.
The contest was over. Ted had finally run out of options. After the
rules vote, he called Carter to congratulate him on his victory.

Ted never got his evening in prime time, as runners-up for the
presidential nomination often get. He spoke instead on three platform
minority reports devoted to the economy. Debate was to be limited to
fifteen minutes, but Ted sailed on like a frigate past forty minutes.

The speech turned out to be a triumph, Ted's manifesto of a lifetime. It was a defense of the liberal wing of the Democratic Party and
drew much of its power from the idea that Reagan, if elected, would

try to erase many of the gains of American liberalism from the New Deal onward. "Government is never more dangerous than when our desire to have it help us blinds us to its great power to harm us," Reagan had intoned at the Republican convention a month earlier.

But Ted would have none of that.

"The commitment I seek is not to outworn ideas, but to old values that will never wear out," he declared. "Programs may sometimes become obsolete, but the idea of fairness always endures. Circumstances may change, but the work of compassion must continue. It is surely correct that we cannot solve problems by throwing money at them; it is also correct that we dare not throw out our national problems onto a scrap heap of inattention and indifference."

And he made clear whom he was speaking for: "Our cause has been, since the days of Thomas Jefferson, the cause of the common man—and the common woman. Our commitment has been, since the days of Andrew Jackson, to all those he called the humble members of society—the farmers, mechanics, and laborers. On this foundation, we have defined our values, refined our policies, and refreshed our faith."

He also went directly after Reagan. "The same Republicans who are talking about the crisis in unemployment have nominated a man who once said—and I quote: 'Unemployment insurance is a prepaid vacation plan for freeloaders.' And that nominee is no friend of labor . . . The same Republicans who are invoking Franklin Roosevelt have nominated a man who said in 1976—and these were his exact words: 'Fascism was really the basis of the New Deal.' And that nominee, whose name is Ronald Reagan, has no right to quote Franklin Roosevelt."

He finished with an emotional plea that would be remembered for decades: "For all those whose cares have been our concern, the work goes on, the cause endures, the hope still lives, and the dream shall never die."

Ted's delivery was smooth, his voice thick with emotion, his body moving seamlessly from one side to the other, as he shifted from reading the teleprompter on the left and the teleprompter on the right. The situation left him no time to look out to the crowd.

But after he spoke, all those assembled in Madison Square Garden knew they had heard something powerful. When the speech ended, there was a spooky silence and then the place exploded into riotous applause and cheering that ran for half an hour.

Kennedy owned the hall. Three minority reports were about to be voted on—one on the need to impose wage and price controls, another on a $12 billion economic stimulus package, and a third to give higher priority to the fight against unemployment than to other parts of the Carter economic plan. Carter's campaign chairman, Bob Strauss, told the president over the phone: "We're going to take a pasting." Carter's delegate counter Tom Donilon was canvassing the state delegate chiefs to see if they were holding. One report came back as follows: "Pennsylvania called and said we didn't have ten votes on the economic planks. Ohio called and said they can't hold their votes."

Caddell says the Carter camp at that point simply let go. "We threw in the towel," he says. "We had to. Teddy had won the hearts of the convention with that speech. We basically weren't going to fight anymore." The debate over the platform planks finally ended when Tip O'Neill, who chaired the convention, gaveled at the speed of sound one victory for Carter against the imposition of wage and price controls and wins for Ted on the other two.

For that evening, all glory belonged to Ted. But he promptly lost altitude and respect two nights later when he was rude to Carter after the president delivered his acceptance speech. Kennedy was supposed to appear on the podium with Carter, join hands, and raise them together in the traditional sign of political unity. He even practiced the clasped hands with Shrum in his room at the Waldorf-Astoria. Shrum made a reluctant Kennedy do it over and over again. As they arrived at the Garden, Shrum said, not for the first time, "Don't forget."

But Ted chose to forget. He arrived late and went straight to the podium, where he disappeared in a sea of dark suits. Carter had to chase him down for what turned out to be a mere handshake. It was surprisingly bitter behavior for a politician once known for his graciousness. After this briefest of appearances on stage, Shrum recalls, Kennedy repaired to his suite at the Waldorf for a small dinner.

It was suddenly all over. Jimmy Carter had won the nomination over Kennedy, 2,129–1,146. The Carter-Kennedy fight had ended and the Carter-Reagan fight would now begin, but not before Carter held a press conference the next morning and distanced himself from some parts of the platform that Ted had won.

In 1981, Hamilton Jordan participated in an oral history project on the Carter presidency at the Miller Center of Public Affairs at the University of Virginia. He, like others, was interviewed at length. Asked how much damage the Kennedy challenge had done to Carter in the general election against Ronald Reagan, Jordan said: "It was the single critical factor in his defeat. When people ask me why we were defeated, I say the hostage crisis—which was seen as a failure of Carter to free the people after being held for so long—the general state of the economy, and the Kennedy challenge. . . . Of those three problems, the most significant was the Kennedy challenge. . . . If we'd had the whole year to pull the party together and to try and work on the economy, I think Carter would, or at least could, have won."

CHAPTER
19

TED KENNEDY RETURNED to Washington in 1981 at sea. He had
lost his race for the Democratic nomination to Carter, who in turn lost
the presidency. And the Republicans had seized control of the Senate
for the first time in twenty-six years. At the end of January, Ted and
Joan would announce that they were getting a divorce. "Rock bottom
is a very good foundation to build on," says Carl Wagner.

Ted had every reason to grieve but he didn't, at least outwardly.
"He'd pray by himself at St. Joseph's church on Capitol Hill. . . . You'd
never really hear it, but he had to be an extremely lonely man," says
Paul Kirk. "Two brothers were gone, a marriage gone. He goes home
to an empty home. That's enormously hard." Ted's friend Senator Joe
Biden watched him in the reentry period and saw a man who stayed
on his feet. "There was no period when Teddy went into a black hole"
over his defeat, says Biden. After Biden himself dropped out of the race
for the 1988 Democratic presidential nomination, he recalls, "Teddy
turned to me and said, 'I promise you there's life after the presidency,
and it's good.' "

Instead of sorrow, friends say, Ted drew on the lessons that helped
him survive a cascade of tragedy in his family. "It was not the worst
thing that ever happened to him," says Bob Shrum about the 1980

defeat. "He was twelve years old when a man walked up to the door and said, 'Your brother Joe has been killed.' His life is a lesson in moving forward. He just doesn't sit."

And Ted decided, with some reluctance, that it was time to move on from his marriage. Conceived in haste—the couple had just a half dozen or so chaperoned weekends during their courtship—the marriage between Ted Kennedy and Joan Bennett died a slow death. Though there were often fond feelings between them, they rarely spent much time together, nor did they share many interests.

In 1977, Joan had moved to an apartment in Boston's Back Bay neighborhood, effectively separating from Ted, who stayed at their home in Virginia. In Boston she began seeing a psychiatrist three times a week and attending Alcoholics Anonymous meetings, while pursuing a graduate degree in education at Lesley College in Cambridge. After she had been sober for a year, Joan talked with reporters about the discomfort she had felt in Washington, the difficulty in making friends and seeking help with her alcoholism in the spotlight there. In Boston, she said, her recovery had been low-key: "I can walk in [to AA meetings] and there's no big flutter. . . . I'm just like any other person who is an alcoholic and who needs help to stay sober."

The couple reunited briefly and superficially for the sake of his presidential campaign. Some friends said Joan was hopeful that spending time together on the campaign trail would lead to a longer reconciliation. She had considered their time campaigning together in the 1960s for Jack's presidential race and Ted's first Senate race to have been among their closest periods: it was the two of them against the world. But when the 1980 campaign was over, it was apparent that the marriage was, too. They had grown too distant during her struggle with alcoholism, an addiction that began after Ted's accident at Chappaquiddick and Joan's subsequent miscarriage. When she dutifully accompanied her husband to Mary Jo Kopechne's funeral, Joan had already suffered two miscarriages and was on bed rest with another pregnancy, which she believes ended because of the arduous flight in a small plane to Kopechne's hometown near Wilkes-Barre, Pennsylvania. While she credits Ted with being a loving father, she always blamed him for pushing her to make the difficult trip.

"The hardest thing for me wasn't that you had another woman, but I was pregnant, up in my bed, and I had stayed in bed with Patrick the whole nine months so I knew that I could have a baby, and I got shots in my rear end . . . So I said, 'Okay, I'm gonna do this one more time so I can give Patrick a little brother or sister.' " But it was not to be. For Joan, who once said that Teddy wanted a huge family like his parents'—and who watched Ethel produce baby after baby—the miscarriage was devastating. She sank into a deep depression.

Although Joan had heard rumors about Ted's womanizing for years, she didn't confront her husband. "It wasn't my personality to make a lot of noise. . . . And so rather than get mad or ask questions concerning the rumors about Ted and his girlfriends, or really stand up for myself at all, it was easier for me to just go and have a few drinks and calm myself down as if I weren't hurt or angry," she once told an interviewer. "I didn't know how to deal with it. And, unfortunately, I found out that alcohol could sedate me. So I didn't care as much. And things didn't hurt so much."

She eventually earned her master's degree. She often played the piano in the Boston public schools and lent her name to benefits for her favorite charities such as Children's Hospital and the Pine Street Inn for the homeless. But neither her husband nor her children were around, and the loneliness led time and again back to the vodka bottle. Ted, who had been supportive during the early years of her struggles, seemed to give up on the marriage.

For decades to come Joan would battle the disease, racking up headlines with DUI arrests, participating in 12-step programs, checking into the famous McLean Hospital in Belmont, Massachusetts, for detox, and eventually having her children take over legal control of her financial affairs. She and Ted would maintain a cordially distant relationship, while she remained close to some other members of the Kennedy family, particularly Ted's sister Eunice Shriver. She would keep her summer home on Squaw Island in Hyannis Port, a short walk down the beach from the Kennedy compound, and she would continue to

attend the Kennedy family's holiday gatherings. She would even agree
to have her marriage to Ted annulled by the Catholic Church, so her
former husband could receive Holy Communion at his mother's funeral. "They thought I'd fight it, but I didn't because I just loved his
mother," she said.

She and Ted would express respect for the other's role as a parent,
and refrain from criticizing each other publicly. Nor would Joan blame
Ted for her drinking; her own mother was an alcoholic. She would
even say the divorce helped free her from the constraints of being a
Kennedy.

"Once you sober up, the whole idea is to become honest with yourself and other people. I mean, all the secrets I've had to keep: mine and
all the secrets of the Kennedy family. I don't have to do that anymore.
It's such a relief to be free. To be a genuine person."

Returning to the Senate after the end of his presidential run and the
end of his marriage, Ted found that many of his closest friends and
colleagues were no longer there. Nine Democratic incumbents had
lost in 1980 — including strong liberal voices like Idaho's Frank Church;
South Dakota's George McGovern, whom Ted had backed for president in 1968 and 1972; Ted's close friend Birch Bayh; and his lifelong
pal from college days, John Culver, who was representing Iowa. Before 1980, Kennedy was one among many liberal voices in the Senate. When he returned, he found himself almost alone as the voice of
American liberalism. But he also felt freer to chart his own course. "He
went from someone who was constantly under pressures of others to
perform in a certain way to someone in charge of his own life," says
David Burke. "What he gained was freedom."

Ted knew he would have to make a fierce defense of his liberal principles in a Senate controlled by the opposite party for the first time in
his Senate career of nearly two decades. Tom Rollins, who served as a
senior aide during this period, calls the time of Republican control in
the 1980s "the darkness." The majority set the agenda and scheduled
hearings. Minority victories were rare. Ted had to choose his issues
carefully.

Civil rights had defined him as a senator and a leader, and he was determined to be the firewall against President Reagan's efforts to roll back some of the hard-won victories of the previous twenty years. It was an issue he had faced in the streets of Boston, where he was forced to see the pain of integration up close. In 1974 the controversy over school busing in Boston had reached a fever pitch, and after months of keeping his distance, Kennedy had felt compelled to step in.

The senator had initially opposed the idea of moving students out of their neighborhood schools in order to achieve more racially balanced classrooms. But as the issue worked its way through the courts, becoming a centerpiece of the civil rights movement, Kennedy changed his position. By the time court-ordered busing was set to begin in Boston, in September 1974, its opponents harbored as much animosity toward Kennedy as they did toward the federal judge who had ruled that it would happen. On September 9, Kennedy showed up unexpectedly at a rally at Government Center, where thousands of angry parents, mostly white women, had gathered to protest the busing of their children to predominantly black city schools.

The demonstration had been planned by a new group known as ROAR—Restore Our Alienated Rights—which was much more radical than those that had come before it. Its outrage, that autumn day, was directed at Kennedy and his colleague Senator Edward Brooke, who also supported busing. Organizers began the program by parading two figures in chicken masks to represent the senators. Many of the protestors were the working-class Catholics who helped build the Kennedy dynasty. They came from Irish neighborhoods like Charlestown and South Boston, and they had long been the most stalwart supporters of the senator and his brothers. Many continued to hang Jack's picture in their living rooms. But on busing, they had come to a chasm they could not cross. Enraged at what they saw as Ted's betrayal, they were ready to erupt.

Ted had planned to address the crowd about the need for Boston to set a peaceful example. He remembered how Bobby had calmed the crowd in Indianapolis after Martin Luther King Jr.'s assassination. Instead, Ted's surprise appearance unleashed a wave of violence. Angry protesters punched him in the shoulder and splattered him with a tomato. Worst of all, perhaps, the crowd turned their backs on him, row by row. Giving up, he retreated to the nearby John F. Kennedy federal office building, accompanied by a hail of vicious insults.

"Why don't you put your one-legged son on a bus," one person yelled.

"Yeah, let your daughter get bused so she can get raped," another shouted.

"You're a disgrace to the Irish," others called.

After Kennedy reached the office building and guards secured the doors, the crowd pounded on the glass, shattering one 6-foot by 2-foot section. Ted tried to defuse the situation, saying afterward, "They're not bigots. They care about the safety of their children." But he was angry, says Robert Bates, his former aide, who was there, because "he was always championing civil rights, and here it was in his own backyard."

Just as busing issues continued to divide the people of Boston for many years, the rift between Kennedy and his blue-collar base would have lasting impact, part of larger changes within the Democratic Party. The experience taught him not to take the Boston Irish for granted, and it spurred him to cultivate support elsewhere, especially among African Americans. But having sacrificed part of his own popularity for the cause of integration, he wasn't going to allow it to fail.

By the time Reagan came along, Kennedy knew what he had to do. His first big fight came quickly, starting in 1981, the year Reagan took office. The Voting Rights Act of 1965, perhaps the greatest of the civil rights measures passed in the wake of Jack's death, was due to expire and needed another extension. The measure applied federal scrutiny to voting decisions in certain states with a particularly hostile racial past, and Reagan, who believed in "getting the government off people's backs," didn't want to renew it. Ted led the charge not only to renew the voting rights bill but to amend the statute in a way that would dilute the impact of a recent Supreme Court decision that had made it more difficult to prove that states had acted in a racially discriminatory way.

Ted reached across the aisle and joined with Maryland's liberal Republican Charles "Mac" Mathias, whose name would appear first on the bill. Ted also won some crucial help from Kansas's conservative Republican Robert Dole and Iowa's conservative Republican Charles Grassley. As always, Ted knew his colleagues intimately and had a clear sense of whom to reach out to among Republicans. He knew, for example, that there were two Doles—the partisan conservative and the injured war veteran who was concerned about helping people in need. Kennedy appealed to Dole's sensitive side to win his support for the voting rights bill. Dole was instrumental in crafting a compromise that would bring the bill into law, and in presenting it as a fait accompli to Reagan in 1982 with a veto-proof margin of 85–8 in the Senate. "If we had lost that battle in 1981–1982, I'm not sure we'd have won anything in the Reagan-Bush era," says Ralph Neas, then executive director of the Leadership Council on Civil Rights, who worked closely with Ted for many years on civil rights issues.

Meanwhile, Ted opted to give up his ranking position on the Judiciary Committee to be the top Democrat on the Labor and Human Resources Committee, so he could play a central role in fighting Reagan's attempts to pare back social programs. "This switch was critical to Kennedy," recalls a former aide. "Instead of dealing with the polarizing issues in Judiciary, he concluded, 'Let's try to deal with pocketbook issues—health, education, workplace safety, employment.' He decided, 'I don't want to be on the front burner on all these social issues. I want to improve the lot of every American.'" Even Stephen Breyer, the future Supreme Court justice who had served as chief counsel of the Judiciary Committee under Kennedy in the late 1970s, said Labor and Human Resources was a better fit for Ted's interests: "The Fair Housing Bill was more consistent to his basic outlook than the criminal code reform."

Ted found that even though his party was outvoted in the Senate, he could score significant victories in the Labor and Human Resources Committee, which determined which bills reached the Senate floor. While a conservative Republican from Utah, Orrin Hatch, chaired the committee, Kennedy made it work. Ted could usually count on the support of liberal New England Republicans Lowell Weicker of Connecticut and Robert Stafford of Vermont. So the effective lineup was often 9–7 against Hatch.

Hatch, who recognized that Ted remained the power behind the committee, eventually developed a close working and personal relationship with him. But Ted wasn't afraid to turn on the chairman when he felt a key union priority was in jeopardy. For example, he beat back the Republican attempt to repeal the Davis-Bacon Act, which had been a longtime target of GOP anger. The law required that all people hired on public works projects would receive the "prevailing wage" of that area—a union-negotiated rate, in most cases. "We worked it to death," recalls Rollins, Ted's top committee aide. "We did fine research, state by state. [Texas Democrat] Lloyd Bentsen was on the fence. There was really good data on Texas. We sent a personal letter to Bentsen indicating how much workers there would lose" if the prevailing wage were dropped.

"The Hatch staff showed that guys were working for $22,000 [a year] instead of $20,000," Rollins adds. "Kennedy looked at me and said, 'God forbid that a working man would make another $2,000 a year.' That affected my reflexes for the rest of my life." The repeal effort died.

Ted's success in picking Republican colleagues to support his causes enabled him to continue to generate legislation, rather than simply block Republican initiatives. He now understood, better than earlier in his career, that people who were opponents of much of his agenda could also be supporters of certain pieces of it. So Hatch, who was often at odds with Ted on civil rights issues, became his ally on public health issues. Dan Quayle, the young Republican from Indiana, joined with Ted to sponsor the Job Training Partnership Act. Alan Simpson, Republican of Wyoming, partnered with Ted on immigration issues. "He is the ultimate pragmatist," says Breyer. When he wanted something done, he'd tell his staff to do whatever it took to cobble together a majority. "He'd say to his staff, 'Work it out.' " The Republicans came on board because they liked and trusted their colleague from Massachusetts. He was fun and energetic, and generous in giving them credit. They also knew that he could deliver. If Republicans could persuade Kennedy to support a bill of theirs, other liberal Democrats would go along, believing if something was okay with Teddy, it should be okay with them.

And Ted eventually found a way around the most painful part of life in the minority—the fact that only committee chairmen could call hearings, thereby depriving him of the ability to explore new possibilities for legislation. Instead of committee hearings, Ted convened his own meetings. "He and I were sitting around one day in February, and it dawned on us, what's to stop us from doing what we've always done and call them policy forums?" recalls his longtime aide Lawrence Horowitz. Ted would hold the meetings in any open room in the Senate, often attended by Republicans as well as Democrats, he says. Experts would talk about a particular issue. Sometimes, senators sat in the audience while speakers from two different sides of an issue went at it. Ted even took the show on the road and held meetings across the country on issues including hunger, arms control, and health care.

In Washington, these policy forums were often associated with dinners that Ted would host at his home across the river in McLean, Virginia. There, he would assemble experts to talk about issues and invite Republicans and Democrats alike to listen in and to build personal relationships. "I'd be invited to his house," recalls John Kerry, the junior senator from Massachusetts. "[Virginia Republican] John Warner would be there, Orrin Hatch. We'd all sit around the table, getting to know each other."

Ted spent much of his personal time alone, even though the gossip columns would often register him escorting a new woman to an event. He would leave the office at night with what staffers called "the bag." It was a big briefcase—sometimes two of them—perched near Ted's office door into which staffers could put memos for him to review. By the end of the day, it would be bulging. Ted would return to his empty house and work on the memos after dinner. He would be back in the office by 7:30 the next morning, the memos full of notations and comments. Rollins would sometimes go to Ted's house in the early morning to brief the senator on upcoming meetings. "It would be 6:30 and he'd be there with a cup of coffee, sitting in the library," Rollins says. "He had a memo from the night before. Then we'd saddle up and continue the briefing in the car."

If he felt lonely at home sometimes, that feeling would disappear when he reached the Senate, where he enjoyed the camaraderie of fellow members. He would hold court from the last row of desks on the Democratic side of the floor, greeting colleagues and telling jokes. "There is always this congregation around him," says Senator Pat Leahy, Democrat of Vermont. "When Kennedy's voice starts, you see people in the gallery trying to lean over. Everyone comes to him. He doesn't go to them." It wasn't just on the floor. Ted would be in the cloakroom telling one story after another, winning over converts, triggering huge roars that could be heard on the Senate floor. One day, the senator who was presiding over the chamber pounded his gavel and pronounced, "There will be order in the Senate—and in the cloakroom."

Behind the bonhomie was an ambitious agenda aimed increasingly at the causes of disadvantaged people.

While Ted had always been a liberal stalwart, he wasn't always on the cutting edge of social change. Bobby had been the crusader in the family. But in the decades that followed Bobby's death, particularly starting in 1980, Ted made himself the embodiment of two of the causes that defined modern liberalism—the rights of women and gays.

The man who had once quipped, back in the 1960s, "You can't give women too much—they get confused," began positioning himself as the leading sponsor of legislation to prevent discrimination against women. He had initially opposed the Equal Rights Amendment, but changed to support it in the mid 1970s, believing it to be a matter of pay equity and fairness. Likewise, before the Supreme Court's *Roe v. Wade* decision made abortion a constitutional right in 1973, Ted had opposed abortion on demand. He held that position as late as his 1972 reelection campaign. A turning point was the Hyde Amendment that passed Congress in 1976 and denied federal funding of abortions through Medicaid. It bothered Ted that the amendment would deprive low-income women of the same constitutionally guaranteed right as women who could afford their own health insurance.

One of his landmark legislative achievements of the 1980s would be the Civil Rights Restoration Act, a law requiring that all institutions that accept federal funds adhere to federal antidiscrimination laws, even in their activities that do not utilize federal funds. The bill was designed as a response to a Supreme Court decision that had severely restricted the application of Title IX, the law guaranteeing equality in education, including women's sports. The effect of Ted's new bill would be that any college or university that accepted federal grants in any of their programs would have to provide equal sports opportunities to women. Kennedy steered the bill through both houses of Congress, but it was vetoed by President Reagan.

Frustrated but determined, Ted resolved to find a way to cobble together a veto-proof majority. He worked feverishly with Dole and Hatch to try to craft a compromise that most Republicans would support. "Senator Kennedy kept all sides working in the Senate into two and three in the morning," recalls Marcia Greenberger, founder of the National Women's Law Center, the leading legislative nonprofit on women's issues. "He was bringing in Chinese food. There was beer, but not for Senator Hatch because he is a Mormon, so he got orange juice. Kennedy would not let anyone leave. He would constantly come in and press the staff to hammer out language. He was always a presence if things weren't on track."

Much of the negotiations centered on the issue of abortion. Catholic institutions opposed the bill because, under student health plans, they would have to pay for abortions. Finally, Kennedy agreed to exempt religious institutions from the abortion requirement, and the Civil Rights Restoration Act became law, 73–24, over Reagan's veto.

Like his work on behalf of women, Ted's advocacy for gays grew over time. Since 1968, he had been friends with David Mixner, a longtime liberal activist and coordinator of the gay fund-raising event for Ted in Los Angeles. Ted had been supportive of Mixner back in the 1970s, when Mixner became open about his homosexuality. But in the

1980s, Ted picked up the cause of gay civil rights. He was a cosponsor of the Employment Non-Discrimination Act to bar workplace discrimination based on sexual orientation. He also fought against a law that prohibited people with HIV from visiting America, believing that the measure discriminated against gays. "You've got to remember the times," says Mixner about the first half of the 1980s. "William Buckley suggested tattoos for people with AIDS. There were quarantine bills, legislation forbidding the distribution of condoms. Jesse Helms filed amendment after amendment to punish people with AIDS, to deny them care and treatment. Ted Kennedy was our protector, our hope. No one was there for people with HIV and AIDS like him."

In 1982, Ted was the first national figure to speak at the annual dinner of the Municipal Elections Committee of Los Angeles, the first gay political action committee in the country. When Mixner went to Kennedy for help getting his partner a new drug to fight AIDS, though, Kennedy said no. "You can't do that," he said, explaining that he couldn't bend the rules for one person. "But I will sponsor a bill to make it available to any American, regardless of cost or need." Which he did.

Ted's advocacy for cutting-edge causes came at a price. While he maintained friendships with many conservative Republicans, he became a reviled figure among many grassroots conservatives, who saw him as the main roadblock to the Reagan Revolution. Soon, the Kennedy name was a staple of the direct-mail appeals that filled the coffers of the conservative movement in the 1980s. And the character attacks that had begun after Chappaquiddick reached a new peak of intensity.

Growing legions of so-called Kennedy haters resented Ted's money and easy, unearned rise to power. The event that fueled their rage was Chappaquiddick, which they believed showed that Ted Kennedy was both a liar and a drunk. They also disapproved of his treatment of Joan. "It's his character combined with his sanctimonious approach," says Richard Viguerie, the pioneer of direct mail fund-raising for conservatives. "He's very hypocritical because of his character. He says, 'I'm a good human being regardless of what I do in my private life.' He's a

Teflon politician, and that aggravates people. He gets a free ride not available to most."

In 1983, Ted received a fund-raising letter mistakenly sent to him by the office of Moral Majority founder Reverend Jerry Falwell. It asked for his support to combat "ultra-liberals like Ted Kennedy." Apprised of the mistake, Cal Thomas, Falwell's press secretary at the time, issued an informal invitation for Kennedy to speak at Liberty University, the conservative Christian institution founded by Falwell. Ted surprised Falwell and Thomas by accepting. Standing in front of a crowd of undergraduates on the Lynchburg, Virginia, campus, Ted quoted what Pope John XXIII said at the beginning of the Second Vatican Council in 1962 to ultra-conservatives in his own church: "We must beware of those who burn with zeal but are not endowed with much sense. . . ." Ted noted that the Pope later called these people "prophets of doom, who are always forecasting disasters, as though the end of the earth was at hand."

Ted delivered the speech in the university's gym after a nonalcoholic cocktail hour and dinner at Falwell's imposing home. The students who packed the gym were respectful, though hardly enthusiastic about Ted's presence. So he softened them up by jokingly asking that Falwell pray for a Democratic president in 1985. Falwell, he said, "might not appreciate the president, but the Democrats would certainly appreciate the prayer." He also appealed to Falwell to allow the students an extra hour before curfew. In return, he promised, he would watch the *Old Time Gospel Hour,* a religious program broadcast from Falwell's Thomas Road Baptist Church in Lynchburg. Ted didn't make many converts that night, but he was well received, and the students seemed to appreciate that he was a real human being and not the enemy of the state described in conservative fund-raising letters.

Despite Ted's success in the Senate, or perhaps because of it, many within the Kennedy camp thought that he would run again for president in 1984. "It was so obvious," says Bill Carrick, who was already helping clear the way for another run. "He learned from 1980. Everybody around him had learned a lot from 1980. It was a good team." By the 1982 mid-term elections, says Carrick, the team was engaged and Ted was showing signs of having the presidential urge again. "He was very definitely, very intensely, 'Okay I'll do all I have to do,' " Carrick says. "We campaigned . . . all over the country. A lot of really hard work went into that. He wanted to reach out to Carter people, expand his base in the minority communities, reach out more to women and the gay activists he first met in the 1980 campaign."

Four people from Kennedy's political staff were dispatched to a meeting of Democratic state party chairmen in New Orleans, assigned to drum up support. "He was clearly positioning himself," says a former staffer. "He had assembled a fund-raising team . . . He was making sure the pieces were in place were he to decide to run."

Ted delivered a strong speech at the Democratic midterm convention in Philadelphia in 1982 that was reminiscent of the rousing midterm speech he gave in Memphis in 1978. He once again challenged his audience to stay true to the soul of the Democratic Party. At the Philadelphia conclave, Ted's campaign committee held a massive reception for him, matching the one for former Vice President Walter Mondale, who was thought to be planning to run against Ted. Facing the Minnesotan Mondale rather than the Georgian Carter would have given Kennedy more than a fighting chance in the South. In preparation, Ted reached out to George Wallace, the former segregationist governor of Alabama who had embraced civil rights. Wallace was planning a comeback and wanted to repair his relations with the Democratic Party. Kennedy talked several times by telephone with Wallace, who told Ted he was the best man for the presidency.

The Kennedy staff's blueprint for the run was crafted early, and it was specific. A robust fund-raising effort would start early to give the campaign the money it had lacked in 1980. A presidential committee would be formed in the first week of January 1983. To mount a serious campaign in Iowa, Kennedy would travel the state by car with the popular former governor and senator Harold Hughes. John Sasso would leave his chief of staff position under Massachusetts Governor Michael Dukakis to run Kennedy's New Hampshire operation. Tim Russert, then an aide to New York Senator Daniel Patrick Moynihan, would be approached to become Ted's campaign press secretary. There was also the belated acknowledgment that Kennedy needed to learn to speak better—in large groups, small groups, and on television. There was even a proposal to schedule another interview with Roger Mudd.

On the day after Thanksgiving in 1982, Ted assembled his three children and other family members at Hyannis Port to seek their opinions on whether he should run for president. Lawrence Horowitz, who was in charge of the planning effort for 1984, was on hand to present the plan. Family members responded in varying ways, from solid support to outright opposition. Over the weekend, Ted talked alone to his three children. "We came on strong [against it]," Teddy Jr. told the *Globe*'s Tom Oliphant. They remembered the separation and chaos of the 1980 campaign, and wanted him with them more. Patrick, who was only fifteen and suffered from frequent asthma attacks, had borne the brunt of his parents' divorce. "Patrick just really was the most sensitive," said Teddy Jr., "and it meant so very much to him, having more time with my father and everything."

Shrum, who as speechwriter was perhaps the most closely attuned to his boss's thinking, had already guessed that Ted was going to back out. A few weeks earlier, Massachusetts voters had overwhelmingly elected Ted to a fifth term in the Senate. Shrum had prepared an expansive speech, addressing important national issues, but Ted rejected it. "I'd written a speech that leaned pretty forward into the idea that we were off and running for president," Shrum recalls. "He looked at it and said, 'I'm not going to say any of that. I want a speech very oriented to Massachusetts.' "

"I said to myself, 'He's not running for president,' " says Shrum, and privately prepared a statement to that effect. Later, after Kennedy had made up his mind, he told Shrum to get something ready fast before the news leaked. Shrum reached in his pocket and said, "It's already written."

Kennedy's announcement on December 1 that he wouldn't run for the 1984 nomination didn't completely end his visions of the White House. Ted briefly contemplated the possibility of running for president in 1988, but pulled out very early in the process, in mid-December 1985. Ted invited Shrum and Horowitz to his mother's house in Hyannis Port to tell them of his intentions. Horowitz directed Shrum into the living room, where Ted gave him a vodka and told him he was done with the White House. It was all over. He would never be president. Shrum made his last, best pitch: Ted would never have a better chance for the White House than in 1988, a year when the Democratic nomination was wide open and the likely Republican nominee would be Vice President George H. W. Bush. "I know, and I don't want to run," Ted replied. Shrum went off to start writing yet another withdrawal statement in the bedroom where Jack had convalesced from his war wounds, and where he and 12-year-old Teddy had taken turns reading aloud from the epic Civil War poem, "John Brown's Body."

Aides knew it was probably the last time they'd go through this routine, because their boss seemed so comfortable with his decision. Many factors came into play, from concern for his family to his own safety. Tom Rollins remembers walking with Ted from the Capitol to his office across the street on a beautiful spring day around this period. "A car backfired down the street, and he's gone," Rollins recalls. "I looked around and he's flat on the ground. He looked up and said, 'You never know.'" In addition, Ted had high hopes that the Democrats would take back the Senate in the 1986 elections, giving him the chairmanship of Labor and Human Services. From there, it was an open road. He could take his Senate career into higher gear, using the legislative skills he perfected while in the minority to produce bold new legislation to help the American people. He was unquestionably the leading Democrat in the body. He liked the job and loved the Senate. "My sense of him is, he just got more inclined to let himself be himself," says Carrick. "With his success in the minority, he knew what he could do in the majority." He also knew that as long as people viewed him as a possible presidential candidate, he would never escape suspicion that every move he made was hatched with the White House in mind.

Earlier that year, for example, he had visited South Africa in an attempt to push the Reagan Administration to apply greater pressure on the South African government to give blacks the right to vote. Flying back to the United States, Ted told Shrum how much he chafed at the endless speculation that the trip was nothing more than a stunt to draw attention to his next campaign. As long as he was a potential contender for the White House, his motives would always be questioned.

"I know this decision means that I may never be president," Ted told a Massachusetts television audience on December 19, 1985. "But the pursuit of the presidency is not my life. Public service is."

CHAPTER
20

Wɪ Rᴏɴᴀʟᴅ Rᴇᴀɢᴀɴ nominated federal appeals court Judge Robert Bork for a seat on the Supreme Court on July 1, 1987, Kennedy was ready. The 60-year-old Bork had been on the Republican short list for the Supreme Court for many years, and when Lewis Powell, a moderate justice who had often been the swing vote in 5–4 decisions on the nine-member court, decided to retire in 1987, Reagan saw an opportunity to put the right's leading legal thinker on the high court.

For two decades, Bork had been the intellectual engine behind the conservative challenge to the perceived excesses of the Supreme Court from the 1950s through the 1970s. During those years, the court took major steps to promote equal rights for minorities, guarantee women the right to an abortion, and ensure that all criminal defendants had proper legal representation, among many other bold strokes. Some of the decisions were based solely on the court's interpretation of the Bill of Rights; in other cases, the court upheld statutes passed by Congress, some of which were authored by Ted and many of which he considered to be part of Jack's legacy.

Bork, for his part, claimed to have no quarrel with the notion of equal rights for women or minorities, but felt those issues were best addressed through the political process, not the courts. And he believed the federal judiciary had overstepped its bounds in overturning laws that were enacted by the various state legislatures. Brilliant, arrogant and provocative, Bork was a forbidding figure with a bushy beard and wild hair. For years, he had engaged in spirited academic debates, carrying the conservative flag into battle against an array of liberal law professors. He believed in a jurisprudence of original intent—meaning that the various provisions in the Constitution should be interpreted in the way that the framers did in their own era. Liberal jurists felt otherwise, claiming that the Constitution was a living document, open to evolving interpretations as the times changed.

During his years as a professor at Yale Law School and later on the U.S. Court of Appeals for the District of Columbia, Bork had produced a long paper trail that was closely scrutinized by the Kennedy team. It revealed some vivid rhetorical excesses, familiar to academia but shocking to the political world. For example, Bork had called the provision of the Civil Rights Act of 1964 that banned discrimination in hotels and restaurants "a principle of unsurpassed ugliness." He found no right to privacy in the Constitution—the right which had been the grounds for the *Roe v. Wade* decision granting abortion rights, along with previous decisions overturning state bans on interracial marriage and the use of contraceptives. He also spoke out against a Supreme Court decision banning the poll tax, and opposed the decision requiring that legislative districts be apportioned evenly, to uphold the principle of one man, one vote. He held that the First Amendment protects only those engaged in political speech, leaving everyone else, including writers and artists, exposed to government restrictions. (He later recanted this, as well as his remarks about the Civil Rights Act of 1964.) And he had played a tangential role in the Watergate scandal. Back in the early 1970s, Bork had been the solicitor general in the Nixon administration, arguing important cases before the Supreme Court. But when the attorney general, Elliott Richardson, and deputy attorney general, William Ruckelshaus, resigned rather than go along with Nixon's order to fire Watergate prosecutor Archibald Cox, Bork, as the department's number three official, was left to do Nixon's bidding. He considered resigning, too, but was urged by Richardson and Ruckelshaus to stay in place to avoid widespread disarray; so he dutifully carried out Nixon's order, making him even more of a pariah on the left.

Still, at the time of Bork's nomination to the Supreme Court, many people in the political and legal worlds assumed he would be confirmed easily. Until that time, the Senate had focused extensively on nominees' personal character and qualifications—not their views on particular legal issues. By those standards, he was an impeccable choice. Bork was a devoted husband whose first wife had died of cancer and whose current wife was a former Catholic nun. Within the legal profession, he was considered a top-notch thinker—one of the finest legal minds in the country.

Up to that time, the Senate had also maintained a tradition of giving deference to Supreme Court nominees during the initial stages of their confirmation process, and waiting until the Judiciary Committee held confirmation hearings to voice concerns about the nominees. Ted decided to break tradition and oppose Bork from the start, setting up an epic confrontation. While the Reagan Administration expected that the focus of Bork's confirmation hearings would be on his stellar legal credentials, Ted would make the hearings a referendum on the civil rights legacy of the 1960s.

Less than an hour after Reagan announced Bork's nomination, Ted stood in the well of the Senate and delivered a blistering attack against the nominee. His speech was already in his coat pocket. The material for it had been gathered by his judiciary aide Jeff Blattner and written by his speechwriter Carey Parker. Ted charged that Bork interpreted the Constitution in a radically different way than it had been read for fifty years, which put him outside the mainstream of American judicial thinking. Ted was especially concerned by Bork's determination to view the law from a bloodless remove, with no consideration of its effects on real people. (When asked why he wanted to be on the Supreme Court, Bork would say it promised "an intellectual feast.") Before Bork could even make a case for himself, Ted painted the judge as both an unfeeling legal technocrat and a right-wing ideologue determined to erase the gains of the past two decades.

"Robert Bork's America is a land in which women would be forced into back-alley abortions, blacks would sit at segregated lunch counters, rogue police could break down citizens' doors in midnight raids, schoolchildren could not be taught about evolution, writers and artists could be censored at the whim of government, and the doors of the federal courts would be shut on the fingers of millions of citizens for whom the judiciary is often the only protector of the individual rights that are the heart of our democracy. America is a better and freer nation than Robert Bork thinks. Yet in the current delicate balance of the Supreme Court, his rigid ideology will tip the scales of justice against the kind of country America is and ought to be."

Blattner, Ted's Judiciary Committee aide, watched him deliver the speech on a closed circuit on C-SPAN and realized that Ted was putting his own credibility on the line. "We better win this one," he said to himself. In anticipation of the nomination, Kennedy's staff had weighed the pros and cons of leveling such a broadside at Bork. A year earlier, the president had nominated a judge with similar views to Bork's, Antonin Scalia, and Democrats had stood down, respectful of Scalia's academic accomplishments and the warm expressions of pride from Scalia's fellow Italian-Americans. Scalia sailed through with a 98–0 vote. "There was a sense early on that Bork could be a kind of Scalia," recalls Bill Carrick. "You couldn't attack him because of his credentials. Then we started hearing more and more in the legal community from professors to look at what Bork has written. . . . Carey [Parker] was one of the first to start reading his stuff. He said, 'You've got to read this.' "

The only question then was whether Ted should try to maintain the appearance of an open mind—what Carrick describes as following "the Kabuki theater" of the confirmation process—or speak out. Ted had no doubts about what approach to take. The speech, which stirred much of the country, would soon become known as the "Robert Bork's America" speech. It was loaded with rhetoric that, depending on where one was on the political spectrum, was either political hardball or plain demagoguery. Phrases like "back-alley abortions" and "rogue police" could be seen as wild overstatements, especially if Bork were to come across in the Judiciary Committee hearings as a measured man of the law. "When Ted went to the floor with that talk about back-alley abortions, oh my God," recalls Alan Simpson, a Republican committee member and a good friend of Kennedy. "I said, 'Ted, I thought that was wretched excess.' He said, 'The man is unfit. He'd be a disaster.' I saw that [Bork] was deep in his craw."

Most Democrats joined the Kennedy cause. "Ted Kennedy had no choice but to lay down that marker," maintains former Democratic Senate Majority Leader Tom Daschle. "This was a wake-up call. It was one of those pivotal moments. He caused the caucus to consider Bork in another light. More than any single speech, this changed the tone of that debate." Ted's comments also forced the Senate to confront the idea that a nominee could be rejected for ideology— a concept that would change the course of judicial nominations for decades. Joe Biden, who, as Judiciary Committee chairman, ran the Bork hearings, delivered a speech at the national convention of the American Bar Association before the hearings, arguing that a Supreme Court candidate's ideas, not just his credentials, were appropriate subjects of inquiry. "We should first address the question of whether we have the right to make a judgment beyond whether or not the person is intellectually and morally qualified," Biden said. "And if you make the conclusion that we do . . . then let's stop pussyfooting around and get to the business of finding out what Judge Bork believes."

Ted's speech, however, was such a radical departure from Senate tradition that it served to freeze many of his colleagues in place, making them guarded in their reactions. The one thing that most senators agreed on was that they wanted much more time to review Bork's record. As a result, Biden scheduled the hearings for mid-September. That meant Ted would have two and a half months to prepare his own questions and to make his case to his colleagues and the American people. Ted repaired to Hyannis Port, where he established his own oceanfront war room, and spent the summer pushing his case. He made hundreds of calls seeking the support of senators, law professors, and interest groups. He sent out pamphlets his staff had put together on Bork's writings. He talked to countless legal scholars and recruited African-American leaders and women's advocates to attest to the dangers of Bork's views.

Ted called, among many other African-American leaders, Ernest

"Dutch" Morial, the influential former mayor of New Orleans. In Alabama, he called Mayor Richard Arrington of Birmingham and Mayor Johnny Ford of Tuskegee. He reached Mayor Andrew Young of Atlanta and Congresswoman Barbara Jordan of Texas, both of whom agreed to testify. He even woke up Reverend Joseph Lowery, head of the Southern Christian Leadership Conference, in the middle of the night to urge him to spread the word about the dangers of Bork in black churches. Lowery did precisely that.

Ted relied on Ralph Neas, executive director of the National Conference on Civil Rights, to pull together grassroots coalitions. Neas rounded up close to 200 groups to work together against Bork. They included women's groups, labor unions, gay groups, and Hispanic groups, along with advocates for the elderly and people with disabilities. Many of the groups dipped into their coffers to pay for advertising against Bork. One ad, which the Kennedy camp found effective and Republicans found despicable, involved the magisterial voice of the actor Gregory Peck warning of a nightmarish future should Bork be confirmed. "It had crumbling columns of the Supreme Court," recalls Simpson with disgust. "It didn't fit anything."

Bork, by contrast, had no organizational superstructure behind him. He had no grassroots network to get his message out. The White House provided him no such support, and maintained its position that a nominee should be judged on his legal credentials alone. Some Democrats agreed. Lloyd Cutler, the prominent Washington lawyer and Democratic stalwart, argued that Bork would be a strong addition to the bench. Cutler called him "a highly qualified conservative jurist who is closer to the moderate center than to the extreme right." Others attacked the Bork opposition for its tactics. David Broder, the Pulitzer Prize–winning columnist for the *Washington Post* known for his measured tone, was one. "The victory that liberals now boast they will achieve in blocking Judge Robert H. Bork's elevation to the Supreme Court could be an expensive one," wrote Broder. "The game of judge-bashing, which they learned from their opponents on the political right, ultimately profits no one. It inevitably damages and could destroy one of the major safeguards of freedom in this society: the independence of the judiciary."

Ted's supporters howled at this: "If Kennedy and Neas are guilty of anything," says Ralph Neas, "it was understatement."

To help him prepare for the hearings, Ted recruited Harvard Law School professor Laurence Tribe, whom some considered to be the Robert Bork of the left. Tribe agreed to play Bork in mock debates with Kennedy held in the senator's office in Boston. "Larry played Bork in our mock hearings better than Bork" himself did, quips Blattner, who was there along with three other Kennedy aides. "He was more nimble. He presciently anticipated where Bork would go." Meanwhile, Bork himself was rejecting advice about how he should tone himself down under the Senate klieg lights. A man of prodigious intellect, if not emotional intelligence, Bork scorned much of the advice from the White House. He came off as the self-appointed smartest guy in the room. "He's a dismissive person," acknowledges Simpson. "He's not a hail-fellow-well-met. He wrote angry books. He puts on the show. The beard irritated people. I spoke to a group of women in New York and asked how many of them didn't like his beard. Half the room raised their hands."

The hearings convened on the morning of Tuesday, September 15, in the ornate Senate Caucus Room, where the Watergate hearings had taken place fourteen years earlier. This was, most agreed, the biggest spectacle since then, and the public tuned in to watch on television in the same large numbers. Over two weeks, there would be ten witnesses other than Bork, along with another ninety-nine advocates on both sides grouped in panels to testify on various aspects of the law. A parade of distinguished legal scholars came and went. But Kennedy also made sure that unconventional witnesses such as the artist Robert Rauschenberg and the writer William Styron were on hand to testify to the possible effects of a Bork appointment on the First Amendment.

The hearings got off to a stumbling start. Former President Gerald Ford led off by paying tribute to Bork, who had served in his administration. However, upon questioning from Democratic Senator Dennis DeConcini of Arizona, it became clear that Ford knew next to nothing about Bork's judicial record. Later, the aged former Chief Justice Warren Burger testified for Bork, but couldn't remember what the

Ninth Amendment was, prompting veteran *Baltimore Sun* Supreme Court reporter Lyle Denniston to stage whisper, "It's the one between the Eighth and the Tenth, Mr. Chief Justice."

Kennedy spoke near the end of the first day, in time for the evening news. He immediately bore in on Bork's opposition to the right to privacy outlined in the 1965 Supreme Court decision that overturned a Connecticut law banning married couples from using contraception. Without a right to privacy, Ted charged, the government could start interfering in the most intimate aspects of people's lives. "As I understand it, under your peculiar constitutional philosophy, you would be prepared to uphold compulsory abortion in America if some future legislature enacted it?" asked Ted. Bork later came back: "What we were talking about here was a generalized, undefined right to privacy which is not in the Bill of Rights. . . . We do not know what it covers." Bork added, "Privacy to what, Senator? You know, privacy to use cocaine in private? Privacy for businessmen to fix prices in a hotel room? We just do not know what it is."

The two also locked horns on civil rights and women's rights in the half hour of questioning that Kennedy was allotted. Ted kept advancing, his voice booming. He challenged Bork on his opposition to the Supreme Court decision that ruled that state legislative districts must be roughly equal in population. Before the court's decision, Southern states drew districts in ways that minimized black representation. Barbara Jordan, the respected African-American congresswoman from Texas, testified that she would not be where she was had the Supreme Court not upheld the principle of "one man, one vote." Bork didn't back down. "There is nothing in our constitutional history that suggests one-man, one-vote is the only proper way of apportioning [legislative districts]," he replied. Ted also challenged Bork's willingness to give state governments more power to pass laws that could discriminate against women or minorities: "I believe, Mr. Bork, that in your world, the individuals have precious few rights to protect them against the majority."

During Kennedy's half hour, Biden discreetly kept score on five-by-eight cards that he showed to Kennedy, who was sitting beside him. Biden started at 6–0 and reached 24–0 with a possible 30–0 by the end. Ted was coming out ahead in volley after volley. The daily showdown demanded extraordinary preparation. "I'd be at McLean at seven and ride in with him," recalls Blattner. "He'd be in his den, notebook open, a fire burning, wearing his reading glasses. Pages were folded over. The intensity was unbelievably dazzling." Then, at night, the Kennedy war council would repair to Ted's office to review the day. Aides would probe for inconsistencies in Bork's statements, look at the holes in Ted's questioning, anticipate what would come the next day.

But some of the drama was taking place outside the hearing room. The Democrats needed at least five of their party's conservative Southern members to vote against Bork, and those senators were deeply concerned about a pro-Bork backlash among white Southerners. The task of persuading them looked daunting until Boston pollsters John Marttila and Tom Kiley polled the country to assess people's views on Bork. What they found was surprising: the last thing that Southern whites wanted to do was refight the civil rights battles of the 1960s, and they worried that Bork would reopen all those painful issues. More predictably, the polls showed that African Americans were strongly opposed to Bork. And, as Ted knew, Democratic senators from the Deep South depended on large African American turnouts to carry them into office. "We knew we'd beat Bork from Marttila's poll," says Pat Caddell, who by then was working for Kennedy. "The South had moved on. The white South wanted nothing to do with this." In the end, says Caddell, "Bork was defeated not by gerbil groups inside the beltway. It was run outside the beltway."

Conservative Democrat Bennett Johnston of Louisiana grasped this early and went out to corral a few of his Senate colleagues against Bork. His fellow senator from Louisiana, John Breaux, also came out against Bork. Richard Shelby of Alabama did, too. At the last minute, so did his fellow Alabaman Howell Heflin. North Carolina's Terry Sanford came out against Bork, as did David Pryor of Arkansas, Lloyd Bentsen of Texas, and even Republican John Warner of Virginia.

On October 6, the Judiciary Committee voted 9–5 to recommend against the nomination. Bork was doomed. The White House wanted Bork to withdraw his name rather than go through a full Senate vote, which he would inevitably lose.

Simpson recalls that a few days before the committee vote, Bork and his wife, Mary Ellen, came to his office. "There was tremendous sadness in her eyes and face, [and] Bob, the air was out of him," Simpson says. "He asked what I would do, withdraw my name, or go to a full vote of the Senate. I said, 'I'll tell you, I'd want my grandchildren to read in the Congressional Record that there were 38 people who thought I was a pretty good egg. That's what I'd do.' " And in the end, Bork decided not to withdraw. The final Senate vote against him on October 23 was by a large 58–42 margin but, recalls Blattner, the Kennedy team was in no mood to crow. There was no exhilaration in the office, but rather a quiet pride. "There was a sense that we had just had a national referendum on the meaning of the Constitution and the Constitution won," says Blattner.

If there had been any question before the Bork nomination of who ran the Senate, there was none after.

CHAPTER
21

On October 25, 1991, a warm fall Friday in Cambridge, Ted Kennedy attended a twenty-fifth anniversary celebration at the JFK School of Government's Institute of Politics knowing he had a huge problem on his hands. A recent Gallup poll had given him a 22 percent national approval rating, shockingly low for a legislator and party leader of his stature. Voters regarded him with personal distaste, and most hoped he would lose his next election.

Ted had long been scheduled to deliver the ceremony's keynote speech, one in which he was expected to pay tribute to an institution he had helped build and to a career, public service, his brothers Jack and Bobby had ennobled. Instead, a few days earlier, Kennedy advised school officials he'd prepared a different speech, "important" and more personal in nature. No advance copy was provided. As word circulated through the media, arrangements were made to accommodate a larger press contingent than normal.

Ted had labored over the speech as friends and advisers watched his public image take a pummeling. Spiced by published reports of heavy drinking and sexual escapades, Kennedy's personal life had become punchline fodder for late-night TV hosts and *Saturday Night Live* sketch writers. At odds with the prevailing political winds, he was now perceived to have lost control of his own appetites as well.

Even more damaging to his political future was an upcoming trial in Palm Beach, where his nephew William Kennedy Smith was accused of raping a woman at the family's estate. While not directly implicated in the rape charge, the senator was a key witness in a tawdry case that had spawned headlines around the world and mocking comments about Ted's inappropriate — many thought reckless — behavior. As details emerged about the Palm Beach incident, *Tonight* show host Jay Leno drew belly laughs when he likened a solar eclipse to nightfall by joking, "The temperature drops, the stars appear, flowers close up. And Ted Kennedy takes his pants off."

Not surprisingly, many people expected the senator to announce he would not run for reelection in 1994 — that it was time to move on after thirty years in Washington and get his personal house in order. In fact, Kennedy was already gearing up for the toughest race of his Senate career. In many ways, this speech was the kickoff.

"We had a conversation," recalls Bob Shrum regarding the gathering storm around Kennedy, "and he said, 'I want to address that. Not in detail, with a bunch of specifics. But people are troubled by things in my private life that I recognize I have to change.'"

Shrum helped Ted shape the tone and content of the speech. Because this was a troubling time for Kennedy personally and not merely a politically challenging one, however, and because talking about himself was not something the senator did naturally or comfortably, he needed all the emotional support he could muster. Accompanying him on the plane ride to Massachusetts was Victoria Reggie, a young Washington lawyer whom he'd been quietly dating for the past several months. The public knew nothing about Vicki. Kennedy asked that she be seated close to the podium — close enough, as it turned out, that the press became suspicious.

The senator entered a reception room accompanied by a small group of family and friends. He did not seem nervous, recalls the then-forum director Heather Campion, who had observed Kennedy in many such situations before. "He's always very focused before big events like these," says Campion. "Always worried about others, managing logistics, always helping to host the event as well as being the center of attention himself."

Ted wore a dark suit, blue shirt, and conservative necktie for the occasion. He walked unsteadily, the result of the bad back from his long-ago plane crash and the weight problem that had grown more severe and made him look older than his sixty years. When it came time to speak, he kept his eyes cast downward and betrayed little emotion. "I am painfully aware that the criticism directed at me in recent months involves far more than disagreements with my positions," he said, "or the usual criticism from the far right. It also involves the disappointment of friends and many others who rely on me to fight the good fight.

"To them I say, I recognize my own shortcomings—the faults in the conduct of my private life. I realize that I alone am responsible for them, and I am the one who must confront them. . . . I believe that each of us as individuals must not only struggle to make a better world but to make ourselves better, too." Unlike his brothers, Kennedy said somberly, "I have been given length of years and time. And as I approach my 60th birthday, I am determined to give all that I have to advance the causes for which I have stood for almost a quarter of a century." He took no questions afterward.

Reaction was, to put it charitably, mixed. In the *New York Times*, Alessandra Stanley called it a "first attempt to fight back, to repair the damage and restore, if not his personal reputation, then his political standing as the voice of American liberalism." The *Boston Globe*'s Mike Barnicle was not even that generous. While his mea culpa was welcome, Kennedy "seemed to mention it merely in passing, as if he were talking about the fact that he didn't brush after every meal or failed to clean up his room," the columnist wrote. Barnicle questioned whether it marked a real turning point, as Kennedy's friends were insisting, quipping that the senator's so-called friends "may not be the wisest counsel available." Nobody singled out the friend whose counsel now meant more to Kennedy than anyone's.

By the late 1960s, Ted's reputation for heavy drinking and womanizing was well established. He provided plenty more to gossip about as he moved into middle age, not always terribly gracefully, during his second bachelorhood in the 1980s and early 1990s.

It was not just his blotchy complexion and yo-yoing weight—he regularly gained and then shed sixty pounds during a twelve-month cycle, going on and off the wagon for weeks at a time—that raised questions about how he lived. Kennedy was a national figure with movie-star wealth and celebrity. His Senate office attracted more than its share of Capitol Hill groupies, young women drawn to men of prestige and power, so much so that the senator and his staff had to develop a strategy for diplomatically spurning their advances. Officially single since his 1982 divorce from Joan, he was very much a man of his generation, embracing the swinging *Playboy* ethos of the 1960s as ardently as he did the spirit of his brother's New Frontier. Asked once to name his "favorite hero of fiction," Ted replied, "James Bond."

So, too, was he incorrigibly his father's son, Joe Sr. having seldom taken pains to hide his extramarital affairs from Rose and the children. In the years after Chappaquiddick, Ted had been largely able to keep his public and private lives separate. More and more, however, the worst of his excesses had begun spilling into public view. As far back as 1979, reputable sources like *Time* magazine—which had previously linked Kennedy romantically to a series of high-profile paramours, among them New York socialite Amanda Burden, Olympic skier Suzy Chaffee, and former Canadian first lady Margaret Trudeau—wrote of his extramarital adventures with a certain hold-your-nose squeamishness. "The mere mention of Edward Kennedy's social life is enough to make an editor's head throb," began one piece titled "Sex and the Senior Senator." It concluded with an anecdote about a Washington dinner party where, according to *New Republic* writer Henry Fairlie, "for a full hour and a half, 14 talented and interesting men and women talked of nothing but the sexual activities of Edward Kennedy."

Other media entities, some more high-minded than others, picked up the thread, adding tales of binge drinking to an accretional portrait of middle-aged dissolution. A 1979 *Washington Monthly* essay by Suzannah Lessard, which bore the title "Kennedy's Woman Problem, Women's Kennedy Problem," reflected upon his long and not terribly

well-concealed history of amorous affairs and frat-boy behavior, adding up to what Lessard called "a severe case of arrested development,
a kind of narcissistic intemperance, a huge, babyish ego that must be
constantly fed."

Rarely did these stories suggest that alcohol was seriously impairing his job performance. If anything, the opposite seemed true: that
Ted was capable of impressive stamina and self-discipline when he was
focused on work, demonstrating greater command of his Senate duties than ever, even as his presidential ambitions waned. Yet as those
dreams faded, along with his patched-together marriage to Joan, Ted's
sense of discretion seemed to have vanished, too, introducing an element of recklessness to his behavior that even Kennedy admirers found
disheartening, if not disturbing. "Ted Kennedy always baffled me to
some degree," says former *Time* correspondent Lance Morrow, who
covered the senator for parts of four decades. "He was so astonishingly
productive as a senator, yet his private life was extremely messy. When
it came to Kennedy's character, you'd feel whipsawed judging it."

After his divorce and the end of his White House ambitions,
"There was a sense of relief, probably, that he hadn't been killed, because his whole life he'd been under that cloud of death threats," observes one family friend. "And with that relief came a desire to kick up
his heels."

Having known many of the women Kennedy dated during this period, the friend adds, "I can say they all loved him dearly. All felt he'd
been a wonderful gentleman and maintained relationships with him
after the [dating] ran its course. There was never any nasty stuff, any
sense of being disrespected or uncompassionate. They were substantive people, too."

Ted's dating habits, even if distorted by the prying eyes and breath-
less headlines of tabloid journalism, grated on many of his supporters
nonetheless, especially feminists who appreciated his support for the
Equal Rights Amendment and access to legal abortion. "The trouble
with Teddy is that he's like the little girl with the curl in the middle of
her forehead," wrote *New York Times* columnist Anna Quindlen. "When
he's good, he's better than anyone else, but when he's bad—oh boy!"

His drinking was another matter. Whether Kennedy was an alcoholic or not was something Lance Morrow, for one, never resolved. The senator denied it in interviews like the one he gave the *Today* show in 1992, when he flatly answered "absolutely not" when asked if he had a drinking problem. His denial did little to quell suspicions, though. In a later interview on *60 Minutes*, Kennedy was again pressed about his drinking. "I went through a lot of difficult times over a period in my life where [drinking] may have been somewhat of a factor or force," he acknowledged uncomfortably. "I never felt that myself." Still, he conceded, "Others did, and I don't question their own kind of assessment of it."

"He seemed to have a pattern of drinking like a fish, then sobering up for a while," says Morrow. "You'd see this funny sequence where he'd seem very dissipated, then relatively healthy. Most drunks, unless they clean up their act, have a long, steady decline. Teddy seemed to go cyclically."

Orrin Hatch, one of Kennedy's closest friends in the Senate, is among the few to acknowledge having confronted Kennedy about his drinking and the toll it was taking on him, physically and otherwise. In 1991, according to an interview Hatch gave several years later, Ted was depressed about how the media had "come down on him like a ton of bricks" over his Rabelaisian behavior. "So I said, 'Now, Ted, it's time for you to grow up and stop acting like a teenager,'" Hatch recalls. "I said, 'You know what you've got to do, don't you?' I said, 'You've got to quit drinking.'" According to Hatch, Kennedy's response was a stunned look followed by a two-word admission: "I know." Adds Hatch, "It was like the first time he'd ever heard that. His eyes got teary . . . and I think he knew that he had to change."

Biting public comments captured Ted's growing image problem. One came after the 1988 Democratic National Convention, at which the senator had delivered a rousing "Where was George?" refrain in attacking GOP presidential nominee George H. W. Bush. "I'll tell Teddy Kennedy where George is," retorted Republican congressman Harold Rogers at a post-convention rally in Kentucky. "He's home sober with his wife."

A year later, vacationing along the French Riviera, Kennedy was stalked by paparazzi, one of whom snapped him having sexual intercourse with an unidentified woman in the back of a motorboat. After the *National Enquirer* ran photos of the tryst—along with many other papers, including the *Boston Herald*, a prime purveyor of Kennedy gossip—Alabama Senator Howell Heflin joked that he was glad to see Kennedy "had changed his position on offshore drilling."

Heflin drew mostly chuckles for chiding Kennedy. Less amusing, and more controversial, was a lurid memoir about life with the senator written by Richard Burke, Kennedy's former personal aide and no relation to David Burke. The book appeared in mid-1992, after Ted's Kennedy School speech acknowledging his need to take responsibility for his behavior. Burke's close proximity to Kennedy from 1971 to 1981 had given him a bird's-eye view of the senator's private affairs. According to *The Senator: My Ten Years with Ted Kennedy,* Burke personally witnessed, and frequently participated in, illegal drug use by the senator, especially cocaine. Girlfriends were plentiful, too, wrote Burke, the senator "grabbing women like so many bags of M&Ms." Burke had his own credibility issues, though, and by the time his memoir appeared, he had already suffered a nervous breakdown and had been charged with filing false police reports while still a member of Kennedy's staff. By 1991, the same year he signed a contract for the book, Burke filed for bankruptcy, raising more questions about his motives. Kennedy himself characterized the book as a "collection of bizarre and untrue stories" in one of his few public comments on anything written about him.

If privately alarmed about Ted's behavior, friends and aides seem to have taken few steps to curb it at the height of its excesses. To this day, the effects of his carousing are often downplayed or dismissed as being much ado about relatively little. Melody Miller, who served as a Kennedy press aide for much of the 1980s, says she would tease the senator as he headed off on vacation each year, reminding him of the ubiquity of telephoto lenses. "He'd laugh about it," says Miller, adding, "He was a bachelor, though, and entitled to a dating life. And who among us could have functioned being spied on incessantly without blowing up? He didn't like it, but what can you do?"

Edmund Reggie, a close friend of Ted's who later became the senator's father-in-law, bought a vacation home on Nantucket in 1982. "Ted came over the first week," says Reggie. " 'Why didn't you tell me?' he said. 'I'd have found you a place near us [on Cape Cod].' But that was during Teddy's party days, and I knew I couldn't go a whole summer with that. I'm not that strong.

"They were good times, fun times, hell-raising times," Reggie, who is only six years older than the senator, continues with a laugh. "I was a lot younger then and could sort of keep up with him." Kennedy would bring girlfriends to the house, says Reggie, and "All those girls would come tell Doris [his wife], 'I know he loves me. We're gonna be married. I'm the one.' " Yet Reggie says he never sensed Kennedy was very serious about these relationships, even if many of the women were. "There was nobody to whom he was going to get engaged," agrees Miller. "He didn't think he'd ever marry again, because he'd already been married and had children. As he later said in interviews, he'd already lost so many people in his life that he'd loved, he didn't want to risk losing another one."

Many close to Kennedy maintain that he was far lonelier than he appeared during this period in his life, that for a man who had made a career out of careful relationship building, and who reveled in the joys of family life, there was something deeply missing.

Ted was such a strong and reliable presence as head of the family, observes David Burke, that "nobody paid much attention" to his emotional needs. Nancy Korman, a political supporter who met Kennedy in the mid-1970s and maintained a close relationship with the senator thereafter, wrote to him often to express her unvarnished opinions on matters both personal and political. "There's an enormously sensitive side to Ted that went unanswered during his bad-boy period, I think," reflects Korman. "He looked bad and felt bad."

The worst blow to his image came in 1990, in a long profile written by Michael Kelly for *GQ* magazine. A talented and resourceful young journalist who later served as editor of *The New Republic* and *Atlantic Monthly*, Kelly spent three months conducting scores of on-the-record interviews. Titled "Ted Kennedy on the Rocks," Kelly's profile fully acknowledged the senator's energy and accomplishments as a legislator. What got tongues wagging, though, were the article's detailed accounts of Kennedy's binge drinking and compulsive womanizing. Unlike his brothers Jack and Bobby, both of whom were remembered for their perpetual youth and handsome features, "Ted is the reality, a 57-year-old living picture of a man who has feasted on too much for too long with too little restraint, the visible proof that nothing exceeds like excess," Kelly wrote.

Kelly's withering judgment of Kennedy's loutish behavior—his alcohol-fueled confrontations in various bars and clubs, his wanton promiscuity, his evolution into "a Senator Bedfellow figure, an aging Irish boyo clutching a bottle and diddling a blonde"—was anchored by a pair of anecdotes that took their place alongside Chappaquiddick in Bad Teddy Kennedy lore. Both incidents took place at a Washington restaurant, La Brasserie, where Kennedy was a regular. One scene, which took place in late 1985, involved Kennedy and his good friend Chris Dodd, the Connecticut senator, sandwiching themselves around a waitress at the end of a lengthy, booze-fueled dinner. The other incident, roughly two years later, captured Kennedy having intercourse with a congressional lobbyist on the floor of a private dining room, in broad daylight. Arrested development "doesn't explain why Kennedy seems to be getting worse as he gets older," wrote Kelly, adding, "I wonder whether Kennedy is really enjoying this anymore."

If nothing else, the rules of engagement governing the senator and the reporters who covered him were changing by the late 1980s and early 1990s, according to former *Boston Globe* correspondent John Aloysius Farrell. Farrell followed Kennedy extensively during the 1990s and was among the first reporters to ask directly about his drinking habits. "Even after Chappaquiddick, Kennedy was given wide leeway by the Capitol Hill press," says Farrell. "For the most part, these were not the boys on the bus from JFK's 1960 campaign but reporters who knew him only as a senator. If we saw a senator come back to work after dinner looking a little rosy-cheeked, we were more inclined to forgive him as long as we saw him functioning well during the day. It was a very serious press corps, and Teddy got a kind of dual protection: from the old guard who went back to the JFK days and a younger generation too bogged down with work to worry much" about his private life.

Still, Kelly's haunting question of whether the senator was really enjoying this any more was on the mind of many after what transpired in South Florida on Easter Weekend 1991.

CHAPTER
22

IN AUGUST 1990, Stephen Smith, Kennedy's brother-in-law and former presidential campaign manager, succumbed to cancer. Married to Jean Kennedy, Ted's closest sibling, Smith had managed the family trusts from his office in Manhattan and functioned as the Kennedys' chief troubleshooter. His death had a profound impact on Ted, who wept openly at Smith's funeral. While enormously painful, the loss of Smith, a valued confidant to whom Kennedy regularly referred as his other brother, was hardly the only blow suffered by the family during a period when the younger generation found itself passing uneasily into adulthood.

In 1983, Robert F. Kennedy Jr. had been arrested for heroin possession. A year later, another of Bobby's sons, David Kennedy, died of a drug overdose in a Palm Beach motel. Kennedy in-law Peter Lawford, a movie actor famously associated with Hollywood's Rat Pack, lost his long struggle with alcohol and drug abuse in 1984, dying from cardiac arrest and liver failure. Other dark chapters would soon be written. Ted's son Patrick checked into a rehab facility in 1986, followed, in 1991, by Teddy Jr., who confessed that his drinking was "impairing my ability to achieve the goals I care about." Christopher Kennedy Lawford, Peter's son, waged his own life-and-death battle with addiction to drugs and alcohol over many years, a battle vividly described in Lawford's 2005 memoir. At one point, according to Lawford, he and his uncle, both besotted, nearly came to blows during a family ski trip in 1982.

"Teddy had moved from the mythic to the human," observed Lawford, a judgment that hovered like a storm cloud over Easter Weekend 1991 in Palm Beach.

With Steve Smith's death weighing heavily upon him, Ted invited a group of relatives and friends to the family's South Florida estate for the holiday weekend. Bought by Joe Sr. in 1933 for $120,000, the six-bedroom house occupied a two-acre site featuring a swimming pool, tennis court, and 176 feet of beach frontage. Designed by Addison Mizner, the architect responsible for many of the Mediterranean-style mansions that sprang up along the Palm Beach waterfront in the 1920s and 1930s, it had originally been commissioned by department store heir Rodman Wanamaker and christened La Guerida, a Spanish term meaning "bounty of war."

For more than half a century, Palm Beach had been the favorite wintertime retreat of Rose Kennedy in particular. As the family matriarch aged, though, eventually becoming too frail to travel south for the season, the property had fallen into conspicuous decline, reaching a state one local official, after roaming around the property in mid-1991, called "seedy." Notwithstanding its rundown condition, La Guerida loomed large in family lore. It was there that Joe and Rose's offspring had fashioned many a happy childhood memory and where, in 1961, Joe had suffered his life-altering stroke while golfing on a nearby course. Jack worked on *Profiles in Courage* at the Palm Beach house and picked his cabinet while relaxing there during a post-election sojourn in 1960. Even Rosemary, who attended few family functions, was ferried to Florida from her residential facility in Wisconsin for occasional visits with relatives.

Much like Hyannis Port, La Guerida had become a nostalgia-tinged gathering spot for large groups of Kennedys, particularly during holidays and other family celebrations. Unlike the Cape Cod compound, however, few local residents had ever set foot inside the place. Nor had they come to embrace the Kennedys as adopted Palm Beachers, political royals masquerading as next-door neighbors. Around Palm

Beach, La Guerida was better known as a Kennedy party house than a southern annex of Camelot. As historian Arthur Schlesinger Jr., a frequent houseguest of the Kennedys, observed, "Palm Beach is not a place where the youngest generation of Kennedys finds sustenance." Rather, he asserted, it was "dedicated to frivolity."

The arm's-length relationship between the town and the Kennedy clan derived from many factors, one being the reality that Palm Beach—a mecca for old-money society types with names like Firestone, Vanderbilt, and Pulitzer—was more conservative Republican than liberal Democrat by nature, more WASP than Irish Catholic. "They're not really considered old guard, although having a president who lived here always fascinated people," commented Roxanne Pulitzer to one reporter in the spring of 1991, speaking about the Kennedys. "They're Catholic, not Episcopalian," she added. "You know, that kind of bitchiness that Palm Beach is known for. But they seemed content to live in their own world, and it didn't seem to matter."

Until the day when a younger-generation Kennedy was charged with raping a local woman during that Easter weekend. Guests at the estate during the three-day holiday included Bobby Kennedy's former bodyguard, William Barry; Ted's son Patrick, a member of the Rhode Island state assembly; and Jean Kennedy Smith and two of her children, Amanda and William, the latter a fourth-year medical student at Georgetown University. According to police reports and trial testimony, a Friday family dinner ended with the senator on the patio, drinking Scotch and chatting nostalgically with his sister and Barry about Steve Smith. The senator retired around 11:30 but was restless and unable to sleep, he said, at which point he invited Patrick and Willie to go out for a drink. The three drove to Au Bar, a hip nightclub widely known as a pickup spot for older men seeking attractive, available women. It was not the first time a group of Kennedy men had visited Au Bar in the wee hours.

After ordering drinks, they were joined at a table by several locals. One, a 29-year-old single mother named Patricia Bowman, wound up dancing with Willie Smith. Sometime around 3:00 A.M.—recollections varied—Ted and Patrick went home, joined there by Michele Cassone, a Palm Beach waitress whom Patrick had invited back for a nightcap. Bowman and Smith arrived separately. According to Cassone, she, Ted, and Patrick sipped wine on the seawall patio before reentering the house around 4:00 A.M. Cassone said she and Patrick then began "cuddling" in a downstairs bedroom until the senator, wearing only a shirt of some kind and nothing else, walked in on them. Ted was "just there with a weird look on his face," she later recalled. "I was weirded out." Disturbed by his appearance, Cassone left the estate shortly thereafter.

Bowman said that she and Willie walked down to the beach, where Willie took off all his clothes and went swimming. Bowman declined to join him and headed toward the house. Willie then tackled her by the swimming pool, according to Bowman, and forced himself upon her sexually. Her screams, she said, drew no response from anyone in the house. Back inside, she said, she confronted Willie, who denied raping her and declared that no one would believe her, anyway. Bowman then called two friends to drive her home. Before leaving, they took an antique vase and several framed photos from the house, ostensibly to prove they'd been inside.

According to statements made by Ted both before and during the trial, he heard no screams that night and, upon seeing Willie the next morning, talked only about playing tennis, not about Bowman. The senator also said he was unaware of the assault charge until days later. But Bowman had gone to the police as early as Saturday afternoon and sworn out a complaint. Officers visiting the house the next day spoke to Bill Barry and came away thinking that neither Willie nor the senator was around. This was not true. The police finally gained access to the house Monday morning, by which time Ted had left Florida. Six weeks later, the senator held a press conference and vehemently denied having deliberately misled investigators. Speculation nevertheless persisted that the family had closed ranks around Smith, making any timely investigation more difficult.

What Ted could not avoid was the media firestorm exploding around a juicy tale involving booze, sex, the police blotter, and America's foremost political family. The first news stories appeared the Tuesday following Easter. Having just ended a prolonged labor strike, New York papers seized on the story, flooding Palm Beach with reporters. Bowman's identity remained shielded—most media outlets adhered to a policy of not publishing the names of rape victims—but not for very long. Meanwhile, the Kennedys chose to play tough: they launched their own investigation of Bowman. "We knew that was the way they were going to play the game," recalls Ellen Roberts, a prosecutor on the Smith case. "Patty certainly was not a bad person. But she did have a past." Several news organizations came out with stories linking Bowman to cocaine use and at least one abortion. Both the *New York Times* and NBC News identified Bowman by name, igniting yet more controversy. While the newspaper ordinarily withheld the names of alleged rape victims, *Times* editors explained, NBC had already made Bowman's name public. NBC news executives justified their decision, in turn, by pointing out that Bowman's name and picture had previously appeared in the *Globe,* a supermarket tabloid. Justified or not, the decision by two of the country's most respected news organizations to break with longstanding policies left Bowman, for one, disillusioned and bitter. Later she would launch a public campaign for victims' rights, telling one audience, "The press has a powerful tool in its hands" that should be used to perpetuate "a free and right society, not as a weapon used against that society."

The Palm Beach case was still in the news, with Willie preparing to go on trial, when President George H. W. Bush nominated Clarence Thomas for a seat on the Supreme Court on July 1, 1991.

Fraught with controversy from the outset, the nomination turned into something more complicated for Ted than a disagreeable choice for the nation's highest court. It ended up placing an additional spotlight on the senator's personal conduct, not merely Thomas's fitness to serve. The Palm Beach incident, once considered part of his life offstage, was now officially infecting Ted's ability to serve effectively on the political stage.

Bush named Thomas, an African American, to replace retiring

Justice Thurgood Marshall, a civil rights hero who had served on the Supreme Court for nearly a quarter of a century. Thomas had served as chairman of the Equal Employment Opportunity Commission before becoming a D.C. Court of Appeals judge less than two years earlier. Few considered him to be Marshall's judicial or intellectual equal. Few believed, either, that, in Bush's words, "the fact that he is black and a minority has absolutely nothing to do" with his being tapped to take Marshall's seat.

As a protégé of Missouri's Republican senator John Danforth, a highly respected moderate, Thomas had a powerful Senate sponsor in his corner. He also had a dramatic life story to tell, having grown up poor in the black belt of Georgia before going on to the College of the Holy Cross, Yale Law School, and a career that spanned corporate law and government policy making.

Thomas's judicial temperament and political ideology, jarringly at odds with Marshall's, made his choice particularly worrisome to civil rights and women's groups. His opposition to affirmative action and racial quotas was well-known. Ted had led the fight against Robert Bork and cast the lone Judiciary Committee vote against Justice David Souter, a more moderate judge appointed to the high court by President Bush the year before. When Thomas was selected for a federal judgeship, Ted had questioned him in perfunctory fashion, ultimately voting in favor of his elevation to the appellate court.

The Supreme Court was another matter. Ted and his allies on the left regarded Thomas's nomination as a cynical ploy to fill the court's "black seat" with a youthful jurist in the conservative Republican mold, a legal lightweight capable of tilting the court rightward for decades to come. Although unhappy with the choice of Thomas, leading civil rights organizations were conflicted over what to do about it. Doubtful that Thomas, who had never litigated a single jury case, was the "best qualified" candidate for the job, they were nevertheless slow to come out against the judge. Civil rights groups feared that making a Borklike attack on an African-American nominee would paint them as hypocrites and deplete their political capital. Faye Wattleton, who ran Planned Parenthood and spoke out strongly against Thomas's candidacy, says many black leaders were in the same quandary she found herself in. "Being an African American, I was in a tough spot," recalls Wattleton.

"Our first impression of Clarence Thomas was that he was not the best choice," recalls former Wyoming Senator Alan Simpson, who sat on the Judiciary Committee with Kennedy and now regards the Thomas nomination as the lowest moment of his eighteen-year Senate career. "At one point Ted said to me, 'The president might have done better.'" There were other black conservatives who would have garnered more bipartisan support, notes Simpson, citing, among others, former transportation secretary William Coleman, a close friend of Marshall's. Ted was especially wary of how Thomas might rule on the abortion issue. Thomas had delivered speeches spelling out his conservative principles and political ideology. But his paper trail wasn't nearly as long as Bork's, making it difficult to pin Thomas down on legal issues. Kennedy's frustration became evident at the start of the Judiciary Committee hearings in September, during which Thomas claimed he'd never discussed *Roe v. Wade* before. Ted, who had otherwise said little during the questioning, suggested that Thomas was distancing himself from past opinions that might derail his nomination. "If we permit [nominees] to dismiss views full of sound and fury as signifying nothing," said Kennedy, "we are abdicating our constitutional role."

The Bush administration worked furiously behind the scenes to smooth Thomas's path, and putting Democrats on the defensive was part of that campaign. Republican strategist Floyd Brown produced a sharp-elbowed television ad aimed at key Democrats on the Judiciary Committee, notably Kennedy and Joe Biden, that called into question their own moral and ethical standing. The architect of the infamous Willie Horton spot that helped sink Michael Dukakis's 1988 presidential campaign, Brown built his ad around headlines such as "Teddy's Sexy Romp," which the *New York Post* had trumpeted during its coverage of the Palm Beach case. A Chappaquiddick reference was tossed in, too. "I'm a member of the 'hit 'em and watch 'em go down' school of politics," boasted Brown, who'd begun work on the ad even before Thomas's nomination, having anticipated a Borklike battle between Senate Democrats and the Bush administration. The White House distanced itself from Brown's ad, which got heavy free play over Labor Day weekend, but the message was clear: Ted's extracurricular life was now undercutting the moral authority he brought to his political one.

After questioning Thomas, committee members split 7–7 on his nomination, sending it to the full Senate without recommendation. In the meantime, Ted focused on reintroducing civil rights legislation that had been vetoed by Bush the year before. Leading civil rights groups like the NAACP and Urban League were deeply invested in that effort, too. Among Kennedy's key allies in that fight? John Danforth, Thomas's sponsor and friend. "Senator Kennedy was going to vote against Clarence Thomas anyway, I knew that," says Danforth, who now practices law in St. Louis. However, he believed Kennedy's opposition was based purely on what kind of justice he thought Thomas would make, not what kind of person Thomas was. Danforth, who had a close working relationship with Kennedy, was confident he had the necessary votes to get Thomas confirmed without Ted's support.

Then Anita Hill surfaced. In the space of a few tumultuous days, the focus shifted from judicial philosophy to personal conduct and veracity. And that meant Kennedy's name was almost guaranteed to be dragged into the same awkward conversation.

Like Thomas, Hill was an African American and a graduate of Yale Law School. She had grown up on a farm in rural Oklahoma. After serving as Thomas's assistant at the Department of Education and Equal Employment Opportunity Commission, Hill had left Washington to teach law back home in Oklahoma. She had never spoken publicly about her dealings with Thomas, with whom she had stayed in periodic touch since leaving Washington. Hill had, however, told a handful of friends about aspects of that association that troubled her. As Thomas prepared to testify before Congress, word about Hill filtered back to Senate aides. Hill was contacted, and with some reluctance she drafted a four-page statement and sent it to committee members. At the direction of Biden, head of the Judiciary Committee, Hill was then interviewed by the FBI. Suddenly the Thomas nomination was in serious jeopardy.

According to Hill, Thomas had subjected her to crude, sexually charged remarks at various points during the years they had worked together, describing XXX-rated films he had seen and bragging about his own sexual prowess. Hill also said Thomas had suggested they "go out socially" on numerous occasions, but she'd always said no. As word of Hill's statements circulated among Senate staffers, pressure mounted to reopen hearings and call Hill to testify.

"At that point I thought it was only a vague inquiry," recalls Hill. "What I told them was, I think you should investigate. But I didn't think my experience was the lone experience" with Thomas's behavior toward women. She adds, "I wasn't thinking this was going to be hard for me to prove. I thought other people had come forward."

Mindful of what had happened to Bork, a former Yale Law professor of hers, Hill also knew how contentious the process could become. "It was one thing to see a nominee get treated like that, though," notes Hill, "and another thing for it to happen to a witness."

Danforth was at home on a Saturday night when Orrin Hatch of the Judiciary Committee called to warn him about an upcoming National Public Radio report on Hill's allegations that, along with a similar report in *Newsday,* left Washington in an uproar. Danforth lobbied hard to block further hearings, without success. In a display of solidarity with Hill, seven female members of the House of Representatives, all Democrats, marched over to the Senate and demanded that she be heard.

Across Capitol Hill, heated discussions took place over what constituted sexual harassment. Because Hill had remained in touch with Thomas, some suggested, his behavior must not have been so bad. Colorado Representative Patricia Schroeder countered with this argument: "Maybe the Senate needs to learn what the Supreme Court laws on sexual harassment are," she said. Writing in the *New York Times,* Maureen Dowd quoted Schroeder and went on to say the debate boiled down to "the different way men and women look at sexual crime because of the vastly different life experiences they bring to the subject."

October 11 opened three more days of testimony. Thomas led off, angrily denying Hill's charges and insisting they'd done "a grave and ir-reparable injustice" to him and his family. Hill followed, testifying for nearly seven hours while millions of Americans watched on television. In often graphic detail, Hill described Thomas's fascination with por-nographic movies of the kinkiest kind imaginable. Committee mem-bers who had only read the FBI report were stunned, recalls Simpson. "There was nothing in them about Long Dong Silver"—a porn-movie star Thomas had allegedly discussed—"or pubic hair on Coke cans," referring to when Thomas allegedly picked up a can of Coca-Cola he was drinking in his office and said, "Who has put pubic hair on my Coke?" Simpson recalls, "If you think America was surprised, how about the committee?"

Republicans mounted a blistering counterattack on Hill, led by Ar-len Specter of Pennsylvania, a former prosecutor, and Hatch, who was also a friend of Ted's. At one point, Specter raised the issue of whether Hill might have perjured herself. When Thomas returned for another round of questioning later that evening, he complained that the whole process had turned into "a high-tech lynching for uppity blacks."

Ted said little while Hill was being questioned, at times looking embarrassed by the graphic nature of her testimony. For two more days, witnesses were called to corroborate or rebut the testimony of both Thomas and Hill. As the process ground on, Hill was portrayed as a combination of spurned woman, sexual fantasist, and pathological liar. By day three, the senator had heard enough, raising his voice to protest what he called the "character assassination" of Hill.

"The issue isn't about discrimination and racism," Ted said angrily. "It is about sexual harassment." He went on, "Are we an old boys' club, insensitive at best—and perhaps something worse? Will we strain to concoct any excuse? To impose any burden? To tolerate any insubstan-tial attack on a woman in order to rationalize a vote for this nomina-tion?"

That did not sit well with Republicans defending Thomas's honor. Sniffed Specter, "We do not need characterizations like 'shame' in this chamber from the senator from Massachusetts." Hatch, in what he later swore was not intended as a reference to Chappaquiddick, said that for anyone who believed Kennedy, "I know a bridge up in Massachusetts I'd be happy to sell them."

In the end, Kennedy's defense of Hill amounted to too little, too late. Thomas won confirmation by a narrow 52–48 margin as polls indicated more Americans believed Thomas than they did Hill. Kennedy was widely criticized, even ridiculed, in the aftermath. On *Saturday Night Live,* a sketch lampooning the hearings had Kennedy (played by cast member Phil Hartman) advising Thomas on dating tactics. "It was obvious he'd been defanged," says Wattleton. "His personal life perhaps mitigated the kind of blazing attack he'd become known for."

Friends say Ted was as troubled by the hearings' outcome as they were by his listless performance. To this day, Hill believes that with his personal life under intense scrutiny and the Palm Beach trial looming, a more spirited defense by Kennedy might have hurt her cause more than helped it. "I'm not saying that's what he was concerned with," says Hill. "But because of the situation he was in, I could see people possibly discrediting both of us. I know a lot of people say he should have been more aggressive. But given the circumstances, I'm not sure it would have made any difference at all. It could even have had a negative impact." Years later, Hill sees Kennedy's performance less as a personal disappointment than "a lesson in how we cannot really fight for equality unless we internalize that fight in our day-to-day lives. In that sense [Kennedy] was no different from anyone else."

Hill never spoke with Ted about her committee appearance. However, after she returned to Oklahoma, he called her mother's house one morning. Told Hill wasn't taking any more calls, he said goodbye and hung up. "The chance to talk to him had passed, and I'd missed it," she says.

More than 500 reporters flocked to Palm Beach for Willie Smith's trial, which began shortly after Thomas's confirmation that fall. Carried live on CNN and Court TV, it became the most watched trial in U.S. history up to that time. Even the television feed was fraught with controversy, recalls Roy Black, Smith's lead defense counsel. Black had initially objected to having cameras in the courtroom, believing they would only add a "titillation" factor while putting his client at a disadvantage. He was dead wrong, says Black.

"This really marked the beginning of professionally presenting trials to a TV audience," he says. "Court TV opened up the courtroom and showed how it operated. It did an excellent, educational job and in that way was a huge sea change from what had come before—one that ironically worked to our advantage."

Smith further benefited from a key decision by Judge Mary Lupo, who disallowed testimony from three women who claimed Smith had also sexually assaulted them. As for Ted, says Black, he was unable to guide his nephew's defense because he was being called as a prosecution witness. And that, according to Black, was a fatal mistake by the district attorney. "They thought they could attack [Ted]," he says, "but they grossly underestimated his charisma, his star power, the fact that he'd survived a lot tougher battles in his life than this one. As soon as he walked into that courtroom, you could tell this was going to be a disaster for the prosecution." Assistant state prosecutor Ellen Roberts recalls that "after we decided to put Senator Kennedy on the stand, he said he wanted to meet with one of us. I was the one. 'What do you want me to say?' he asked. 'Well, Senator,' I said, 'the truth would be nice.' "

Bowman and Smith were the star witnesses. Her face hidden from television viewers by a blue dot, Bowman testified for nearly ten hours. At one point, she said, Smith "had me on the ground and I was trying to get up because he was crushing me. And I was yelling 'no' and 'stop'. . . . He slammed me back on the ground and then he pulled my dress up and he raped me. I thought he was going to kill me." Smith contended he was being victimized by a woman who had turned a consensual sex act into rape. After calling her by the wrong name while they embraced, said Smith, "She sort of snapped. She got very, very upset and told me to get the hell off her." Asked if family members might have tailored their stories to fit his, Smith shot back, "If you're implying that my family would lie to protect me, you're dead wrong."

Most analysts agreed that neither Bowman nor Smith had been seriously challenged during cross-examination, setting up a he-said, she-said scenario that favored the defense. After all, Smith would have to be found guilty "beyond a reasonable doubt."

Ted took the stand on December 6. In the courtroom were his sisters Jean Smith and Pat Lawford along with Vicki Reggie, who had helped prepare him to testify. During 45 minutes of questioning, he appeared relaxed and confident, flashing an occasional smile as jurors listened intently. No, said Ted, he did not hear any screams that night. Yes, he regretted not having gone for "a long walk on the beach" rather than inviting his son and his nephew out drinking. Only when Bill Barry and Steve Smith were mentioned did Ted become visibly emotional, saying Barry had been the one who "knocked the gun out of Sirhan Sirhan's hand" after Bobby Kennedy had been fatally shot. Smith, he continued in a husky voice, "was very special to me" and had been much in his thoughts that night. "We're a very close family," the senator averred. Standing over by the defense table, Black sensed that the ballgame was over. "Suddenly it wasn't the Kennedys out carousing but a sense of melancholy hanging over them that the jury saw," says Black.

Ted left the courthouse hugging Jean Smith. Five days later, the jury took seventy-seven minutes to acquit Willie of all charges. Expressing satisfaction with the verdict, Ted said, "Most of all, I hope that Willie, whom I love very much, can resume his life and his medical career, and that other members of our family who are private persons can regain their privacy."

In late 1993, the Kennedys put their Palm Beach estate on the market. It was bought eighteen months later by a Manhattan bank executive for an undisclosed sum.

CHAPTER
23

NINETEEN NINETY-ONE WAS a year that transformed Ted's life, thanks in part to a June party celebrating Edmund and Doris Reggie's fortieth wedding anniversary. The Reggies were old, cherished friends who'd supported Ted during bad times and good. A retired Louisiana judge and former banker, Edmund had ties to the Kennedy family dating back to 1956, when, as a young aide to Governor Earl Long, he had marshaled Louisiana Democrats to support Jack's vice-presidential bid. Edmund had gone on to manage presidential campaigns in 1960 (for Jack), 1968 (Bobby), and 1980 (Ted) in Louisiana. Doris was a feisty party chairwoman who, resisting a push to have Jimmy Carter nominated unanimously, had cast the only Louisiana floor vote for Ted at the 1980 Democratic Convention. "I could never vote for anyone but Teddy," she had proudly declared.

In a political world where alliances ebbed and flowed, the Kennedys had no more loyal friends than the Reggies of Crowley, Louisiana. If the bond between the two families was originally built on politics, though, it had grown over the years into something deeper. The Reggies were Lebanese-Americans with Deep South roots. The Kennedys were Irish-Catholic Northeasterners. Their superficial differences notwithstanding, the Reggies and their six children had more than a little Kennedy in them. Edmund was an unabashed liberal from the heart of Dixie, a civic and civil rights leader admired around the state, a trusted confederate whom President Kennedy had dispatched on a 1961 diplomatic mission to the Middle East. He was an immigrant's son living the American Dream and relishing every minute of it. "Last one in the pool is a Republican!" the judge was known to bellow at his kids. He and the senator, gregarious men with robust senses of humor, loved each other's company. After Bobby died, says Edmund Reggie, "I considered Ted my best friend." His nickname for Ted? The Commander.

In ways Ted could scarcely have anticipated during periodic visits to Crowley in the 1970s and 1980s, the Reggies would soon become even more pivotal to his life. Crowley, population 15,000, is located in southwest Louisiana on the outskirts of the Atchafalaya Swamp, a three-hour drive west of New Orleans. Its principal engines of commerce are rice, soybeans, and crawfish. And while it seems just a charming small town on the surface, it has always had a special political sophistication as the home to, among others, former Senator John Breaux and ex-governor Edwin Edwards, a close friend of the Reggies. In 1959, Jack and Jackie Kennedy visited the town at Edmund's invitation to celebrate its annual International Rice Festival.

Photos of the event show a smiling JFK sporting an elegant, rice-studded fedora, an incongruous portrait of the famously hat-averse Jack, but one that helps explain how he carried Louisiana in the 1960 presidential campaign, even though southwest Louisiana is, in the words of one local newspaper executive, "far, far from liberal."

The future president and his charismatic wife were greeted by a cheering throng of 135,000. Afterward, they attended a lavish reception at Edmund and Doris's home, where such gatherings had become de rigeur for vote-seeking politicians, famous or not. "If you were running for office in Louisiana, any office," observes Gregory Reggie, the fourth of six Reggie children and now a practicing lawyer in Crowley, "a visit to our house was practically mandatory."

Southwest Louisiana is also home to a large, vibrant community of Lebanese-Americans for whom education and entrepreneurship have long been driving forces. Both of Edmund's parents emigrated from Lebanon to Crowley, raising their children in a home where both Arabic and French were spoken. Doris's father, Frem Boustany, settled in nearby Lafayette, bought a local bakeshop, and turned it into the largest bakery chain in the state. Their offspring were encouraged to study hard and make the most of their opportunities.

Edmund and Doris Reggie exemplified those values and instilled them in their own children. After graduating from Tulane Law School, Edmund became the youngest sitting judge in the country when, at age twenty-four, he took over a vacated city judgeship. He remained on the bench for the next twenty-six years, turning down a federal judgeship offered by then Attorney General Bobby Kennedy because he thought it would be boring. As a city judge, he acquired a reputation for firmness but fairness, especially in cases involving juvenile offenders. In 1952, he desegregated his courtroom—without incident. Beyond the courthouse, he spoke forcefully for civil rights when it was not always popular, backing a strong Democratic Party civil rights platform in 1957, just two years after Martin Luther King Jr. led the Montgomery, Alabama, bus boycott. He also served Louisiana in several high-profile capacities, always pro bono, including welfare commissioner, member of the Commission on the Status of Women, and gubernatorial counsel. In that role, he oversaw a sweeping reorganization of state government in the 1970s.

In 1959, Edmund founded Acadia Savings & Loan of Crowley. The bank and its demise would become a blemish on an otherwise admirable record of business enterprise and public service. Acadia failed in 1987, part of a nationwide S&L collapse that rocked America's financial institutions. For Edmund, who served as board chairman, the collapse had particularly painful repercussions. Federal prosecutors looking into questionable lending practices during the bank's steep decline targeted Reggie, whose close association with Governor Edwards (in 1998, Edwards was convicted on multiple counts of racketeering, mail fraud, and extortion, drawing a ten-year prison sentence) didn't help him. Their lengthy investigation led to a thirteen-count indictment and two separate trials for Edmund, who ultimately pled no contest to one count of misapplying bank funds. Noting that Edmund had not profited personally, the trial judge imposed a $30,000 fine and ordered three years' probation plus four months' home detention. Maintaining his innocence to this day, Edmund says he's rejected any talk of a presidential pardon because, "I'd have to say I was guilty and I'm sorry, but I'm not—because I didn't do anything wrong."

If life in Crowley had a small-town flavor in the 1960s and 1970s, it was seldom boring in the Reggie household, where family, food, faith, and friends took precedence over nearly everything else. "We grew up Mayberry-like," Gregory Reggie recalls. "Our father came home from work every night, and everyone sat around the dinner table. There was no TV on. We said grace, ate dinner, and talked about what was going on in the world. We were all encouraged—no, expected—to participate. 'Are you reading a newspaper?' he'd ask."

It was, in more ways than just the dinner conversation, an updated version of Joe and Rose's household, where closeness and competition went hand-in-hand. Friends and schoolmates were constantly swirling through the house, which boasted a swimming pool, pool table, jukebox, and pinball machine. Like old Joe Kennedy, Edmund even procured first-run movies to show at home. One of Edmund's clients, a movie distributor, supplied the hit films every week for a backyard theater Edmund installed, complete with popcorn machine and projectionist. Thursday night was movie night. "It was pretty cool for a small town," Gregory says, looking back. The Reggie children attended parochial schools in Crowley and took summer courses at Choate, the Connecticut school where Jack Kennedy prepped. Three of the six went to law school. Once they began heading off to college, Doris and Edmund installed a home WATS line so they could chat every day. It was that kind of family.

The anniversary party took place at the home of Vicki Reggie, thirty-eight, the couple's second-oldest child, who lived in the Woodley Park section of Washington. Two decades younger than Ted, she came from a different generation, a different place in life than the senator. Despite the close family ties, she had no recollection of even having met Ted Kennedy until the summer of 1976, when she interned in his Senate office mailroom. She and the senator barely interacted that summer, sharing only a brief conversation and photo op as her internship was coming to an end. After a stellar high school career—straight As, an "all-around everything," as family members describe her—Vicki had gone on to graduate with high honors from H. Sophie Newcomb Memorial College, an auxiliary of Tulane University in New Orleans, preparing to enter law school. In the fall of 1976, Vicki began Tulane Law School, where she served as editor of the law review on her way to graduating summa cum laude in 1979.

She married telecommunications lawyer Grier Raclin after both clerked for the same federal appellate judge in Chicago. Other than occasionally crossing paths with Ted on Nantucket, Vicki had seen little of the senator since her internship while busy building her career and starting a family. After Chicago, Vicki and her husband moved to Washington, where she worked for a small firm specializing in tax law. By the late 1980s, that firm had been taken over by Keck, Mahin & Cate, a larger, Chicago-based firm seeking more of a professional foothold in the nation's capital. In November 1982, Vicki gave birth to a son, Curran, embarking on a demanding path juggling motherhood and professional life. A daughter, Caroline, came along in 1985.

But her marriage to Raclin didn't last. After their divorce, in 1990, Vicki retreated from the Beltway social circuit. Being a single parent while managing a demanding career precluded having much of a dating life. She had also made partner at her firm, combining what colleagues say was an ability to master complex financial transactions with a striking degree of emotional intelligence and a vivacious personality that impressed colleagues, clients, and legal adversaries alike. "Vicki was a real star," says Steven Engelberg, who ran the law office where Reggie worked. "Not only was she a great lawyer, she had tremendous political skills and a great sense of humor."

Her specialty was managing so-called work-outs, cases in which the firm's clients—mostly banks—needed to restructure financial arrangements with debt-ridden customers. By their nature, work-outs often created tensions between lender and lendee. In one instance,

Vicki's firm was trying to cultivate a relationship with a large bank in the D.C. area. Bank executives had steered a couple of smaller test cases their way, recalls Engelberg, and Vicki was assigned a lead role. Six months later, the bank became a major client, one executive confiding to Engelberg that Vicki was a big reason why. Whereas most bank lawyers treated defaulting customers like criminals, he noted, Vicki understood they might become valued customers again some day. Instead of burning bridges, she labored to rebuild them. "There are very few lawyers who know how to do this," Engelberg says admiringly. "And Vicki was the best."

Ted quickly witnessed many of the qualities that made Vicki such an outstanding lawyer—sharp elbows combined with an even sharper wit—after he rang the doorbell the night of the anniversary party. "What's the matter," she said, smiling at the senator, "you couldn't get a date?" He followed her into the kitchen while she finished making dinner. They talked for several hours more, mostly just the two of them, more than they ever had before, as the party wore on. A few days later, Kennedy asked her out on a bona fide date. More social than romantic at first, their meetings gradually deepened into a mutual affection that took both by surprise.

"Vicki would call and tell me, 'Oh, Mom. We're just friends,' " says Doris Reggie. "Then one day, I sensed a change of tone in her voice. To me, they started out as friends and fell in love."

What made Vicki different from the scores of other dates Kennedy had pursued and discarded over the years? She was youthful and attractive, certainly: 5'8" with hazel eyes and a sophisticated air about her. Intelligent, politically savvy, a lover of opera and pro football, an accomplished cook, fluent in French. More significant, perhaps, she was raising two young children who were central to her life. For all his middle-aged roistering, Kennedy loved children and never seemed happier than when surrounded by them.

Vicki, too, put her children first and was charmed to discover that Ted enthusiastically agreed. One evening at Vicki's house, she apologized for constantly having to dash upstairs to tend to her children, then eight and six. "A child calling for its mother is the most beautiful sound in the world," Ted said to her. "Don't ever apologize for that." Heather Campion, a longtime Kennedy friend, recalls what a radical change Vicki caused in Ted. "His life was going in a very different direction when they met, then it all came together afterward. Vicki made Ted Kennedy much more accessible to us than he'd been before. None of us had ever seen or known him that way, as a family man, a romantic man. He became much more of a complete human being after meeting Vicki."

Unlike Joan and other wives of Kennedy men, Vicki also shared his political interests, enabling her to serve as partner and troubleshooter in all aspects of his life. As her years of negotiating financial work-outs proved, she also had the skills necessary to manage the ebbs and flows of a large group of people with sometimes competing interests, which is what the Kennedy family had become by the early 1990s. Ted had worked desperately hard to keep his extended clan together, but it was becoming harder and harder as divorces, deaths, and scandals were pulling at the fabric of the family. He needed help.

After they'd been dating for a few weeks, Vicki later recalled, Ted was stuck on Capitol Hill and could not make it to her house for dinner, where he'd gotten used to helping with the children's homework and reading them bedtime stories. At that moment, she said, "I started to realize more and more that this man was very important in my life." To Pamela Covington, a close friend of Vicki's, the couple's affection for one another was immediately obvious. Well aware of the senator's past reputation, Covington also says she was unconcerned that Vicki would go the way of other Kennedy girlfriends. "Vicki, for all her sense of humor, can take care of herself," says Covington. "She's a big girl. I knew that whatever decision she made would be the right decision."

Edmund Reggie, who had seen plenty of what he calls Kennedy's "wild side," was similarly unconcerned. "There was no romance before Vicki, none," he asserts, believing that once Ted found the right partner, there would be no more cheating. "I knew how strong his religious faith was. And I knew in the end that was going to prevail." Vicki would later be asked about Kennedy's reputation for womanizing and whether it had given her pause. "I know him," she responded. "I know the tremendous respect he has for me, and for his daughters, and for his mother. I think that says it all."

That Halloween, Ted asked if he could escort Vicki's children as they went trick-or-treating in the Woodley Park area. Neighbors had already taken notice of his frequent comings and goings at Vicki's house—there was no more recognizable person in Washington than Ted Kennedy—yet even they were startled to see the senator, sans costume, ringing doorbells with two small children in tow. With phones ringing up and down the block, Ted appeared on the doorstep of the home belonging to the Chinese cultural attaché. A man answered the doorbell, saw Ted standing there, invited him to sit down, and raced upstairs to tell his boss who had dropped by. Vicki and Ted burst out laughing when they heard a voice say, "You stupid fool! That's someone in a Ted Kennedy mask!"

By November, Ted had decided where he wanted this relationship to go. Relaxing at Vicki's house one evening, the pair was listening to a recording of *La Bohème* when the senator asked if she would like tickets to an upcoming production at the Metropolitan Opera in New York. She agreed, and one early December day Kennedy sailed from Hyannis Port to Nantucket to pay a call on Edmund and Doris Reggie. "I want to marry Vicki," he announced, "and I want your permission."

The Reggies happily said yes. Still, it was not until January that he formally proposed while they were at the Met and not until a subsequent trip to the Virgin Islands, where the couple stayed with Ted's sister Pat, that Vicki received her diamond and sapphire engagement ring, which Ted had discreetly placed on a piece of coral for Vicki to discover while scuba diving. Their engagement remained a private affair until March, when Caroline Raclin mentioned it in kindergarten one day to a classmate whose parents worked for the *Washington Post*. Once the news broke, Kennedy phoned close friends and associates, including several former girlfriends and his ex-wife, Joan, to share the news.

Vicki put her house on the market, preparing for her new life as the senator's wife. On July 3, 1992, they were married in a civil ceremony held in the living room of Kennedy's McLean, Virginia, home. Escorted by Edmund, Vicki wore a knee-length dress of white lace over silk and carried three white roses. Guests included Eunice and Sargent Shriver, Jean Smith, Patricia Lawford, Ethel Kennedy, two of the senator's three children (son Patrick was unable to attend), and Vicki's mother, siblings, and children. During the half-hour ceremony, family members read passages from George Eliot and Elizabeth Barrett Browning, culled from a poetry anthology borrowed from Rose Kennedy's library. The Irish-born singer Maura O'Connell performed. The senator's wedding gift to Vicki was an acrylic painting of daffodils he'd made. Guests received a reproduction of the painting with an inscription by Wordsworth: "And then my heart with pleasure fills/ And dances with the daffodils." They dined on hummus and pita bread, Louisiana lump crab, and filet mignon, circling the bride and groom as they danced to "You'll Never Know," Vicki and Ted's favorite song. The couple honeymooned in Vermont, then showed up in New York for the Democratic National Convention and Bill Clinton's coronation.

The news stunned many who had taken Kennedy at his word that he'd never marry again, raising suspicions that he was doing so only for political reasons. The Palm Beach scandal had turned his chaotic personal life into a political issue. Suspicions about his motives for marrying Vicki were all the greater for the fact that their courtship, while lasting nearly a year, had somehow escaped much attention amid swirling coverage of Willie Smith's rape trial. Edmund Reggie dismissed such talk as foolishness. Nobody in his right mind, he told one reporter, would look to improve his political standing by committing his whole life to a woman with two young children.

As for the possibility that the marriage could help him with his own legal difficulties in the upcoming bank fraud case, he quipped, "As good a friend as Ted is, I doubt he'd marry my daughter" just to rescue an old friend. Privately, he advised his daughter to keep the marriage in perspective. "I told her," he says with a laugh, "that the order in which Teddy holds you is as follows. First comes the Senate, second is *Mya* [his sailboat]. Third and fourth are his dogs. You're fifth, and you've got to understand that." Vicki, he recalls, grinned while replying, "I know what you're saying so well."

CHAPTER
24

WITH HIS PERSONAL life stabilized, Ted still had work to do to restore his political life. The summer of 1994 was winding down when David Burke, who had left Ted's office decades earlier, fielded a call from fellow Kennedy loyalist Milton Gwirtzman. Gwirtzman wondered if Burke had been following the senator's reelection campaign, which appeared to be in serious jeopardy. To Burke, it was unimaginable that the senator would have trouble winning in Massachusetts. In every race since 1962, Ted had captured at least 60 percent of the vote. He had raised $3.6 million for this race. He had steered hundreds of millions of federal dollars toward the Bay State, whose economy remained mired in recession. It was a great record, Burke thought. Unfortunately, the poll numbers and news columns told a different story.

Ted's 20-point lead had shrunk to practically zero. The twenty-fifth anniversary of Chappaquiddick had been widely noted. Joan was seeking a new divorce settlement. Ted's noticeable girth and unsteady gait, the result of chronic back pain, called unwelcome attention to his age and physical condition. Old demons were proving hard to escape and old friends were suddenly harder to win over. Pundits who had been kind to Kennedy in the past were now writing about his political career in the past tense. "If Democrats were thinking about the future," observed the *Boston Globe*'s Martin F. Nolan, describing a September Democratic Party "unity breakfast," "they were thinking aloud about a future without Kennedy." Despite having widely traveled throughout Massachusetts since the Palm Beach trial, spending more than 100 days a year crisscrossing the state, Ted was having difficulty defining himself to voters. According to one focus group, many remained unsure of his position on national health care, a legislative issue on which Kennedy had long taken a leading role. Yet they knew quite a lot about Willie Smith and Au Bar.

Tactically the campaign had gambled—and lost—by suspending advertising for six weeks in an effort to conserve badly needed cash. As a result, the airwaves had been left to Kennedy's likely Republican foe, Mitt Romney, who would go on to seal the GOP nomination in mid-September. Romney had taken full advantage, going after Kennedy with guns blazing on issues like welfare and crime. In one ad, a ponderous Kennedy was shown lowering himself slowly onto a park bench, an image that contrasted sharply with Romney's manifest youth and vitality.

Indeed, Kennedy, sixty-two, had never faced an opponent as well-funded and telegenic as the 47-year-old Romney, a wealthy, Harvard-educated venture capitalist who had jumped into the race after Governor William Weld had decided not to. Romney had deep political roots of his own, being the son of former Michigan Governor George Romney, a gregarious, charismatic figure who was once considered the Republicans' best answer to the Kennedys. Now, with Republicans across the country poised to blow away the Democrats, Ted particularly resented Romney implying that the senator's time had passed. Recalls one campaign staffer, "He was offended that someone like that could come along and take his Senate seat by buying it."

Burke phoned Kennedy, offering to help any way he could. Ride around the state with me in my campaign car, Kennedy asked him. Nothing else, just ride along. A kid's job, thought Burke. "What he really needed," Burke recalls, "was an older hand like me to talk to."

In fact, a platoon of old hands was being summoned back to shore up the campaign. Bob Shrum was already writing speeches and advising on media strategy. John Sasso and Paul Kirk had enlisted, too. Tom Kiley and Jack Corrigan were running polling and research, Rick

Gureghian the press office. Ranny Cooper arrived shortly after Burke did, immediately smoothing lines of communication between the candidate and his young campaign staff.

Michael Kennedy, one of Bobby's sons, held the campaign manager's title; although well-liked, he had never run a campaign before and ceded many of the day-to-day details to more experienced aides. Charles Baker and Robert Donahue beefed up field operations that had languished badly since Kennedy's 1988 race against a then-little-known Republican named Joe Malone. Joined by Vicki and Edmund Reggie, all were veterans of presidential-level campaigns and knew what it took to wage all-out war in a tight race against a formidable enemy. "It's like the Marines," says one former legislative aide, speaking about the loyalty Kennedy has accrued over the decades. "There's no such thing as an ex-Marine."

Money was a major concern. Romney had pledged to spend as much as $8 million on the race. Kennedy's staff had drawn up two budgets, one if they held a comfortable lead, the other if the race was close. Plan B was now operative. With expenditures eventually toping $10 million, it provided for a series of negative ads targeting his opponent, a tactic Kennedy had never used before. While the Kennedys remained well off—just how well off had long been a subject of speculation—scores of Kennedy heirs and relatives were now living in part off Joe Sr.'s various trusts and businesses. Ted couldn't simply write a check for his campaign expenses, and he went so far as to take out a second mortgage on his McLean mansion to help pay the bills.

Romney understood that defeating Kennedy would not be easy. At the outset he calculated no better than a 10 percent chance of winning. "A Republican, white, male Mormon millionaire in Massachusetts had no credible chance," he later noted. As the gap narrowed, though, Romney began liking his chances better. His strategy: sell himself as a job-creating executive and Washington outsider, a family-values Mormon with moderate views on social issues like gay rights and abortion. Kennedy, by contrast, was old, out of touch, soft on crime, and beholden to special interests. Only the senator's personal life was off-limits, Romney told his staff. "People in Massachusetts knew that stuff already," recalls Romney campaign strategist Charles Manning. "And the national audience didn't vote here anyway."

Kennedy's challenge? Reintroduce himself to voters and grassroots party organizers, reenergize his core constituencies such as organized labor, and reeducate himself on a state economy in rapid transition. That, and teach Romney a lesson in hardball politics, if necessary. "He may have been right out of central casting, but Romney had a glass jaw," says Burke. "He'd never been in a fight where someone could be as mean to him as he'd been to others," he adds, referring to Romney's reputation for being an aggressive, to some even ruthless, corporate takeover artist.

What he would not do, vowed Kennedy, was run away from his liberal record. Earlier in the campaign, Romney had suggested that the solution to what he called the "welfare crisis" was to deny further aid to welfare mothers who bore more children—an idea that was gaining widespread currency across the country. Shrum, for one, encouraged Kennedy not to oppose the idea outright. Kennedy flatly rejected that advice, telling Shrum he would rather lose his Senate seat than endorse a plan that would hurt underprivileged families.

A September 18 staff meeting set the tone for a campaign that would grow increasingly uncivil—and expensive—as it barreled toward election day. Gathered at the senator's Back Bay apartment were a dozen top aides, including Shrum, Sasso, Kiley, Michael Kennedy, Edmund Reggie, and Vicki. With Kiley's latest poll showing Ted a point behind Romney, the mood was one of "looking into the abyss," as several attendees later put it. More focused than agitated, Kennedy waved away any talk about dwindling campaign funds, declaring that henceforth the budget would be "whatever Bob [Shrum] says it is."

Shrum, backed by Vicki, recommended going harder after Romney by recasting him as a ruthless corporate raider. Romney had no voting record on which to run. However, his firm, Bain Capital, was a major player in the complex financial world of mergers, acquisitions, and leveraged buyouts.

The campaign had hired The Investigative Group Inc., a corporate research firm run by former Watergate committee counsel Terry

Lenzner, to investigate Bain's holdings. Through union contacts, Kennedy's staff learned that a Bain Capital subsidiary, Ampad Corp., had bought an Indiana paper plant, SCM, which had then laid off workers in a cost-cutting move, precipitating a bitter strike. "I said we should go out there and film them," recalls Shrum. "Vicki said, smart. I wrote a script in case they had trouble [on camera], but when my partner Tad Devine met with them, he called me twenty minutes later saying, 'These people are unbelievably powerful, telling their story.' I said, 'Throw the scripts away.' "

Kennedy struck paydirt. Ads built around the interviews sharply undercut Romney's image as a job-creating chief executive in synch with middle-class voters. "I would like to say to Mitt Romney: If you think you'd make such a good senator, come out here to Marion, Indiana, and see what your company has done to these people," challenged one out-of-work packer. Because Romney had been on leave during the Ampad acquisition, he and his staff did not take the attack ads seriously at first. When a "truth squad" made up of six striking workers journeyed east to confront Romney, he refused to meet with them for three days, keeping the story unnecessarily alive while the candidate's negatives crept upward. Kennedy took full advantage, pressing his case with blue-collar voters across the state.

"Labor hated Romney, yes. But they also loved Ted," notes Baker. "I remember the AFL-CIO national political director saying, 'Look, just tell me what you need and we'll do it.' "

"Romney was toast after the Ampad story broke," remembers another campaign aide.

The race shifted into high gear. Romney ran ads highlighting his long, happy marriage and five clean-cut sons, a not-so-subtle reminder of Ted's turbulent familial past. Ted touted all he had done for Massachusetts, an arm draped affectionately around Vicki in one ad. Other spots underscored issues and constituencies friendly to Kennedy: senior citizens and Social Security, college students and student loans, unemployment benefits, women's issues, emerging technology companies. He boasted of saving nearly 2,000 jobs by persuading defense contractor Martin Marietta not to close its Pittsfield plant. He scolded

Romney for opposing an increase in the minimum wage while pocketing more than $11 million over the previous two years. The overriding message? Ted Kennedy is Our Guy, Mitt Romney is not.

Romney's efforts to neutralize that strategy often backfired, sometimes badly. Late in the campaign, Romney said he had attended a rally in Dorchester where a Kennedy supporter had held up a "Kennedy Country" sign. "I looked around and saw boarded-up buildings and I saw jobs leaving and I said, 'It looks like it,'" Romney quipped, linking the phrase to failed liberal policies championed by Ted. But Dorchester was a diverse community of about 90,000 people.

Quickly, a billboard sign went up next to Boston's main commuting artery proclaiming itself "Kennedy Country and Proud of It!" Local politicians including Thomas Menino, Boston's popular mayor, assailed Romney for taking "a cheap shot at Dorchester" and calling it evidence of Romney's upper-class cluelessness. When Dorchester residents got around to voting, Ted promised, "We are going to board up Mitt Romney and put him out of business."

The race was not just about Ted reintroducing himself to voters, though, or even tarnishing Romney's shiny CEO image. It was also a chance for Ted to acquaint himself more deeply with the Massachusetts that had become a center of a new post–industrial economy. "There was a sense that Massachusetts had become a 495/128, economically conservative Republican state," notes Baker, referring to the highways circling Boston where dozens of high-tech and biotech startup companies flourished. "He filled his schedule with visits to hundreds of those companies. It was counterintuitive, but if you could show people you could be a progressive Democrat and pro-business at the same time, you had a real advantage."

Meanwhile, a political all-star team led by Bill and Hillary Clinton, John Kerry, Jesse Jackson, and Caroline and John F. Kennedy Jr. stumped the state on Ted's behalf. Vicki was constantly by the senator's side as well, reinforcing his profile as a candidate, and a man, transformed.

The senator and his vibrant young wife hosted a series of gatherings at their Boston apartment, establishing a personal connection with party officials that proved invaluable down the stretch run. "Think how much more difficult this campaign would be without her," mused Democratic consultant Ann Lewis, adding that having Vicki next to him "conveys an image of him in an obviously settled, happy relationship. It's an image we want to see."

While both campaigns largely refrained from personal attacks, Ted's nephew and then-Congressman Joseph Kennedy II touched off a brushfire by publicly questioning the Mormon church's exclusionary policies toward African Americans and women, calling Romney a member of a "white boy's club." The senator's nephew apologized, but Ted kept the fire burning by saying the church's record on African Americans was fair territory. Furious, Romney pointed out that Ted had pledged not to raise the religion issue and accused the senator of hypocrisy, given Jack's 1960 presidential campaign, in which he had confronted prejudice against Irish Catholics. Ted's and Joe's remarks, the Romney campaign declared, were further proof, if any were necessary, that the Kennedys would do anything to take down an opponent. Meanwhile, Romney aides feared the Mormon church's opposition to legalized abortion would be tough to overcome, underscoring doubts about Romney's avowed support, at the time, for *Roe v. Wade*. Every time Mormonism is brought up, said Romney research director Christopher Crowley, "It makes women think, 'Is he really pro-choice?'"

With their candidate surging ahead in the polls, Ted's advisers were divided over whether to debate Romney. Burke and Sasso were among those strongly in favor. "My argument was, I'm in the back of the car, and fifty microphones are going to come through the window asking why we won't debate," Burke recalls. "This is crazy, I said. Of course he's going to debate. He's better than the other guy." Shrum, for one, thought it was risky—until the Boston media, including the *Globe, Herald*, and all three network TV affiliates, began calling for debates. To ignore them "would have been a big problem," acknowledges Shrum. "So we got very serious about debate prep."

The campaign set up headquarters in offices near Park Square, in downtown Boston, for the last few days before the October 25 debate.

Ted's aide David Smith played the role of Mitt Romney. Shrum functioned as debate moderator, while Sasso, Corrigan, and Parker stood in for reporters firing questions at the candidates. Shrum felt he had at least one ace up his sleeve. Romney had been hammering away at a Washington, D.C., real estate deal involving the Kennedy family trusts. Convinced it would come up in the debate, Shrum had the senator practice a line he would use to devastating effect when he and Romney squared off. "Mr. Romney," Kennedy said solemnly, "my family did not go into public service to make money. And frankly, we've paid too high a price."

They finished practicing on the morning of the first debate. Kennedy left for the JFK Library, where he went to rest and compose himself in the familiar place where the legacies of Jack and Bobby were preserved.

At Faneuil Hall, another small but telling detail was being addressed by Kennedy staffers. Concerned about the senator's weight, which made him look older and frailer than his sixty-two years, they arranged for a pair of specially designed podiums to replace the old models already in place. The morning of the debate, Romney aide Charles Manning was checking out the hall when Kennedy aide Paul Kirk approached him. The senator's back has been bothering him, Kirk said. Would it be all right to substitute a more comfortable set of podiums? No problem, said Manning. But when he came back that afternoon, Manning was surprised to find two podiums so large only the candidates' upper torsos could be seen.

A large and noisy crowd filled the hall that night. They were joined by national pundits eager to see if Kennedy still had what it took. Outside the hall thousands of supporters, the overwhelming majority of them pro-Kennedy, waved signs and shouted passionately for their favorite candidate. Ted's car pulled up as the senator, accompanied by Vicki Kennedy and Burke, reviewed his briefing book one last time. Burke tapped him on the shoulder. "What, what?" said Kennedy, clearly annoyed at the interruption. Burke grinned. "I just wanted to know," he said, "why [former Kennedy staffer] Steve Breyer is sitting on the Supreme Court and I'm sitting in this [expletive] car with you?"

With a hearty laugh, Ted tossed aside the briefing book and headed inside.

He waited in a small room flanking the hall while Sasso and Shrum stood outside. Romney was already onstage. As the clock ticked down toward the start of the nationally televised debate, the senator's aides held him back, a bit of psychological gamesmanship aimed at unsettling the less experienced Romney. Three million Massachusetts voters tuned in as Kennedy walked onstage to a thunderous ovation. "When is the fun going to start?" asked Romney playfully as the two shook hands.

Heavy on his feet yet clear-eyed and brimming with confidence, he hit Romney hard on abortion rights ("You're not pro-choice, but multiple choice") and health care. When Romney went after Kennedy for attacking his business record, the senator delivered the line he and Shrum had rehearsed about the Kennedys not profiting from public service. The crowd inside the hall cheered wildly. And when Kennedy had a chance to question Romney directly on the cost of his health plan, Romney protested that it was impossible to put a precise number on it. "But Mr. Romney, that's exactly what you have to do as a legislator," Kennedy retorted.

The crowd, and most pundits, judged Kennedy the clear winner. Writing in the *Boston Globe*, longtime Kennedy watcher Robert Healy summed up what had made the debate a national event, not just a local one: "The event was tied to the notion that Romney would destroy Kennedy, and the old progressive who has fought consistently for liberal programs would come crashing down. More than the political end of the last Kennedy brother, it would have been a strong score for the end of liberalism. It didn't happen."

There was one more debate to come, but it had little effect on Kennedy's 22-point lead by late October. Massachusetts voters re-elected the senator by an 18-point margin in a year when Democrats lost eight Senate seats to the GOP.

Although he would later develop a warm personal relationship with Kennedy, Romney remained bitter about his treatment during the campaign, especially the indirect jabs about his faith. "Ted's real formula for success," wrote Romney in an op-ed column seething with resentment, "was a personal, negative, coordinated and distorted attack."

Election night 1994 was the happiest campaign staffers had ever seen Ted, they say. "It was the first election he knew was a personal victory, not one he got because he was Edward Kennedy, Brother of . . ." Baker reflects. "He hadn't let down his family or staff or all the people who believed in him. It was probably his most fulfilling victory ever." Savoring that victory with an ebullient Vicki by his side, Ted Kennedy had faced his harshest critics, his most formidable opponent, and a host of old demons — and prevailed.

PART THREE

THE REDEMPTION

"He has always been there
for everyone who needs him."

—Caroline Kennedy, speaking in 1999 of her Uncle Teddy

CHAPTER
25

TED'S DECISION TO remarry caught many people off guard. But Vicki Kennedy wasted little time making clear their partnership had been long in the making, and that she had no intention of playing the retiring backstage wife.

The public unveiling of their alliance had come over Labor Day weekend in 1992, when the couple invited more than a dozen interviewers to the family compound in Hyannis Port. Giggling and holding hands, surrounded by Kennedy family mementos and the seascape he so loved, the newlyweds sat for a series of glowing portraits that contrasted sharply with the ugly press he'd gotten a year or two before. A slimmed-down Ted seemed more relaxed than he had in years, using the term *stability* to sum up the changes marriage had already wrought in his life. "I don't think there's any question that my relationship with Vicki has had a very profound, welcome, happy impact," he told one reporter. A beaming Vicki described her husband as a devoted stepfather ("He's the flame, and they're the little moths to the flame") who'd brought much happiness and fulfillment to her life as well. Asked if the union could prove politically advantageous to Ted, Vicki did not duck the question, conceding that it might. But, she added, "It's certainly not why we went into this."

A few weeks after the Labor Day interviews took place, a dozen of Boston's most prominent professional women gathered in a downtown hotel to meet the senator's new bride. None of the women knew Vicki well, although most considered themselves friends and political allies of Ted's. Vicki stood up during the luncheon and did something wholly unanticipated. "I thought the best thing I could do," she told the gathering, "is tell you a little bit about myself and how my relationship with Ted Kennedy developed." She went on to recount how their friendship had blossomed into courtship and how two people who had never expected to marry again had made a deep commitment to each other. She talked about her children and how important Ted had become to their lives, too. The women were stunned by her candor. It was, says Heather Campion, one of the attendees, "the way you'd talk to your best friends. Everyone fell in love with her." None of the women there had ever had such a personal conversation with the senator, she notes.

Back in Washington, Vicki moved her family into Ted's home in McLean, and made plans to give up her law practice. As the spouse of a powerful senator, she faced too many potential conflicts of interest to continue her legal career. Meanwhile, Ted's office schedule was filling up with soccer games, music recitals, PTA meetings, and school plays as he settled into the role of attentive stepfather. His staff was learning not to schedule appearances that conflicted with the family dinner hour. For important events, Vicki almost always was by his side. "She's very protective of him," observes one former staffer. "She was setting new rules in his life, providing structure that wasn't there before."

Before the marriage, Ted's work hours spilled over throughout the day, but Vicki reined him in, in part to make sure he got enough rest. Ted tended to wear down as the week wore on, the former aide notes, "and Vicki didn't want the tired, irritable Ted going out there" in public.

"Clearly Vicki was becoming more involved in the senator's political life," adds Steve Engelberg, her former law colleague. "She loved practicing law and was great at it, but like a lot of spouses in Washington—men and women—she had to tread very carefully [to avoid conflicts of interest]. Also, I'm guessing that [Ted] wanted more of her time anyway as he began to rely on her more politically." Many women in her situation would have hated dealing with crowds or greeting voters one-on-one, he adds. "She instinctively likes it."

Politics had not figured prominently in the relationship at first, friends of the couple say. Once Ted made it clear he wanted Vicki as a partner, though, not waiting at home at the end of the workday, her political skills were fully deployed. Whether studying the history behind a piece of legislation or getting to know Ted's colleagues, she was a quick study. Never shy about voicing her opinions, she soon became a trusted adviser and sounding board. Ted's style of decision making—he loathed yes-men—thrived on pushback and hearing opposing views. Vicki was more than capable of giving them, often with a dash of humor that kept Ted from taking himself too seriously. Early in their courtship, Ted had joked that Vicki was the only person in his life who waited three hours before returning his phone calls.

"Vicki is a brilliant woman, and I don't say that just because I'm her father," says Edmund Reggie. "Ted is a person who's sure of his position in politics, no doubt. Vicki's a woman who's sure of her position, as a mother, a lawyer, whatever. He admired that in her and she admired that in him." Adds Reggie, "I was surprised she'd absorbed Teddy's politics so quickly, though."

At the same time, the structure Vicki was imposing on Ted's personal life, one that had been conspicuously absent before they met, had a ripple effect on younger family members for whom Uncle Teddy had not always been the ideal role model. Ted looked better and felt better, presiding over family gatherings with renewed energy while making certain his stepchildren were fully assimilated into the Kennedy clan.

Meanwhile, Vicki was taking charge of family matters large and small, including helping other members cope with their own stresses and illnesses and losses. In January 1995, Rose Kennedy died peacefully of pneumonia at the age of 104. She had continued to be a forceful presence in her surviving children's lives until 1984 when, at ninety-three, she suffered a debilitating stroke. Thereafter she lived quietly in Hyannis Port, attended by nurses.

As Rose's only surviving son and her youngest child, Ted had played an important role in her life as she aged. He was very protective of her, and traveled from Washington to Hyannis Port on weekends to be with her. His booming baritone would fill the house and penetrate the near deafness of the old lady: "Mother? Mother? It's Teddy. Teddy's home! Let's say our prayers, Mother! Hail Mary, full of grace. . . ." Even if she hadn't spoken in a while, Rose would invariably begin repeating the rosary with her son. Granddaughter Caroline Kennedy once described the "special bond" between Rose and Ted: "Her face always lit up when she heard Teddy's voice from miles away."

In a speech at Georgetown University in 1977, Ted had described the large role his mother played in her children's and grandchildren's lives. "She did everything nine times. And now she's doing everything twenty-nine times again. For half a century, she has been gently stretching each child and grandchild toward her goal of excellence." When she turned 100 in July of 1990, he presided over a weeklong celebration. He spoke of her ongoing ability to inspire the younger generations of Kennedys. "Sometimes the aging process diminishes those abilities," he said. "With my mother, it's quite the contrary. We all continue to draw enormous strength from her."

By the time of her death, Rose had outlived by decades her husband and four of their nine children. The night after she died, Ted gathered his sisters and Rose's grandchildren together to share memories. Each stood and relayed poignant or humorous tales about her. Later, in a foreword to *Her Grace Above Gold*, a book of family essays he put together about Rose, Ted wrote of her impact on the Kennedy family.

"It is obvious that she had instilled in the next generation the enduring bonds of faith and love that tie us together as a family." In his own essay, he fondly recalled a scene from six decades earlier, when he had whooping cough, "having Mother all to myself as she nursed me back to health." The memories he most cherished were those that involved just the two of them. "As the last of nine children, such private times were not always easy to come by," he said. Despite having spent many lonely days as a child while Rose was away on her many extended trips, Ted was fiercely defensive of his mother and proud of her role as family matriarch. He credited her with the enduring religious faith that helped get the family through the tragedies.

After she died, he honored her memory by going to Mass every day for a year.

❧

Rose left to Ted the family's fabled Hyannis Port home, basically unchanged since the Camelot era. Knowing the depth of Ted's attachment to the place, Vicki oversaw an extensive renovation and also replaced the old family cook with one who specialized in healthier cuisine. It was a characteristic gesture for Vicki: protective of Ted, proactive in seeking to anticipate problems and ward them off, and also signaling a new orderliness in the Kennedy establishment.

Still, Vicki's sharp-elbowed way of doing things sometimes took adjusting to. She posted signs around the Hyannis Port swimming pool declaring it off-limits to anyone but Ted and his children and stepchildren. One day Joan was visiting with Kara and her children and jumped in the water. Walking by, Ethel Kennedy saw her and gasped, "Joansie! What are you doing in the pool?"

"I'm babysitting Ted's grandchildren!" Joan shouted back.

But for all of Vicki's strong will, there was a lightheartedness to her style that veteran Ted watchers could not help but notice and applaud. The senator loved parties—his annual Christmas party on Capitol Hill attracted hundreds of friends and colleagues, as did the February celebrations for his own and Vicki's birthdays. The Christmas parties often included skits performed by the couple, in costume and in character. One year they showed up as Beauty and the Beast, another year as Rhett Butler and Scarlett O'Hara, another as players for Ted's beloved Red Sox. They would exchange a few lines of ribald patter that at least once included a Viagra joke. In a few short years, Ted had gone from being the butt of Jay Leno's jokes to the subject of his own self-deprecating humor.

As Vicki came to share Ted's passion for sailing, he presented her with her own sailboat, a blue-hulled Herreshoff 12 1/2 model prized by antique-boat buffs as a classic training boat. The couple christened the vessel *La Bohème*. To celebrate their wedding anniversary each summer, Ted and Vicki would set sail on the *Mya* for several days, just the two of them, Ted plotting a course that typically took them around

Nantucket Sound to visit friends and relatives en route. It was, says one close family friend, their "special time," when the two of them would swim off the boat and stay at cozy seaside inns.

As her children grew older, Vicki threw herself into public policy issues separate from those on Ted's Senate office agenda. During the 1994 Senate race, she had gotten to know Boston developer John Rosenthal, who would go on to found Stop Handgun Violence, a Massachusetts-based organization advocating gun safety. Through Rosenthal, Vicki became active in a movement that obviously touched the Kennedys personally. Rosenthal also sat on the board of the Brady Center to Prevent Gun Violence, in Washington, a board Vicki herself later joined. "Vicki and I both grew up around guns—I'm a gun owner myself—and we agreed we needed to replicate the Massachusetts approach to handgun safety," recalls Rosenthal.

Borrowing from the mantra of Stop Handgun Violence—it pushed accountability for owners, dealers, and manufacturers of firearms—Vicki founded Common Sense About Kids and Guns, a national organization dedicated to gun safety and gun-owner responsibility. Using her national contacts, with Ted's full support, she reached out to groups representing educators, child welfare, and safety organizations, even the National Shooting Sports Association. At the Brady Center, Vicki became what others say was a primary force in revamping the board and its fund raising capability. "The issue for her was definitely personal," says Phyllis Segal, a lawyer and fellow Brady board member. Beyond the passion Vicki brought to the firearms safety issue, adds Segal, was "a real analytical and strategic sense" of what would work and how to make it happen.

The stability that Vicki brought to Ted's life enhanced his Senate career. It was one area of his life that had never lacked discipline, but colleagues noticed a new calmness behind his usual confidence. Once again, the Republicans were in control of the chamber, based on their eight-seat pickup in the 1994 elections. But just like in the 1980s, being in the minority party enabled Ted to showcase the growing range of his legislative techniques. And by his fourth decade in the Senate, he was being compared to the greatest legislators in American history.

"He came to the Senate as a very young man," says the political scientist Ross K. Baker. "In a sense his formative years were in the Senate, as was his maturity. If anyone can be said to be shaped by the institution, it's Ted Kennedy. There are people who are there a long time, who crack the code. That's what he did. He found the Rosetta Stone of how to prosper there."

Ted's sense of that senatorial code, and the mix of tradition and status that formed it, developed over the years, as he realized that the Senate, not the presidency, would be the focus of his career.

Jack's and Bobby's remarkable impact on the political process had lain in their being the first to recognize, and exploit, a newfound importance of personal image in both campaigning and governing. Where previously party affiliation and professional record had mattered most, a media age focused on the individual and his personal attributes. As it happened, the Kennedy brothers had in abundance several of the characteristics post–World War II America came to prize: youthfulness, energy, good looks. Yet, useful as such attractive qualities would prove to be in electoral politics, they were at best irrelevant to success in the Senate. The senior brothers' negligible legislative careers testify to that. One image, and one image only, mattered within the august confines of the Senate: the institution's own.

That image stood in contrast to how late twentieth century American society saw itself. Dynamic, egalitarian, forward-looking, unpretentious: these qualities the United States possessed in abundance, and the Senate not at all. The Senate was slow moving, hierarchical, obsessed with precedent and almost comically devoted to a sense of its own grandeur. In fact, the Senate had been explicitly intended by the framers as a brake on the new democracy. For one thing, it wasn't even democratic; not until 1913 were senators directly elected by voters. (State legislatures had chosen them prior to that.) As James Madison explained, the Senate would "protect the people against the transient impressions in which they themselves might be led." The very name "Senate" declared an institutional opposition to youthful enthusiasms and political faddishness. It comes from the name for the Roman Senate, Senatus, which in turn derives from the Latin *senex*, "old man."

There's a well-known anecdote about Thomas Jefferson and George Washington discussing the Senate. Jefferson, who had been serving as U.S. ambassador to France at the time of the Constitutional Convention, asked Washington what had led him to support inclusion of the Senate in the new federal government. The first president replied with a question of his own. "Why did you pour that coffee into your saucer?" "To cool it," Jefferson responded. And that, Washington told him, answered Jefferson's question. "We put legislation in the senatorial saucer to cool it," Washington said.

The Senate's greatest period of influence, which came in the decades leading up to the Civil War, memorably demonstrated this cooling capacity. A succession of ineffectual presidents coincided with the presence in the Senate of three of the leading figures in its history: Henry Clay, of Kentucky; Daniel Webster, of Massachusetts; and John C. Calhoun, of South Carolina. They dominated the national imagination, and their ultimate failure to avoid the Civil War should not obscure just how large they had loomed, and with them the Senate, in the antebellum period.

In the century that followed, as if to compensate for its diminishing prominence and achievement, the Senate had most certainly not diminished in self-importance. "Senators do not grow," President Woodrow Wilson complained, "they swell." Swelling brought with it swollen verbiage and protocol. "The distinguished gentleman from here," "my esteemed colleague from there": the courtliness of senatorial forms of address eventually became a national joke. The most famous member of the Senate for much of the middle years of the twentieth century was the clownish Senator Claghorn, a character on Fred Allen's radio show. What made him so funny was how little his blow-hard magniloquence departed from the actual senatorial norm.

What was said on the Senate floor was simply the most public form of how a senator behaved in its halls. Protocols there were equally elaborate, and violations of them were simply unacceptable. The Senate was "the world's most exclusive club," after all, and clubs have their rules. (And exclusiveness has its demography: the Senate was much older than the population at large, almost entirely male, and almost entirely white.) It's generally assumed that what earned the late Wisconsin Senator Joseph R. McCarthy censure from his fellow senators was his bullying of witnesses, misstatements of fact, and slanderous charges against public officials during his campaign to root out communists. What the censure resolution condemned was McCarthy's conduct being "contrary to senatorial traditions" and the fact it "tended to bring the Senate into disrepute." (Disrepute is a relative concept. During Prohibition, senators had their own private bootlegger, known as "the man in the green hat.")

McCarthy's downfall illustrates another curious aspect of life within the Senate chamber. Having a national following was, if anything, a drawback there. It was, in effect, an affront to institutional pride: an indication that events outside the Capitol mattered more. Even at the height of his popularity, McCarthy was at best put up with by fellow senators, when not politely disdained. An even better example might be his fellow Wisconsin Republican Robert M. La Follette. The foremost Progressive champion during much of the 1910s and 1920s, he was practically a pariah in the Senate. Not the least of Ted Kennedy's achievements in the Senate was an ability to be so important a political figure both within its halls and in the nation as a whole.

The institution that liked to think of itself as "the world's greatest deliberative body" was seldom great but always deliberate. Six-year terms gave senators an altogether different time sense from representatives and presidents, with their two- and four-year terms. The vigor that Jack and Bobby so prided themselves on was wasted in the Senate, which equally prided itself on never being hurried. Ted, however, learned to turn the Senate's eccentricities to his advantage. If it functioned as an old-fashioned men's club, he would serve as a kind of membership chairman, squiring new senators through his memento-filled office, bestowing little kindnesses on colleagues, and keeping track of members' personal interests.

But while many senators lost their sense of urgency in the gilded halls of the Capitol, Ted marshaled all the Senate protocols and courtesies to the service of a quietly aggressive political agenda. His high-powered staff was, by the late 1990s, the body's chief engine of legislation. It was like a school of government whose graduates included a future Supreme Court justice, senior White House aides, Democratic party bigwigs, and corporate leaders.

Ted himself—the man whose intelligence had so often been derided in comparison with Jack's and Bobby's—mastered the details of the various bills before the chamber better than any other senator, his colleagues agreed. He also developed an unerring sense of timing, maintaining steady pressure to advance his agenda, but knowing when to hold off and when to make the dramatic push that would finally make his legislative wishes a reality. From immigration to housing discrimination, from rights for the disabled to providing more help to poor children and struggling college hopefuls, Kennedy adopted the long view, wearing down the opposition until he got part of what he wanted. Then he'd come right back with a new proposal to get a bit closer to his ultimate goals.

Among the twentieth-century senators, only Texas's Lyndon Johnson, the man whose career was intertwined with Jack's, could compare with Ted as a driver of legislation. But, colleagues note, Johnson relied on threats as often as on charm to prod his fellow senators into line, while Ted's salient quality, beside his passion for the issues, was his patience. Unlike Johnson, says Ted's friend Jay Rockefeller, the longtime senator from West Virginia, "he's not a bully."

Still, Ted's determination could sometimes exasperate his slower moving colleagues. Representative George Miller of California, who worked with Ted to increase the minimum wage—an effort ten years in the making—recalls Ted's response during a jubilant rally to celebrate the House's passage of the bill. He gave a rousing speech on the grounds near the Russell Senate Office Building to thank supporters. Still clapping his raised hands, Ted leaned over to Miller. "I'm introducing a new bill to increase the minimum wage again," Miller recalls him saying. When an incredulous Miller noted that they hadn't even finished celebrating the latest wage hike, Ted replied, "I know, but we've got to move on this."

Although he was the prime mover of broad swaths of legislation, Ted was especially generous in sharing credit, which was unusual in the often competitive Senate. It allowed other, less active senators to claim Ted's accomplishments as their own, but he didn't mind at all—as long as the bill went through. Although Ted had worked on a Patient's Bill of Rights for decades, he tried at various points to cobble together a majority by giving the credit to other senators, particularly those with presidential ambitions. He "wanted McCain's name to be first, mine second, and his third," remembers John Edwards, who in the late 1990s was a junior North Carolina senator. When that effort failed, Ted immediately began recruiting a new team of cosponsors.

Ted also made a point of phoning his colleagues and their family members at times of personal crisis, a gesture made even more powerful by the implicit reminder of the tragedies Kennedy himself had endured. He was among the first to call Oregon's Republican senator Gordon Smith after his son committed suicide. Ted stood by West Virginia's fragile and elderly Democrat Robert Byrd when he lost his wife of sixty-eight years, Erma. After Joe Biden suffered an aneurysm and his doctors declared that his life was in danger, Ted jumped on a train to visit the Delaware Democrat at his Wilmington home, spending more than fourteen hours with the Biden family before heading back to Washington.

The expressions of care and concern were deeply genuine, an outgrowth of his own experiences. But they became, by the later decades of his career, a bond with his colleagues that often helped him overcome the ideological and procedural hurdles that are necessary to move bills through the Senate. "He realized he would have to win small battles to try to piece together some sort of plan or goal," says Senator Richard Durbin, an Illinois Democrat who has worked with Ted on a range of issues. "I can't imagine how many thousands of compromises [he's made], or how many times his heart has been broken [as] he tried to put together not all that he wanted, but what he could get."

Unlike other senators, Ted did not adhere to the protocol that required more junior members to make the trek through the Capitol's cavernous walkways and subways to visit the offices of their more senior colleagues. He found that as he aged and became more leonine and imposing, his efforts to reach out to younger senators often bore even more fruit. "It's flattering to have Ted Kennedy come up to you," says Rockefeller, who joined the Senate in 1985. "You could have been here twenty years, and it's still flattering."

When Ted himself was a freshman in the 1960s, he had paid his respects to his legendary elders and received his memorable rebuke by Richard Russell, the legislative kingpin who disputed Ted's suggestion that they both were similar by virtue of having come to the Senate in their early thirties. "He was a bit green," former Senator George McGovern says about Ted when he entered the Senate. In later years, Ted would relate the Russell anecdote himself, an expression of humility that disarmed colleagues who were in awe of the man who by then commanded prime office space in the Senate building named for Russell.

Ted's offices—both the imposing suite in the Russell building and his "hideaway" in the Capitol, a perk given only to senior senators— served their own roles in Kennedy's legislative mission. Visitors to Kennedy's Russell Building office would walk into a reception area featuring a life-sized photo of Ted as a Harvard football player, along with vintage family photos and a cartoon drawing of *The Simpsons* fictional Mayor Quimby, a character with a suspiciously Kennedyesque accent. His inner office holds drawings from his grandchildren alongside photos of Kennedy with presidents and civil rights leaders. And if Ted's history had not already stirred invitees to the office, there was the framed, hand-written note from Jack to Rose soon after baby Teddy was born, asking if he could be Ted's godfather.

Ted used the venues both to charm visitors, including freshman members of the Senate, and to throw them off balance, as he did with Supreme Court nominee John Roberts. The youthful appeals court judge was being squired around Capitol Hill by former Tennessee Senator Fred Thompson, who sat in on the meet-and-greets with senators on the Judiciary Committee, the body that would decide whether to endorse Roberts's nomination to the high court.

Ted, however, refused to invite Thompson into his inner office, and instead asked the Supreme Court nominee to come in for a one-on-one chat. Ted knew that Roberts's confirmation was likely and wanted to send a message to the man who could end up influencing the laws of the land for four decades. As Roberts perched next to a wall containing pictures of Reverend Martin Luther King Jr. and JFK, Ted lectured the conservative nominee about the importance of never backsliding on civil rights. Roberts listened attentively. Both men knew the power of the Kennedy name and legacy, and Ted's willingness to approach and engage conservatives in a respectful way surprised those who knew only of his reputation as a liberal crusader.

After a young Republican named Peter Fitzgerald won a Senate seat from Illinois by defeating the incumbent Democrat Carol Moseley Braun, he didn't expect to be greeted warmly by senior Democrats. But Ted introduced himself early on, teasing the young senator about how he could possibly be a Republican with a name like Fitzgerald. On St. Patrick's Day, Kennedy gave Fitzgerald a copy of Doris Kearns Goodwin's book *The Fitzgeralds and the Kennedys,* inscribed with a warm note. Now a banker in northern Virginia and no longer involved in politics, Fitzgerald proudly keeps the tome in his bookcase at work.

Also on St. Patrick's Day, Ted once brought shamrock-shaped, green-speckled sugar cookies—on a china plate—to the notoriously irascible Representative Bill Thomas, a California Republican who chaired the powerful Ways and Means Committee. Ted knew that Thomas would be pleased, because Ted had a shrewd sense of his colleagues' temptations. In the case of former Representative Jack Brooks, a conservative Democrat who was a longtime power on the House Judiciary Committee, the penchant was for cigars. In fact, it was rare to see the Texan without a stogie in his mouth. In a last-ditch effort to get Brooks on board for an immigration bill, Ted acquired some high-quality cigars, put them in a plain manila envelope, and went over to the House side of the Capitol for a meeting with Brooks and other legislators. Ted opened the envelope to give Brooks a peek inside, then put it on the table. When things were going Ted's way, he would nudge the envelope—whose contents were unknown to everyone but Ted and Brooks—closer to the Texan. And when Brooks balked, Ted pulled it back. A tickled Brooks ended up letting the immigration bill go forward.

Kentucky's Republican Senator Mitch McConnell—a political foe on many issues—recalls inviting Ted to come to his home state to deliver a speech to scholars in an academic program McConnell sponsored. Not only did Kennedy deliver a world-class speech, McConnell says, but he unearthed an old photo of Jack Kennedy with former Senator John Sherman Cooper, a Kentucky Republican for whom McConnell had worked as a young man. McConnell was surprised and moved by what Ted inscribed on the picture: "To the McConnell Scholars, with great respect and warmest wishes to the past, present, and future McConnell Scholars in their pursuit of leadership, scholarship, and service. I know how much President Kennedy admired John Sherman Cooper in the Senate and so did I. Mitch McConnell is part of that great Kentucky tradition and it is a privilege to serve with him today (not that we always see eye to eye on the issues)," Kennedy wrote in his long looping scrawl.

As much as Ted valued his Senate relationships, the ultimate aim of his exertions was clear to all: advancing his liberal policy agenda. As an example of how Ted's charm and intimidation could push through landmark bills, many senators hearkened back to the Americans with Disabilities Act, a 1990 law that Ted considered one of the most important civil rights measures of his career.

Helping people with disabilities was a personal issue for Ted. His sister Rosemary had been mentally disabled since her failed lobotomy, and Teddy Jr. wore an artificial leg to replace the one he lost to cancer. If a mentally disabled person or someone in a wheelchair was ever in a conversation with Ted, his staff knew not to interrupt: his bad back notwithstanding, Ted would always bend down to the eye level of the disabled person speaking to him, and would not be rushed through the encounter.

Ted had already won piecemeal protections for people with disabilities, including expanding the jurisdiction of the Civil Rights Commission in 1978 to include disabled people, requiring public schools to provide equal education to handicapped children, and mandating that polling places be accessible to all Americans. But Kennedy longed for something more sweeping: a federal law that would protect disabled Americans from job discrimination and guarantee them access to a long list of public and private facilities.

Ted needed the help of Senator Tom Harkin, an Iowa Democrat whose brother was deaf and who therefore shared a similar personal interest in the empowerment of Americans with disabilities. As Harkin pondered his committee assignments, Kennedy offered him a deal: if Harkin came onto Kennedy's Health, Education, Labor and Pensions Committee, Kennedy would let him chair the subcommittee handling issues for the disabled. And while Ted, as chairman of the HELP Committee, was well within his rights to take the publicity and power of managing the bill on the floor, he gave the assignment to Harkin, a gesture that Harkin never forgot.

"It was one of the most generous, kindest things anyone has ever done for me," Harkin says.

Meanwhile, Ted deployed many of the strategies that had made him successful over the years: he found the best experts on the issue, hosted them at his home, and hashed out the language for the new law. He also identified his allies and his potential nemeses—quickly singling out the imperious former New Hampshire governor John Sununu, then chief of staff to President George H. W. Bush, as the bill's leading skeptic. Sununu was philosophically opposed to placing costly new requirements on businesses.

Robert Burgdorf, a University of the District of Columbia professor who wrote the framework for the original bill, recalls dining with other experts at Kennedy's McLean home, an estate with tennis courts, ten bathrooms, and a Jacuzzi. Despite the palatial setting, Ted made the starstruck guests feel at home, serving a meal of chowder and crab before settling into the hard work of sketching out the bill.

The Bush administration had been dragging its feet on the matter, the guests told Ted. The president had seemed sympathetic to their cause, and a number of key Republicans on Capitol Hill supported it. The problem, the disability experts told Kennedy, appeared to be Sununu, who was refusing even to issue an administration position on the measure, thus preventing lawmakers from knowing where to begin to compromise.

Ted nodded, picked up the phone, dialed some numbers, and quickly reached his target. "John! When can we expect a position from you?" Kennedy asked jovially. A startled Sununu told him he would get one soon.

"I felt it was that [call] that had broken the logjam," Burgdorf says.

But Sununu continued to fight, nitpicking at the legislation in Capitol negotiating sessions with Harkin, Kennedy, other key Democratic and Republican senators, and several cabinet secretaries. "He had this knee-jerk thing against it," an exasperated Harkin recalls of Sununu. On point after point, Sununu would object, claiming the bill said one thing; a senior Harkin aide, Bobby Silverstein, would respond that the bill actually said something else.

Finally, Sununu lost his temper, shouting at Silverstein. Harkin was stunned. But Ted leapt up and slammed his open hand loudly onto the table, inches from Sununu.

"You want to yell at someone? You yell at me, Sununu. You don't yell at our staff. You don't treat our staff that way," a red-faced Ted shouted before the stunned group, banging the table repeatedly.

"I really thought [Ted] was going to punch him," Harkin recalls.

But the tactic worked. In a single, dramatic explosion of anger, Kennedy had changed the dynamics of the meeting. Instead of focusing on their differences, the group joined in silent admonition of Sununu.

"Everybody sitting across the table thought Sununu was out of line. All the Republicans thought he was out of line. We were all kind of agreeing that Sununu was the odd person out," Harkin says. And far from responding in kind, the fiery Sununu "just shut up. He just froze. Nobody had ever called him on that before."

Chastened, Sununu allowed a deal to go forward.

"Kennedy ate his lunch," recalls Orrin Hatch, who was at the meeting. Later, Ted chuckled at Sununu's worries that the measure would impose burdens on businesses.

"If Sununu only knew what was in that bill," he'd be horrified, Ted told Hatch.

Businesses did object to the new law, but eventually almost all of them complied. Millions of access ramps, wheelchair-accessible restrooms, hand-operated amplifiers in movie theaters, and other accommodations are the legacy of one of the most sweeping civil rights bills of the century.

CHAPTER
26

To watch Ted Kennedy by the late 1990s was to watch a man in pain. He would walk, slightly bent, from the senators-only elevator on the ornate second floor of the Capitol to the Senate chamber, his face often grimacing. It wasn't age and it wasn't aggravation over stalled legislation: Kennedy's back, broken in his 1964 plane crash, was a constant source of discomfort.

At critical moments in the Tuesday afternoon caucus lunches, when senators gathered with colleagues of their own party to discuss legislation, he would slowly raise himself to his feet and exhort his fellow Democrats to push harder for the health and education measures he believed in. But while such passionate exhortations came naturally to Kennedy, the movement itself did not. "Ted Kennedy, by any objective measuring stick, is disabled," says Durbin, Ted's Senate colleague since 1997. "At any given moment, you can look and see the pain. He doesn't wince. He doesn't complain. But when he reaches for that chair, you know he's pushing himself more than anyone could."

Health care was always a personal issue for Kennedy, not only because of his and his family's various illnesses. Ted's father, who witnessed tremendous medical advances during his lifetime, was a strong believer in the importance of seeking the latest treatments—a practice that didn't always work to his family's benefit. But it meant that throughout his childhood, Ted frequently saw his father reaching out to the most famous researchers for the latest cures, a privilege that came along with Joe's great wealth. Ted, who would also develop a habit of contacting the top researchers for advice on his family's and friends' illnesses, had frequent occasion to realize that all Americans don't have the same access to specialists.

His personal exposure to health care challenges only strengthened his determination to achieve his central goal in the Senate, the mission that drove both his daily schedule and his long-term agenda: he wanted every man, woman, and child in America to have access to decent health care. In theory, it was a goal that could be accomplished with one, big national health care program, a plan that would ensure that pregnant women would have prenatal care, that children would get their vaccinations, that sufferers of rare diseases would have access to the medicines they needed, that workers could change jobs without worrying about losing their health insurance, and that seniors would not have to choose between food and prescription drugs. In practice, Kennedy would spend decades trying to make those things happen piece by piece.

In the back of his mind, Kennedy knew he had missed a great chance early in his career. In 1971, President Richard Nixon unveiled a plan to expand health care to nearly all Americans through their employers, with the federal government subsidizing insurance premiums for the poor. The plan was strikingly similar to those that Democrats would put forth in subsequent years. But in the early 1970s, the then 39-year-old senator wanted more. He stubbornly held out for a straight-up, national health care system funded through general revenues and Social Security taxes.

"It's really a partnership between the administration and insurance companies," Kennedy griped in 1971 about the Nixon plan, his youthful face showing an irritation that would become very familiar to his colleagues in later years. "It's not a partnership between patients and doctors of this nation." In the end, neither the Nixon plan nor the Kennedy proposal passed, and Kennedy would wonder, decades later, if he had missed his only chance to install a plan—even an imperfect one—to provide coverage to every American.

Perhaps, Ted said later, "we should have jumped on that." Had Ted and his allies approved the Nixon plan, they could have built on that frame later, adding to it over the passing years. Instead, Ted had sentenced himself to an arduous path, involving years of coalition building and massaging of competing interest groups, to get, piece by piece, a series of benefits and protections for Americans of all ages and incomes. And while he never gave up on the idea of achieving a universal health plan, Ted always had a more modest proposal in the works to help him get a step closer to his ultimate goal.

By the 1990s, the list of health programs he enacted read like a bowl of alphabet soup. In 1972, he was one of the architects of the Women, Infants and Children (WIC) program that provides food assistance and access to health services to low-income women and their children. In 1986, Ted won approval of one of his biggest health care initiatives, the Consolidated Omnibus Budget Reconciliation Act, or COBRA, that now allows workers to temporarily continue their health insurance while between jobs. He would follow with the Health Insurance Portability and Accountability Act, or HIPAA, which limited the ability of insurance companies to use preexisting conditions to deny coverage to patients.

Nor did Ted ignore the more narrowly targeted health care concerns: He kept a close eye on the Food and Drug Administration, battling back efforts to weaken the agency's authority. In 1990, he worked with his friend Chris Dodd to give the FDA the same control over medical devices that it had over drugs. He also helped win passage of amendments to the Orphan Drug Act, providing incentives for drug companies to seek cures to rare diseases.

Ted was also the prime Senate mover of the so-called War on Cancer, winning approval in 1971 of a measure that quadrupled funding for cancer research at the National Institutes of Health. He later followed up with the Mammography Quality Standards Act to improve screening for breast cancer. He became a strong supporter of legislation to increase research on blood cancers such as leukemia and lymphoma, whose level of funding did not match their high incidence in the population. He pushed for legislation to expand the availability of colorectal cancer screenings.

"The conquest of cancer is a special problem of such enormous concern to all Americans," Ted said the day before the passage of his 1971 cancer bill. "I think every one of us in this body, and most families across the country, have been touched by this disease one way or the other."

Mental health, too, was an ongoing priority for Kennedy. His son Patrick had been treated for drug dependence and depression. Starting with the Mental Health Systems Act of 1980, which helped mentally disabled people stay in their homes and receive community care instead of being institutionalized, he spent years working for bills that would expand the availability of this kind of treatment and remove the stigma associated with it.

But the Holy Grail of health care—a universal program to guarantee health coverage to all citizens—continued to elude him.

In 1993, Ted thought he had a shot at it. Until that point, the health care battle had been framed largely around the uninsured—people who lacked treatment largely because they lacked money. Increasingly, though, middle-class Americans were getting frustrated with the limits of their health plans, while businesses who sought to insure their workers confronted skyrocketing costs. Politicians began reframing the battle less around the uninsured than around the adequacy of the entire system, and the need to root out inefficiencies and control costs.

Harris Wofford, one of Jack's former White House aides, won a surprise victory for a Senate seat from Pennsylvania over President George H. W. Bush's attorney general, Dick Thornburgh, in a special election fought largely over the need for health care reform. Wofford's campaign was overseen by an up-and-coming consultant from Louisiana named James Carville. His advice to other Democratic candidates was to promise action on health care.

For the 1992 presidential election, Carville signed on early with Arkansas Governor Bill Clinton, who believed that what had worked against Thornburgh in Pennsylvania could work across the nation against President Bush. In the end, Clinton won a solid victory over Bush and a third-party candidate, Ross Perot, who emphasized balancing the federal budget. Many economic frustrations had fueled

Clinton's victory, but he believed he had won a mandate to revamp the entire health system. And he had a key adviser who was eager to make it her crusade—his wife, Hillary.

Ted was thrilled, hailing the new Democratic administration for its commitment to all the hard work and politicking it would take to pass health care reform; the Clintons, he felt, would do what Carter had so vexingly failed to do: deliver on the central promise of the Democratic Party, to provide health care for all. But, as Ted knew, there were powerful reasons why America had never embraced a national health system, despite his and many other Democrats' belief that it was necessary. For starters, many Americans were skeptical of ceding to the government such a large portion of the American economy. Unlike people in European countries, many of which developed large social safety nets after World War II, most Americans believed that the private sector was the best source of innovation, and that government intervention usually choked off progress. In addition, while many Americans disliked the restrictions imposed by their insurance companies, they were also afraid that the government would do the same thing. And while the middle class may have been sympathetic toward the uninsured, they also worried about too many of their tax dollars going to pay for the health care of lower-income people.

Then there was the health care industry itself—an amalgam of insurance companies, hospitals, drug companies, and medical professionals who felt they had much to lose through health care reform.

Before the battle could even begin on Capitol Hill—where Ted was waiting to play his customary leading role—Hillary Clinton convened a special task force and took it on the road, hoping to draw on the experiences of average Americans in crafting a plan that could be presented, in completed form, to Congress. But each meeting of the task force seemed to yield another series of leaks and rumors about what services or procedures the final plan might, or might not, cover, and opposition coalesced around each potential change or oversight.

Republicans, then in the minority in both chambers of Congress, were quick to predict that "Hillarycare" would put most Americans in a heavily bureaucratic, socialist system in which they could not choose their own doctors. The health care industry chipped in with an advertising campaign that came to be defined by the "Harry and Louise" ads. Aired even before the Clintons delivered their plan to Capitol Hill, the ads showed a fictitious married couple, seated at a kitchen table, worrying aloud about the impact of the health care changes on their lives.

Ted privately felt that Hillary Clinton had not handled the politically delicate matter well. After decades in the Senate, he knew that such a historic policy change required much negotiation, consultation, and compromise—especially with minority-party Republicans still smarting over their losses in 1992. Like many presidents before him, Clinton had come to Washington eager to shake things up and make big changes; many on Capitol Hill saw the first lady's approach to health care as an example of the new administration's arrogance.

Some Democratic House members were annoyed at being asked to sign on to a dramatic policy change that the White House was writing with little input from them. The long time that the Clintons spent developing the plan slowed its momentum, allowing opponents to stoke voters' fears, while supporters, unaware of the shape of the final plan, could say little in its defense. But Ted also knew that the first lady had faced a difficult situation. Republicans were not eager to hand President Clinton an early victory, and some lawmakers were uncomfortable with the high-profile role the president's wife had assumed in developing policy.

Momentum stalled, and the plan fell apart on Capitol Hill before a vote could be taken. Ted, despairing over the lost opportunity, made a last-ditch effort in September of 1994 to revive health care reform, saying he would agree to a watered-down version. But by then the public, the administration, and much of Congress had moved on. Democratic leaders said the idea was finished for the year—at least. And when Republicans, capitalizing on public discontent over the health care plan, took back control of both the House and Senate that November, the idea would be moribund for many years to come.

Having missed for the second time a chance at national health care, Ted turned to his backup strategy: expand the availability of coverage to disadvantaged people, group by group, while trying to cure as many of the flaws in the existing system as he could. It was a mission that would yield mixed results, as Kennedy sought to navigate an increasingly partisan Congress.

Strengthening health care coverage for children was the easiest case to make, and Ted saw an opening in early 1997. Massachusetts had developed a plan to subsidize insurance policies for children, and Ted pondered whether the idea could be implemented across the nation. While many lawmakers were reluctant to approve subsidies for able-bodied adults, believing that they would lose the incentive to buy insurance on their own, no one could make the same point about children. And kids, who made up a disproportionate share of the uninsured, are relatively inexpensive to cover.

Paying for a bold new initiative in children's health was a thornier problem. Ted was intrigued by the Massachusetts plan, which relied on a tobacco tax to cover children's care. But it carried political risks; not only would Ted have to wheedle support from Republicans leery of a tax hike, he would have to convince Democrats from tobacco-producing states to go along. Dr. Barry Zuckerman, chief of pediatrics at Boston Medical Center, made his pitch to Ted at a Boston meeting, arguing that a nationwide plan funded by tobacco tax revenues could vastly expand coverage for uninsured children. But Zuckerman came away discouraged. Kennedy, he was sure, would not push the idea with his colleagues.

Back in Washington, though, Ted was thinking about how he could cobble together a coalition to pass such a program, and he identified a critical ally: his longtime friend and conservative colleague Orrin Hatch.

Hatch, a devout Mormon with a manner as proper and dignified as Kennedy's was florid and chummy, was concerned about children's health and abhorred smoking, making him a natural partner on the bill. But Ted sensed his friend was also nervous about the idea of a tax hike and afraid the plan—to be called the State Children's Health Insurance Program, or SCHIP—would give too much power to the federal government.

Characteristically, Ted brought all his weapons into battle—including friendship and humor. He corralled his then chief of staff, Nick Littlefield, an accomplished singer, to learn some of the patriotic songs that Hatch, a passionate musician, had written, and deliver a command performance in Hatch's office. Littlefield serenaded the Utah Republican with one of Hatch's signature tunes, "Freedom's Light." Hatch was impressed. "He can really belt out a song," Hatch says of Littlefield, adding, "It was one of [Ted's] ways of trying to placate me."

The song broke the tension in negotiations, and Ted followed up by inviting Hatch to dinner in McLean, where the two shared a leisurely meal with Vicki. By the end of the evening—which a charmed Hatch told Ted was one of the loveliest he'd ever spent—Hatch was sold, agreeing to Kennedy's $20 billion price tag, including an extra $1 billion that Vicki had suggested at the close of the evening.

In return, Ted worked with Hatch to find mutually acceptable terms to govern how the money should be spent, and, in the end, agreed to give states more authority in administering the program.

Kennedy and Hatch set about wooing their respective parties. Hatch tried to reassure Republicans that they were not ushering in the beginning of a national health care plan. Ted met with resistance in his own caucus: Jay Rockefeller wanted to simply expand Medicare to cover more kids. Ted fought back, arguing that such an idea would not gain enough GOP support to pass. Ted also assuaged the liberal interest groups, persuading health care and children's advocates that having the states run the program was a good idea. Hatch, meanwhile, took on the Republicans who swore they would never support a tax increase of any kind.

Eventually, both Ted and Hatch felt confident that they had enough votes to pass the measure, and sought to attach it to a budget reconciliation bill. Such bills cannot be filibustered, meaning that Hatch and Kennedy needed to eke out only a single-vote majority in the Senate.

The roadblock, as it turned out, came from an unexpected source: President Clinton. He, too, had plans for expanding health care. Both

Bill and Hillary Clinton were deeply committed to insuring kids; Hillary had served on the board of the Children's Defense Fund, and was herself looking for a vehicle to expand children's health care. But the president had made a deal with the Republican leaders who controlled Congress: no new programs or amendments would be added to the budget bill. To Ted's annoyance, the president called Democratic senators to lobby against the children's health amendment. Even in the final hours, Ted thought he might still have enough votes; he had heard—erroneously, it turned out—that Vice President Al Gore was on his way to the Hill to break a tie to pass the measure. Instead, the amendment was defeated, and an angry and frustrated Kennedy feared that he had lost a rare chance for victory on an issue he cherished deeply.

It was Hatch, ultimately, who would come through for his friend and ensure passage of the program.

Orrin Hatch despised Kennedy long before he loved him. A Pittsburgh-born lawyer who put himself through school before settling with his wife and six children in Salt Lake City, Hatch had never intended to go into politics and waited until the last day to file for the U.S. Senate race in Utah in 1976. He won in an upset after securing an endorsement from Ronald Reagan.

The former Mormon missionary had a single goal in entering Washington politics—"to fight Ted Kennedy." To be clear, Hatch notes, it was not to fight the Democrats, or control government spending, or advance a social agenda consistent with Hatch's abstemious ways. This was personal. Kennedy was the target, and Hatch thought he was the person who could bring down the Senate's most vocal emblem of East Coast liberalism. "I thought he stood for everything I did not," Hatch recalls. "I thought someone had to take him on, and I just didn't see anyone that was doing it."

But Hatch soon warmed to Kennedy, if only because the cold hard facts of power made it necessary. In 1981, Hatch assumed the chairmanship of the Senate labor committee—a perfect venue for a conservative mission—but he faced a double wallop. First, Kennedy came onto the committee as a member—"some said to put a curse on me," Hatch half-jokes—and the Massachusetts liberal, with his outsized personality and determination, started blocking some of the things Hatch wanted to achieve.

Even tougher for Hatch was the presence of two left-leaning Republicans on his labor team: senators Robert Stafford of Vermont and Lowell Weicker of Connecticut, both of whom had long-standing relationships with Ted. So Hatch summoned all he could muster of his public service ethic and approached the man he had castigated as the root of evil in Washington. "I can't run this committee without you," Hatch told Kennedy frankly. "I know it. You know it. I'm going to need your help."

Ted agreed to work with Hatch when he could, although he said he would not be willing to team up on legislation opposed by labor unions. Hatch continued to shepherd through some bills opposed by organized labor, including one lowering the minimum wage for teenagers and another converting some federal labor programs into block grants for states. Ted opposed him on each one. But the two would find common ground on other bills aimed at helping workers—such as a law banning private employers from forcing their workers to take lie detector tests—and pretty soon Hatch and Kennedy were teaming up on some of the most significant public health legislation of the era.

The alliance baffled Democrats and infuriated Hatch's Republican colleagues. Surely, there was hardly an odder couple in the Senate. There was Ted, his face and body showing the wear of the plane crash, his drinking over the years, and his periodic attempts at dieting, taking the Senate subway from the Russell Building to the Capitol to vote, struggling with his bad back. And then there was Hatch, his face almost translucent and unnaturally taut for a man about the same age as Ted, walking crisply from his office to the Senate chamber with the alacrity of one who had religiously eschewed alcohol and tobacco his entire life.

Hatch was perhaps organized labor's single biggest foe in the Senate; Kennedy was the movement's favorite senator. Hatch was instrumental in defeating the Equal Rights Amendment, while Kennedy overcame his early opposition to keep reintroducing the measure, even though momentum had long since waned. Still, there was a symmetry that bound them. Both had clear missions—one liberal, one conservative—and were relentless in fighting for them, even if it meant mounting filibusters that ruined the schedules of their colleagues. Both ended up making unsuccessful bids for their parties' presidential nominations. And while Kennedy got much closer to the goal line than Hatch, who ended his 2000 bid early in the process, both men learned the common lesson that the popularity each enjoyed among a certain sector of his party did not extend to the national support needed to become president. And both, despite their deep passions for often disparate issues, knew when to make a deal.

In an emotional tribute on Ted's seventieth birthday, Hatch tried to explain their unlikely relationship to colleagues on the Senate floor—and merely underscored the reasons fellow senators were so confused by their alliance.

"It is no secret that Ted and I are close friends, even though I am a conservative, he is a liberal; I am a westerner, he is an easterner; I am a physical fitness fanatic, he is—well, never mind," Hatch said, drawing chuckles from fellow senators.

"It is no secret that many, if not most, of my constituents in Utah disagree with Senator Kennedy on almost every issue," he continued. "I will never forget a letter I got from one of my constituents many, many years ago. From a senior citizen in Southern Utah, a very conservative part of the state. She said, 'Senator Hatch, when we heard you might run for office, we supported you. When you actually ran for office, we voted for you. And when we heard you were friends with Senator Kennedy, we prayed for you!'"

But as Hatch lovingly noted, the political partnership between the two men grew into more than a working relationship. In the odd way that opposites sometimes attract each other, Kennedy and Hatch formed a mutually reinforcing alliance, alerting each other to excesses in the other's personality. Far from fighting Ted Kennedy, Hatch stood by him as a friend through difficult times. When Ted was under public assault for his role in the Palm Beach scandal, he asked Hatch if he could send reporters to him for a vote of confidence. Hatch said he could, but he accompanied the assent with some blunt advice: Kennedy had to get his act together. If his friend kept getting into those sorts of difficulties, Hatch warned, he would have to send the Mormon missionaries to him. A chastened Kennedy, Hatch recalls, said, "I'm ready."

"A lot of my memories of [the two of] them are when Kennedy was footloose and doing a lot of crazy things, mostly with Chris Dodd, and Hatch was always the straitlaced guy," says Tom Harkin. "There were all these jokes back and forth, Hatch telling him he should straighten up, Teddy telling him he should loosen up."

But Kennedy, too, was a source of support for Hatch in difficult times. Hatch was accused in the early 1990s of impropriety involving the Bank of Credit and Commerce International (BCCI), which was closed for money laundering. Hatch was devastated, not only because he ended up paying $250,000 in legal fees before he was cleared of any wrongdoing, but because he couldn't bear to be accused of violating his oath of office. No one from the Senate called to offer support, Hatch said, except Ted, who reached Hatch from a pay phone.

"Don't let that bother you. We know you're honest," Ted told Hatch.

"He was the only one who did that," in either party, Hatch recalls.

Ted admired Hatch's sincerity, and his courage in openly aligning himself with a man so deeply distrusted by his own constituents. For Hatch, the friendship was even more profound: Hatch had lost his only brother in World War II, and Ted, the Utah senator says, became a late-life replacement for the brother he had lost.

When Rose died, Hatch came uninvited to the funeral, and Kennedy made sure his Utah friend was seated prominently in front. And when Hatch's father died, Ted and Vicki traveled to Utah to attend the services, a gesture deeply moving to Hatch. When Hatch saw them at the funeral, he immediately sat the couple in the first row with Hatch's family.

And when Hatch's grandson developed a serious case of colitis, requiring surgery, Ted stepped in to help. The procedure had not gone well, and the boy developed an infection. While Hatch prayed and fasted for his grandson, Ted contacted one of the top surgeons in the world, a doctor at Massachusetts General Hospital. "He'll take your call, call your doctor out there, and make sure everything turns out," Hatch recalls Ted telling him.

Their politically peculiar alliance became critical to passing key health legislation over the years, from funding community health centers to amending the Orphan Drug Act, the law providing incentives for private researchers to develop cures for rare illnesses. While the bills required much legislative wrangling, most of the health initiatives Hatch and Kennedy pursued were relatively uncontroversial, appealing to the desires in both parties to help sick people.

But when it came to devoting federal dollars to anything associated with AIDS, the two senators hit a roadblock. In the 1980s, it had been difficult to convince fellow senators to throw money behind treatment of the disease. With AIDS still regarded as a "gay disease," lawmakers were skittish about directing government health funds toward programs meant to stop the spread of the HIV virus, much less to find a cure. But Ryan White ended up changing that dynamic on Capitol Hill.

White was a 13-year-old boy who contracted AIDS from a blood transfusion. The tragedy of his illness — and the indisputable fact that he had not been infected through any act of his own — made him the face of a new awareness in Washington that AIDS was not just a condition affecting drug users and gay men, but a public health crisis for people of all ages and sexual orientations.

Kennedy had already secured funding in 1988 for programs to expand home and community care for AIDS patients, easier access to experimental drugs, and a new national commission to establish AIDS policy. But as with other health measures, Kennedy had not obtained nearly as much government action as he wanted. So in 1990, the year White died of AIDS, Kennedy and Hatch teamed up on a measure to provide emergency relief to the top thirteen U.S. cities hit hardest by the epidemic. Their alliance proved critical to gaining passage of the "Ryan White Act," but their success raised the ire of Senator Jesse

Helms, a North Carolina Republican known as "Senator No" for his obstruction of liberal initiatives.

Helms was bent on killing funding to fight the disease, which Helms deemed the outcome of "degenerate" gay behavior. And having failed to defeat the measure in 1990, he tried again when the Ryan White Act came up for renewal in 1995, offering an amendment saying that the money could not be used to advance homosexuality. The amendment put senators in both parties in a politically awkward position; would-be presidential hopefuls, in particular, could imagine the attack ads that would spring up if they voted against a measure that called for the federal government to avoid promoting homosexuality. But from a practical perspective, the amendment was unworkable, since teaching patients how to practice safe sex was a critical part of controlling the disease.

The Ryan White Act was on track for renewal, and then "in sashays Jesse Helms," Hatch recalls of the July 1995 day when the North Carolina legend offered the amendment he hoped would doom the whole AIDS bill. "That was just ingenious—all of the [future] Democratic presidential candidates were standing around saying, 'What are we going to do? We're going to have to vote with Jesse Helms'" to avoid appearing too liberal.

Ted, caught unaware and unable to convince Helms to back down, was furious, red in the face, and shouting at increasing decibel levels. Hatch wanted to step in to help. Staffers advised Hatch to let Kennedy handle it. But Hatch knew his conservative credentials would carry more weight with his fellow GOP lawmaker, and so he confronted Helms on the Senate floor.

"Senator, I know you're sincere," Hatch told his fellow conservative. "But this is not a gay rights bill. This is a public health bill."

Hatch's statement gave senators of both parties the cover to oppose Helms. The 1995 reauthorization for the Ryan White bill passed, and it was extended again in 2000, when Kennedy and others secured $9 billion for the program. Since then, more than half of all Americans living with AIDS have relied solely on Ryan White program funds to manage their disease.

The relationship between Ted and Hatch remained an elaborate dance even after decades of working together. Each maintained a slight wariness of the other, warning their colleagues about the other's shortcomings as negotiator. One Democratic senator said that when he told Ted he was going to approach Hatch to work with him on a bill, Kennedy advised him, "Watch out for Orrin. He says he's with you, but then he gets nervous and starts backing away." With that in mind, the Democratic senator went to Hatch, mentioning Kennedy. "Oh, you need to watch out with him. You think you agree on something, and then he tries to get something else," Hatch said. And yet the two continued to collaborate on numerous bills, ranging from Food and Drug Administration reforms to job training. The Mormon Hatch and the Catholic Kennedy even teamed up to pass a religious freedom bill—later declared unconstitutional—that put the burden on states to justify limits on religious expression.

And the dance continued when Hatch stepped in to rescue their children's health bill. Having been thwarted by Clinton in his and Ted's attempt to add it to the 1997 budget bill, Hatch tried again with a different version of the bill—one less generously funded—and offered it up in the Senate Finance Committee, then controlled by Republicans. Hatch remembers the day with pride, as his fellow Republicans rallied to his side. New York Senator Al D'Amato got up and said Hatch was right—they needed to expand children's health care. Curmudgeonly Senator Frank Murkowski of Alaska agreed, declaring, "Orrin is right."

The children's health care plan was given a second chance. Kennedy, Hatch was sure, would be thrilled. When Hatch got back to his office, his staff told him Kennedy was on the phone. Hatch took the call, eager to hear what he assumed would be words of praise. But Ted was furious. "Orrin, I have never been so betrayed in my entire time in the U.S. Senate," he thundered. A perplexed Hatch asked why. "Because of what you just did!" Ted felt sold out, feeling Hatch had pushed through a smaller package without consulting him.

The next day, a sheepish Kennedy walked over to Hatch's office to make amends. "He wouldn't [actually] say 'I apologize.' That's how he apologized"—by showing up in the office, Hatch says. The two went back to work, lobbying fellow lawmakers in a second-round attempt to pass SCHIP. The White House came on board, with Hillary Clinton personally arguing for the measure in frequent conversations with members of Congress. When SCHIP was finally signed into law in August 1997, it was authorized for $24 billion over five years—more even than Ted had envisioned. It was just one piece, one small segment of the uninsured who would have a chance for health coverage, but Kennedy was delighted.

"That's his secret of legislating," says former Senator Alan Simpson. "You take a crumb when you can't get a loaf."

And he relies on whomever can help him—Hatch as much as anyone. For that reason, many of Hatch's fellow Republicans complain that Kennedy has gotten the better end of the pairing—that Hatch has been seduced by Ted. "I don't think he's gained anything by it," fumes a frustrated Paul Weyrich, the conservative activist who remains dismayed by the Kennedy-Hatch alliance. Weyrich sought early on to discourage Hatch from aligning with Kennedy—to no avail. "He thought he had a strong enough personality and could bring Kennedy around," Weyrich says. "I thought to myself, 'You fool.' You talk about ego. You really have to have an extraordinary ego to think that somebody as dogmatic as Kennedy is, and as important to the left in this country as he is, that he is somehow going to be changed because you are interacting with him."

Had he heard it, Ted would have appreciated the tribute.

CHAPTER

27

Even though he had just lost a key vote in the Senate on a cherished piece of legislation—the Patient's Bill of Rights, his first major initiative after children's health—there was a lightness to Ted Kennedy's step and a smile on his face as he strode out of the Capitol on a Thursday night in mid-July of 1999.

For one thing, he knew the legislative battle was not over. "We'll be back to fight and fight and fight again," Kennedy vowed after the vote. But what really buoyed the senator's spirits was the prospect of the wedding that weekend of his niece Rory, the youngest child of Bobby, at the family compound in Hyannis Port. Rory had been born six months after her father was assassinated in June 1968—a turning point in Ted's life, the moment when, though only thirty-six, he was thrust into the role of family patriarch.

The wedding promised to be the kind of family event that Ted absolutely reveled in, and as he made his way down the Capitol steps, he talked animatedly about how much he was looking forward to it. Ted knew that the white clapboard houses of the Kennedy compound would fill up with more than two dozen nieces and nephews to whom he was known, affectionately, as the Grand Fromage—French for "the big cheese." He had been a surrogate dad to many of them throughout their youth: shepherding them on camping trips to the Berkshire mountains of Massachusetts, beaming up at them from the pews at their First Communions and from the seats at their graduations.

As they grew to adulthood and began having children of their own, Ted had worked to establish similar relationships with the young ones. In 1997, he had taken dozens of the younger Kennedys for an excursion on a make-believe pirate ship, and in 1998, he had organized a huge family reunion that brought together more than 100 Kennedys (half of whom were thirteen or younger) at Hyannis Port. To ensure a permanence to the memories, Ted hired a photographer and a cinematographer to record the proceedings. He was such a jovial fixture in the life of Caroline Kennedy's family that by 1999 Caroline's 11-year-old daughter Rose was drifting off to sleep each night clutching a stuffed animal she called Uncle Teddy.

He had built his entire life on personal relationships, but the deepest relationships of all were with those who also bore the name of Kennedy. "He's more than an uncle to his nieces and nephews," says Caroline. During the worst period of his life, after Chappaquiddick, Jacqueline Kennedy Onassis had asked Ted Kennedy to become Caroline's godfather to replace the slain Bobby. Ted had taken the responsibility seriously. To deepen Caroline and John Jr.'s understanding of their father's legacy, Ted had worked intensively to involve both of them in the place Ted himself cherished most as a memorial to JFK: the Institute of Politics at Harvard's John F. Kennedy School of Government. Thanks to Ted's efforts, Caroline says, she has been able to "have the connection to my father and my whole family history."

However, his attempt to perform that task for so many nieces and nephews had come at considerable cost. After Bobby's death in 1968, "Uncle Teddy was left to pick up the pieces and be harshly judged for his humanity," according to one of his nephews, Christopher Kennedy Lawford. In Lawford's view, "it all fell on him. If he hadn't stepped up and carried us all on his back for the next thirty-plus years, the family would have disintegrated many years before."

As he grew older, Kennedy was sometimes bedeviled by fears of that very outcome. Once, as he sipped a vodka and tonic in the kitchen of his sister, Patricia Lawford, Kennedy surprised the younger Lawfords by blurting out: "I'm glad I'm not going to be around when you guys are my age." When a puzzled Christopher asked him why, Kennedy replied gloomily: "Because when you guys are my age, the whole thing is going to fall apart."

His native optimism would sooner or later assert itself, though, and he would redouble his efforts to foster a sense of togetherness, and to prevent that falling apart of the family that he so dreaded. It didn't always work—some of the younger Kennedys went through protracted periods of wildness and irresponsibility, and Ted himself was far from the best role model—but when they needed him he was dependable, a rock. "He gave us a sense of continuity," says Kerry Kennedy, who was just eight years old when her father, Bobby, was killed. "That sense of a role model, someone I could depend on, was very, very important."

But Ted also sought to teach the next generation what it meant to be a Kennedy, and to inspire them to a life of service. So he had made sure to take the younger Kennedys to John F. Kennedy's birthplace in Brookline, and to the church in Boston's North End where Honey Fitz had his daughter Rose baptized. "[Ted] told us stories about politics, American history, our family," says Kerry Kennedy. Ted wanted to make sure all the kids saw the family ethic playing out in the present tense as well, so they were always welcome in their uncle's Senate office. "At twelve or thirteen, I felt free to walk in, talk to the staff," Kerry recalls. "That was just what we did."

The message Ted sent them was clear: Our family is part of the sweeping American story, which confers not just status but obligation. Public service is not just a legacy; it can also be a destiny. It was always clear to Caroline that Ted was intently focused on "passing on that [commitment to] public service and history." Adds Caroline: "All that takes a tremendous amount of time and care. But he somehow makes it a priority."

As Ted left Washington and headed for Rory's wedding, there was reason for him to feel some satisfaction that his three decades of effort had paid off. Bobby's first-born child, Kathleen Kennedy Townsend, was lieutenant governor of Maryland. After serving in Congress for twelve years, Joseph P. Kennedy II, Bobby's oldest son, had returned to Citizens Energy, a nonprofit company that he had founded to provide low-cost heating oil to poor people in the Boston area. Bobby's namesake, Robert F. Kennedy Jr., was making a substantial name for himself as an environmental lawyer and activist in the Hudson River Valley. And Rory, preparing to be married that weekend, had already won acclaim as a documentary filmmaker whose work sought to capture the lives of the poor.

Caroline had recently coauthored a book about the civil rights ramifications of the Bill of Rights. John Jr., known primarily in his younger years for his matinee idol looks and for dating celebrities including the singer Madonna, was winning new respect as the cofounder and publisher of *George*, a lively magazine of politics and pop culture. Tim Shriver had taken the helm of the Special Olympics, a favorite Kennedy cause that had been founded by his mother, Eunice, and his brother, Anthony, had created Best Buddies, a charity that recruited high school and college students to work with the mentally challenged.

As for Ted's own children, Patrick was a Democratic congressman from Rhode Island who, showing some of his father's appetite for campaigning, had also recently been named chairman of the Democratic Congressional Campaign Committee. Kara worked for Very Special Arts, a creative offshoot of the Special Olympics. Teddy Jr. had launched a nonprofit firm to help poor people move out of lead-contaminated homes.

Ted, they said, was their inspiration. But there was another, sadder duty for which the Kennedy family had long relied on its patriarch. "When things are going badly he is somebody who you can turn to," says Joe II. "Our family has gone through too many crises, too many sad times, as other families have. But every time it happens, he is the guy that people look to." Caroline puts it succinctly, saying that at any time of crisis, "He's the first person who calls, the first person who shows up."

It was that grim duty—rather than singing, dancing, and toasting at Rory's wedding—that Ted Kennedy would have to shoulder, once again, that summer weekend in 1999. And it was Caroline herself who would especially need Ted's support.

He arrived in Hyannis Port on Friday, July 16, 1999. A festive air surrounded the wedding preparations. Nearly 300 guests had been invited, and a large white tent billowed on the lawn overlooking Nantucket Sound. That night, Ted and Vicki attended Rory's wedding rehearsal dinner. Later on, Kennedy was awakened with the news that John Jr.'s plane was overdue. John, thirty-eight, was piloting a single-engine Piper Saratoga with two passengers: his 33-year-old wife, Carolyn Bessette Kennedy, and her sister, 34-year-old Lauren Bessette. He had been due to land on Martha's Vineyard about 10:00 P.M., drop off his sister-in-law, and then continue on to Hyannis Port. But it was after midnight, and there was no sign of John.

Ted quickly got out of bed and began making calls while Vicki made a pot of coffee. One of his first calls was to John's loft in the TriBeCa neighborhood of New York City. When a friend who was staying in the apartment answered the phone, Ted asked him whether, perhaps, the plane had not left yet. The friend told Ted that it had. Around 2:00 A.M., a family friend telephoned the Coast Guard at Woods Hole to report a missing plane. The caller did not at first identify the pilot and passengers, saying only that three people were on board. Coast Guard officers called back within minutes and learned their identities. By early morning, a rescue mission was in full swing, with Coast Guard cutters, Air Force planes, and Air National Guard helicopters searching the waters.

Back in Hyannis Port, a heartsick Ted stepped into the role he had played so many times before. Caroline was not there—she was on a rafting vacation in Idaho with her husband and their three children—but the senator did his best to console other members of the family. He had faced this kind of news too many times to have false hopes. Even if by some miracle John, Carolyn, and Lauren had survived a plane crash, he knew that they could not live for long hours in the 68-degree water off Martha's Vineyard.

Still, Ted kept in constant contact with the officials in charge of the search, including those at the very top: Jane Garvey, head of the Federal Aviation Administration; William Cohen, Secretary of Defense; Rodney Slater, Secretary of Transportation; and leaders of the National Transportation Safety Board. "Kennedy was intimately involved in managing everything," recalls a former aide who was working for the senator at that time. "The senator was trying to hold up the [Kennedy] family, and keep [the Bessette] family in the loop. The thing was coming at us very fast." Around 2:00 P.M. Saturday, an aide finally persuaded Kennedy to take a nap. He had not slept since the phone call the night before alerting him that John Jr.'s plane was missing. Before he would consent to shut his eyes, though, Kennedy told the aide to put together a checklist of steps that would need to be taken, and in what order, if searchers located the remains.

On Sunday—which was, by grim coincidence, the thirtieth anniversary of Ted's accident on Chappaquiddick—three priests said a private Mass for the Kennedy family under the white tent that had been set up for Rory's wedding. As the service ended, Ted held the communion chalice and offered wine to Rory, to her mother, Ethel, and to other members of the family. Later that day, Ted took several family members sailing on the *Mya*.

Sailing could not help but evoke memories of JFK Jr. In the years following President Kennedy's death, Ted had often taken Caroline and John Jr. out in their father's boat. When John was eight years old, Ted had let him take the helm and had stood behind the boy as they sailed to Newport, Rhode Island, to watch the beginning of an annual sailboat race to Bermuda. Often, Ted, Caroline, and John Jr. had walked along the beach at Hyannis Port, talking and skipping stones across the water.

The drama of the missing plane riveted the nation and cracked the heart of anyone old enough to remember little John's salute at his father's funeral. Inevitably, the loss of John also revived talk of a Kennedy curse. Ted knew it was time for a public statement. On Monday, he released one on his Senate letterhead. It began: "We are filled with unspeakable grief and sadness by the loss of John and Carolyn and Lauren Bessette. John was a shining light in all our lives and in the lives of the nation and the world that first came to know him when he was a little boy."

Meanwhile, Caroline had returned to her home on Long Island, traveling on the private jet of movie star Arnold Schwarzenegger, who was married to Ted's niece Maria Shriver and would go on to become governor of California. Ted himself wanted to visit Caroline, but did not want to trigger a media circus. Reporters and cameramen had staked out the Kennedy compound, making it impossible for him to leave unnoticed. After pondering the matter, the senator and his staff devised a ruse.

Several times over the course of a couple of hours, Kennedy's driver transported other passengers—ostentatiously holding newspapers or coffee cups so they were plainly visible—down the long private driveway and out onto the road. The idea was to get the assembled media horde accustomed to seeing the car go by. It worked: eventually, Ted got into the back seat of the car, and a blanket was draped over him. The car slipped past the reporters without causing a stir. It took Ted to the Hyannis airport, where he boarded a private plane for a flight to Long Island and made his way to Caroline's house.

Exactly thirteen years earlier, to the day, Ted had given Caroline away at her wedding to Edwin Schlossberg. And less than two months earlier, Caroline and Ted had been together for the annual Profiles in Courage dinner at the John F. Kennedy Library. Guests were shown archival footage of JFK, including an image of the president and the toddler John Jr. walking on a beach together, father gazing down at son. Caroline had joked at the ceremony about the "pointless task" of introducing Ted, a man who needed no introduction. But then she turned serious, and said: "He has always been there for everyone who needs him."

At the time, the words had seemed unremarkable, even banal, the kind of tribute that might be conferred on the guest of honor at a Rotary luncheon. Yet they were words that captured the essence of how Kennedy had come to see his role in his family and beyond. And they were words that now carried a haunting echo, because Caroline herself now needed her uncle.

Ted visited privately with Caroline and her husband and children inside their brown-shingled, two-story summer home in Sagaponack, New York. He had consoled Caroline after the death of her father in

1963, and her mother, Jackie, who had succumbed to lymphoma in 1994. Now, with the death of John Jr., Caroline was the sole surviving member of the family that had made the Kennedys a national name. Ted promised Caroline that he would identify John's body when it was found, sparing her that grim task.

At one point, Ted decided Caroline's kids needed a break, so he brought Rose, 9-year-old Tatiana, and 6-year-old John outdoors and engaged them in a spirited game of pickup basketball. It was a humid day, so the 67-year-old Ted played shirtless. He bantered with the children, and his laughter punctuated the slap-slap-slap rhythm of the basketball as he called out the shots.

After Ted returned to Hyannis Port, the bad news was not long in coming. Late Tuesday night, a section of the plane's fuselage was discovered, upside down on the ocean floor seven miles southwest of Martha's Vineyard, with John's body still strapped in the cockpit seat. The bodies of Carolyn and Lauren Bessette lay nearby. Around noon on Wednesday, July 21, 1999, a helicopter touched down on the lawn of the Kennedy compound. The chopper took Ted and his two sons to a Coast Guard boat that transported them to a Navy salvage vessel, the USS *Grasp*. At 4:30 P.M., the bodies of John, Carolyn, and Lauren were brought to the surface. Ted stood stoically, wearing dark glasses, with Patrick and Teddy Jr. at his side. He helped identify John's body. His remains and those of the Bessette sisters were placed in metal caskets.

One day later, Ted led the funeral party as it left the family compound. He carried John's ashes as they boarded the USS *Briscoe*, a Navy warship, for a private ceremony. Family members cast John's ashes, and those of Carolyn and Lauren, over the ship's stern and into the ocean.

The next day, at the requiem Mass at the Church of St. Thomas More, in Manhattan, Ted tried to put the family's grief into words. He delivered the eulogy for his nephew, as he had for his own brother Bobby in 1968 and for his mother, Rose, in 1995.

"From the first day of his life, John seemed to belong not only to our family, but to the American family," Ted said. "The whole world knew his name before he did." Ted fondly recalled the time when the young JFK Jr. was asked what he would do if he were elected president, and how John replied with a grin: "I guess the first thing is call up Uncle Teddy and gloat." Said Ted: "I loved that. It was so like his father."

Ted's voice cracked when he spoke of the times he had gone sailing on Nantucket Sound with John Jr. and Caroline. It cracked again when he ended his tribute to John by paraphrasing "In Memory of Major Robert Gregory," a poem by William Butler Yeats: "We dared to think, in that other Irish phrase, that this John Kennedy would live to comb gray hair, with his beloved Carolyn by his side. But like his father, he had every gift but length of years." After Ted concluded his ten-minute eulogy, Caroline rose from her pew and clasped him in a hug. Always close, the two would grow closer still as they tried to move on from this latest, terrible blow.

"Nobody was more amazing than Teddy last summer," Caroline would say a year later. "He was everywhere. He took care of everything." After John's death, she says, she and her uncle "worked together much more. I stepped into some of the stuff John was doing. I had a chance to work on the Profiles in Courage award, a chance to see [Ted] as a leader."

Ted had never expected to become the custodian of his family's sorrows. But when the role was thrust upon him, he learned to submerge his own pain enough to provide strength and reassurance for the rest of the family. As for himself, he coped by making room in his memory for the good times as well as the bad. "You try to live with the upside and the positive aspects of it, the happier aspects and the joyous aspects, and try to muffle down the other kinds of concerns and anxiety and the sadness of it, and know that you have no alternative but to continue on," Ted said less than a year after John Jr.'s death. "And so you do."

It underscored the evolution that surprised so many who knew the Kennedys: Teddy, the baby of the family, the chubby kid in short pants who was eclipsed for so many years by his brothers and who grew into a man who could sometimes be dissolute and reckless, had become the steady, indispensable patriarch, the one the family turned to in good times and bad.

In times of crisis, he seemed to draw on equal parts faith in God and faith in action. In 2002, his daughter Kara would be diagnosed with inoperable lung cancer and told that she might have only a year to live, but Ted would refuse to accept that prognosis. He would find a top surgeon to operate on Kara, and he and Vicki would go with Kara to her chemotherapy treatments. After the treatments, Ted would often go to Mass and pray for his daughter. At no point would he betray his own fears in his conversations with Kara, repeatedly exhorting her to have faith that she would pull through. She would do just that, and by 2008 Kara would be cancer-free and running five miles a day.

As always, he would attribute his strength to Joe Sr. and Rose. They had been strict and demanding, but he had chosen to remember their benevolence. The teachings of his mother were important enough to Ted that he tried to impart them to succeeding generations. His privately published book of remembrances of Rose, *Her Grace Above Gold,* saluted her for laying down the foundation of family solidarity. As the family expanded through marriages and births, he made simple but deliberate gestures at maintaining those bonds: No matter where he was, he would make annual birthday phone calls to every single member of both his own extended Kennedy family and that of Vicki—a total of more than 120 people.

The loving son had turned into a loving father and grandfather, the paterfamilias of a sprawling clan far larger than Joe Sr. ever presided over. Tellingly, that evolution played out in Kennedy's public life as well. When he first ran for the Senate at age thirty, he was seen as a callow opportunist riding Camelot's coattails, someone who sought public office as an entitlement. Yet after nearly five decades in the Senate, he remained consumed by the ham-and-egg details of constituent service. He grew, if anything, even more determined to be known as the man to call in a pinch. Having become a nurturing patriarchal presence in his own family, Ted seemed to feel a similar obligation to his constituents in Massachusetts as well.

It was as if he knew, deep down, that if his life were to be marked by a heroic quality, it was not to be the lit-by-lightning kind his martyred brothers had, but rather by the sort of day-to-day doggedness that John Updike captured in his classic *New Yorker* essay, "Hub Bids

Kid Adieu," on the final game of another Boston legend named Ted, one of Kennedy's boyhood heroes: Theodore Samuel Williams.

"For me, Williams is the classic ballplayer of the game on a hot August weekday, before a small crowd, when the only thing at stake is the tissue-thin difference between a thing done well and a thing done ill," Updike wrote. "Baseball is a game of the long season, of relentless and gradual averaging-out."

So is politics. And in the long season of Ted Kennedy's political career, any averaging out would have to take into account his indefatigable exertions on behalf of people in need, at those times when to them and, in a way, to him, too, everything was at stake.

As a new century dawned, that quality would be tested anew by two convulsive events: the terrorist attacks of September 11, 2001, and the war in Iraq.

CHAPTER

28

In the decades since his 1980 presidential race, Ted's reputation outside the Senate had hardened. Respected on the left, he remained the symbol on the right of a spent ideology, the perfect embodiment of political and personal self-indulgence. Even in his own party, his liberalism had seemed, at times, outmoded as the "third way" of the Clintons gained ascendance in the Washington of the 1990s.

But as Ted entered the twenty-first century with unflagging energy and stumped for Democratic presidential nominee Al Gore in 2000, he drew some of the most enthusiastic crowds of his career. Part of that outpouring of affection came from liberals who wanted to show their appreciation to him for carrying their standard through long periods of conservative dominance. On the right, meanwhile, as the full scope of Ted's career became visible, some of his conservative foes began to concede that there was something admirable in fighting that relentlessly and skillfully on behalf of the people and the principles he cared about. This grudging respect underlay an amiable exchange in July 2000 between then Texas Governor George W. Bush, the GOP nominee for president, and Kennedy at a memorial service for Republican Senator Paul Coverdell of Georgia. "I've heard of you," Bush told Kennedy jokingly, then added: "I understand that what you do, you do very well."

Then, in early 2001, Ted made a decision that jolted and dismayed some Democrats: he opted to forge a partnership with the new President Bush. It would be hard to imagine a more unlikely scenario than the leader of the reigning Republican dynasty and that of the most famous Democratic dynasty joining forces. To make the alliance all the more striking, Bush's election in 2000 had ushered in an era of bad feelings on Capitol Hill. Democrats seethed at what they viewed as a stolen election in the state of Florida, allowing Bush to defeat Gore, and many had not accepted the idea that the cowboy-boot-wearing Texan would occupy the White House.

Adding to the Democrats' pain was the ensuing situation in the Senate. Democrats had picked up four seats in the election, causing an unusual 50–50 split. With Dick Cheney in the vice president's chair to cast the tie-breaking vote, the Republicans took over, with all the attending rights to appoint committee chairmen and subpoena witnesses. Bush was not only going to be president, he was going to have the advantage of a House and Senate controlled by his own party.

Ted wasted little time being disappointed by Gore's loss or agonizing over his party's quandary in the Senate. Adept after nearly four decades in office at adjusting to the frequent power changes in Washington, Ted came to a simple conclusion: he was going to try to work with George Bush on education.

If health care was Ted's central passion on Capitol Hill, education ran a close second. Going back to the War on Poverty in 1964, he had been an early and aggressive advocate of Head Start, which provides both classroom instruction and social services to pre-kindergarten-age children from low-income families. He was a chief sponsor of the 1965 law creating the National Teacher Corps, which gave scholarships to young people willing to add education courses to their collegiate studies. The Education for All Handicapped Children Act of 1975, a program later called the Individuals with Disabilities Education Act, guaranteed a free and appropriate public education for all disabled children, regardless of the severity of their disabilities.

He was a strong advocate for higher education funding as well, both for universities and students seeking help with tuition. He sponsored the 1993 Direct Lending Program for college students and, under President Clinton, the bill that created AmeriCorps, which gave students scholarships in exchange for agreeing to do volunteer work.

Still, he believed that much remained to be done. His central goal had long been a major expansion of federal funding of elementary and secondary education, traditionally the provinces of state and local governments, and he was prepared to work with Bush to try to make it happen. The new president, for his part, viewed himself as a cross-party man. He had sold himself during the 2000 campaign as a "compassionate conservative" and a "uniter not a divider." He was proud of the fact that he had developed a close relationship with Texas's Democratic lieutenant governor, Bob Bullock. Like many Democrats, Bullock had initially rebuffed Bush's entreaties, but eventually the men became friends and allies — so much so that Bullock, on his deathbed, asked Bush to deliver the eulogy at his funeral.

As president-elect, Bush had ideas about joining with Democrats to reform education, touting what he had done in Texas — combining higher funding of schools with strict new testing to make sure each school was improving its academic performance. This formula, which provided the basis for Bush's and Kennedy's collaboration on the No Child Left Behind Act, was always destined to be more controversial at the federal level. Conservatives had long resisted the idea of greater federal control of schools, believing that decisions should be left to parents and local school districts. In the traditional Republican view, it was the teachers' unions — who made it much too difficult to fire bad teachers or reward good ones — who were the prime obstacles to quality schools.

The Democratic view, long represented by Ted, was quite different: the unions, seeking decent wages and protections for their members, were hardly the problem. Instead, the system of local control produced schools of wildly uneven quality. In wealthy districts, homeowners easily paid the high property taxes necessary to fund quality schools; in poorer districts, where the most troubled students lived, schools often lacked the funding for even basic educational tools. States were usually unwilling to fill in the gaps between districts, so

Ted believed that the federal government needed to step in in a big way, or whole generations of children would suffer.

Bush seemed to see both sides, recognizing the necessity of more federal resources to help poorer districts, but also a need to impose tough new testing requirements to make sure schools were using the money wisely. And Bush was determined to make improved education his legacy. Even before taking office, he summoned Republican and Democratic congressional leaders to meet with him at the gubernatorial mansion in Austin, hoping to begin work early on the reforms that would establish him as the Education President. Kennedy, however, was not invited. Bush didn't see the Massachusetts liberal as a genuine reformer, and looked to California Representative George Miller as his Democratic partner. Miller had been critical of the Clinton administration on some matters, indicating that he might be less tied to party orthodoxy than Kennedy.

But after his inauguration, Bush quickly realized he would need Kennedy, who was the senior Democrat on the Health, Education, Labor and Pensions Committee. Bush called a meeting at the White House, inviting Kennedy, Miller, and Republican congressional leaders to discuss education.

When Kennedy and Bush met, each was surprised to find things to like in the other. Both believed in setting standards for schools and holding districts accountable for meeting them. And while it was clear that the two men had philosophical disagreements on education—especially on using federal funds to subsidize vouchers to help parents pay for private schooling—both saw a bipartisan opportunity at the dawn of one of the most partisan eras that Washington had seen in many decades. "The president was far more knowledgeable, passionate, deeply committed, experienced, and intelligent about this issue than I would have guessed Senator Kennedy would have predicted," says Sandy Kress, Bush's chief education adviser and the administration's pointman on No Child Left Behind. "And Senator Kennedy was far more respectful, collaborative, willing to join together, passionate and knowledgeable than the president might have anticipated. It was a beautiful thing to have experienced."

At the end of the meeting, the new president from Texas made a gentle request of the venerable senator from Massachusetts. There are a lot of reporters waiting outside, wanting to know what went on here, Bush told him. We clearly have some disagreements, Bush said, but we also have common goals. I would urge you to emphasize what we agree on, not what separates us. Ted was impressed with Bush's desire to put policy ahead of politics, and announced as he left the White House that he was ready to work with the administration on a sweeping package ushering in a historic expansion of federal involvement in elementary and secondary education.

Ted met with Bush repeatedly in the first two weeks after the inauguration. The president even invited his new friend to the White House to watch *Thirteen Days,* a movie about President Kennedy's handling of the Cuban missile crisis. The two men, joined by some family members, shared hamburgers and ribs during the unusual four-hour get-together. Afterward, much of Washington gossiped about how Bush had wooed Kennedy with his signature "charm offensive." In truth, Ted hated to see movies about his brothers, but he accepted Bush's gesture as a sincere attempt to reach out. And Bush was oddly deferential to Kennedy. The new president had quickly assigned nicknames to Washington players — most of them undignified, like dubbing former New Hampshire Representative Charlie Bass "Bassmaster," a reference to a stomach-churning *Saturday Night Live* sketch featuring fish in a blender. It was Bush's way of taking ownership of Washington, giving his own names to the city's major players. But Kennedy, almost alone among the capital elite, was given a far more respectful moniker: "The Senator."

During the movie night at the White House, Bush humbly showed Kennedy the desk he had chosen for the Oval Office — it was the one Jack had used — and the two men chatted about the fact that both had relatives who had occupied that same famous room. Ted, for his part, showed that he wasn't awed by the White House, frequently bringing one or both of his large dogs with him for meetings with Bush, a move that would have been considered audacious at best for most visitors to the country's most famous address. But the president was happy with the senator's informality, even giving a bone to Ted's dog Splash that he said was a gift from his own dog, Barney.

Despite these cozy overtures, the alliance of Kennedy and Bush was based less on a genuine friendship than on hardheaded political calculation. Having lost the popular vote in 2000, Bush's advisers knew he was on unstable political ground, and would need to score some early bipartisan victories to set himself up for reelection in 2004. And while Bush's staff was full of conservatives on foreign policy, his White House advisers took a far more pragmatic approach toward domestic policy. Ted, meanwhile, was in legacy-building mode, eager to complete landmark legislation on his two pet issues—health care and education—before he left the Senate. If it took working with a Republican president inaugurated after a bitterly disputed election, he was prepared to do it.

Besides, the truth was that while Ted had famously sparred with presidents over the years, he always maintained a deep respect for the office itself. He almost never referred to JFK as "my brother" or even as "Jack": It was always "President Kennedy." And he had never had much taste for the Capitol Hill gamesmanship that sought to deny presidents of the opposing party key victories: it was, in Ted's view, putting politics ahead of the country's problems.

When the No Child Left Behind bill emerged, crafted by the White House with Ted's close involvement, many Democrats were shocked. Goaded on by unhappy teachers' unions, they argued that the provision to punish schools that did not meet "adequate yearly progress" markers, as defined by steadily improving test scores, was arbitrary and unfair, and failed to take into account the challenges many poor districts faced with at-risk children.

Ted, though, used his considerable clout with both his colleagues and the unions to argue that the testing standards were exactly the way to identify struggling schools and to get help to children in need. And the bill would inject billions of new dollars per year into the nation's school systems, most of the money aimed at the weakest districts. Eventually, Ted wore down enough Democrats, while Bush did the same with skeptical Republicans, to get the bill through.

Despite the bipartisan success, Kennedy's budding relationship with Bush would prove to be less sturdy than his partnership with Orrin Hatch or other Republicans. Some Democrats would grumble that Kennedy's love of the deal had obscured his better judgment—that in this case he had given away too much, especially with the testing requirements, to win his proverbial half a loaf. Tom Harkin, who said Kennedy had convinced him to back the bill, would eventually state frankly that he was "sorry I voted for the darn thing." Ted would also confront the wrath of his longtime ally, the National Education Association, whose members grew angrier and angrier at the provisions in the law holding teachers accountable for student performance.

Rather than defend the deal, Ted blamed Bush for reneging on his side of the bargain. Within a year after No Child Left Behind took effect, Kennedy's office would claim that the Bush administration had shortchanged the program by $9 billion—a big chunk of the $29.2 billion that was authorized for the program that year. Ted declared that he had been betrayed, saying Bush had looked him "in the eye" and promised to fund the program up to the ceiling that Congress had approved.

The White House argued that it was still spending record amounts of money on education. Administration officials would point out that many programs are "authorized" at a certain spending level, but given less in an actual appropriation. And if Ted felt betrayed, so did Bush. Having carefully set up bipartisan meetings at the beginning of his presidency to find areas of common ground, Bush increasingly felt he was under partisan attack. The president seemed genuinely baffled that he could not have the same comity with Democrats in Washington as he did in Texas, where Democrats tended to be more conservative.

On September 11, 2001, Ted was in his office, awaiting a visit from First Lady Laura Bush when he spotted something on the TV set. "That can't be a mistake," he said grimly. It was shortly before 9:00 A.M., and he was standing stock-still in his outer office. A television on the desk of his chief of staff, Mary Beth Cahill, had just shown a plane crashing into the World Trade Center in New York City. Ted, who had spent much of his life in the air, sensed immediately that it was no accident.

But the magnitude of the crisis was not yet known, and Mrs. Bush was slated to arrive at his office at that very moment. They had scheduled a meeting that morning because the first lady was going to testify later in the day on education issues before the Senate Committee on Health, Education, Labor and Pensions.

Mrs. Bush walked into the office. She had heard about the plane, but, like Ted, did not yet know that it was part of a terrorist attack. The two of them went into his private office and began to talk. Then the second plane hit. Cahill hastily scribbled a note, got up from her desk, and hurried into the senator's office. She handed Ted the note. He told Mrs. Bush what had happened. The two of them hastened to the outer office and stood with their eyes glued to the TV coverage until Secret Service agents hustled Mrs. Bush away to a secure location.

Ted accompanied the first lady until she was off the Capitol grounds. She was his guest, and he felt a responsibility for her safety. Then he turned back toward his office. There would be a lot of work to be done—the kind of private and public comforting that Ted had long since mastered—in the days ahead.

CHAPTER
29

W HEN C INDY M C G INTY of Foxborough, Massachusetts, heard
the booming voice on the other end of the telephone line, so instantly
recognizable with its impossibly broad vowels, she wondered who had
chosen the worst possible time to play a prank on her. That couldn't
really be Ted Kennedy, could it?

It was September 12, 2001. One day earlier, McGinty's husband,
Mike, who was on the ninety-ninth floor of the World Trade Center for
a business meeting, had been killed in the worst terrorist attack in U.S.
history. Cindy McGinty lost her husband, and her two sons, ages seven
and eight, lost their father. "I was totally grief-stricken, scared out of
my mind," recalls McGinty. But now Ted Kennedy—for it was indeed
he—was on the line, calling to share her grief. Ted told McGinty how
sorry he was for her loss, and said that his family and the entire nation
shared that sorrow. He asked if there was any way he could be helpful,
and told McGinty that if there was anything she needed—anything
at all, then or in the future—she should contact his office. There was
nothing rote about Kennedy's words, she recalls; no sense that he was
hurrying through a list. He spoke like a man who knew, insofar as any
other human being could possibly know, what she was going through.

McGinty was grateful but a bit stunned to hear from such a famous figure. Yet the reality was that for all his fame, Ted prided himself
on his personal connection to his constituents, the incarnation of the

old-school ethos he absorbed from his grandfather, Honey Fitz. His standing instruction to Barbara Souliotis, the woman in charge of his Boston office, was to respond to every one of the 300 letters the office received each week, and to every one of the hundreds of phone calls as well. "I know what gets me elected," he would say to Souliotis. But he—and she—knew there was more to it than that. The Kennedy name would likely have been enough to get him reelected every six years. Yet tens of thousands of Massachusetts residents have personal memories of Kennedy's interventions on their behalf on matters large and small. If an elderly and ailing veteran was having trouble gaining access to a VA facility; if a family was facing bankruptcy due to medical costs; if fishermen in Gloucester were struggling to cope with new federal regulations; if a mayor needed a federal grant to help turn around a struggling city; if a family was desperate to get a wounded son or daughter out of a war zone: if these or a thousand other eventualities occurred, Kennedy invariably got the call.

In 1995, when a huge explosion and fire devastated the textile complex Malden Mills, Kennedy wrangled millions of federal dollars to retrain the company's employees for the high-tech manufacturing methods used at the mill after it was rebuilt. In the late 1990s, Kennedy began to tell allies that he wanted to try to double the budget for the National Institutes of Health—a goal that many thought was farfetched. But sure enough, from 1998 to 2003 the NIH budget did double—and because it distributed the money to some of the nation's top teaching hospitals and medical research institutions, Kennedy's home state got a major share of the funds.

But along with such grand gestures, Ted kept his eye on micro matters as well. Nothing, it seemed, was too small to garner his attention if it would benefit his home state. When he learned of a grant available from the Department of Energy that would be helpful to a single company in western Massachusetts, he called Jim Brett, head of the New England Council, which monitors federal legislation that could affect the region's businesses, to urge that the council apply for the money. Another time, when the Senate approved a research and development tax credit that would help Boston-area biotech firms, he called Brett late at night from the floor of the Senate to let him know, then returned to the legislative fray while an astonished Brett watched on C-SPAN.

To be sure, many constituents go to their senators for help in dealing with the government. But Ted had become more than just a legislative fixer: he was a friend and comforter to people who were afflicted. Those who lost loved ones to sudden death were a special concern of his. His office even had an operator who specialized in finding people's cell phone numbers, so he could reach out to people who were confronted by tragedy.

That is what he did after September 11, 2001. In the month following the attacks, Kennedy called each of the 177 families in Massachusetts who lost loved ones on that day, many on the two flights that were hijacked out of Boston's Logan Airport and flown into the World Trade Center. One of the family members was Sally White, who describes herself as a "dyed-in-the-wool conservative Republican," and whose daughter, Susan Blair, died in the 9/11 attacks. The last person whose voice she expected to hear on her answering machine was that of the quintessential liberal Democrat. "I had not heard from one local politician, one medium politician, or certainly any federal guy. Nothing," says White. "He was the first one to call and offer assistance, or even sympathy, which meant a great deal to all of us."

When she called him back, Ted framed his comforting words to White in the most personal of terms: He told her that his family's experience of loss had well acquainted him with the pain it causes, and he talked about the time he had spent with Caroline after John Jr. was killed. He asked the grieving mother about Susan, what she had been like. "He was very interested and very sincere," recalls White. "He talked to me like he was my next-door neighbor, my best friend. He was amazing. He had all the time in the world for me. I was totally blown away. I was just overwhelmed by a person of his stature reaching out to me. He did it for all of us, but he made it seem like it was just me. That was what was so impressive and so meaningful."

Those initial phone calls were just the beginning of a special relationship that he forged with the families. The terrorist attacks would become a defining moment in Ted's career, albeit one of the less-known chapters in a very public life. "He saw this from the very beginning as a huge moment in the country's history," says Mary Beth Cahill, who was Kennedy's chief of staff from April 2001 until November 2004. "The fact that [two of] the planes took off from Boston: he insisted that this become a special task for the office. It became calls to the families on a daily basis."

Kennedy had a special kinship with the 9/11 families. Like him, they had experienced shattering personal losses that occurred in full public view. Like him, they had to grieve with the eyes of the world upon them. So he cut bureaucratic red tape, but he also performed numerous acts of personal kindness that were not written into the job description of United States senator. "Who knew how much he did for the 9/11 families? Nobody does," says McGinty. "He doesn't talk about it. He wanted to protect our privacy, which was at the time being so invaded."

A month after that initial phone call in September 2001, McGinty received an invitation from Kennedy's office, asking her to come to Boston for a meeting at the Park Plaza hotel in downtown Boston. By that point, McGinty, like many other 9/11 relatives, was feeling out-gunned in a bureaucratic battle. The agencies that were supposed to help them were drowning them in paperwork instead. In the chaotic aftermath of 9/11, getting something as simple as a death certificate, which was necessary in order to receive death benefits, was a bureau-cratic nightmare. It was unclear to the families what benefits they were eligible for, or how to apply.

McGinty rode the train in to Boston, practicing what she was go-ing to say. She walked into a ballroom at the Park Plaza, and there they sat: scores of people just like her. It was the first time the 9/11 family members had had a chance to meet one another. In itself, that pro-vided its own kind of comfort. A good many enduring friendships were forged that day.

Ted knew the emotional value of such a group meeting, but he had a pragmatic agenda as well. Arrayed around the room were represen-tatives from the FBI, the Red Cross, the Salvation Army, the Social

Security Administration, the Massachusetts Office of Victims Assistance, and other governmental agencies and nonprofit aid organizations. He walked to the front of the room and addressed the families directly. "What are your needs?" he asked them. "What do you need that is not being met?" He told them that the assembled representatives were there to help them.

McGinty drew a deep breath, got to her feet, turned to the agency representatives, and spoke bluntly. "You people have no idea how hard this is for us," she told them. "I know you want to help, but you're not being helpful." The other family members applauded. Kennedy looked startled. But as he left the meeting, he turned to an aide and said: "I don't want to ever hear that Mrs. McGinty or one of the other families has this problem. Fix it!"

Shortly after the meeting, Ted arranged for an advocate, whose task was to help with the paperwork and applications for assistance, to be available to each 9/11 family. He assigned two staffers to work for a full year on the needs of the group. He also played a key role in pushing through legislation to provide health care and grief counseling for the families. He urged Senate Majority Leader Tom Daschle to support the appointment of a former Kennedy chief of staff, Kenneth Feinberg, as the special master of the 9/11 Victim Compensation Fund. But Kennedy and his staff remained a vital lifeline for the families, often working behind the scenes.

For example, Mike McGinty had served in the U.S. Navy for twelve years, and his wife wanted to have an honor guard at his memorial service. But Navy officials told her there could be no honor guard unless she could produce Mike's discharge papers. Cindy couldn't find them, and the Navy couldn't locate a copy for her. She called Kennedy's office, and within a day the papers had been located. An honor guard was present at Mike McGinty's memorial service.

She thought that would be all, but in the summer of 2002, the phone rang again in the McGinty home. A Kennedy staffer asked McGinty: "What are you doing this weekend? How would you like to go sailing with the senator?" That weekend, McGinty and her two sons, along with her sister, her brother-in-law, and their son, sailed in the waters off Hyannis on the *Mya*, with the 70-year-old senator at the helm, cracking jokes, putting the children at ease. Afterward, they went back to the Kennedy house. McGinty had grown up watching television footage of the Kennedys playing football on the lawn of the family compound. Now she was standing on that lawn herself. She turned to her sister and said: "My God, we're standing in history." A year or so later, McGinty found herself sitting at the same table as Ted during a 9/11 commemoration ceremony. He scribbled something on his program, then pushed it across the table to her. "How are your two little sailors doing?" the note read.

When Ted learned that Christie Coombs of Abington, Massachusetts, whose husband, Jeff, was killed on 9/11, had set up a charitable foundation in her husband's name, he began sending her watercolors, painted and signed by himself, to be auctioned off. When he learned that White, the dyed-in-the-wool conservative Republican, was running a fund-raiser in her daughter Susan's name for special needs kids, Kennedy sent her a signed painting he had done of the *Mya*.

As the anniversary of September 11 neared each year, Ted made sure to send a letter to each of the 9/11 families in Massachusetts. To Coombs, he wrote on September 11, 2005: "Dear Christie, Vicki and I wanted you to know that we are thinking of you and your entire family during this difficult time of year. As you know so well, the passage of time never really heals the tragic memory of such a great loss, but we carry on, because we have to, because our loved one would want us to, and because there is still light to guide us in the world from the love they gave us."

In those words—"we carry on, because we have to"—Coombs sees evidence that Kennedy's own losses have given him insight into hers. "It feels very personal," she says, gazing at the note in her home south of Boston. "This just tells me that he knows. He gets it. And so few people do."

Kennedy seemed to need to put a human face on even the most far-reaching legislation. When the Senate approved the Intelligence Reform and Terrorism Prevention Act on December 8, 2004, which had been recommended by the 9/11 Commission, he would call Carie Lemack, of Framingham, Massachusetts, right after he voted for the bill. Lemack is the daughter of Judy Laroque of Framingham, who was aboard American Airlines Flight 11, one of the planes hijacked by terrorists and flown into the World Trade Center. Lemack wasn't home, but Kennedy left her a message. He told Lemack that he voted for the bill, and that he had been thinking about her mother when he cast the vote. Lemack, the cofounder, with her sister Danielle, of a group called Families of 9/11, says: "To think that someone like him was thinking about my mom. . . ."

Sally White has remained a proud Republican, but her encounters with Kennedy have prompted her to reexamine some of her views. "Since this has happened, I have looked a little more closely at his politics and what he has meant to Massachusetts and for the country," says White. "I have changed my opinion in some areas." McGinty was an independent who leaned right. Because of Kennedy, she is now a Democrat.

But ultimately, Kennedy's impact on the 9/11 families cannot be measured by any votes he might have obtained along the way. By the summer of 2008, Cindy McGinty would sum it up this way: "I can't imagine getting through the last seven years without him. I honestly mean that."

It was early in the morning of November 4, 2003, and Brian and Alma Hart of Bedford, Massachusetts, were preparing to bury their only son—and preparing to meet Senator Edward M. Kennedy.

The Harts were at Arlington National Cemetery, surrounded by friends and relatives from their native Texas. Two weeks earlier, 20-year-old John D. Hart had been killed in Iraq. But there was a chilling backstory to John's death, and it was that story that Brian and Alma Hart wanted Kennedy to know.

From the beginning, Ted had viewed the war in Iraq as a mistake. He had supported the Tonkin Gulf resolution in 1964, which allowed President Lyndon Johnson to greatly increase United States involvement in Vietnam. Since then, Ted had been on guard when presidents began beating the drums of war.

The Bush administration had begun laying the groundwork for

the Iraq war in the summer of 2002 with a series of strongly worded speeches. By the time Congress returned to Washington that fall, the president had signaled that he would ask for military authority to strike against Saddam Hussein unless the Iraqi dictator gave up the weapons of mass destruction that Bush insisted he was hiding. Ted researched the issue, meeting day after day with experts from across the spectrum. Each evening he went home for dinner, and then returned to Capitol Hill to spend hours poring over the documents that were provided to him and other senators on the activities of Hussein. "He didn't immediately dismiss the president's position, and he didn't immediately dismiss Colin Powell's representation," says Cahill, then his chief of staff. "But he wanted to find out as much as he could."

What he read, and what he heard, left him convinced that Bush had not made the case that Iraq was an imminent threat to the United States. Along with West Virginia's Democratic Senator Robert Byrd, Ted soon emerged as one of the most vocal critics of the administration's march to war. His stance would put him at odds with a then-popular president, many close Democratic colleagues in the Senate, including his fellow Massachusetts senator John Kerry, and even his own son, Patrick, then in his eighth year representing Rhode Island in the House of Representatives.

Ted consistently urged the administration to work through the United Nations to stop Iraq's alleged weapons programs. He also prodded the administration to commit to reaching out to other nations if military force became necessary, and to provide a clearer picture of its long-range plans for Iraq. "As of today, many questions still remain unanswered: Is war the only option? How much support will we have in the international community? How will war affect our global war against terrorism? How long will the United States need to stay in Iraq? How many casualties will there be?" he asked Defense Secretary Donald Rumsfeld at a Senate Armed Services Committee hearing on September 19.

But many other Democrats, fearful of losing seats in the midterm elections, were more accepting of the Bush administration's approach. On September 26, Democratic Senate leaders announced a deal with

Republicans on a war resolution that gave Bush what he desired: authority to use force against Iraq to enforce United Nations resolutions. On the day the deal was unveiled, Ted said he was inclined to vote against it because it allowed Bush to go to war without explicit backing from the U.N. Security Council.

The next day, he amplified his objections to the president's unilateral approach in a speech to the School of Advanced International Studies at Johns Hopkins University. The address drew a fiery reaction from Republicans. "The argument advanced by Senator Kennedy irresponsibly relies on a benign view of Saddam's relationship with terrorist organizations," said GOP House Leader Tom DeLay, who accused Kennedy of "subcontracting our national security to the United Nations."

Ted formally announced on October 4 that he would vote against the war resolution. In casting his no vote a week later, he said on the Senate floor: "The power to declare war is the most solemn responsibility given to Congress by the Constitution. We must not delegate that responsibility to the president in advance."

Ted was unable to persuade nearly enough members of Congress to take his position, even as he reinforced his arguments in private conversations with his colleagues. A total of seventy-seven senators supported the authorization, including Kerry. Years later, in his 2007 book, *No Excuses*, Robert Shrum, who worked for both Kennedy and Kerry, would claim that political calculation played a part in Kerry's decision. Shrum would write that Kerry called him the night before the vote and asked whether he could still be a viable presidential candidate if he voted against the war authorization. Shrum replied that it would be "impossible to predict the political fallout." He also noted that Kennedy had lobbied Kerry against the war vote up until the last moment, including on the Senate floor. Ted "passionately contended that even if it looked like good politics now, siding with Bush was wrong on the merits — and even politically," Shrum wrote.

As it turned out, the war vote was the last chance Congress would have to influence the Bush administration's policy. Using the authority granted in the October vote, Bush went to war on March 20, 2003. After the invasion began, Kennedy joined other senators in taking to the floor to express his support for the troops. The speech did not mention his own opposition to the war. Instead, he closed by reciting the famous poem "Abraham Lincoln Walks at Midnight," by Vachel Lindsay, which ends with the lines:

> *It breaks his heart that kings must murder still.*
> *That all his hours of travail here for men*
> *Seem yet in vain. And who will bring white peace*
> *That he may sleep upon his hill again?*

Later, as the Iraqi insurgency grew, Ted jumped out ahead of most leading Democrats in declaring Iraq to be "Bush's Vietnam." He called the war a "fraud" built on a lie that would lead to needless deaths and damage the United States for many years to come. Bush called Ted's comments "uncivil," a rare personal rebuke of a specific lawmaker by a sitting president. Meanwhile, many other senators were shielding their opposition in the name of supporting the troops. In Kennedy's view, though, he was supporting the troops—and he took a personal interest in soldiers from Massachusetts. By October 2003, more than a dozen Massachusetts troops had lost their lives in Iraq. Twenty-year-old John D. Hart of Bedford was the latest.

As he did with the other soldiers, Ted picked up the phone and called the parents of John Hart. He asked for permission to attend John's burial. Brian said yes; he told the senator there was something about John's death he wanted to discuss with him. So on that November morning, a black Navigator pulled up inside Arlington National Cemetery and Ted's bulky figure emerged, accompanied by two aides. They and the Harts went into the office of the cemetery administrator for a private conversation, where Kennedy offered some personal advice. "The best time to visit Arlington is the morning," Ted told the grieving parents. "That's when I visit. It's cooler, and the crowds aren't there yet." Brian and Alma Hart had moved to Massachusetts in 1989 and therefore were not as steeped in Kennedy lore as some other Bay Staters were, but they knew why the senator was so familiar with Arlington National Cemetery: because John F. Kennedy and Robert F. Kennedy are buried there.

Brian and Alma told the senator that their son had been killed while riding in a canvas-topped Humvee that had no armor, no bulletproof shields, not even so much as a metal door. And they told him this haunting detail: John had predicted that very scenario just a few days earlier, in an anxious phone call home to his father. "We're going to get killed," John said. "Dad, can you do something?" Brian Hart says that after he hung up the phone, he paced back and forth. He and Alma agonized over what to do. How could they help their son without landing him in hot water with his superiors? Brian began to draft a letter to his congressman, and he began calling people for advice. But one week after that call, John Hart was killed. "He thought he would be ambushed and killed on the road," says Brian Hart. And that's what happened. He adds quietly: "It's one of those things that haunts a parent."

Brian told Ted how, since John's death, he had dug into the issue of armored vehicles and body armor, conducting research online and calling manufacturing plants. He told Ted his research indicated armored Humvees were not being manufactured at nearly the necessary rate and that many other U.S. soldiers were at risk in Iraq.

Ted's face tightened as he listened. He said little, asking the occasional question while his aide, who specialized in military affairs, took notes, but the senator had already been tracking this issue. Of the Massachusetts soldiers killed in the first phase of the war, fully a third had died in unarmored trucks or Humvees. Kennedy told the Harts that he would prod the Senate Armed Services Committee to hold a hearing on the matter. Still, it was hard not to feel at least some skepticism about a politician's—any politician's—promise. "Do you think we'll ever hear from him?" Alma asked Brian as they walked to the gravesite.

During the burial, Ted stood at the back of the crowd, and when mourners formed a line to walk past the coffin and place flowers on it, the senator went to the end of the line. One of Alma Hart's best friends, who had known John all his life, was wracked by sobs as she stood before the coffin. She felt someone gently patting her shoulder. She turned to see who had made the comforting gesture. It was Ted. "He just behaved like a gentleman," says Alma Hart. "The relatives from Texas were knocked over." She pauses, then adds with a slight laugh: "You know, he's not beloved in Texas. But they were like 'Wow, he's a nice guy.'"

Two weeks after John Hart's burial, Kennedy was grilling the Army chief of staff and the acting secretary of the Army in a hearing about the shortages of armored Humvees and body armor for the troops. When they told him it would take two years to produce a sufficient supply of armored Humvees, Kennedy told them that was not good enough and demanded to know whether manufacturing plants were running twenty-four hours a day. "When I was out at Arlington for Private First Class Hart's burial, the parents said, 'If you can do anything to make sure that other soldiers who are over there are not put in the kind of danger that my son was put in, and lost, that would be the best thing we could ever think of in terms of our son,'" said Ted.

Kennedy and Brian Hart became a sort of Mr. Inside–Mr. Outside team, working together to pressure Congress and the Pentagon to speed up the approval and acquisition process for Humvees, to provide body armor for troops in Iraq, and to generally build better-protected military vehicles.

Brian would tell the congressmen the story of his son, who always dreamed of following the military tradition of his family. When John played soldier as a boy, he went so far as to dig a foxhole. As a teenager, he watched HBO's *Band of Brothers*, set during World War II, and the camaraderie appealed to him. But he also believed deeply in service. His parents wanted him to go to college and then join the service as an officer, but after September 11, 2001, there was no stopping John from enlisting. One year later, on his nineteenth birthday, he joined the Army as a private. He was sent to northern Iraq in 2003. He participated in several battles and won a Combat Infantryman Badge in his first week.

Brian's work on the outside, and Ted's work on the inside, began to pay off. In early March 2004, the acting secretary of the Army announced plans for a doubling, from 220 to 450 a month, of heavily armored Humvees. But on February 3, 2005, Kennedy and the Harts published an op-ed piece in the *Boston Globe* arguing that still more armored vehicles were needed. "The number one priority of the Department of Defense this year should be to supply our troops with all the protection they need to get their job done and return safely home," they wrote.

Kennedy cosponsored legislation to provide $213 million to ensure that every Humvee that rolled off an assembly line was adequately armored. On April 21, 2005, the legislation passed, 60–40. On the wall of the dining room of Brian and Alma Hart's home stands a large, framed tally sheet that records that Senate roll-call vote. It bears an inscription: "To Brian & Alma, This one was for you and for John. We couldn't have done it without you. April 05." It is signed "Ted Kennedy."

CHAPTER 30

DESPITE TED'S FURY over the Iraq war and his still-simmering sense of grievance over No Child Left Behind, he was willing to engage with George W. Bush again—this time over Ted's most urgent concern, health care. Shocking to many of his colleagues, Ted's decision was in keeping with his long-standing belief that, legislatively speaking, it made sense to grab opportunities whenever they presented themselves. And Bush, who was approaching a difficult reelection fight with an increasingly unpopular war on his hands, was eager to fulfill a promise from his 2000 campaign: prescription drug coverage for the elderly.

The political world was awash in stories about senior citizens who were forced to cut pills in half to save money on prescriptions, or who confronted the choice between eating or taking their blood pressure medicine. Ted felt the best way to help them was to pay for their prescription drugs as part of their guaranteed Medicare benefits.

A big obstacle, however, was the pharmaceutical industry. Democrats delighted in characterizing Big Pharma, as the industry was often known, as heartless and money-grubbing, eager to wrest the biggest chunk they could from the Social Security checks of senior citizens. In fact, Ted was more willing to engage with pharmaceutical industry leaders than was commonly assumed. Years earlier, when President Clinton was still in office, Ted had begun his own lobbying effort with select drug company CEOs to see if they could reach some type of compromise on costs.

Big Pharma's main sticking point was with having drug coverage be a part of Medicare: seniors were the biggest users of prescription drugs, and having them covered by the government would give enormous power to Medicare officials, who might try to save money by trimming reimbursements or by forcing drug companies to negotiate lower prices. That could hurt drug company profits, yes, but also deplete the amount of money available for research into new cures. The drug companies preferred that the benefit be given only to seniors who joined Medicare-sponsored health maintenance organizations, thereby limiting the power of any one organization to dictate drug prices.

Ted and the drug industry CEOs had continued to meet in the late 1990s, with Ted dominating their encounters through sheer force of personality. At one point, they went to the White House for a talk with President Clinton, recalls David Nexon, a senior Kennedy aide at the time. But Republicans on the Hill got wind of the visit and urged the executives to hold out for a better deal under the next president, Nexon says.

Bush came into office having promised to help seniors pay for their drugs, and in 2003 he let it be known that he would allot up to $400 billion over ten years to do it—a stunning commitment from any administration, and particularly from a Republican reluctant to expand federal benefits.

Some of Ted's fellow Democrats warned against handing a political bonanza to the Republican Party, and urged Kennedy to back off. After having been burned by Bush on the No Child Left Behind bill, many Democrats wondered aloud how Kennedy could be lining up to help the president achieve another big domestic victory.

Besides, many Democrats believed, the benefit that Bush was proposing was not even that generous: It had a "doughnut hole" in the coverage, reimbursing seniors for 75 percent of their first $2,250 of drug costs, nothing at all for costs between $2,250 and $5,100, and then 95 percent of the costs after that. The idea was to make sure that the seniors with highest drug costs got the most help, while those with more moderate needs paid a significant share of their costs. In terms of fiscal restraint, the idea made sense, but some Democrats worried that seniors would be furious as soon as they hit the $2,251 mark—and would blame Congress for it.

With the memory of his missed chance in the early 1970s to undertake a massive health care restructuring under Nixon, Ted warned his Democratic colleagues that it could be a long time before another president threw $400 billion into the health care pool. Maybe decades. Maybe never. Yes, the benefit was imperfect, he said, and there were provisions that he himself didn't like. But Congress could always fix it later. "It was probably one of the most emotional of all the discussions and debates we ever had in the caucus," recalls Daschle, then the Senate Democratic Leader.

Ted prevailed, convincing a grudging Democratic caucus to work with Bush and the Republicans in Congress to develop a bill. Ted assumed they could reach a compromise acceptable to all the disparate groups—Democrats, Republicans, the pharmaceutical industry, and the AARP, a powerful advocacy group for seniors. But the final bill—heavily influenced by the White House and by the pharmaceutical industry, which sent 600 lobbyists to Capitol Hill to make its case—was unacceptable to Ted. For the first time, the measure allowed private HMOs to compete with Medicare for patients, a change Ted felt would threaten the very integrity of Medicare.

He marshaled his forces to amend the bill, determined to get the prescription drug coverage without giving a boost to HMOs. But then came an unexpected blow from a longtime ally: the AARP endorsed the Republican-written bill. AARP leaders hadn't even told Ted of their decision before making an announcement, and he felt betrayed and angry. AARP head Bill Novelli says he hated defying a longtime Senate ally but felt the group had no choice. "We thought of this as [an opportunity] whose time would not come again anytime soon," Novelli recalls.

House Democrats tried to help Kennedy, initially succeeding in defeating the bill on the House floor. But Republican leaders kept the vote open for an unprecedented three hours while they worked on their exhausted colleagues. At the White House, Bush's aides woke the president before dawn so he could make calls to potential vote switchers. Just before 6:00 A.M. — three hours after the voting began — Bush and the Republican leaders prevailed. The bill passed by a 220–215 margin.

An angry Kennedy voted against the bill in the Senate, but it passed anyway. Some of Ted's Democratic colleagues believed he was sending a message to the AARP — don't break with me like that again. Others thought that Ted, having been burned on No Child Left Behind, felt that this latest compromise had gone too far: Half a loaf was, in this case at least, worse than none at all. In the future, Ted declared, he would insist on "preconferencing" big bills — making sure the final details of legislation were clear and agreed on well in advance of votes.

Novelli, who says he "still has the scars" from the fight with Kennedy, worked hard to repair his relationship with AARP's critical Senate ally. And in retrospect, Novelli says, the law ended up giving Ted a lot of what he wanted. Novelli still credits the prescription drug benefit to Kennedy's advocacy. "I think the lesson he learned from the Nixon era is a lesson that history teaches us: you should not let the perfect be the enemy of the good," Novelli says. "The Medicare Modernization Act was certainly not perfect, but the idea was, get it done, and improve it over the coming years."

An impish grin on his face, Ted Kennedy took the microphone in a packed high school gymnasium in Davenport, Iowa, on a cold night in January 2004, and proceeded to play a little let's-make-a-deal with the crowd.

Iowa was the place where Ted's presidential hopes had begun to crumble in 1980. The state had soundly rejected him then, choosing President Jimmy Carter instead in the Iowa caucuses. Now Ted had returned to Iowa — older, grayer, heavier, having abandoned his presidential ambitions long ago. He was there to stump for Senator John Kerry, his Massachusetts colleague, whose bid for the Democratic presidential nomination was facing an uphill climb in the all-important state with the caucuses less than two weeks away. Two months earlier, Kerry had fired his campaign manager and then, at Kennedy's urging, hired Mary Beth Cahill, Kennedy's chief of staff, as his replacement.

Many of the spectators in Davenport had come to see Kennedy rather than Kerry. Plenty of them remembered his Iowa flop in 1980. They waited expectantly. Ted began to speak. "You voted for my brother!" he exclaimed, then paused expertly. "You voted for my *other* brother!" Another pause. "You *didn't* vote for me!" The crowd roared with laughter. Ted continued, bellowing: "But if you vote for John Kerry, I'll forgive you!" More laughter, followed by applause.

When Ted finished his roof-raising speech that first night in Davenport, "Love Train," the 1973 hit by the soul group The O'Jays, began pumping in over the PA system. Ted, improbably enough, began to dance, his massive bulk swaying from side to side. He looked over at Cahill and winked. He was having the time of his life.

Ted crisscrossed Iowa on a two-seater plane for much of the next two weeks. He stumped everywhere for Kerry, drawing fervent crowds. Because of his old back injury, he had to sit through most events. But when he stood and took the microphone, he was electrifying. "He played an enormous role in attracting attention to Kerry, in wrapping Kerry in the Democratic tradition, and also in looking like it was fun," says Cahill. "Tip O'Neill might have said it, but Kennedy lives it — that all politics is personal."

In speech after speech, Kennedy tapped into his deep reservoirs of goodwill among minority voters, liberals, and blue-collar workers, especially union members. When they clapped and cheered, it was as if they were applauding the political tradition he represented and his own dogged advocacy for them, however out of vogue they had been at times. Between 1980 and 2004, Kennedy carried the liberal flag through sixteen years of conservative Republican presidencies: two terms for Ronald Reagan, one term for George H. W. Bush, and, at that point, one term for George W. Bush. Of the eight years of the Clinton Administration, six were spent with Republicans in control of Congress. Iowans noticed how persistently Kennedy fought on the issues of health care, education, and workers' rights throughout that long period. They noticed, too, that sometimes he seemed to be the only one doing the fighting. In Iowa, Ted spoke their language unapologetically. "He's not necessarily made for the TV age, or the cool age, as a candidate," notes Dan Balz, national political correspondent for the *Washington Post*. "But in those settings, he's pretty much pitch-perfect."

At the age of seventy-one, nearly a quarter-century after his last national run, Ted found in 2004 that his zest for campaigning was very much alive. As the caucus date approached, he began urging Kerry operatives to utilize him even more fully. He would call Cahill and say: "You've asked for me to be there Friday and Saturday night, but I think I'll stay till Tuesday." On a cold January evening, Kennedy galvanized a packed house in Cedar Rapids, bellowing: "Tonight, the New England Patriots are playing the Tennessee Titans, but I said: 'No, I want to be in Cedar Rapids, Iowa!' " After the crowd roared in approval, Kennedy couldn't resist a follow-up quip: "Do you believe that?" Again the crowd roared, this time with laughter. "He was effervescent, he was happy, he was having fun," recalls David Yepsen, a political columnist for the *Des Moines Register*, who was there that night. "All these stops he made, there was a lot of poking fun at himself. He was even teasing the audience." Massachusetts Democratic operative Paul Pezzella, who had volunteered for Kennedy's 1980 presidential campaign and went to Iowa in 2004 to work on Kerry's behalf, saw not just a looseness in Kennedy's performance, but a redemptive quality. He had been given a chance for a do-over on the national campaign trail, and he seized it. "It was like going back and doing his own victory lap," says Pezzella.

Thanks in part to Ted, Kerry pulled off an upset and won the Iowa caucus. On caucus night, Cahill, along with top operative Michael Whouley and other staffers, was in a hotel conference room in Des Moines that was serving as the campaign's "boiler room." Suddenly, the door opened and in walked Ted. He stayed for several hours, right in the middle of the give-and-take, as the votes were counted.

Ted wasn't finished after Iowa. He stumped for Kerry in New Hampshire, then told Cahill: " 'I think I'll go to Wisconsin." Soon, he was fashioning his own campaign itinerary. He would say to Cahill: "We could go to New Mexico," and then tick off the names of party leaders in that state.

In the end, Kerry won the Democratic nomination but fell short of winning the White House. Still, the campaigning experience of 2004 reassured Ted that he still had plenty of clout on the national landscape. In short, he still had political capital to spend—and he would spend it in dramatic fashion in the next presidential election.

Despite his reelection, Bush proved to be a damaged president, as worsening conditions in Iraq sapped his credibility. A slow government response to Hurricane Katrina in 2005 damaged any notion of him as a can-do leader, and Democrats rode a wave of voter disgust to take back control of Congress in the 2006 elections.

Faced with spending the final two years of his presidency sparring with a Congress controlled by the opposing party, Bush identified one issue, at least, where he felt he had a lot of common ground with the opposition: curbing illegal immigration.

For decades, millions of undocumented workers had entered the country, either by slipping over the border with Mexico or by coming as tourists and overstaying their visas. Lost to American law enforcement, the undocumented aliens were living and working in the shadows of American cities and towns. The workers' lack of legal status was a danger to them as much as anyone else: undocumented workers were regularly exploited, forced to work for less than the legal minimum and often under unsafe conditions.

Many conservative Republicans advocated an "enforcement only" approach to the problem—essentially taking dramatic steps to seal the border and to deport any illegal workers who could be caught. But most political leaders acknowledged that rounding up the estimated 12 million illegal immigrants would be impossible; and forcing them even further underground with threats of tough treatment would only compound the existing problems.

Ted and Bush happened to agree that solving illegal immigration required multiple changes to existing laws. Both were open to taking stronger steps to seal the border with Mexico, but also felt that the best way to discourage illegal immigration would be to clear away some of the obstacles to legal immigration. As for the people already in the country illegally, they could be offered a temporary visa to serve as "guest workers," before returning home to apply to reenter the United States legally.

For Kennedy, who regarded undocumented workers as an exploited minority, reforming the nation's immigration laws was akin to protecting people's civil rights. And immigration had been the subject of one of Kennedy's earliest legislative initiatives. He was a chief advocate of the landmark Immigration Act of 1965, which ended the built-in preferences for northern and western Europeans that had defined the nation's immigration laws for forty-one years. The measure, Kennedy said at the time, reflected the nation's changes in attitude toward ethnic minorities.

In 2007, Ted thought he had the chance for another landmark bill, one that would allow the undocumented workers to "come out of the shadows," and receive a temporary visa if they paid a fine and passed a background check. Needing a bipartisan team to have any chance at passing a bill, Ted brought together an improbable collection of senators to take part in the negotiations. There was Lindsey Graham, a conservative first-termer from South Carolina whom Ted had identified early as a potential ally on certain issues; Dianne Feinstein, a moderate California Democrat worried about how the changes in immigration laws might affect her state's farm industry; and two Hispanic senators—Mel Martinez, a Republican from Florida, and Ken Salazar, a Democrat from Colorado—both of whom were concerned about the anti-Hispanic rhetoric of some of the arch-opponents of illegal immigration.

Arizona's Republican Senator Jon Kyl, whose state was the entry point for millions of illegal immigrants, was also on the negotiating team. And Illinois Senator Barack Obama, already a Democratic candidate for president, occasionally joined in the talks, impressing Ted, who knew the immigration issue was politically explosive and risky for a presidential aspirant.

The start of the 2008 campaign was, in fact, a deadline of sorts for

Ted, who knew Congress would never approve a deeply controversial bill in an election year. The summer of 2007, Ted believed, was the latest that Congress could move on a bill without having it get tangled up in the campaign.

The negotiations, going for several hours, two or three times a week, were contentious. Liberals worried that the guest worker provision would create a permanent underclass of low-paid workers, driving down wages and taking jobs from Americans. Conservatives insisted on strong border control measures, and severe punishments for breaking the law.

Lawmakers on both sides were inundated with calls and e-mails from constituents. One member of the negotiating team—Trent Lott, the Mississippi Republican who was among the most conservative members of the Senate—received death threats. In trying to bring the group together, Ted alternated between playing the exasperated high school principal and the sympathetic guidance counselor. One night, he got so angry with the pace of talks that he walked out, telling his colleagues they would have to come back at it the next day.

Then, at another tense negotiation, he came up with an inspired way to change the atmosphere. He asked each senator to tell the group how his or her family came to America. It was a poignant moment, one that created a bond that would help the odd team of negotiators to get through heated fights over the details of the legislation.

They finally emerged with a compromise that all could support. But outside the negotiating room, opposition ran deep and wide. Immigration skeptics argued that no more foreigners should be allowed into the country until the borders were secured. Some liberals opposed the part of the bill that would build a fence along the southern border, saying it would be a sign of hostility to the rest of the world. Lawmakers from states with high unemployment worried that people who got "guest worker" visas under the bill would take jobs from Americans. Immigrant-advocacy groups thought the fines and fees that undocumented residents would need to pay to become guest workers were unrealistically high. Some Latino groups declared that the bill was unfair to Hispanics, because it defined "family" as only spouses and children, while Latin American cultures considered aunts, uncles, and cousins to be immediate relatives.

Bush delivered a prime-time Oval Office address, explaining that the measure was the best compromise possible to secure the border while dealing firmly but fairly with the 12 million people already in the country illegally. But the speech—coming from a president with little political capital left to spend—did not change many minds.

The Senate, in the end, defeated the measure. Ted slumped resignedly in a chair at the front of the chamber as he watched the results of his hard work go down the drain. One by one, colleagues in both parties approached the veteran lawmaker to pay their respects. Mel Martinez, who rarely voted with Ted on other matters, stuck out his hand in condolence. "Thank you, my friend," Ted told him.

Less than an hour after the loss, Ted had adopted a philosophical view about it. It always took an average of three Congresses—at least six years—to develop the necessary momentum for any kind of civil rights legislation, he declared. The first time the Senate had voted on a housing anti-discrimination bill, it had the backing of only a handful of senators, he said. But by the time the measure was approved, it passed overwhelmingly, and sponsors were able to expand it to include age and parenthood as factors landlords could not use to reject tenants.

Immigration, Kennedy vowed, would be back. "His view is . . . if it takes fifteen years to get a bill, then let's do it in fifteen years," says Jay Rockefeller with admiration. "He's always had the long view and the big picture in mind."

And by 2007, Ted was as much a part of the Capitol as the dome or the Rotunda beneath it. And no one doubted that the senior senator from Massachusetts, then seventy-five, would be around in fifteen years to help illegal immigrants finally emerge from the shadows.

CHAPTER
31

TED SAW PIECES of himself in almost all of the 2008 Democratic presidential candidates. There was his pal Chris Dodd, with whom he had shared many raucous and liquid evenings during their lonely second bachelorhoods. There was Joe Biden, another close friend who had been his Judiciary Committee colleague since the 1970s. There was John Edwards, whom Ted—with his eye for up-and-coming Democrats—had taken under his wing in the late 1990s. There was Hillary Clinton, who shared his passion for health care policy. And there was also Barack Obama, the first-term senator from Illinois.

Obama had turned to Kennedy as one of his mentors after joining the Senate in January 2005. Less than two years later, he sought Ted's advice about whether to jump into the presidential race. Remembering how people had advised Jack to defer to Lyndon Johnson in 1960, and how they told Ted himself that he was too young to run for the Senate in 1962, Ted didn't put much store in the argument that Obama needed more seasoning. Ted advised Obama to go for it, since he might never have as promising an opportunity again. Considering Ted's own roller-coaster ride through presidential politics—the years he probably could have made it, but passed up the chance; the time he finally did run, and lost—it was important advice, and Obama took it seriously.

However, Kennedy explained that he would remain neutral in the presidential race, in part because of his loyalty to Dodd. Ted knew that Dodd's candidacy was a long shot at best, but he wasn't willing to undermine his friend by endorsing someone else. And as the campaign heated up, Ted took pains not to praise any one candidate more than the others. Meanwhile, donations from members of the Kennedy family were split among Clinton, Obama, and Dodd. Former Maryland Lieutenant Governor Kathleen Kennedy Townsend campaigned actively for Clinton, who also had the backing of Bobby Jr., now a respected global environmentalist.

But when Dodd dropped out of the presidential race in January 2008, following his disappointing showing in the Iowa caucuses, Ted began to consider endorsing Obama, who shared so much of Jack's charismatic style, and who—also like Jack—was drawing young people into politics. Ted felt grateful for Obama's help on the failed 2007 immigration reform legislation, but there was still a sticking point between them. It stemmed from a video that surfaced late in 2007, showing Obama making a disparaging remark about Ted several years earlier. Dick Durbin, Obama's fellow senator from Illinois, had been pressing Kennedy to endorse Obama, but one day a clearly miffed Ted took Durbin aside. He was brandishing a newspaper. "I've got to show you this clip," Ted told Durbin. "It's something Barack said about me a few years ago."

In June 2003, in an address to AFL-CIO members, Obama, who was then a state senator in Illinois, had contended that the proposed Medicare prescription drug benefit bill did not go far enough in helping seniors. He called on Democrats to "get some backbone" and vote it down. Then he added: "We've got to call up Ted Kennedy and say, 'Ted, you're getting a little old now, and you've been a fighter for us before. I don't know what's happening now. Get some spine and stand up to Republicans.'"

In fact, Ted had turned against the prescription drug benefit for many of the reasons Obama was citing. He was perturbed to learn of Obama's blithe dismissal. "I could tell he was not happy about it," Durbin recalls. Durbin immediately went back to his office and looked up a video clip of Obama's speech; the quote criticizing Kennedy, Durbin noted to his chagrin, was accurate. Disheartened, Durbin called Obama to inform him that Kennedy was upset at Obama's suggestion that he was out of touch and politically pliant.

"I didn't say that," Obama exclaimed.

Durbin replied: "Barack, it's on the video."

So Obama went to Ted to apologize. "It was a stupid thing to say," a sheepish Obama told the older senator. Ted accepted his apology, and then offered an apology of his own. "Oh, by the way, I'm sorry I called you Osama by mistake," Ted told Obama, referring to a time when he was answering questions at the National Press Club and fumbled for Obama's name, calling him "Osama bin . . . Osama Obama."

When it came to Hillary Clinton's candidacy, Kennedy had some serious doubts. He flatly told the Massachusetts congressional delegation at a private dinner in early 2008 that she could not win. That verdict came despite the harmonious, though not especially close, relations that had existed between their two families when Bill Clinton was president. In one much-photographed episode, Ted and Vicki and Jacqueline Kennedy Onassis had taken the first couple boating in the waters off of Jackie's farm on Martha's Vineyard. Years later, Bill Clinton unleashed the full resources of the federal government to search for John Jr.'s plane, and then to help with his funeral. Meanwhile, Bill turned to Kennedy for support and guidance while facing impeachment, holding numerous private conversations with a sympathetic Ted.

When Hillary entered the Senate in 2001, Ted contributed some helpful advice. With a famous political name, a family connection to the White House, and a brother who had also been a senator from New York, Ted was probably the only lawmaker on Capitol Hill who fully understood what she would be going through. Her colleagues would be wondering whether she had joined their ranks not by merit, but by family connections—an experience Kennedy understood. But ultimately, he told her, everyone in the Senate respects hard work: immerse yourself in your issues, learn about your colleagues, and make friendships on both sides of the aisle. Always a dutiful student, Hillary followed Ted's advice closely: it was common to see her during Senate votes, working the room. She always made a point of approaching the ailing Senator Strom Thurmond, the South Carolina Republican who had once been a segregationist candidate for president. Thurmond always greeted her with a smile.

But while maintaining a sense of respect for each other, Ted and Hillary never really clicked on a personal level. She was pragmatic, a hard worker with an ambitious agenda. Her style differed greatly from that of the jovial Ted, who worked assiduously at developing personal relationships to get legislation passed. Still, when she launched her campaign for the White House, Ted was ready with some more advice: make sure the Secret Service, who guarded Clinton at all times because she was a former first lady, does not keep you from connecting with voters.

But as the campaign unfolded, Ted was increasingly drawn to Obama. The opinions of his family members always weighed heavily with Ted, and even though Kathleen and Bobby Jr. were firmly in Hillary's camp, there was also strong pro-Obama sentiment among many of his children, nieces, and nephews. Ted's admiration of Obama grew after he watched the young senator's victory speech following the Iowa caucuses on January 3, 2008. He had long been waiting for a candidate who could energize young voters and African Americans, and in Obama he saw, in Mary Beth Cahill's words, "a meeting of the man and the moment."

Word of Ted's feelings reached the Clinton camp, whose hardball tactics had helped solidify Ted's decision to back Obama. While campaigning for Hillary in South Carolina, which was going to hold its primary on January 26, Bill made remarks that were perceived as racially divisive for suggesting that Obama was succeeding only because of his support from African Americans. Ted was unhappy, and had appealed directly to Clinton to stop, but to no avail.

In a series of Kennedy family conclaves, Caroline urged Ted to declare for Obama, saying that she was prepared to endorse him herself. Two days before the South Carolina primary, on Thursday, January 24, Ted notified the Obama campaign that he and Caroline were both ready to offer their support. And, in a carefully planned rollout, Caroline wrote an op-ed column, "A President Like My Father," which was published in the *New York Times* on January 27.

Later that morning, the news broke that Senator Kennedy would endorse Obama the next day—a huge blow to the Clinton campaign and one that undermined Hillary's argument that Obama was too inexperienced for the presidency. Ted called Bill Clinton that day to explain his decision. (The front page of the next day's New York *Daily News* screamed "ShafTED.")

On the morning of January 28, 2008, Obama and Kennedy appeared together before an overflow audience at Bender Arena on the campus of American University in Washington. Standing alongside them were Caroline and Patrick, who had previously endorsed Dodd but was now free to support Obama. The fact that Jack had given a famous speech at American University in June 1963, where he called for a nuclear test ban treaty with the Soviet Union, added to the symbolic echo of the historic moment. "Every time I've been asked, over the past year, who I would support in the Democratic primary, my answer has always been the same," Ted told the cheering crowd. "I'll support the candidate who inspires me, inspires all of us, who can lift our vision." He invoked his late brother and said: "It is time again for a new generation of leadership. It is time now for Barack Obama."

Ted's words left little doubt that he saw his endorsement as the passing of a torch: Jack's torch, Bobby's torch, and his own. He was, in effect, making Obama an honorary Kennedy. At one point, while Ted spoke, Obama closed his eyes and kept them closed, as if he wanted to fully absorb the moment, and the fact that Ted Kennedy, who was famous before Obama was born, was pronouncing him the best candidate for president.

The next day, three of Bobby's children—Kerry, Kathleen, and Bobby Jr.—published an op-ed column in the *Los Angeles Times* reiterating their support for Clinton. The public family split was unusual. "I've been in the family thirty years, and I've never seen that," said California Governor Arnold Schwarzenegger, whose wife, Maria Shriver, sided with Ted in backing Obama. Still, it was the senator's endorsement that drew the most headlines and had the greatest effect on the race. Edwards, who had held out hope for a Kennedy endorsement to revive his faltering campaign, suspended his candidacy on January 30 in New Orleans.

The endorsement of Obama surprised some Kennedy insiders and infuriated many of the women's groups that were backing Clinton. They unleashed a wave of denunciations. The New York chapter of the National Organization for Women issued a scathing statement, widely circulated over the Internet, implicitly raising the issue of Ted's past dalliances: "Women have just experienced the ultimate betrayal. Senator Kennedy's endorsement of Hillary Clinton's opponent in the Democratic presidential primary campaign has really hit women hard. Women have forgiven Kennedy, stuck up for him, stood by him, hushed the fact that he was late in his support of Title IX, the ERA, and the Family and Medical Leave Act to name a few. . . . And now the greatest betrayal! We are repaid with his abandonment! He's picked the new guy over us. He's joined the list of progressive white men who can't or won't handle the prospect of a woman president who is Hillary Clinton."

Clinton operatives, meanwhile, began dismissing the significance of the Kennedy endorsement she had so aggressively pursued. Kennedy only did it, the operatives said, because he was miffed that Hillary had mentioned LBJ and not JFK when discussing the civil rights triumphs of the 1960s—a suggestion the Kennedy team laughed off as absurd. But Ted, who had felt similarly burned by colleagues who sided with Carter over him in 1980, took it in stride. He had done what he thought was right and was ready to deal with any repercussions.

No sooner had Ted endorsed Obama than he hit the road for him. The timing was perfect: Ted had come out for Obama just eight days before Super Tuesday, the day when the move would have the most impact. Obama was struggling with Latino and union voters, two constituencies with whom Kennedy had substantial influence. So three days after delivering the endorsement, Ted brought his trademark gusto to New Mexico; a day later, he was in California. In both states, he focused on Latino voters who had great respect for Ted, especially after his exertions on the previous year's immigration bill. "Are you glad to see me, Santa Fe?" he bellowed at a rally before a large crowd at a community college. The reply came back: "Yes!" Chants of "Viva

Kennedy" were heard; one man held an "Obama 2008, Kennedy 2016" sign. Ted visited a restaurant called the Flying Tortilla in Santa Fe and went from table to table, then gathered the kitchen employees together for a photo.

Ted also spoke to an audience of 200 at the National Hispanic Cultural Center in Albuquerque, saluting the Latino soldiers fighting in Iraq and Afghanistan. "We have looked in the eyes of the young, a young generation that said they're not interested in being involved," Ted told the crowd. "There is one person, one candidate, one individual, who has the ability to bring together that enthusiasm. . . . His name is Barack Obama." The next day, Ted went to East Los Angeles. He sang a song in Spanish on a radio program, and jokingly challenged Schwarzenegger—a Republican who was backing John McCain—to arm wrestle on the air to decide who should be president.

Many political observers had felt that Obama couldn't compete with Clinton in the twenty-two states voting on Super Tuesday; her name recognition, and the gratitude that many Democrats felt toward her husband, would ultimately win out in what some were calling a national primary. Ted, with his own reservoirs of fame and gratitude among Democrats, helped to even the playing field for Obama. On that night, Obama held Clinton to a draw, thwarting her drive to the nomination and setting himself up for a run of eleven straight victories that helped seal the prize for him. Among the Super Tuesday states, Ted's native Massachusetts went for Hillary, which her supporters cited as a rebuke of him. Still, Ted's endorsement had delivered something potentially more important—the credibility in the Democratic Party that the Kennedys had earned over four decades. He had given many Democrats the courage to take a chance on Obama. "A lot of us want us to take bigger steps than we do, but sometimes you say, 'If I take that bigger step, do we fall?' " Representative Michael Capuano, Ted's Massachusetts colleague, said at the time. Ted "is telling people it's okay to take that bigger step—we can do it, we can win."

As he stumped with and for Obama over the next few months, Ted was reveling in his role as a kingmaker. But at 8:15 A.M. on Saturday, May 17,

2008, everything changed. He suffered a seizure in his Hyannis Port home. After being rushed to Cape Cod Hospital he was then transported by helicopter to Massachusetts General Hospital. His three children—Kara, Teddy Jr., and Patrick—hurried to his side, as did Caroline. Obama, who was campaigning in Eugene, Oregon, immediately called Vicki. "He's just been an extraordinary senator but he's also been an extraordinary friend to me," Obama said, adding, "Our job is to support him and his family in this difficult time."

By Tuesday, though, doctors had identified the cause of Kennedy's seizure, and the diagnosis left little room for optimism: Kennedy had a malignant brain tumor. At the age of seventy-six, he had been on the national scene for so long and with such force that the news seemed almost unthinkable, and the political world reacted with shock. In some cases, word of Ted's illness hit Republicans as hard as Democrats, a reminder of the bipartisan ties of this most ardently liberal of politicians. President Bush said he and his wife, Laura, were "concerned to learn of our friend Senator Kennedy's diagnosis," adding: "Ted Kennedy is a man of tremendous courage, remarkable strength, and powerful spirit." John McCain, who would soon become the Republican presidential nominee, said he hoped Ted would experience a full recovery and described him as "the single most effective member of the Senate if you want to get results." Senator John Warner, Ted's longtime Republican colleague from Virginia, said he was "so deeply saddened I have lost the words."

As Ted confronted a fight for his life, some of the 9/11 families reached out to the man who had given them so much support. Christie Coombs sent him an e-mail urging him to keep his spirits up. Then she wrote about Kennedy's illness in the journal she keeps, addressing her thoughts, as always, to her late husband, Jeff. As for Cindy McGinty, she said that when she heard about Ted's illness, she felt as if she had been punched in the stomach. But then she rallied and said to herself: "This cancer doesn't know what it's up against." She sent Kennedy several get-well cards, along with a book titled *Listening Is an Act of Love*. "He's shown me through his own personal struggles how to really put one foot in front of the other and really move forward," she says.

But like many others of his well-wishers, she had no idea whether

Ted would be well enough to continue fighting to make Obama president, a prospect that was seeming more and more likely as he drew closer to the Democratic nomination. Obama would be the first African-American nominee in history. That was something that heartened the old civil rights warrior in Kennedy, who had once described the upholding of civil rights as "the defining aspect of the American political experience: who we are or are not going to be—the helping hand to the dispossessed."

In fact, Obama had evoked Kennedy's civil rights history in his reaction to the announcement of Ted's brain cancer. "I think you can argue that I would not be sitting here as a presidential candidate had it not been for some of the battles that Ted Kennedy has fought," said Obama. "He is somebody who battled for voting rights and civil rights when I was a child. I stand on his shoulders."

CHAPTER
32

On Wednesday, May 21, 2008, Ted left Massachusetts General Hospital, flanked by family and greeted outside the door by his dogs, Sunny and Splash.

Ted and Vicki offered smiles and thumbs up in the face of the bad news announced the day before. They drove back home to Cape Cod in their black Chevrolet sport utility vehicle, news helicopters trailing overhead. They traveled through the winding roads of Hyannis until they arrived in the small neighborhood of Hyannis Port. Dozens of people—plus TV satellite trucks and cameras—gathered along the tree-lined streets, waving and calling out encouragement to the senator. One supporter wore a Kennedy campaign button older than many of the reporters there. A homemade banner hanging over a line of bushes greeted him: "Welcome home."

The SUV stopped briefly so Ted could lean out from the passenger side and shake a few hands, ever the progeny of Honey Fitz. Once he was standing outside his house, he took a breath of Cape Cod air and looked out at the water. He was home. Within hours he had changed out of his dark suit and into his sailing gear of beige corduroys, a red jacket, and a black knit hat pulled down over his ears. He watched with a smile as the dogs swam and rolled in the sand. "They'll be sleeping on her side of the bed tonight," he said, pointing to Vicki.

He, Vicki, and the dogs set out for a sail on the *Mya*, its mahogany hull cutting through the waves. Like its owner, the *Mya* is a creature of the Cape, a schooner built a little farther along the Massachusetts coast in Duxbury, in 1940. It is, in the eyes of admiring fellow boat owners, a sailor's dream. And for Ted, the *Mya* gave him a chance to reconnect to the sea, which is his fastest way to tranquillity. As Jack Kennedy said in a speech in 1962 before the start of the America's Cup Races, "All of us have in our veins the exact same percentage of salt in our blood that exists in the ocean, and, therefore, we have salt in our blood, in our sweat, in our tears. We are tied to the ocean. And when we go back to the sea—whether it is to sail or to watch it—we are going back from whence we came." That day, Ted was sailing on Nantucket Sound as he had done thousands of times since he was a young boy. Only a small square bandage on the back of his head suggested the challenging straits ahead.

The next day he announced he would not be speaking at Wesleyan University's graduation ceremony that Sunday as planned. It would have been a family affair; his stepdaughter Caroline was graduating from Wesleyan and his son Teddy Jr. was celebrating his twenty-fifth class reunion. Instead, Ted asked Barack Obama to make the speech, and Obama graciously agreed. Then Ted set out to sail again. "This is the best place in the world," he said as he looked out at the Sound.

Two days later, Vicki urged him not to participate in the 37th annual Figawi, a race across Nantucket Sound he had competed in for years, even winning the return leg in 2007. The day before the races began, as the other sailors stocked their boats with provisions, Ted's participation seemed unlikely. "There's definitely a void without him," the chairman of the Figawi board of governors, J. David Crawford, said. Yet on that Memorial Day, a week after Ted received his diagnosis, it was a glorious sailor's dream of a day: southwest winds 10 to 20 mph, with 40 mph gusts, and seas running two- to four-foot waves. Ted set out to compete. "The wind was just right," his spokeswoman, Stephanie Cutter, explained. With a team that included Chris Dodd on deck, Ted led the *Mya* to a second place finish on the 19.7-mile return leg of the race. "He was at the helm the whole way, doing what he always does, guiding the boat to the head of the fleet," said David Nunes, a family friend who helped crew the schooner. Ted, sporting a blue Red Sox cap, seemed pleased. "It's a tradition out here and we had a great day," he said.

Just days later, though, he was forced to confront his illness. Despite his nearly lifelong exposure to doctors and hospitals, Ted was agitated about what lay ahead as he faced the crucial decision on how to proceed with the growing tumor in his head. Less than a year before, he had undergone surgery to repair a near-complete blockage in his left carotid artery that had been discovered during a routine exam. And he constantly lived with the effects of his broken back from the 1964 plane crash. A malignant glioma in the left parietal lobe was the most serious battle yet.

Many who receive such a devastating diagnosis visit more than one doctor looking for answers, seeking out second and third opinions. Ted, too, sought expert advice, as he had done when Teddy Jr. battled cancer as a child and when his grown daughter Kara had lung cancer. But his stature ensured that advice came flooding in. "Kennedy worked the other way around," said Dr. Henry Brem, the director of neurosurgery at Johns Hopkins University. "Everybody came to him." Experts from some of the nation's elite neurosurgical centers, including the University of California at San Francisco, Johns Hopkins, and Duke University, met on a Friday at Massachusetts General Hospital to discuss the options. Allan Friedman, a 59-year-old surgeon from Duke, cancelled his plans to leave for a Canadian vacation that day upon hearing that he might be needed by Ted Kennedy.

The Mass. General team suggested chemotherapy and radiation but no surgery. Others argued that trying to remove as much of the tumor as possible could help. Still, none of the doctors promised a cure. This was not something that could be fixed. It was a question of extending the senator's life. Ted chose the most aggressive route: surgery. And in doing so, he skipped over his home hospital, choosing Friedman and his team at Duke University's Preston Robert Tisch Brain Tumor Center. The next day, a Saturday, he called Senate Majority Leader Harry Reid to discuss the reauthorization of a bill regarding student loans and another requiring health insurance to cover mental illness. He hoped his colleagues would pass the legislation during the last weeks of the summer session, even without him there to push the bills through. Before the operation, Ted issued a statement that bore his trademark optimism: "After completing treatment, I look forward to returning to the United States Senate and to doing everything I can to help elect Barack Obama as our next president."

That Monday, June 2, hordes of reporters and nine satellite TV trucks camped outside Duke University Medical Center awaiting news about the delicate and dangerous surgery occurring inside. The operation was a complicated three and a half hour ordeal. Such surgeries typically begin by opening the scalp and removing a piece of the skull to expose the brain. The team kept the senator awake for some portions, asking him questions as they probed his brain to ensure they weren't affecting crucial areas that controlled his speech or understanding. The brain tissue doesn't have nerve endings, so the patient feels no pain. But the testing is a crucial step, because each brain is somewhat different. "When you look at the brain," Friedman later explained, "it's not color-coded." The surgical team mapped a route to the tumor, then excised as much of the mass and its tentacles as they could. But it was unlikely they were able to remove all of the cancer. "A malignant tumor is not like a cherry in a bowl of Jell-O," Friedman said. Radiation and chemotherapy would attack what remained.

For Friedman, an acclaimed surgeon who would later operate on political columnist Robert Novak, it was a high-profile operation, yet similar to so many others he had performed in his thirty-four years in medicine. "It's not like you play your B game all the time, and now you're going to play your A game," said Friedman, an avid Duke basketball fan. Shortly after 2:00 P.M., Friedman deemed the surgery a success. The surgeon said it met his goals and he did not expect that Kennedy would have any adverse neurological effects from the procedure.

"I feel like a million bucks," Ted told Vicki immediately afterward. "I think I'll do that again tomorrow." He spent his first night in intensive care. The next day, he walked the hospital hallways, spent time with Vicki, Patrick, Kara, and sister Jean Kennedy Smith, and also caught up on the news of the day. He had survived the first twenty-four hours—the most dangerous after such a surgery—without apparent complications. But the senator kept a low profile in the following week, staying out of the camera's eye and even refraining from using the phone. Guards patrolled hospital hallways, and he was taken to the hospital's heliport for secluded exercise and fresh air.

As the danger subsided, the television trucks and photographers also left. Still, Ted had many hours of treatment and uncertainty ahead. He returned home June 9, a week after his surgery, wearing a straw hat and accompanied by Vicki. He was at his home, with his family beside him, but he was still thinking of his unfinished business. He told his loved ones he wanted to draft legislation on universal health care to be ready in January should Barack Obama win the presidency.

Ted spent time with his family over the next several weeks, continuing to sail and enjoying what time he could in between his regular trips to Boston for medical treatments. As they had every summer for Ted's reunion with his buddies, old friends John Culver and John Tunney came to see him, go sailing, and reminisce about the old days. The Fourth of July had always been the biggest celebration among the extended family, a time when all the Kennedys—some ex-spouses included—returned to the compound and crowded the lawn in a show of togetherness. And family members say that July 4, 2008, was especially significant. As three generations came together at the Kennedy compound to party, Joan Kennedy, for one, couldn't help but notice that the mood was more somber than in previous years. "I was talking to some of my nieces and nephews . . . and they're very upset about Ted's being sick," she says. "It's like [he] was their real—like their father."

But Ted had often confounded people's expectations. Just a few days after the Fourth of July gathering, he took a surprising detour on his trip to Mass. General, and headed to Washington, D.C., despite the fretting of his doctors. That day, July 9, the Senate was poised to vote on legislation in which Ted had a deep interest. It was a Democrat-sponsored bill to prevent planned cuts in Medicare reimbursements for doctors. The bill had come up once before in the Senate, but Democratic senators had failed by one vote to override a Republican filibuster. For Ted, monitoring the issue from Hyannis Port, being away from this moment was torture.

The secretary of the Senate was calling out the roll-call vote that day when suddenly Ted walked in from the back of the chamber, flanked by Patrick Kennedy, Barack Obama, Chris Dodd, and John Kerry. Ted's features seemed puffy from the steroids he took to prevent additional seizures, but he looked like himself, and flashed a big smile. An enormous cheer went up as the senators saw their ailing colleague. All of them—even the Republicans, who were taken by surprise and had no time to scrounge up another vote, and thus knew they were about to lose—were on their feet, applauding. Robert Byrd, who was one of a few senators who knew that Ted was coming, had stationed himself by the door in his wheelchair so he could be the first to greet Ted as he arrived in the chamber. Ted joyfully yelled "Jay!" as he saw Rockefeller. Dodd and Kerry tried to keep fellow senators from hugging Ted, since it might compromise his immune system. Eventually, the senators let him pass, and Ted walked to the front of the chamber. He looked at the secretary of the Senate, ready to state his vote, but the cheers continued. Ted threw up his hands in mock-exasperation, and the chamber quieted. Ted then lifted his arms, thumbs up, and said: "Aye!" The Senate chamber exploded in applause.

The surprise appearance overwhelmed his colleagues. Obama was so distracted that a fellow Democrat had to nudge him, reminding him to cast his own vote on the bill. "I return to the Senate today to keep a promise to our senior citizens," Ted said. "Win, lose, or draw, I wanted to be here."

And Ted wasn't close to finished. In the seven weeks after his diagnosis, his office had released nineteen statements on topics ranging from reactions to the Supreme Court's ruling on Washington, D.C.'s gun ban to the importance of carrying out the student loan acts.

Two weeks later, on his last day of the six-week round of chemotherapy and radiation, Vicki e-mailed friends and family with news that Ted was staying strong despite "this shock and awe phase" of the treatment. "Even in the midst of this very serious business, we've shared a lot of laughter," she wrote. "But that's not surprising to those of us who love and know Teddy—there's always laughter when he's around."

Kara, Teddy Jr., and Patrick all made a point of spending much of the summer in Hyannis Port, along with Ted's four grandchildren. His two stepchildren also came. Ted was thrilled to be able to spend more time with family on those summer days when the Cape can seem like the best place to be, and Ted can find constant reminders that he belongs there.

Hyannis is a community where the Kennedy name—and influence—shows up everywhere. During the summer of 2008, Hyannis officials discussed naming a new terminal at the Barnstable Municipal Airport for the senator and giving the Kennedy moniker to a training ship at the Massachusetts Maritime Academy. The *Barnstable Patriot* editorialized that a Cape Cod baseball team should consider changing its name to the Hyannis Senators in honor of the famed clan and its "dream infield" of Jack, Bobby, and Teddy.

Barnstable County already boasts the Lt. Joseph P. Kennedy Jr. Skating Rink, the John F. Kennedy museum along Hyannis's main drag, and the JFK memorial along its harbor. It claims both the Rose Kennedy Park and the Eunice Kennedy Shriver Park. The pediatric wing of the hospital is named for John F. Kennedy Jr. Some town members grumbled in letters to the editor and online chats about the newest naming proposals: "That should be enough for any family."

But residents of the town of Barnstable and its six villages besides Hyannis are also fiercely proud—and protective—of their famous neighbors. It's a community where a woman who works at the visitor center admits she doesn't tell people how one can walk along the beach to see the Kennedy homes up close. It's a place where locals won't correct the many tourists who take photos of a columned white house, wrongly assuming it is part of the Kennedy compound. And it's a place where the illustrated visitors' map conveniently ends right where the compound begins.

Hyannis Fire Chief Harold Brunelle understands the allure of the

Kennedy family. The 53-year-old chief remembers watching motor-cades for President John F. Kennedy rolling through town when he was a child. He remembers seeing the Kennedy brothers attending his church, St. Francis Xavier. And today, a portrait of the late president and photographs of the chief posing with Ted over the years line the walls of his office. "The Kennedy family has kind of put Hyannis on the map, so to speak," Brunelle said. "When you travel, they may never have heard of Barnstable. They don't know it. You say 'Hyannis Port, where the Kennedys live.' They say 'Oh, I know where you're from.' "

But locals such as Brunelle watched the same newscasts and read the same reports as others around the world, and they said there was little chance that Ted could make it to Denver, where the Democrats were meeting in August to nominate Obama for the presidency. The senator, as it turned out, had another surprise in him.

Ted Kennedy, old and sick, stood on a stage in Denver on August 25, 2008, and saw a party that still needed him. He had flown across the country a day earlier, determined to speak on the first night of the convention. By all medical logic, he should not have been anywhere near the Pepsi Center. It was less than three months since his surgery. His face remained bloated from the anti-seizure medication. His mane of white hair was slightly thinner at the crown, the by-product of six weeks of chemotherapy and radiation treatments. For a cancer patient, the cross-country flight posed the risk of blood clots, not to mention the chance of brain swelling due to the thin air in the Mile High City, or the possibility he could further compromise his immune system.

On top of that, from the moment he had arrived in Denver on a charter flight, Ted had been in severe pain. After a sleepless night, he went to the University of Colorado Hospital, where doctors diagnosed kidney stones unrelated to the brain tumor.

Just two hours before his scheduled time slot for addressing the convention, Ted was still in a hospital bed. All in all, it appeared likely that the only image of Ted the convention would see would be in the short tribute film about his 46-year Senate career that had been prepared by documentarian Ken Burns. But Ted told Vicki and the doctors that he wanted to speak. A physician and several paramedics accompanied him on the trip to the Pepsi Center, and he was ferried inside on a golf cart, along with Vicki and Caroline.

In a demonstration of Ted's continuing clout, Caroline had been part of the three-person vetting team that examined prospective running mates for Obama. He ultimately settled on Ted's friend Joe Biden. As Caroline had grown older, she and Ted had developed a playful rapport. She felt free to tease him. On May 11, 2008, just six days before Ted had his seizure, she had introduced him, as usual, at the Profiles in Courage dinner at the John F. Kennedy Library. It was the twentieth anniversary of the dinners, but it was also, Caroline noted, Mother's Day. So she talked about Ted's relationship with Rose Kennedy, noting that Rose gave Ted "her love of politics, poetry, and history, and her belief that everyone we ever met was a voter whose vote we might need in the next election." Caroline added mischievously: "As you all know, he also believes that he inherited her musical talent. And mariachi bands in primary states across the Southwest have humored him in this delusion."

When it came Ted's time to speak, he noted with a smile: "Caroline sometimes forgets that one of the family traditions is a camping trip. And I'm still the chief camp director. And where you end up putting your sleeping bag is still up to me. So I'll tell Caroline where she's going to end up, after this evening." Then he added, beaming and gesturing toward her in the audience: "Isn't she something else? Isn't Caroline something else? Doesn't she make it all worthwhile?"

Now it was Caroline's task to introduce Ted again, this time in Denver, with a national television audience looking on. "I am here to pay tribute to two men who have changed my life, and the life of this country: Barack Obama and Edward M. Kennedy," Caroline said. "In our family, he's known as Uncle Teddy." She spoke of how her uncle had "never missed a First Communion, a graduation, or a chance to walk a niece down the aisle," and said his sixty great-nieces and great-nephews experienced the same devotion.

After Caroline's introduction, Ted walked to the podium, to tumultuous applause. Thousands of delegates, many of them far from dry-eyed, waved blue placards with KENNEDY in white letters.

Obama was squaring off in a presidential election against GOP nominee John McCain, who was saddled with the weight of his ties to the very unpopular President Bush. In theory, Democrats should have been in the highest of spirits. Yet before Ted took the stage, several television commentators remarked on the strange absence of passion and a coherent message inside the Pepsi Center. If there was anything Ted knew how to deliver, it was a passionate message. He accepted a kiss from Vicki, stepped to the lectern, and began to speak. "It is so wonderful to be here," he told the delegates, and gave a little laugh. "Nothing—nothing—is going to keep me away from this special gathering tonight."

For the next seven minutes, Ted proceeded to give the convention a much-needed jolt of adrenaline. In a voice that was sometimes ragged around the edges but still capable of rhetorical thunder, he spoke with eloquence and urgency. He touched on the groundbreaking nature of Obama's candidacy, touting him as a force for unity and promising that the nominee would "close the book on the old politics of race, gender, and group."

"Together, we have known success and seen setbacks, victory and defeat," Ted told the crowd and the national TV audience. "But we have never lost our belief that we are all called to a better country and a newer world. And I pledge to you, I pledge to you, that I will be there next January on the floor of the United States Senate.

"For me, this is a season of hope," he added. "New hope for justice and fair prosperity for the many and not just for the few. New hope— and this is the cause of my life—new hope that we will break the old gridlock and guarantee that every American—north, south, east, west, young, old—will have decent, quality health care as a fundamental right and not a privilege. We can meet these challenges with Barack Obama. Yes, we can. And finally, yes, we will."

If it was a last hurrah, it was a resolutely forward-looking one. Even when language was borrowed from the past, it was pressed into the service of the future. To galvanize the young voters Obama needed to win the presidency, Ted evoked the words that Jack had spoken at his inauguration in 1960. "This November, the torch will be passed again to a new generation of Americans," he said. He closed by evoking the words he himself had spoken nearly three decades earlier, at another Democratic convention, saying that "the work begins anew, the hope rises again, and the dream lives on." The final three words of his 1980 convention speech, "shall never die," were changed to "lives on," suggesting the passing of that symbolic torch.

It was a performance of sheer, unstoppable will. Ted lumbered away from the podium to chants of "Teddy! Teddy!" There, waiting for him, was Vicki, who had barely left his side in the previous three months, and Caroline, his children, and several members of the younger generation of Kennedys. All of them stood waiting for the patriarch.

And there were others following his words intently from afar. There was Jessica Katz, whom Ted had gotten out of the Soviet Union in 1978. Jessica got engaged in May 2008, on the very weekend Ted had his seizure. She built her life along lines inspired by Ted, making public service her top priority. She works for the city of New York, helping to find housing for homeless and disabled people. "I definitely feel a debt that has to be repaid," she says. "He saved my life." But her debt to Ted goes beyond her choice of career. "I think of him after major life events," says Jessica. "When my grandmother died, I thought of him. When I got engaged, I thought of him. Anytime I'm feeling lucky to be alive, that's when I need to feel grateful to him."

There was Brian Hart, the father of slain soldier John Hart, whose emotional homage to Ted was featured in the tribute film shown at the Denver convention. Determined to prevent more deaths like John's, Hart founded a company that builds robotic vehicles that disable car bombs and roadside explosives like the ones used in Iraq. In the summer of 2008, with Kennedy's support, Hart won a contract from the Pentagon to continue that work.

There were the impoverished clients of the Codman Square Health Center in the Boston neighborhood of Dorchester, where Ted is such a familiar figure that staffers call him "Uncle Ted" and where the center's founder, Bill Walczak, maintains that "for everything having to do with poor people's health care, Ted Kennedy is the most important person of the last two generations."

And there was Cindy McGinty, the 9/11 widow who sat, her eyes filled with tears, and watched Ted's Denver speech from her living room couch. "There's just nothing that keeps that man down," she said to herself. She thought of all that Ted had done for her and her sons, and for many others like them who had been in need over the past half century. There had been an undeniable largeness to Ted's flaws during that time. But there had been an undeniable largeness of spirit, too. As McGinty looked at the television screen, she saw not a legend but a friend, not Kennedy the myth but Kennedy the man. "He's a real person," she says. "He's not just a picture in a history book."

EPILOGUE

On a warm spring day in 2007, Ted Kennedy and his old friend and father-in-law Edmund Reggie sat on the porch in Hyannis Port, staring at the view that Ted had enjoyed for seventy-five years. When showing visitors his home, Ted would sweep his arm out toward the gray churning ocean and express amazement that his view had never changed. It was the only thing in his life that hadn't. And now he, too, was changing—stooped and old and every bit as fat as Joe Sr. and Rose had feared he would become, back in their missives of seven decades earlier.

Neither Edmund nor Ted was much for baring his soul. For them, friendship was about doing things together and having fun, not talking about life. Ted, especially, never liked to sit down and think about his place in the world. Constant movement was like therapy for him. He kept going, even when it wasn't clear to those closest to him if he was moving away from something or toward something.

His ability to take the long view in politics, the ultimate shifting landscape, impressed all who knew him. But what Ted thought of his own life was far less apparent. No one could imagine what he pondered as he sat in the pews of St. Francis Xavier or the other churches he attended, sometimes more than once a day. Some thought it was simple devotion to Rose. Others imagined the sense of comfort he would feel in escaping the judgment of the world and submitting himself to a higher power.

Whatever the reason, the hours in church calmed him and kept him going, just like his mother always said they would. But Edmund, who was just six years older than Ted, wondered if his friend could ever just sit back, enjoy life, and achieve the kind of peace and acceptance that retirement can bring.

"You're nuts to beat yourself to death like this on the Senate floor," Edmund said in the blunt, no-nonsense way in which the two men communicated. "Passing a new law won't be any more glorious for you than the reputation you've made. Some people say you and Daniel Webster are the greatest senators of all time."

Ted seemed taken aback, not by the prospect of retirement but at the suggestion that another senator might have achieved as much as he had.

"What did Webster do?" Ted responded in a jesting tone.

Edmund could only marvel again at the Kennedys' competitive spirit, and the straight line that could be drawn from the dinner table of the 1930s in that very house to the conversation on the porch that spring afternoon. Pointing out toward Nantucket Sound, Edmund said: "You have all this. You and Vicki love to travel. Why are you beating your brains out? You've got all the money you need. Your kids are all raised."

"No," said Ted. "I don't think so. I'll stay in the Senate."

Daniel Webster, as it happened, also spent more than four decades on the national stage, always on the periphery of the presidency. He was constantly mentioned as a contender but the only time he actually ran, as a favorite son from New England in 1836, he drew only 2.7 percent of the vote. It wasn't a debacle—the fractured Whig party ran four different candidates, hoping to throw the election to the House of Representatives—and Webster emerged with his reputation intact. But he would never be president.

Instead, he built a career in the Senate. Nonetheless, parallels between Daniel Webster and Ted Kennedy go only so far. In Webster's era, the Senate was less a fount of legislation than a debating society, where speeches were carefully prepared, memorized, and then printed for distribution throughout the country. And with the country riven by the slavery issue, and the constitutional question of whether states could secede, Webster stood as the foremost unionist until the emergence of Abraham Lincoln.

Like Lincoln's, Webster's ideas were put into words, and the words meant more than any law, policy, or social welfare program. In his great valedictory statement, in a speech in New York in 1852, Webster compared the United States to Rome, begging that all Americans protect and preserve their country's Constitution, so there would be "no decline and fall."

Webster was, in short, a model of the kind of erudite New England statesman that Ted's early critics — the Harvard scholars who doubted his abilities — yearned for. But the Senate had long since ceased to be a debating society, and Ted, like Lyndon Johnson before him, would help transform it into a legislative body.

Ted's record isn't limited to the roughly 2,500 major bills he authored over forty-six years, of which at least 300 became law. In whole areas of policy — civil rights, immigration, health care, and education — he dominated the Congress for almost a half century.

Other than Supreme Court justices, he was the only architect of the liberal transformation of the 1960s to make it into the 1970s, and he kept fighting well into the twenty-first century. His legislation provided health care to tens of millions of people, and funded cures for diseases that struck tens of millions more around the world. His Immigration Act of 1965 ended the national-origins test that had, for forty years, choked off immigration from non-European countries. The multicultural America of the twenty-first century is the fruit of his legislation.

He could, of course, claim only partial credit for the civil rights bills and health care achievements of the 1960s because he worked with a liberal majority in the Congress and an activist president in Johnson. Quite possibly, but by no means certainly, those bills would have passed without his leadership.

But in the 1980s, when a Republican president and Senate were determined to roll back those programs, he led the fight to keep them alive. His defeat of Ronald Reagan's attempts to modify civil rights laws, and his epic confrontation with Robert Bork, set the boundaries for the conservative era in American politics. And against the greatest of legislative odds, he continued to expand government's role in extending civil rights to the disabled, providing health care to children, and giving loans to college students, among many other initiatives.

While presidents will always be judged by how they confronted the challenges of their moment in history, Kennedy, from his perch in the Senate, defined policy over a longer term: his accomplishments belong to the glacial movements that shape the challenges of presidents.

And yet, while his impact may be measured against that of Webster or Richard Russell or other Senate leviathans, his career was unique. Russell may have been a self-made man, as he reminded the young Ted, but he didn't carry the burden of expectations that Ted did, and no expectations were ever greater.

And it is there, in many people's minds, that Ted failed to measure up.

When Jack Kennedy died so suddenly and shockingly, jolting the country, Ted bore up well. Like Jackie and Bobby, he took to burnishing Jack's legacy in ways that conformed to his own image. Jackie, who invented the Camelot analogy, made her husband, in death, a figure of enduring charm and glamour, like herself. Bobby made him an iconic figure of righteousness—superhuman, like Bobby himself aspired to be. Ted made his brother a liberal.

Jack was a cautious politician who ran for president in 1960 to the right of the Eisenhower administration on foreign policy, and who promised an across-the-board tax cut—not more social programs—to stimulate the nation's economy. Jack became more progressive over time, making meaningful overtures toward arms control and civil rights. Still, many historians regard him as a latecomer to the issue of equal rights for blacks, and doubt that he would have expended much political capital on an issue that would alienate the South from the Democratic Party for generations.

But Ted, in his Senate speech introducing the Civil Rights Act of 1964, portrayed the bill as the last wish of the assassinated president, summoning all the nation's grief behind the cause of equal rights for blacks.

And so, when later generations expressed their disappointment that Ted hadn't lived up to the virtuous legacies of Jack and Bobby, they were citing legacies shaped by Ted himself. No one remembered the cautious Jack. And few would remember the "ruthless" Bobby, who once aligned himself with Joe McCarthy, served as a political fixer for Jack, and maintained a destructive rivalry with Lyndon Johnson. Ted helped mold Bobby's saintly image by eulogizing him as a man of simple convictions, "who saw wrong and tried to right it, saw suffering and tried to heal it, saw war and tried to stop it."

Ted was entrapping himself in a Kennedy myth he could never escape, though he did use it for his own purposes—to build support for ambitious legislation, yes, but also to escape political death. After Chappaquiddick, when millions of people demanded explanations, he spoke of having wondered, in those terrible early-morning hours when he did nothing to report the accident, if there really was a curse on the Kennedys. During his nephew's rape trial, he reminded jurors of the family tragedies by noting how Stephen Smith, the nephew's recently deceased father, had been like a surrogate brother to him. In the 1994 Senate race, when Mitt Romney attacked a Kennedy real estate deal, Ted declared that the Kennedys had paid "too high a price" to ever profit from public service.

Evoking Jack and Bobby was his free pass, but also his yoke. When he needed a national image of his own, in 1980, he couldn't escape the comparisons with his brothers. Their youthful profiles would be compared to his thickening one, their gilded words to his fractured syntax. His fate was less Shakespearean than something out of a fantasy story—the child who was touched by magic but forever haunted by death.

Bobby's assassination, leaving Ted the head of the family at thirty-six, with the weight of the country's expectations on his shoulders, overwhelmed him. It eventually became clear that the central moral question at Chappaquiddick was not whether he was taking Mary Jo Kopechne to the ferry or to the beach, or even if he had been drunk or sober. It was: Why didn't he get help? Was his failure one of princely indulgence, assuming he could do anything and have others clean up, or something closer to the opposite — the faltering of a grief-stricken and damaged psyche, unable to confront his responsibilities?

People will forever disagree, but the disintegration of Ted's personal life continued for a quarter century. The robust politician was dogged by obvious weaknesses, from drinking to problems maintaining relationships; his furious work ethic couldn't outrun his personal problems.

After his 1980 presidential defeat, it appeared that his story was all over but the telling, that he was fated to live out his years repeating the pattern of periodic legislative successes and personal disappointments.

But there was another act to come.

Ted's marriage to Vicki Reggie seemed, at first, a gesture to appease his critics or, perhaps, his many concerned friends. But it soon proved to be a love match, and a very adult partnership. She fully inhabited his personal life and found space in his political life, too — so much so that some wondered if she should one day be heir to his Senate seat.

His step-parenthood of her children Curran and Caroline revived what had always been a warm place in his life: his love for children, and his eager embrace of his role as family patriarch. With Vicki providing the stability that was missing in the Kennedy family for decades, Ted became a more robust patriarch to his own extended family, as well.

And while Joseph Kennedy Sr.'s commitment to public service was indistinguishable from his quest for power, Ted's emphasis on public service — passed on as the Kennedy creed to the next generation — was more generous. As his own ambition shifted from the presidency to advancing particular issues, Ted's allegiance to his causes became more personal. Friends saw an element of expiation in his commitment to issues above all, with little concern for personal credit or political glory;

with his own Senate seat secure after 1994, he was working only for others, and redeeming himself for his earlier wrongs. His thousands of phone calls per year to people coping with losses was another way to give back to society, to draw on his misfortunes to make others feel less alone in their grief.

Under Ted's guidance, his younger family members found meaning in their own endeavors. The Kennedys were acting out the spirit of noblesse oblige that Joe Sr. had once admired in the New England Protestants and sought to supplant. But Joe's grasping sense of ambition undermined the family's good works and added an element of distrust to the way the Kennedys were perceived. Only after Ted renounced any further interest in the presidency, and his nieces and nephews slowly surrendered their own political ambitions, did the Kennedys become more purely charitable.

Taken together, their good deeds represented significant bodies of work, from founding African universities to helping thousands of poor people heat their homes more inexpensively; from boosting the self-esteem of people with disabilities to promoting awareness of global warming.

And yet Ted failed as patriarch in the way that meant the most to his father: in grooming a future president. Despite their large numbers, the generation of Kennedys after Ted's has fallen short on the goal of producing political leaders. Bobby's eldest children, studious Kathleen and jaunty Joe, both won elective offices. But Kathleen's career lacked the magic that buoyed the earlier generation. After serving eight years as lieutenant governor of Maryland, she lost her race for governor. And Joe, at one time a rising star in Congress, declined to run again after a scandal surrounding his brother Michael's relationship with his family's underage babysitter and Michael's death soon afterward in a skiing accident.

Patrick, Ted and Joan's youngest child, remained in Congress, but suffered from alcohol and drug addictions; his political future seemed more likely to lead to a Rhode Island Senate seat than to the White House. Caroline, who spent so long on the sidelines, didn't catch the political bug until well into middle age.

So Ted, in his later years, sought to pass on the Kennedy chalice—the hopes, the dreams, the mythic promise surrounding Jack's unfinished presidency—to others. First was John Kerry, Ted's junior colleague from Massachusetts. Kerry was often thought of as an ersatz JFK, down to mimicking Jack's mannerisms; but Kerry earned Ted's gratitude by deferring to him on most domestic issues, and seemed, for a while, to have caught the Kennedy magic. Kerry's presidential race, however, ended in a close defeat.

Next was Barack Obama, who evoked comparisons to JFK for more substantive reasons: he made young people feel excited about politics. And Ted, just weeks before his brain tumor diagnosis, undertook a physically demanding campaign tour to assist Obama. Joined by Caroline, Ted stressed the parallels between President Kennedy and the youthful Obama, who was two years old when Jack died.

At times, it seemed as if Ted and Obama were using each other. After almost forty-five years, the Camelot mystique was losing its luster, and Ted was hoping Obama could restore its power. But Obama, who had youthful charisma to spare, craved the support of the Kennedys for a different reason. He wanted what Ted could give him, not Jack.

He wanted the very real credibility that the senator had earned from a grateful Democratic Party, not the fading promise of the long-dead president.

On November 4, 2008, Ted and Vicki, joined by friends and aides, watched as Barack Obama was declared the forty-fourth president of the United States; the following day the two men had a private chat.

In several essays published around election time, Ted compared Obama to Jack and Bobby and cited their "capacity to inspire a nation and a world." But in paying tribute to Obama, as to his own brothers, Ted was also defining the new president as a liberal in the mold of Ted himself. He was keeping memories of Jack and Bobby alive, but also the political agenda that was his alone. Perhaps no one understood the power and limits of charisma better than Ted; he wanted to make sure that Obama's inspiration yielded actual accomplishments, not just promises.

When Ted returned to the Senate in late November after five

months of cancer treatments, with Vicki and their two dogs by his side, he was smiling and robust, but once again haunted by death— this time his own. It was in the air along with the too-tight smiles of his Senate staff members and the moist eyes of others who worked there. But with Ted's anointed candidate soon to be inaugurated and big Democratic majorities in the House and the Senate, it felt as much like the rebirth of the Kennedy era as its end. He used his father's cane in a gesture of continuity, and greeted the Capitol police as if he planned to be back for a long time.

Ted Kennedy returned to the Senate for a reason. Some senators had quietly been assuming he would take a backseat and that his great cause—universal health care—was in danger of being left behind. It was too expensive, too much to expect the new president to tackle in his first months or year in office.

Ted was there to remind everyone—including Barack Obama— that he expected to pass a universal health care bill early in the new year. Other needs might press in, but Ted's cause would endure. No one could know how much he really believed in the politics of hope, in the mystique he himself had carried so fitfully for so long. Maybe Obama would move mountains. Maybe he wouldn't. But in any case, Ted was pushing forward the way he had learned to do over five decades.

Relentlessly, with hard work and no illusions.

ACKNOWLEDGMENTS

This book drew from all corners of the *Boston Globe,* past and present, to help produce a definitive look at Senator Kennedy's life.

The book was the vision of Simon & Schuster Editor-in-Chief Priscilla Painton, whose journalistic expertise helped frame the entire narrative. She was ably assisted by Associate Director of Copyediting Gypsy da Silva and Production Manager Mike Kwan.

The *Globe*'s editor, Martin Baron, provided support, and Book Development Editor Janice Page helped edit and coordinate the project. Lane Zachary and Todd Schuster, the *Globe*'s literary agents, offered editing and writing input.

Mark Feeney, the *Globe*'s senior arts critic, contributed writing and research, and offered helpful advice and insights on the entire narrative. *Globe* correspondents Kytja Weir and Alan Wirzbicki researched and drafted key portions of the book. Stephanie Vallejo of the *Globe*'s Washington bureau oversaw fact-checking, with the help of former assistant national editor Richard Dill.

Senior editors Mark Morrow and Scott Heller provided valuable editing advice. Brian McGrory, who covered Kennedy in Washington and as metro editor oversaw coverage of his illness, helped organize interviews and offered insights. Fiona Luis and Stephen Greenlee contributed staff time and resources to the project.

The book also drew on the reporting and insights of many generations of *Globe* writers and editors, including former Washington bureau chiefs Robert Healy, Martin Nolan, and Stephen Kurkjian. Political writers John Aloysius Farrell and Thomas Oliphant, who covered Kennedy extensively over the decades, provided important input, as did former *Globe* editor Matthew V. Storin, who covered Kennedy in the 1960s and '70s.

The *Globe* is also grateful to many other staff members who contributed to its Kennedy coverage, including managing editors Caleb Solomon and Mary Jane Wilkinson, national politics editor Jim Smith, photo editor Paula Nelson, graphics editor David Schutz, video editors Thea Breite and Ann Silvio, librarians Lisa Tuite, Betty Grillo, and Jeremiah Manion, online coordinator Tito Bottitta, photo licensing manager Bruce Pomerantz, product development director Nancy Buzby, and researcher Liberty McHugh Pilsch.

The *Globe*'s publisher, P. Steven Ainsley, offered his full support and cooperation, for which we are grateful.

NOTES

INTRODUCTION

PAGE

1 *At 8:19 A.M. on Saturday, May 17, 2008:* Hyannis Fire Department log report; and Fire Department members including EMS Supervisor Michael Medeiros, Chief Harold Brunelle, interviews by Kytja Weir, October 13–14, 2008.

1 *Arriving at the house, the ambulance pulled up beside a billowing:* Heather Schatz, Best Buddies, interview by Kytja Weir, October 22, 2008.

2 *When the ambulance arrived at Cape Cod Hospital:* Cynthia McCormick, *Cape Cod Times*, May 21, 2008.

2 *His wife, Vicki, his inseparable partner:* Harold Brunelle, interview by Kytja Weir, October 14, 2008.

2 *He had used a tennis racket:* Michael Levenson, *The Boston Globe*, May 20, 2008.

3 *The ambulance arrived five minutes later:* Hyannis Fire Department log, May 17, 2008.

3 *But while en route to the hospital:* Cynthia McCormick, *Cape Cod Times*, May 21, 2008.

3 *the 600-acre air field:* Barnstable Municipal Airport Manager Frank Sanchez, interview by Kytja Weir, October 14, 2008.

4 *It was a gray, wet morning:* National Climatic Data Center, Barnstable Municipal Airport, May 17, 2008.

4 *As the helicopter arced over Plymouth:* John M. Broder and Jeff Zeleny, *New York Times* online, May 18, 2008.

4 *John McCain of Arizona, the presumptive Republican:* McCain campaign website, May 17, 2008; campaign trail group interview, May 20, 2008.

5 *Obama was campaigning in Oregon:* The Politico, May 17, 2008.

5 *Meanwhile, at the Kennedy compound, the celebrations:* Heather Schatz, Best Buddies, interview by Kytja Weir, October 22, 2008.

5 *Anthony Shriver, hosting the event on:* K. C. Myers, *Cape Cod Times*, May 18, 2008.

5 *He added, later that day:* Peter Schworm and Matt Viser, *Boston Globe* online update, May 18, 2008.

6 *it was he who quadrupled federal spending:* Dr. Phillip A. Sharp, speech text, November 24, 2008.

6 *Indeed, as he walked out of Mass. General after:* AP, May 21, 2008.

7 *He knew, even as he gazed:* Karen Jeffrey, *Cape Cod Times*, May 22, 2008.

7 *It was there, in 1969:* Rita Dallas with Jeanira Ratcliffe, *The Kennedy Case* (New York: G. P. Putnam's Sons, 1973), 338.

CHAPTER ONE

PAGE

12 *"Separate 'society columns' "*: Rose Fitzgerald Kennedy, *Times to Remember* (Garden City, NY: Doubleday, 1974), 51.

13 *The couple often:* Laurence Leamer, *The Kennedy Men, 1901–1963* (New York: William Morrow, 2001), 57.

13 *"I became so incensed"*: Rose Kennedy journal notes, 1972, Rose Kennedy Papers, JFK Library, Boston.

13 *Decades later, she would:* ibid.

13 *"It is the night before exams"*: John F. Kennedy letter to his mother, February 22, 1932, Joseph P. Kennedy Papers, JFK Library, Boston.

13 *"Everyone is crazy"*: Kathleen Kennedy, March 27, 1932, Joseph P. Kennedy Papers, JFK Library, Boston.

14 *"Biscuits and Muffins"*: Mary Jo Clasby, interview by Bella English, July 2008.

14 *"I was scared to death"*: John F. Kennedy, ed., *As We Remember Joe* (Cambridge, MA: University Press, privately printed, 1945), 59.

14 *"We tried to keep"*: Robert Sherrill, *The Last Kennedy* (New York: Dial Press, 1976), 20.

14 *"Thank you very much"*: Edward M. Kennedy to Santa Claus, Christmas 1937, Joseph P. Kennedy Papers, JFK Library, Boston.

15 *"I think I am going to get"*: Edward M. Kennedy to Joseph P. Kennedy, 1939, Amanda Smith, ed., *Hostage to Fortune* (New York: Viking, 2001), 389.

15 *"My name is Moe"*: *Times to Remember*, 282.

15 *"He had to fight harder"*: William Peters, "Teddy Kennedy," *Redbook*, June 1962, 36.

15 *"I got dressed up"*: Edward M. Kennedy to Joseph P. Kennedy, 1939, Smith, *Hostage to Fortune*, 397.

15 *"I have never experienced"*: David Nasaw, interview by Bella English, September 2008.

16 *"Don't hesitate to interrupt"*: Edward M. Kennedy, ed., *The Fruitful Bough* (privately printed, 1965), 194.

16 *"You and Bobby are the worst"*: Joseph P. Kennedy to Edward M. Kennedy, September 11, 1940, Smith, *Hostage to Fortune*, 470.

16 *"I wish you would get hold"* Joseph P. Kennedy to Jean Kennedy, August 2, 1940. Rose Kennedy Papers, JFK Library, Boston.

16 *"I certainly wish you could"*: *Times to Remember*, 272.

17 *"If I wanted to contribute"*: Edward M. Kennedy, *Her Grace Above Gold* (privately printed, 1997), 37.

18 *"I hope when you grow"*: *The Fruitful Bough*, 203.

18 *"No losers"*: ibid., 200.

18 *"He wouldn't let any"*: ibid., 203.

19 *"Rose, this is a helluva"*: *Times to Remember*, 221.

19 *"The Kennedys were the royal family":* Will Swift, interview by Bella English, July 2008.

19 *Joe Sr. gave their nanny:* footage from Hearst *Metrodome*, biography of Joseph P. Kennedy, 1938–1940, JFK Library, Boston.

20 *"I can't get the King's":* Joseph P. Kennedy to Edward M. Kennedy, July 23, 1940, Joseph P. Kennedy Papers.

20 *Further alienating Winston Churchill:* Will Swift, *The Kennedys Amidst the Gathering Storm, A Thousand Days in London, 1938–1940* (New York: HarperCollins, 2008), 199.

20 *"Well, they brought it on":* Leamer, *The Kennedy Men*, 115.

21 *During the Blitz:* Swift, *The Kennedys Amidst the Gathering Storm*, 281.

21 *"I never want to see":* ibid., 294.

21 *Soon after, Roosevelt made:* ibid., 295.

22 *"For us younger children":* Mary Jo Clasby, interview by Bella English, July 2008.

22 *"Children, your brother":* The Fruitful Bough, 207.

23 *"They'd cut bridle paths":* Mary Jo Clasby, interview by Bella English, July 2008.

23 *"Teddy, make sure":* ibid.

23 *"We'd say":* ibid.

23 *The summer of 1944:* Robert Shrum, interview by Bella English, July 2008.

24 *"Jack told him never":* John Culver, interview by Bella English, July 2008.

CHAPTER TWO

PAGE

25 *"I went to classes":* William Peters, "Teddy Kennedy," *Redbook*, June 1962, 36.

25 *"You've got to learn":* Adam Clymer, *Edward M. Kennedy* (New York: William Morrow, 1999), 14.

25 *"That was hard to take":* Laurence Leamer, *The Kennedy Men, 1901–1963* (New York: William Morrow 2001), 165.

26 *"I think Ted":* John Culver, interview by Bella English, July 2008.

26 *"I am still":* Joseph P. Kennedy to John F. Kennedy, October 5, 1943, Joseph P. Kennedy Papers.

26 *"Ted is getting":* Eunice Kennedy to Joseph P. Kennedy, November 20, 1939, ibid.

26 *"Thinking of you":* Rose Kennedy telegram to Joseph P. Kennedy, 1940, ibid.

27 *"Although I do not want":* Her Grace Above Gold, 50.

27 *"My only complaint":* ibid., 52.

27 *"You still spell 'no' ":* Joseph P. Kennedy to Edward M. Kennedy, January 31, 1946, Smith, *Hostage to Fortune*, 624.

27 *"Teddy is the same":* Joseph P. Kennedy Sr. to Joseph P. Kennedy Jr., December 7, 1943, Joseph P. Kennedy Papers, JFK Library, Boston.

27 *"You didn't pass"*: Joseph P. Kennedy to Edward M. Kennedy, October 5, 1943, Smith, *Hostage to Fortune*, 569.

27 *"A mother knows"*: Rose Kennedy speech, 1962, *Her Grace Above Gold*, 17.

28 *"Dear Jack, this is a note"*: Smith, *Hostage to Fortune*, 684.

28 *"What are you going to do"*: David Nasaw, interview by Bella English, September 2008.

28 *When the inquisitive Eunice*: *Her Grace Above Gold*, 43.

29 *"If he gets too excited"*: Rose Kennedy to Robert F. Kennedy, 1958, Joseph P. Kennedy Papers, JFK Library, Boston.

29 *"I just said"*: *Her Grace Above Gold*, 141.

29 *Dinner was always*: ibid., 22.

30 *Rose was obsessed*: ibid., 36.

30 *"Remember, too"*: ibid., 49.

30 *"I wish you would"*: ibid., 38.

30 *"I noticed"*: ibid., 38.

30 *"I watched you speak"*: ibid., 38.

31 *When he was ten*: *The Fruitful Bough*, 32.

31 *"In the old days"*: Rose Kennedy Papers, JFK Library, Boston.

31 *"I can still see"*: *Her Grace Above Gold, 32*.

32 *"Jack was the pitcher"*: Terrill Griggs, interview by Bella English, July 2008.

32 *"Then we all voted"*: *McCalls*, August 1957, 35.

32 *"He said, 'We've got'"*: Dick Clasby, interview by Bella English, July 2008.

32 *a "vital and vibrant"*: Frank Millet, e-mail message to Bella English, September 8, 2008.

33 *"about the biggest dance"*: Edward M. Kennedy to Joseph P. Kennedy, 1948, Rose Kennedy Papers.

33 *Once, playing hockey*: Edward M. Kennedy to Rose Kennedy and Joseph P. Kennedy, December 12, 1946, ibid.

33 *"I have now dropped"*: Edward M. Kennedy to Rose and Joseph P. Kennedy, December 12, 1946, Rose Kennedy Papers.

33 *His senior yearbook photo*: *The Orange and Blue* (Milton Academy yearbook), 1950, 18.

33 *The boys began*: ibid., 46.

33 *"His standards were"*: *The Fruitful Bough*, 203.

33 *"Mother supplied the"*: *Her Grace Above Gold, 34*.

34 *"I wish you could"*: Edward M. Kennedy, letter to the editor, *Newsweek*, December 15, 1969, 14B.

34 *"Teddy was more"*: Bob Healy, interview by Bella English, July 2008.

34 *While at Milton, Teddy borrowed*: Edward M. Kennedy to Joseph P. Kennedy, April 25, 1948, Rose Kennedy Papers.

34 *"a definite blow"*: Edward M. Kennedy to Joseph P. Kennedy, 1948, Rose Kennedy Papers.

35 *"The pay was usually"*: William Peters, "Teddy Kennedy," *Redbook*, June 1962, 36.

35 *At Milton Academy: The Fruitful Bough*, 204.

35 *at Harvard:* ibid., 205.

35 *"ahead of the masses":* ibid.

35 *He often went to:* Edward M. Kennedy to Joseph P. Kennedy, May 10, 1948, Rose Kennedy Papers.

35 *Back in 1944, when Teddy:* Joseph P. Kennedy Sr. to Joseph P. Kennedy Jr., April 7, 1944, Joseph P. Kennedy Papers.

35 *"Your youngest brother":* Lawrence Leamer, *The Kennedy Men* (New York: William Morrow, 1974), 202.

CHAPTER THREE

PAGE

37 *"They said he had no qualms":* Robert F. Kennedy to Joseph P. Kennedy Sr., December 1950, Rose Kennedy Papers, JFK Library, Boston.

38 *"Ted was a bright guy":* Ron Messer, interview by Bella English, July 2008.

38 *"Teddy didn't manage himself":* Burton Hersh, interview by Neil Swidey, July 2008.

38 *"He got no special":* Joseph Maguire, interview by Bella English, August 2008.

39 *"I hope you will make up":* Joseph P. Kennedy Sr. to Edward M. Kennedy, July 18, 1951, Joseph P. Kennedy Papers, JFK Library, Boston.

39 *"I think he got to know":* James Sterling Young, interview by Bella English, September 2008.

40 *"People like Ted":* Joseph Maguire, interview by Bella English, August 2008.

40 *"Keep after the books":* Joseph P. Kennedy Sr. to Edward M. Kennedy, January 9, 1951, Joseph P. Kennedy Papers.

40 *Not only that, he:* Edward M. Kennedy to Rose and Joseph P. Kennedy Sr., 1951, Rose Kennedy Papers.

41 *"So the best thing to do":* Rose Kennedy to Edward M. Kennedy, June 20, 1952, Joseph P. Kennedy Papers.

41 *"Rose, are you out?":* Her Grace Above Gold, 38.

41 *Teddy was looking forward:* ibid., 33.

41 *"His girl, the nurse":* Rose Kennedy to Joseph P. Kennedy Sr., 1953, Joseph P. Kennedy Papers.

42 *"He may weigh 215":* Jean Kennedy to Joseph P. Kennedy Sr., 1953, Joseph P. Kennedy Papers.

42 *"Several little fellows":* Edward M. Kennedy to Rose and Joseph P. Kennedy Sr., 1952, Joseph P. Kennedy Papers, JFK Library, Boston.

42 *"He was dead serious":* Claude Hooten, interview by Bella English, August 2008.

42 *"He put on the pads":* Ted Carey, interview by Bella English, September 2008.

43 *"We'd go to the Stork Club":* Dick Clasby, interview by Bella English, August 2008.

43 *"He had such a zest"*: Claude Hooten, interview by Bella English, August 2008.

43 *"We had classmates thinking"*: Dick Clasby, interview by Bella English, August 2008.

43 *"He had a twinkle"*: ibid.

44 *"I fell over trees"*: ibid.

44 *"We were as close"*: Ted Carey, interview by Bella English, September, 2008.

46 *"Kennedy, what's going on?"*: ibid.

46 *"I'll never forget it"*: John Culver, interview by Bella English, July 2008.

47 *"So Ted and I went"*: Dick Clasby, interview by Bella English, July 2008.

47 *In the Kennedy family:* Her Grace Above Gold, 34.

48 *"Through her we have"*: ibid., 39.

48 *"After I spilled"*: ibid., 121.

48 *Her brother Joe:* ibid., 123.

48 *Bobby Jr. said:* ibid., 126.

48 *But amid the fun:* John Culver, interview by Bella English, July 2008.

CHAPTER FOUR

49 *"Why don't you get?"*: Dick Clasby, interview by Bella English, July 2008.

50 *"I remember a lot of"*: William Peters, "Teddy Kennedy," *Redbook*, June 1962, 70.

50 *He followed a sultan:* Edward M. Kennedy to Joseph P. Kennedy Sr., August 1956, Joseph P. Kennedy Papers, JFK Library, Boston.

50 *Teddy pored over:* Edward M. Kennedy to Joseph P. Kennedy Sr., May 1958, Joseph P. Kennedy Papers, JFK Library, Boston.

50 *"He'd gone to Harvard"*: John Tunney, interview by Bella English, August 2008.

51 *"Now, you try to run"*: ibid.

53 *"You did a great job"*: Joseph P. Kennedy Sr. to Edward M. Kennedy, April 21, 1959, Joseph P. Kennedy Papers, JFK Library, Boston.

53 *"It was the first time"*: Ted Sorenson, interview by Bella English, August 2008.

54 *"If you're going to make"*: Joseph P. Kennedy Sr. to Edward M. Kennedy, May 2, 1958, Amanda Smith, ed., *Hostage to Fortune: The Letters of Joseph P. Kennedy* (New York: Viking, 2001), 680.

54 *Joe, once again:* "Kennedy Names Brother to Head Senate Campaign," *Boston Globe*, May 2, 1958.

54 *Then he released:* "Kennedy's Brother in Court—Left Auto License at Home," *Boston Globe*, June 4, 1958.

CHAPTER FIVE

PAGE

55 *In this respect:* John Tunney, interview by Bella English, August 2008.

55 *"I was not intimidated":* Joan Kennedy, interview by Bella English and Neil Swidey, July 2008.

56 *Eunice, who was on:* Rose Kennedy, *Times to Remember* (Garden City, NY: Doubleday, 1974), 262.

56 *"It was a command":* Joan Kennedy, interview by Bella English and Neil Swidey, July 2008.

56 *"You know, in the 1950s":* ibid.

57 *"What do you think?":* Rose Kennedy, *Times to Remember*, 432.

57 *In fact, Joan says:* Joan Kennedy, interview by Bella English and Neil Swidey, July 2008.

57 *"Dearest Connie":* Rose Kennedy to Joan Bennett, September 14, 1958, Rose Kennedy Papers, JFK Library, Boston.

57 *Joan would later reason:* Joan Kennedy, interview by Bella English and Neil Swidey, July 2008.

57 *Later, watching the film:* Laurence Leamer, *The Kennedy Men*, 1901–1963 (New York: William Morrow, 2001), 399.

58 *During the reception:* Adam Clymer notes, JFK Library, Boston.

58 *"You could walk right out":* Joan Kennedy, interview by Bella English and Neil Swidey, July 2008.

58 *"One of his abiding":* Gerard Doherty, interview by Bella English, August 2008.

59 *"Would you consider":* ibid.

59 *"Here's to 1960":* Adam Clymer, *Edward M. Kennedy* (New York: William Morrow, 1999), 26.

60 *"I said, 'Ted' ":* Ted Carey, interview by Bella English, September 2008.

60 *"He was adorable":* Joan Kennedy, interview by Bella English and Neil Swidey, July 2008.

60 *"Evidently only the hardier souls":* Letter from Edward M. Kennedy to Rose and Joseph P. Kennedy Sr., August 1958, Rose Kennedy Papers.

61 *"Teddy's role was that":* Bob Healy, interview by Bella English, July 2008.

61 *"My best friend":* Tom Oliphant, interview by Bella English, July 2008.

61 *"Teddy was a good":* Bob Healy, interview by Bella English and Neil Swidey, July 2008.

62 *"Joan Kennedy—Too Beautiful":* Joan Kennedy, interview by Bella English and Neil Swidey, July 2008.

62 *"I told him":* Claude Hooten, interview by Bella English, August 2008.

63 *"He's the hardest working man":* ibid.

63 *"Teddy said, 'You can do it' ":* Robert Shrum, interview by Bella English, July 2008.

63 *According to the: Philadelphia Inquirer*, January 1962.

64 *At the last minute:* Rose Kennedy, *Times to Remember*, 378.

CHAPTER SIX

PAGE

65 *Bobby, too, gave him:* Burton Hersh, interview by Neil Swidey, August 2008.

65 *The* Denver Post *put:* Thomas P. Morgan, "Teddy," *Esquire*, April 1962, 151.

65 *A joke spread:* William Peters, "Teddy Kennedy," *Redbook*, June 1962, 37.

66 *"Can I come back":* Burton Hersh, *The Education of Edward Kennedy* (New York: William Morrow, 1972), 146. Also, Hersh, interview by Neil Swidey, August 2008.

66 *He still used:* Rita Dallas, July 2008, and Burton Hersh, interviews by Neil Swidey, August 2008.

66 *They talked about how:* Claude Hooten, interview by Neil Swidey, August 2008.

66 *As Ted became more serious:* Adam Clymer, *Edward M. Kennedy* (New York: William Morrow, 1999), 31.

66 *"The disadvantage of my position":* Betty Hannah Hoffman, "What It's Like to Marry a Kennedy," *Ladies' Home Journal*, October 1962.

67 *"His main reason for wanting":* Redbook, June 1962. Also see Joan's interview in the May 26, 1962 *New Bedford Standard-Times* referenced in Murray B. Levin, *Kennedy Campaigning* (Boston: Beacon Press, 1966), 7.

67 *"All I remember":* Joan Kennedy, interview by Bella English and Neil Swidey, July 2008.

67 *It would take too long:* Eunice Shriver essay in *The Fruitful Bough*, 220.

68 *"I'll hear whether":* Clymer, *Edward M. Kennedy*, 31.

68 *Joe was adamant:* Stewart Alsop, "What Made Teddy Run," *Saturday Evening Post*, October 27, 1962, 17.

68 *"Fervent admirers of the Kennedys":* Harold H. Martin, "The Amazing Kennedys," *Saturday Evening Post*, September 7, 1957, 48.

69 *He told author:* Bela Kornitzer, "Here Comes Ted Kennedy," *The Boston Advertiser*, October 14, 1962, 1.

69 *Fellow prosecutor:* Newman Flanagan, interview by Neil Swidey, July 2008.

70 *A subsequent* Saturday: Alsop, *Saturday Evening Post*, October 1962.

70 *On the eighth floor:* Newman Flanagan, interview by Neil Swidey, July 2008.

70 *In February 1961:* "Ted Kennedy's First Case Lures Flock of Lawyers," *Boston Globe*, February 17, 1961.

70 *"Dear Dad":* Letters from Ted Kennedy to Joseph P. Kennedy, Rose Kennedy Papers, JFK Library, Boston.

71 *He often began:* Newman Flanagan, interview by Neil Swidey, July 2008.

71 *They both loved:* Joan Kennedy, interview by Bella English and Neil Swidey, July 2008.

71 *Joan would voice:* ibid.

72 *"They think we're weird":* ibid.

72 *Presidential advisor Ted:* Ted Sorenson, interview by Bella English, August 2008.

72 *Jack also knew that:* ibid; also, Milton Gwirtzman, interview by Neil Swidey, July 2008.

72 *In the summer of 1961:* Letter from Ted Kennedy to Joseph P. Kennedy Rose Kennedy Papers. An illegible word in the final sentence of that quotation has been omitted in the text of this book.

73 *In the fall of 1961:* Gerard Doherty, interview by Neil Swidey, July 2008. Also, William M. Bulger, *While the Music Lasts* (Boston: Houghton Mifflin, 1996), 91.

73 *Ted rushed from Boston:* James MacGregor Burns, *Edward Kennedy and the Camelot Legacy* (New York: W. W. Norton, 1976), 76.

73 *His brothers came:* "Teddy and Kennedyism," *Time*, September 28, 1962.

73 *Ted once compared him:* A&E Biography, *Ted Kennedy: A Portrait*, A&E Home Video, 1994.

CHAPTER SEVEN

PAGE

75 *"If you are talking":* Transcript of *Meet the Press*, NBC, March 11, 1962.

75 *"I am aware":* "Ted Announces Bid for Senate," *Boston Evening Globe*, March 14, 1962, 1.

75 *"I don't want to":* O'Neill, interview in PBS series *The Kennedys*, Part II (coproduction of WGBH-Boston and Thames Television), 1992.

76 *Family and friends say:* Edward J. "Skip" McCormack III, June 2008, and Sumner Kaplan, July 2008, interviews by Neil Swidey.

76 *One of his pamphlets:* "The Qualified Candidate," 1962 campaign material from the McCormack family.

76 *Harvard Law School professor:* Various press accounts. Also, John Culver, interview by Neil Swidey and Bella English, July 2008.

76 *Influential* New York Times: James Reston, "Another Kennedy Reaches for the Brass Ring," *New York Times*, March 11, 1962, 8.

76 *A Chicago satirist:* Burns, *Edward Kennedy and the Camelot Legacy* (New York: W. W. Norton, 1976), 79.

76 *Burly, round-faced Knocko:* Skip McCormack, interview by Neil Swidey, June 2008.

77 *(Many in the Jewish community):* Sumner Kaplan, interview by Neil Swidey, July 2008.

77 *As attorney general:* "Edward J. McCormack Jr., 73; Influential Politician, Lawyer," *Boston Globe*, February 28, 1997, E15.

77 *Among McCormack's eager:* Gerard Doherty, interview by Neil Swidey, July 2008.

77 *The president summoned:* Bob Healy, interview by Bella English, July 2008.

77 *The article did not:* Robert Healy, "Ted Kennedy Tells About Harvard Examination Incident," *Boston Globe*, March 30, 1962, 1.

77 *At the height:* Bob Healy, interview by Bella English, July 2008; also, Burton Hersh, *The Education of Edward Kennedy* (New York: William Morrow, 1972), 158.

77 *A few minutes:* Gerard Doherty, interview by Neil Swidey, July 2008.

78 *He fit the part:* Hersh, *The Education of Edward Kennedy*, 155.

78 *With Ted's brothers:* Gerard Doherty, interview by Neil Swidey, July 2008.

79 *Yet Joan lacked:* Sue Seay, "A New Mrs. Kennedy," *Look*, February 26, 1963, 23.

79 *"Let's show them":* Joan Kennedy, interview by Bella English and Neil Swidey, July 2008.

79 *Asked about how: Esquire*, April 1962, 147.

79 *"It was just us":* Joan Kennedy, interview by Bella English and Neil Swidey, July 2008.

80 *At one Harvard function:* Milton Gwirtzman and John Culver, interviews by Neil Swidey, July 2008.

80 *About one, Crimmins cracked:* Hersh, *The Education of Edward Kennedy*, 152.

80 *"I was trying to give":* John Culver, interview by Bella English and Neil Swidey, July 2008.

80 *The academics who:* Sam Beer, interview by Neil Swidey, July 2008; also Burton Hersh, interview by Neil Swidey, August 2008.

80 *A few days before Easter:* Gerard Doherty, interview by Neil Swidey, July 2008.

80 *These included Kenny:* Gerard Doherty, interview by Neil Swidey, July 2008; also, Alsop, *Saturday Evening Post*, October 27, 1962.

81 *"It was the first time":* Arthur Schlesinger Jr. diary entry from April 27, 1962, Adam Clymer Papers, JFK Library, Boston.

81 *"That meeting," Doherty:* Gerard Doherty, interview by Neil Swidey, July 2008.

81 *"It's pressure, pressure":* "Pressure, Pressure," *Time*, June 15, 1962, 14.

82 *"When we knew":* Sumner Kaplan, interview by Neil Swidey, July 2008.

82 *He could go all:* Campaign schedules, in Joseph P. Kennedy Papers, JFK Library, Boston.

82 *At one stop:* Gerard Doherty, interview by Neil Swidey, July 2008.

82 *If campaign aides:* ibid.

82 *And he refused:* John Culver, interview by Neil Swidey and Bella English, July 2008.

82 *One day his advance:* Charles Tretter, interview by Jenna Russell, September 2008.

83 *"If you have a":* Burton Hersh, interview by Neil Swidey, August 2008.

83 *Although he was:* Gerard Doherty, interview by Neil Swidey, July 2008.

83 *One day, he was shaking:* John Culver, interview by Neil Swidey and Bella English, July 2008; also, Eddie Martin, interview by Adam Clymer, De-

cember 17, 1992, transcript, Adam Clymer Papers, JFK Library, Boston, and Bulger, *While the Music Lasts*, 99.

83 *He rented an empty office:* Gerard Doherty, interview by Neil Swidey, July 2008.

84 *McCormack wore his:* Full-length footage of South Boston High School debate, August 27, 1962, JFK Library, Boston.

84 *His speechwriter:* Milton Gwirtzman, interview by Neil Swidey, July 2008.

84 *As he walked:* Gerard Doherty, interview by Neil Swidey, July 2008.

85 *"All I can remember":* Sumner Kaplan, interview by Neil Swidey, July 2008.

85 *Gwirtzman was struck:* Milton Gwirtzman, interview by Neil Swidey, July 2008.

85 *Meanwhile, Kaplan and:* Sumner Kaplan, interview by Neil Swidey, July 2008.

85 *So few were the towns:* Skip McCormack, interview by Neil Swidey, June 2008.

CHAPTER EIGHT

87 *Kennedy's old Harvard:* John Culver, interview by Neil Swidey, July 2008; also, "Family Reunion," *Newsweek*, January 4, 1963, 21.

88 *It didn't take them long:* Eastland's beverage of choice from "Personality, Press, and Private Life" section of the James O. Eastland Collection, the University of Mississippi Libraries; also, Jim Flug, interview by Neil Swidey, July 2008.

88 *So rather than argue:* Clymer, *Edward M. Kennedy*, 46.

89 *Once, when fellow:* George McGovern, interview by Adam Clymer, April 14, 1994, transcript, Adam Clymer Papers, JFK Library, Boston.

89 *As much as Bobby:* Burton Hersh, *Bobby and J. Edgar* (New York: Carroll and Graf, 2007), 236, referencing Harris Wofford, *Of Kennedys and Kings* (New York: Farrar, Straus, Giroux, 1980), 25.

89 *Just a month after:* "Ted Kennedy Seizes Film, Faces Charge," United Press International, accessed from archives of *Long Beach Press-Telegram*, February 25, 1963, 1.

89 *He was photographed:* "Mrs. Nhu Sees Senator Kennedy at Lunch in Belgrade," *New York Times*, September 14, 1963, A1.

90 *Erich Kocher, the chargé:* Eric Kocher letter to Adam Clymer, January 12, 1994, Adam Clymer Papers, JFK Library, Boston.

90 *"We are determined":* "Senator Kennedy, in Belgrade, Says U.S. Fights Racial Bars," *New York Times*, September 17, 1963, 25.

90 *At a news conference:* Footage, A&E Biography, *Ted Kennedy*.

91 *Actually, in an echo:* "Further Crises in Store for U.S., President Says," *Boston Globe*, October 20, 1963, 1.

91 *Later, he cracked:* Tom Wicker, "Kennedy Defends Moves to Relax War Tension," *New York Times*, October 20, 1963.

91 *When it was his turn: Boston Globe*, October 20, 1963. Also, Burns, *Edward Kennedy and the Camelot Legacy*, 102.

92 *Ted was using the time:* William Manchester, *Death of a President*. (New York: Harper & Row, 1967), 197.

93 *The avuncular Texan:* Claude Hooten, interview by Neil Swidey, August 2008.

93 *Gwirtzman raced his:* Milton Gwirtzman, interview by Neil Swidey, July 2008.

93 *Ted was the first to find:* Claude Hooten, interview by Neil Swidey, August 2008.

93 *"He's dead," Bobby said:* Manchester, *Death of a President*, 255.

94 *He preferred to concentrate:* Various Kennedy aides and family members, including Joan Kennedy, Milton Gwirtzman, and John Culver, interviews by Neil Swidey, July and August 2008.

94 *Occasionally, he would needle:* Letter from Ted Kennedy to Rose Kennedy, April 15, 1966, Rose Kennedy Papers, JFK Library.

94 *Once again, Ted:* Milton Gwirtzman, interview by Neil Swidey, July 2008.

94 *He called Eddie Martin:* Eddie Martin, interview by Adam Clymer, December 17, 1992, Adam Clymer Papers, JFK Library, Boston.

95 *The patriarch became increasingly:* Manchester, *Death of a President*, 372; also, Rita Dallas and Jeanira Ratcliffe, *The Kennedy Case* (New York: G. P. Putnam's Sons, 1973), 18; and Rita Dallas, interview by Neil Swidey, July 2008.

95 *"I thought maybe I'd":* Dallas, *The Kennedy Case*, 255; Rita Dallas interview by Neil Swidey, July 2008.

95 *Joan, who was crumbling:* Clymer, *Edward M. Kennedy*, 62. Her instructions to caterers comes from Joan Kennedy interview by Bella English and Neil Swidey, July 2008.

96 *On the morning of the president's:* Manchester, *Death of a President*, 576.

96 *The next morning, his children's:* Rita Dallas, interview by Neil Swidey, July 2008, also, Dallas, *The Kennedy Case*, 254.

97 *During a talk on May 29:* Edward Behr, "A Day of Joy and Sadness," *Saturday Evening Post*, July 11, 1964, 36.

CHAPTER NINE

PAGE

98 *"My brother was the first":* E. W. Kenworthy, "Rights Plea Made by Sen. Kennedy," *New York Times*, 23.

98 *(This came in contrast):* Comments by Adam Clymer to Howard Baker, during interview of Baker by Adam Clymer, January 13, 1994, transcript, Adam Clymer Papers, JFK Library, Boston.

98 *It was a year to the day:* E. W. Kenworthy, "Civil Rights Bill Due to Be Passed by Senate Today," *New York Times*, June 19, 1964, 1.

99 *Joan, who had recently:* Joan Kennedy, interview by Bella English and Neil Swidey, July 2008.

99 *Moss, who had a quick wit:* Carol Moss Mulcahy, interviews by Neil Swidey, August 2008.

100 *"You should make some kind":* Wilfrid C. Rogers, "Moss, Ted Like Twins in Travel," *Boston Globe*, June 21, 1964, 12.

100 *Kennedy and Bayh had joined:* Birch Bayh, interview by Neil Swidey, July 2008.

100 *Ted had asked Howard Baird:* Dallas, *The Kennedy Case*, 280.

100 *Birch and Marvella Bayh:* Reconstruction of accident from Birch Bayh interviews by Neil Swidey as well as extensive coverage in days following the accident in the *Boston Globe* and the *Boston Evening Globe*. All direct quotations involving Bayh come from Swidey's interview of Bayh.

101 *"We are over the Z marker":* "Ideal Plane, Expert Pilot . . . Why Flying So Low?" *Boston Globe*, June 23, 1964, 10.

101 *A short time later, the big-bellied:* ibid.

102 *He tracked down Captain Baird:* Dallas, *The Kennedy Case,* 81.

103 *When Bobby arrived at the hospital:* William V. Shannon, "How Ted Kennedy Survived His Ordeal," *Good Housekeeping*, April 1965, 190.

103 *He was in the room when doctors:* Rita Dallas, interview by Neil Swidey, July 2008; also, Dallas, *The Kennedy Case,* 284.

103 *When Jack had undergone:* Ted Sorensen, *Counselor: A Life at the Edge of History* (New York: HarperCollins, 2008), 105; also, Laurence Leamer, *The Kennedy Men, 1901–1963* (New York: William Morrow, 2001), 340.

104 *Instead, Ted was confined:* Stryker CircOlectric Bed 460/470 product description, Adam Clymer Papers, JFK Library, Boston.

104 *And the media ate it up:* Campaign coverage in the *Boston Globe*, the *Boston Evening Globe*, the *Boston Herald*, and the *Boston Traveler*, including Eleanor Roberts, "Magic Combination for a Vote-Getter," *Boston Traveler,* October 13, 1964, 1.

104 *"I never got over my stomach":* Charles Tretter, interview by Jenna Russell, September 2008.

104 *"When you are lying in bed":* Undated letter from Rose Kennedy to Ted Kennedy, Rose Kennedy Papers, JFK Library, Boston.

105 *Even his blistering critic:* Burns, *Edward Kennedy and the Camelot Legacy*, 122.

105 *When George Lodge, his Republican:* Hersh, *The Education of Edward Kennedy*, 202.

105 *During one bedside talk:* Gerard Doherty, interview by Neil Swidey, July 2008.

106 *As the clock ticked past:* Eddie Martin, interview by Adam Clymer, June 2, 1993, transcript, Adam Clymer Papers, JFK Library, Boston.

107 *While it was clear to everyone:* David Burke, interview by Neil Swidey, June 2008.

107 *Just a few weeks before his plane:* Milton Gwirtzman memo to Edward Kennedy, Spring 1964, Milton S. Gwirtzman Papers, JFK Library, Boston.

108 *For twenty-two minutes:* Footage of Bobby Kennedy's speech in PBS series, *The Kennedys,* Part II.

108 *Afterward he went to the Moss:* Carol Moss Mulcahy, interview by Neil Swidey, August 2008.

109 *When Ted ribbed his brother:* Footage of hospital news conference from PBS series, *The Kennedys,* Part II.

109 *A photographer told Bobby:* "Topics," *New York Times,* January 4, 1965.

CHAPTER TEN

PAGE

110 *In the summer of 1965:* Birch Bayh, interview by Neil Swidey, July 2008.

111 *"Robert Kennedy looked at me":* Hersh, *Bobby and J. Edgar,* 456.

111 *Many of them looked down:* Frank Mankiewicz, interview by Adam Clymer, July 5, 1995, Adam Clymer Papers, JFK Library; also, Jim Flug, interview by Neil Swidey, July 2008.

111 *On visits with his father:* Rita Dallas, interview by Neil Swidey, July 2008.

112 *Ted told Burke to put together:* David Burke, interview by Neil Swidey, June 2008.

112 *Ted and Burke sounded out:* ibid.

114 *A young compact guy:* ibid.

114 *When, on occasion, Eastland denounces:* Meg Greenfield, "The Senior Senator Kennedy," *The Reporter,* December 15, 1966, 22.

115 *As his detractors liked to joke:* "Morrissey Named Federal Judge," *Boston Globe,* September 27, 1965, A1.

115 *For his unfailingly tentative:* Bulger, *While the Music Lasts,* 94.

116 *In September 1964, in one:* Attorney General Robert Kennedy to President Lyndon Johnson, September 2, 1964, Adam Clymer Papers, JFK Library, Boston.

117 *For added insurance:* Arthur Schlesinger Jr. quoted in Clymer, *Edward M. Kennedy,* 74.

117 *"For the past seven years":* Press briefing agenda, September 26, 1965, Adam Clymer Papers, at JFK Library, Boston.

117 *When Ted met with Senate:* David Burke, interview by Neil Swidey, June 2008.

118 *While Ted still felt he might:* David Burke interview by Neil Swidey, June 2008; also, Burke comments to Clymer, quoted in transcript with Frank Mankiewicz, July 5, 1995, Adam Clymer Papers, JFK Library, Boston.

118 *Joan idolized her mother-in-law:* Joan Kennedy, interview by Bella English and Neil Swidey, July 2008; selected correspondence between Joan

Kennedy and Rose Kennedy throughout the 1960s, Rose Kennedy Papers, JFK Library, Boston.

118 *And by the middle of the decade:* Joan Kennedy, interview by Bella English and Neil Swidey, July 2008.

119 *Like Joan, Ted also came to rely:* Milton Gwirtzman and other former aides, interviews by Neil Swidey, July 2008.

119 *At meetings, he'd often impress:* John Culver and other former aides, interviews by Neil Swidey and Bella English, July 2008.

120 *"I support our fundamental":* Burns, *Edward Kennedy and the Camelot Legacy,* 134.

121 *Touring with Kennedy, Burke:* David Burke, interview by Neil Swidey, June 2008.

121 *"My state, as the other states in the North":* Copy of speech Kennedy delivered to the Southern Christian Leadership Conference, Jackson, Mississippi, August 8, 1966, Adam Clymer Papers, JFK Library, Boston.

121 *Still, there was a limit:* Joseph H. Miller, "Senator Kennedy Opposes Busing of Students," *Philadelphia Inquirer*, April 23, 1964.

122 *He enlisted support from:* Jim Flug, interview by Neil Swidey, July 2008.

122 *During a string of speeches:* Alan L. Otten, "The Other Kennedy," *Wall Street Journal*, November 3, 1966.

CHAPTER ELEVEN

124 *In March of 1967:* William V. Shannon, *The Heir Apparent* (New York: Macmillan, 1967), 115.

125 *A confidential telegram:* December 1967 telegram from the U.S. Embassy in Saigon to the secretary of state in Washington, DC, declassified, from National Security File, Vietnam 7 F 2 (b) — Congressional Attitudes and Statements, Adam Clymer Papers, JFK Library, Boston.

125 *During one stop at a military:* David Burke, interview by Neil Swidey, June 2008.

125 *In a speech before the World:* Text of address before the World Affairs Council of Boston, January 25, 1968, Rose Kennedy Papers, JFK Library, Boston.

126 *As Ted began his remarks:* David Burke, interview by Neil Swidey, June 2008.

128 *One day in the Senate gym:* Clymer, *Edward M. Kennedy*, 105.

129 *"That was pure Ted":* Frank Mankiewicz, interview by Adam Clymer, July 5, 1995, Adam Clymer Papers, JFK Library, Boston.

129 *"It's going to be all right":* Rita Dallas interview, PBS series, *The Kennedys*, Part II.

129 *It also didn't help that:* Gerard Doherty, interview by Neil Swidey, July 2008.

129 *"The family is divided":* March 28, 1968, memo from a presidential aide recounting Cardinal Cushing's conversation with Eugene Rostow, Adam Clymer Papers, JFK Library, Boston.

130 *In reality, Bayh cared little:* Birch Bayh, interview by Neil Swidey, July 2008.

130 *They kept their eyes on:* Gerard Doherty, interview by Neil Swidey, July 2008.

131 *"Martin Luther King has been":* ibid.

132 *On the primary night of June 4:* David Burke, interview by Neil Swidey, June 2008.

133 *The next day, after it became:* Frank Mankiewicz, interview by Jenna Russell, July 2008.

134 *There, they summoned:* Jim Flug, interview by Neil Swidey, July 2008.

134 *"You are invited to attend":* Telegram, June 7, 1968, Joseph P. Kennedy Papers, JFK Library, Boston.

135 *Now, grieving like the rest:* Milton Gwirtzman, interview by Neil Swidey, July 2008.

135 *But to one confidant:* Hersh, *The Education of Edward Kennedy*, 330.

135 *He joined the family:* Clymer, *Edward M. Kennedy*, 118.

135 *"The enormity of this series":* John Culver, interview by Neil Swidey, July 2008.

136 *"There was this crushing drive":* ibid.

136 *"Each of us":* "Ted Assures Nation: Kennedy 'Dream Still Remains,' " *Boston Sunday Globe*, June 16, 1968, 1.

137 *"With Jack, it was the death."* Rita Dallas, interview by Neil Swidey, July 2008.

137 *"But when he wasn't with Mr.":* ibid.

138 *"It was like a gruesome nightmare":* John Tunney interview, PBS series, *The Kennedys*, Part II.

138 *Ted's closest friends and advisers:* John Culver, interview by Neil Swidey, July 2008, and David Burke, interview by Neil Swidey, June 2008.

139 *"There's no safety in hiding":* "Partial Text of Speech by Senator Kennedy," *Boston Evening Globe*, August 21, 1968, 29.

139 *"I'm going to hold off for forty-eight hours":* Peter Maas, "Ted Kennedy— What Might Have Been," *New York*, October 7, 1968, 34.

139 *By Tuesday afternoon, Smith:* Details drawn from Maas's *New York* article as well as Richard Goodwin, "The Night McCarthy Turned to Kennedy," *Look*, October 15, 1968, 102.

140 *"I am deeply grateful to those":* Letter from Ted Kennedy to Carl Albert, August 28, 1968, JFK Library, Boston.

140 *Ted's reluctance to quash:* John Culver, interview by Neil Swidey, July 2008.

141 *"He felt understandably":* ibid.

CHAPTER TWELVE

PAGE

145 *Almost 80 percent of voters:* Robert Sherrill, *The Last Kennedy* (New York: Dial Press, 1976), 56.

146 *"There was all this rising, boiling feeling":* Robert Bates, interview by Jenna Russell, July 2008.

146 *At a raucous St. Patrick's:* Matthew V. Storin, interview by Jenna Russell, July 2008.

146 *"Whatever his own wishes":* David S. Broder, "Politicians, Pundits Played God with Edward Kennedy's Life," *Washington Post*, July 29, 1969.

146 *Two weeks after he had turned down:* Burton Hersh, *The Education of Edward Kennedy* (New York: William Morrow, 1972), 352.

146 *At times he tried recklessly:* Adam Clymer, *Edward M. Kennedy* (New York: William Morrow, 1999), 138.

147 *"I thought he was willing himself":* Charles Tretter, interview by Jenna Russell, September 2008.

147 *He had brought Kennedy's car:* Edgartown District Court, *Inquest into the death of Mary Jo Kopechne* (New York: EVR Production Inc., 1970), John B. Crimmins testimony, 49.

147 *After a stop for fried clams:* ibid., Edward M. Kennedy testimony, 3.

147 *Ted wanted a swim:* ibid., Crimmins, 49.

148 *Just a handful of families:* Nan Robertson, "Tourists Flock to Scene of Kennedy Accident," *New York Times*, August 25, 1969.

148 *He had rented the modest cottage:* Edgartown District Court, *Inquest into the Death of Mary Jo Kopechne*, Crimmins, 54.

148 *It was not the first reunion:* Hersh, *The Education of Edward Kennedy*, 338, 390.

148 *"It was almost like war veterans":* Anonymous source, interview by Jenna Russell, August 2008.

149 *It was a buzzing:* K. Dun Gifford, interview by Jenna Russell, July 2008.

149 *The boiler room workers were chosen:* Hersh, *The Education of Edward Kennedy,* 321.

149 *Serious-minded and "notorious":* Edgartown District Court, *Inquest into the Death of Mary Jo Kopechne*, Esther Newburgh testimony, 97.

149 *She cheered for the Boston Red Sox:* Martin F. Nolan, "Real Tragedy Not in Hyannis," *Boston Globe*, July 28, 1969.

149 *After Bobby's death, Kopechne had joined:* Ken O. Botwright, "Ted First to Call Victim's Father," *Boston Globe*, July 20, 1969.

149 *She had known him well:* Hersh, *The Education of Edward Kennedy*, 385.

150 *After Robert Kennedy was killed:* Robert L. Ward, "Nun Recalls Mary Jo: An Active, Popular Girl," *Boston Globe*, July 20, 1969.

150 *Friday morning the group of friends:* Edgartown District Court, *Inquest into the Death of Mary Jo Kopechne*, Maryellen Lyons testimony, 99.

150 *After the regatta, the men convened:* ibid., Joseph Gargan testimony, 32.

150 *Ted asked Crimmins:* ibid., Paul Markham testimony, 42.

150 *Tretter, who was also along:* Hersh, *The Education of Edward Kennedy*, 392.

150 *A sixth man:* ibid., Raymond LaRosa testimony, 14.

151 *Tretter would later say:* Hersh, *The Education of Edward Kennedy,* 392.

151 *Seeking to lighten the mood:* Edgartown District Court, *Inquest into the Death of Mary Jo Kopechne*, Tretter, 22.

151 *According to Crimmins:* ibid., Crimmins, 51.

151 *The only hint:* ibid., Newburgh, 58.

153 *The next thing Ted knew:* ibid., Kennedy, 6–8.

154 *"The senator said to me":* ibid., Gargan, 33.

154 *"I felt there was only one thing":* ibid., Gargan, 35.

154 *"He was sobbing":* ibid., Markham, 45.

155 *He thought about the phone calls:* ibid., Kennedy, 9.

155 *Weakened by his ordeal:* ibid., Kennedy, 9–11.

CHAPTER THIRTEEN

PAGE

157 *Steve Ewing, then a 17-year-old:* Steve Ewing, interview by Jenna Russell, September 2008.

158 *There was no reason for Arena:* Dominick Arena, interview by Jenna Russell, July 2008.

158 *Wearing a wetsuit:* Edgartown District Court, *Inquest into the Death of Mary Jo Kopechne* (New York: EVR Production Inc., 1970), John Farrar testimony, 78–79.

159 *"If you'll forgive me":* Richard Powers and Robert Kennedy, "Kennedy Vows Full Statement," *Boston Globe*, July 23, 1969.

159 *Then the chief returned:* Edgartown District Court, *Inquest into the Death of Mary Jo Kopechne*, Dominick Arena testimony, 85.

159 *He says he was not in awe:* Dominick Arena, interview by Jenna Russell, July 2008.

159 *Ted hung up:* Edgartown District Court, *Inquest into the Death of Mary Jo Kopechne*, Arena, 85.

159 *"I was taken aback":* Dominick Arena, interview by Jenna Russell, July 2008.

159 *"What would you like for me to do":* Edgartown District Court, *Inquest into the Death of Mary Jo Kopechne*, Arena, 85.

160 *When Arena told Walter Steele:* Dominick Arena, interview by Jenna Russell, July 2008.

160 *"He said, 'Jesus, Bob,'":* Robert Carroll, interview by Jenna Russell, July 2008.

160 *"to get him off the island":* ibid.

160 *Just 230 words:* James E. T. Lange and Katherine DeWitt Jr., *Chappaquiddick* (New York: St. Martin's Press, 1993), 100.

161 *But from the first discussions:* K. Dun Gifford, interview by Jenna Russell, August 2008.

161 *They did not learn until later:* Ken O. Botwright, "Ted First to Call Victim's Father," *Boston Globe*, July 20, 1969.

162 *There, he acted more like a brother:* K. Dun Gifford, interview by Jenna Russell, August 2008.

162 *Among the flowers:* Jeremiah V. Murphy, "Kopechne Girl's Funeral Today," *Boston Globe*, July 22, 1969.

162 *Gifford faced his grimmest task:* K. Dun Gifford, interview by Jenna Russell, August 2008.

162 *Wilfred Rock, the pilot:* Wilfred Rock, interview by Jenna Russell, September 2008.

162 *Arena gave in at about 3 P.M.:* Dominick Arena, interview by Jenna Russell, July 2008.

162 *In fact, they were fast:* Edgartown District Court, *Inquest into the Death of Mary Jo Kopechne*, Newburgh, 62.

163 *The young woman had not:* Carl Cobb, "What Alcohol Tests Mean," *Boston Globe*, July 25, 1969.

163 *To reach .09, Kopechne:* Edgartown District Court, *Inquest into the Death of Mary Jo Kopechne*, John McHugh testimony, 41.

164 *To step the charge up:* Dominick Arena, interview by Jenna Russell, July 2008.

164 *In that Monday morning's:* Richard Harwood, "Kennedy Cleared of Any Negligence," *Washington Post*, July 21, 1969.

164 *She was floating:* John Farrar, interview by Jenna Russell, September 2008.

164 *Officials had to cover:* Richard Powers and Robert Kenney, "Kennedy Vows Full Statement," *Boston Globe*, July 23, 1969.

165 *Behind closed doors:* Robert J. Rosenthal, "Ten Years Later, How Chappaquiddick Shaped Kennedy's Life," *Boston Globe*, July 15, 1979.

165 *One of those present:* Hersh, *The Education of Edward Kennedy*, 409.

165 *Girls swarmed close:* Richard Harwood, "Accident Victim Buried," *Washington Post*, July 23, 1969.

165 *"This is the biggest thing":* Jeremiah V. Murphy, "Kopechne Girl's Funeral Today," *Boston Globe*, July 22, 1969.

165 *The town's mayor:* ibid.

165 *Just before the funeral Mass:* Richard Stewart and Jeremiah V. Murphy, "Ted's Wife, Ethel Join Mourners at Rites for Cape Accident Victim," *Boston Globe*, July 22, 1969.

166 *Later, Joseph Kopechne told:* ibid.

166 *A lone bell tolled:* ibid.

166 *"My advice in all situations":* Frank Mankiewicz, interview by Jenna Russell, July 2008.

166 *A Newsweek story:* Hersh, *The Education of Edward Kennedy*, 413–414.

166 *During a long walk:* Robert J. Rosenthal, "Ten Years Later," *Boston Globe*, July 15, 1979.

166 *"He was seriously considering leaving":* Milton Gwirtzman, interview by Neil Swidey, July 2008.

166 *On Wednesday, Arena met:* Dominick Arena, interview by Jenna Russell, July 2008.

167 *But Arena had canceled:* Jeremiah V. Murphy, "No Further Press Conferences," *Boston Globe*, July 25, 1969.

167 *One TV crew paid:* Stephen Kurkjian, "Swim Called 'A Feat,'" *Boston Globe*, July 27, 1969.

167 *Medical examiner Dr. Donald Mills:* Richard Powers and Robert Kenney, "Senator Kennedy to Be in Court Today," *Boston Globe*, July 25, 1969.

167 *Arena and Steele told reporters:* Laurence Stern, "Drinking Reports Probed," *Washington Post*, July 23, 1969.

167 *Writing in the* Washington Post: Rowland Evans and Robert Novak, "Hopes for a Kennedy Explanation Fade," *Washington Post*, July 24, 1969.

167 *Ted crossed from Hyannis:* Stephen Kurkjian and Richard Powers, "Kennedy Given Suspended Sentence," *Boston Globe*, July 26, 1969.

168 *Judge James Boyle:* ibid.

168 *The 9:00 A.M. hearing began:* Edgartown District Court, Court transcript of proceedings in Kennedy case, *New York Times*, July 26, 1969.

169 *He still regrets the words:* Dominick Arena, interview by Jenna Russell, July 2008.

169 *"I watched things get worse":* Milton Gwirtzman, interview by Neil Swidey, July 2008.

169 *It was Gwirtzman's idea:* ibid.

170 *A crew from WHDH-TV:* George McKinnon, "Emotions Restrained in Speech," *Boston Globe*, July 26, 1969.

170 *He began with an attempt:* Lange and DeWitt Jr., *Chappaquiddick* (New York: St. Martin's Press, 1993), Appendix A, text of Kennedy's television address.

171 *In South Boston, the last light:* Jeremiah V. Murphy, "It's Tough Break for Ted; Gimme Another Drink," *Boston Globe*, July 26, 1969.

172 *At the* Boston Globe, *the phone:* "Callers React 2–1 in Favor of Kennedy," *Boston Globe*, July 26, 1969.

172 *"It was a straightforward story":* AP, "Muskie Applauds Statement," *Boston Globe*, July 26, 1969.

172 *Even Gwen Kopechne:* AP, "Kopechnes Hope He Won't Resign," *Boston Globe*, July 26, 1969.

172 *Western Union delivered:* [from news dispatches], "Messages Flood Hyannis Port; Thousands Back Kennedy," *Washington Post*, July 27, 1969.

172 *A certain hometown pride:* Christopher Lydon, "A Special Kind of Grief in Massachusetts," *New York Times*, August 3, 1969.

172 *By midweek, aides had confirmed:* Jeremiah V. Murphy, "Aides Say Kennedy Won't Resign," *Washington Post*, July 29, 1969.

172 *A national Gallup poll:* "Kennedy Reported in Gallup Poll to Be Losing Public Esteem," *New York Times*, August 3, 1969.

172 *"Pro-Kennedy Democrats":* Rowland Evans and Robert Novak, "Kennedy's Choice to Say Nothing More on Fatal Accident," *Washington Post*, July 31, 1969.

173 *Another Gallup poll:* "Kennedy Reported in Gallup Poll to Be Losing Public Esteem," *New York Times*, August 3, 1969.

CHAPTER FOURTEEN

PAGE

174 *Kennedy returned to the Senate:* William Greider, "Kennedy: 'I'm Glad to Be Back,' " *Washington Post*, August 1, 1969.

175 *On August 5, Kennedy canceled:* Reuters, "Kennedy Cancels Trip," *New York Times*, August 6, 1969.

175 *Two days later:* UPI, "Official Presses, Exhumation Move," *New York Times*, August 8, 1969.

175 *A week later, in an interview:* Matthew Storin, "Kennedy: I Can Live With Myself," *Boston Globe*, August 14, 1969.

175 *Three days later, in an interview:* "Mrs. Kopechne Is 'Confused' by Daughter's Death," *New York Times*, August 17, 1969.

175 *On Martha's Vineyard, August:* Nan Robertson, "Tourists on Ferry Flock to Scene of Kennedy Accident," *New York Times*, August 25, 1969.

176 *On August 28:* "Joan Leaves Hyannis Hospital," *Boston Globe*, August 31, 1969.

176 *Her pregnancy, still in the early:* Leo Damore, *Senatorial Privilege* (Washington, DC: Regnery Gateway, 1988), 221.

176 *Because of her previous miscarriages:* Joan Kennedy, interview by Neil Swidey and Bella English, July 2008.

176 *Judge Boyle had declared:* Joseph Lelyveld, "Kopechne Inquest Put Off by Judge," *New York Times*, September 3, 1969.

176 *In Edgartown, crews pulled down:* Lacey Fosburgh, "Edgartown Made Its Plans in Vain," *New York Times*, September 3, 1969.

176 *The press had "essentially decided":* Robert Bates, interview by Jenna Russell, July 2008.

177 *Late that fall:* Clymer, *Edward M. Kennedy*, 159.

177 *But his role as patriarch:* ibid., 156.

177 *Only a day or two earlier:* Rita Dallas with Jeanira Ratcliffe, *The Kennedy Case* (New York: G. P. Putnam's Sons, 1973), 345–346.

177 *Just four months before:* ibid., 338.

177 *The night before his father's funeral:* Matthew Storin, interview by Jenna Russell, July 2008.

178 *His lawyers had another reason:* Beverly Ford, "Ted K Aides Got Kopechne Case Info," *Boston Herald*, February 12, 1991.

178 *Forty photographers trailed:* Jeremiah V. Murphy, "Boiler Room Girls Center of Attention," *Boston Globe*, January 7, 1970.

178 *Barred from the proceedings:* Stephen Kurkjian, interview by Jenna Russell, July 2008.

178 *His legislative aide:* Clymer, *Edward M. Kennedy*, 163–165.

178 *"When it started":* Jim Flug, interview by Jenna Russell, August 2008.

179 *"It was a learning experience":* Jim Flug, interview by Jenna Russell, August 2008.

179 *The voters "need to see me":* R. W. Apple Jr., "Kennedy Is Running Hard Against His '64 Vote Total," *New York Times*, August 27, 1970.

179 *When firecrackers popped:* Burton Hersh, *The Shadow President: Ted Kennedy in Opposition* (South Royalton, Vt.: Steerforth Press, 1997), 8.

179 *Death threats arrived:* Ken Clawson, "Constant Threat of Death Affects Kennedy's Life," *Washington Post*, February 5, 1971.

179 *The threat was so much a part:* Robert Bates, interview by Jenna Russell, July 2008.

179 *Joan Kennedy confided her fears:* AP, " 'I worry all the time whether Ted will be shot,' says Joan Kennedy," *Boston Globe*, June 30, 1970.

180 *They made their decision:* Damore, *Senatorial Privilege*, 389.

180 *Later, some jury members:* Beverly Ford, "Witnesses Break Years of Silence on Chappaquiddick," *Boston Herald*, July 2, 1989.

180 *Based on the testimony at the inquest:* Edgartown District Court, *Inquest into the Death of Mary Jo Kopechne*, Report of James A. Boyle, Justice, 125–126.

181 *The charge the judge seemed to advocate:* Lange and DeWitt Jr., *Chappaquiddick*, 148–149.

181 *Kennedy, nonetheless, rejected:* Warren Weaver Jr., "Kennedy Statement Rejects Findings," *New York Times*, April 30, 1970.

181 *In a separate finding:* Damore, *Senatorial Privilege*, 397.

181 *During the summer, a $141,000:* Text of Sen. Kennedy's letter to the *Globe* editor, *Boston Globe*, November 3, 1974.

181 *They reelected him:* Bill Kovach, "Kennedy Gets 500,000-Vote Plurality," *New York Times,* November 5, 1970.

181 *Ted was bitter:* Clymer, *Edward M. Kennedy*, 171–173.

181 *He became the chairman:* ibid., 173–176.

182 *He was also deeply concerned with the war:* Dale de Haan, interview by Jenna Russell, July 2008.

182 *Battling for the least powerful:* Paul Kirk, interview by Jenna Russell, July 2008.

183 *Senator Edward Brooke, his Republican colleague:* Edward Brooke, interview by Jenna Russell, July 2008.

183 *A study in 1971:* K. Dun Gifford, "An Islands Trust: Leading Edges in Land Use Laws," *Harvard Journal on Legislation* 11:417 (1974): 422–426.

183 *"The legislation will not make":* "Kennedy Introduces Islands Trust Legislation," *Vineyard Gazette*, April 14, 1972.

184 *The reaction was immediate:* Gifford, "An Islands Trust: Leading Edges in Land Use Laws," 429.

184 *In the end, facing inescapable:* Ronald Rappaport, interview by Jenna Russell, July 2008.

184 *Almost anything he did:* William Honan, "Ted Kennedy Keeps His Options Open," *Boston Sunday Herald Traveler*, November 28, 1971.

184 *"Short of self-immolation":* S. J. Micciche, "Ted Kennedy: Moving Party or Himself?" *Boston Globe*, November 21, 1971.

185 *Ted had acknowledged:* R. W. Apple Jr., "Despite His Lead in Gallup Poll, Kennedy Insists He Won't Run," *New York Times*, May 24, 1971.

185 *His defeat as whip had freed:* Honan, "Ted Kennedy Keeps His Options Open," November 28, 1971.

185 *Ted called Nixon's list:* ibid.

185 *At a breakfast meeting in September:* Drew Steis, "Administration Moves Kennedy into Spotlight," *Boston Herald Traveler*, November 4, 1971.

185 *His staff started tracking:* Jim Flug, interview by Jenna Russell August 2008.

185 *But as the Senate moved:* Clymer, *Edward M. Kennedy*, 194.

186 *The head of the AFL-CIO:* ibid., 186–187.

186 *Frank Mankiewicz, then McGovern's:* Frank Mankiewicz, interview by Jenna Russell, July 2008.

CHAPTER FIFTEEN

PAGE

187 *When he traveled with his father:* Eleanor Roberts, "The Ordeal of Teddy Kennedy Jr.," *Boston Sunday Herald Advertiser*, December 2, 1973.

187 *The senator had never barred:* Melody Miller, interview by Jenna Russell, August 2008.

188 *The senator "was as devastated":* ibid.

188 *Of course, for all the secrecy:* Roberts, "The Ordeal of Teddy Kennedy Jr.," *Boston Sunday Herald Advertiser,* December 2, 1973.

188 *"The last song was":* Melody Miller interview by Jenna Russell, August 2008.

188 *Emerging from his surgery with:* Lester David, "Teddy: One Year Later," *Boston Herald*, October 10, 1974.

189 *As he recovered, some 30,000:* Roberts, "The Ordeal of Teddy Kennedy Jr.," *Boston Sunday Herald Advertiser,* December 2, 1973.

189 *It had turned out:* David, "Teddy: One Year Later," *Boston Herald,* October 10, 1974.

189 *The drugs caused crushing nausea:* Melody Miller, interview by Jenna Russell, August 2008.

189 *But Teddy Jr. never lamented:* David, "Teddy: One Year Later," *Boston Herald,* October 10, 1974.

189 *"It was very rough":* Hersh, *The Shadow President*, 18–19.

189 *Although Teddy's progress was:* Joan Kennedy, interview by Neil Swidey and Bella English, July 2008.

190 *In June, she was hospitalized:* UPI, "Joan in Hospital for Treatment," *Boston Herald*, June 22, 1974.

190 *In September, she checked:* AP, "Joan Kennedy Enters a Clinic in California," *New York Times*, September 14, 1974.

190 *The senator, attentive to her:* Anonymous source, interview by Jenna Russell, August 2008.

190 *"Of course they hurt my feelings":* Joan Braden, "Joan Kennedy Tells Her Own Story," *McCall's*, August 1978.

191 *Once, according to a family:* Melody Miller, interview by Jenna Russell, August 2008.

191 *Bobby had been the first:* Christopher Kennedy Lawford, *Symptoms of Withdrawal* (New York: William Morrow, 2005), 105.

191 *It fell to Ted to try:* ibid., 107.

192 *The adults were mired:* ibid., 107.

192 *"The mistrust and estrangement":* ibid., 108.

193 *It was Ted who took Joe II:* Adam Clymer, *Edward M. Kennedy* (New York: William Morrow, 1999), 120.

193 *"a relentless quest":* Lawford, *Symptoms of Withdrawal*, 151.

193 *The young Kennedy, who had attracted:* UPI, "Robert Kennedy, 17, Fined for Loitering; Pleads No Contest," *New York Times,* August 24, 1971.

193 *"Teddy was mythic in my life":* Lawford, *Symptoms of Withdrawal,* 167.

194 *Ted would sometimes call their sister:* Clymer, *Edward M. Kennedy,* 142.

194 *During summers in Hyannis:* Kerry Kennedy, interview by Jenna Russell, October 2008.

194 *When she fled the spotlight:* Clymer, *Edward M. Kennedy*, 129–130.

194 *According to some friends:* Bill Adler, "Guilt, Drugs, Despair Haunt David," *Cape Cod Times*, November 14, 1980.

195 *"He [took] us on all these history trips":* Caroline Kennedy, interview by Susan Milligan, August 2008.

195 *"I think that came":* John Culver, interview by Bella English and Neil Swidey, July 2008.

195 *Usually Dowd drove the Winnebago:* Don Dowd, interview by Don Aucoin, July 2008.

195 *One day in the mid-1970s:* Larry Morrison, interview by Don Aucoin, June 2008.

196 *But on many excursions:* Don Dowd, interview by Don Aucoin, July 2008.

196 *In the fall of 1978:* Peter Davis, interview by Jenna Russell, July 2008.

196 *"I think that he's been":* Joan Kennedy, interview by Bella English and Neil Swidey, July 2008.

197 *At the end of September 1974:* Gloria Negri, "Kennedy Decides Not to Run," *Boston Globe*, September 23, 1974.

197 *This time, he made the decision:* Mary McGrory, "Kennedy Made Up His Mind Alone—and It Wasn't Easy," *Washington Star*, September 24, 1974.

197 *Concern for his family:* Paul Kirk, interview by Jenna Russell, July 2008.

CHAPTER SIXTEEN

PAGE

198 *Asked, before the election:* Eleanor Roberts, "Kennedy Hits the Campaign Trail," *Boston Herald*, August 8, 1976.

198 *He did send two aides:* Clymer, *Edward M. Kennedy*, 246.

198 *His aide Paul Kirk:* Stephen Wermiel, "Kennedy Invited Too Late to Unity Night, Aide Says," *Boston Globe*, July 17, 1976.

199 *A few weeks later in Boston:* Robert Turner, "Kennedy Finally Gets His Turn on a Convention Soapbox," *Boston Globe*, August 24, 1976.

199 *"He became really aware":* Melody Miller, interview by Jenna Russell, July 2008.

200 *"He saw it as his job":* Dr. Lawrence Horowitz, interview by Jenna Russell, September 2008.

200 *"One hundred and sixteen days":* Rachelle Patterson, "Kennedy Presses Carter for Commitment on Comprehensive Health Insurance," *Boston Globe*, May 17, 1977.

200 *He widened his longstanding:* Robert Hunter, interview by Jenna Russell, July 2008.

201 *"What bothered me":* Boris, Natalya, and Jessica Katz, interview by Don Aucoin, June 2008.

204 *"A mandatory minimum sentence":* Edward M. Kennedy, "Punishing the Offenders," *New York Times,* December 6, 1975.

204 *Kenneth Feinberg, a former assistant:* Kenneth Feinberg, interview by Jenna Russell, July 2008.

204 *Through the summer, McDaniel:* Paul McDaniel, interview by Jenna Russell, July 2008.

205 *Senator Barry Goldwater lashed back:* AP, "Goldwater Says Kennedy Lacks Basis to Criticize Watergate," *Boston Globe*, July 13, 1973.

205 *The voters did not think so:* Reuters, "Kennedy Favored in Poll," *Boston Globe*, August 14, 1978.

206 *Mary Jo Kopechne's parents:* Howard Blum, "Kopechnes Say They Don't Have 'The Whole Story' on Accident," *New York Times,* July 18, 1979.

206 *At the outset, Kennedy had:* Text of Chappaquiddick interview with Senator Kennedy, *Boston Globe*, October 27, 1974.

206 *But by the end, the senator:* Stephen Kurkjian, interview by Jenna Russell, July 2008.

206 *Ted again dismissed the testimony:* "Text of Chappaquiddick interview with Senator Kennedy," *Boston Globe*, October 27, 1974.

206 *They quoted an anonymous source:* Gerald O'Neill, Stephen Kurkjian, and Peter Cowen, "Chappaquiddick: The conflicts are still unresolved 5 years later," *Boston Globe*, October 29, 1974.

206 *They quoted Gwen Kopechne:* Gerald O'Neill, Stephen Kurkjian, Peter Cowen, and Robert Turner, "Kopechnes Got $140,923 in Settlement," *Boston Globe*, October 30, 1974.

207 *No one did:* Gerald O'Neill, Stephen Kurkjian, Peter Cowen, and Robert Turner, "The Men: Nothing Left to Say," *Boston Globe*, October 30, 1974.

207 *Ted reacted angrily:* "Text of Sen. Kennedy's letter to the Globe editor," *Boston Globe*, November 3, 1974.

207 *"Until Senator Kennedy or someone else":* "Our Rationale for the Chappaquiddick Series," *Boston Globe,* November 15, 1974.

207 *On the tenth anniversary:* Russell Garland, "Kopechne Service at Chappaquiddick," *Boston Globe*, July 19, 1979.

CHAPTER SEVENTEEN

PAGE

208 *On October 12, 1979, CBS:* Roger Mudd, *The Place to Be: Washington, CBS, and The Glory Days of Television News* (New York: Public Affairs, 2008), 355.

208 *"Well, I'm—were I":* ibid., 355–356.

209 *"It revealed that he":* Roger Mudd, interview by Sam Allis, July 16, 2008.

209 *As of June, only 28 percent:* Gallup Poll, June 12–17, 1979.

209 *as the nation suffered from: Time*, November 19, 1979.

210 *"He never called me":* David Burke, interview by Sam Allis, July 8, 2008.

210 *"There was a lot of anger":* former Vice President Walter Mondale, interview by Sam Allis, July 12, 2008.

210 *But speculation about:* Clymer, *Edward M. Kennedy*, 280.

210 *Carter's weakness became:* ibid., 283.

210 *"We can see this crisis":* Text of Carter speech, "Jimmy Carter," *American Experience*, 2002.

210 *Carter' standing dropped again:* Clymer, *Edward M. Kennedy*, 283.

210 *Gallup poll taken:* Gallup poll, August 14, 1979.

210 *His longtime counselor Paul Kirk:* Paul Kirk, interview by Sam Allis, July 14, 2008.

211 *"I said, 'I'm not sure' ":* ibid.

211 *Many leading Democrats:* Thomas Oliphant, interview by Sam Allis, July 2, 2008.

211 *"It was an event that had to":* David Burke, interview by Sam Allis, July 8, 2008.

211 *A Lou Harris poll taken:* Harris poll, June 13–17, 1979.

211 *"It was understood that this":* Paul Kirk, interview by Sam Allis, July 14, 2008.

211 *"The Carter campaign will be"*: Richard Stearns, interview by Sam Allis, October 8, 2008.

212 *"Sometimes," he declared:* Text of speech from Office of Senator Edward Kennedy.

212 *"The son of a bitch is going"*: Patrick Caddell, interview by Sam Allis, August 3, 2008.

212 *The price was simply too high:* Stuart Eisenstadt, interview by Sam Allis, September 3, 2008.

212 *"If Carter had said"*: Carl Wagner, interview by Sam Allis, July 1, 2008.

212 *"We were down to the real"*: Stuart Eisenstadt, interview by Sam Allis, September 3, 2008.

212 *But Carter's economic and political:* ibid.

213 *"Once they had the challenge"*: Patrick Caddell, interview by Sam Allis, August 3, 2008.

213 *He called Bob Shrum, Carl Wagner:* Patrick Caddell, interview by Sam Allis, November 6, 2008.

213 *Ted's people countered that:* Thomas Oliphant, interview by Sam Allis, July 2, 2008.

213 *Three days after the Mudd interviews:* Thomas Oliphant, interview by Sam Allis, July 2, 2008.

213 *Not Ted. He and his staff:* Clymer, *Edward M. Kennedy*, 292.

213 *"For months we have been sinking"*: Text of speech, Office of Senator Edward Kennedy.

214 *"I've got 45 percent"*: Anonymous, interview by Sam Allis, July 9, 2008.

214 *"Step one was"*: ibid.

214 *"We asked people, 'Okay' "*: Patrick Caddell, interview by Sam Allis, August 3, 2008.

215 *Ted's team, for its part:* William Carrick, interview by Sam Allis, July 29, 2008.

215 *Accompanied by Carrick:* ibid.

215 *"John Lewis [the iconic figure]"*: ibid.

215 *Meanwhile, Ted's brother-in-law:* Thomas Oliphant, interview by Sam Allis, November 8, 2008.

215 *It was dubbed "Air Malaise"*: ibid.

215 *"No one could capture it"*: William Carrick, interview by Sam Allis, July 29, 2008.

216 *"He couldn't articulate an English"*: Edward Fouhy, interview by Sam Allis, July 8, 2008.

216 *He talked about "fam families"*: Thomas Oliphant, interview by Sam Allis, July 2, 2008.

216 *"lust" in his heart:* Jimmy Carter, *Playboy* interview, November 1976.

216 *"He was a rollicking man"*: Anonymous, interview by Sam Allis, July 9, 2008.

217 *"What do you want me to do"*: ibid.

217 *On November 4, 1979:* Nazila Fathi, *New York Times*, November 5, 2006.

217 *Then, to further scramble:* Clymer, *Edward M. Kennedy*, 299.

217 *On December 28, Carter announced:* ibid.

217 *"This guy's a peanut farmer":* David Yepsen, interview by Sam Allis, July 10, 2008.

217 *When Carter imposed a partial:* Barry Schweid, AP, January 4, 1980.

218 *Back in the late spring of 1979:* Thomas Oliphant, interview by Sam Allis, July 2, 2008.

218 *"Our mistake was thinking we were":* Robert Shrum, interview by Sam Allis, July 17, 2008.

218 *And the message the campaign heard:* Les Francis, interview by Sam Allis, July 15, 2008.

218 *"We massively underestimated":* ibid.

218 *Kennedy lost the caucuses:* Clymer, *Edward M. Kennedy*, 300.

218 *"Kennedy will get out":* ibid., 23.

219 *Afterward, he polled them:* Shrum, *No Excuses*, 90.

219 *"Let's get ready and go":* ibid.

CHAPTER EIGHTEEN

PAGE

220 *During the run-up to the New York primary:* Shrum, *No Excuses*, 101.

220 *"Do the right thing, Jim":* ibid., 102.

220 *On January 28, he went after Carter:* Robert Shrum, interview by Sam Allis, July 17, 2008.

221 *"It is less than a year since":* Text of speech provided by Office of Senator Edward Kennedy.

221 *Ted drew clear distinctions:* ibid.

221 *Ted had a point about the shah:* Hamilton Jordan, *Crisis* (New York: G. P. Putnam's Sons, 1982), 74, 77–87.

221 *He opposed Carter's plan:* Text of speech provided by Office of Senator Edward Kennedy.

221 *"I have only just begun to fight":* Shrum, *No Excuses*, 93.

221 *"It really rallied people":* William Carrick, interview by Sam Allis, July 28, 2008.

222 *"Bullshit":* Jordan, *Crisis*, 141.

222 *He proceeded to lose the Maine caucuses on February 10:* AP, April 23, 1980.

222 *the New Hampshire primary on February 26:* Thomas Oliphant, *Boston Globe*, February 27, 1980.

222 *and the Vermont primary on March 4:* Wayne Davis, AP, March 5, 1980.

222 *Carter's strategists had believed:* Les Francis, interview by Sam Allis, July 15, 2008.

222 *But he soon found himself trapped:* ibid.

222 *She had been elected as an insurgent:* Douglas Martin, *New York Times*, November 17, 2002.

222 *The parade was a disaster for both:* ibid.

223 *"Catholics west of the Susquehanna River":* Patrick Caddell, interview by Sam Allis, August 3, 2008.

223 *When the counting was done:* William Carrick, interview by Sam Allis, July 29, 2008.

223 *But a bright spot quickly:* Thomas Oliphant, *Boston Globe*, October 21, 1979.

223 *On screen was Carroll O'Connor:* Nazila Fathi, *New York Times*, November 5, 1980.

223 *On March 1:* Text of U.N. Security Council Resolution 465.

224 *Bob Shrum started writing the speech:* Clymer, *Edward M. Kennedy*, 307.

224 *But Caddell's numbers told:* Patrick Caddell, interview by Sam Allis, August 3, 2008.

224 *"New York and Carter were":* William Carrick, interview by Sam Allis, July 29, 2008.

224 *Kennedy beat Carter in New York:* Clymer, *Edward M. Kennedy*, 307.

224 *"It meant we lived to fight":* Paul Kirk, interview by Sam Allis, July 14, 2008.

225 *Ted turned to him and said:* Shrum, *No Excuses*, 104.

225 *Lost in all the attention:* William Carrick, interview by Sam Allis, July 29, 2008.

225 *According to Caddell's polls:* ibid.

225 *"That's when I pulled the trigger":* ibid.

225 *So Pennsylvania voters saw a series:* Clymer, *Edward M. Kennedy*, 309.

225 *The coda to the primary season:* Clymer, *Edward M. Kennedy*, 310.

225 *The young and talented Ron Brown:* Anonymous, interview by Sam Allis, July 11, 2008.

226 *In retrospect, says Shrum:* Robert Shrum, interview by Sam Allis, July 17, 2008.

226 *Ted became the first presidential candidate:* David Mixner, interview by Sam Allis, July 14, 2008.

226 *The fund-raiser was held at the Hollywood Hills:* ibid.

226 *He promptly stopped his campaign:* ibid.

226 *On June 25, Jordan:* Jordan, *Crisis*, 306–309.

226 *"The Kennedy challenge hurt us":* ibid.

227 *He then instructed Susan Estrich:* Carl Wagner, interview by Sam Allis, July 1, 2008.

227 *The signature fight at the convention:* A. O. Sulzberger Jr., *New York Times*, July 31, 1980.

228 *Jordan was adamant:* Paul Kirk, interview by Sam Allis, July 14, 2008.

228 *he would prevent Kennedy from speaking:* Robert Shrum, interview by Sam Allis, July 17, 2008.

228 *"Have you ever heard the sound":* Carl Wagner, interview by Sam Allis, July 1, 2008.

228 *Kirk spent two days with:* Paul Kirk, interview by Sam Allis, July 14, 2008.

228 *Carter beat him on the all-important:* Jordan, *Crisis*, 324.

228 *After the rules vote:* Clymer, *Edward M. Kennedy*, 316.

228 *He spoke instead:* Carl Wagner, interview by Sam Allis, July 1, 2008.

229 *"The commitment I seek is not":* ibid.

229 *"Our cause has been":* ibid.

229 *"The same Republicans who are talking":* ibid.

229 *"For all those whose cares":* ibid.

229 *Ted's delivery was smooth:* Tape in the Adam Clymer Papers, JFK Library, Boston.

230 *Three minority reports were:* Jordan, *Crisis*, 324.

230 *Bob Strauss, told the president:* ibid., 325.

230 *One report came back:* ibid., 327.

230 *"We threw in the towel":* Patrick Caddell, interview by Sam Allis, August 3, 2008.

230 *The debate over the platform planks:* Jordan, *Crisis*, 328.

230 *Shrum made a reluctant Kennedy:* Shrum, *No Excuses*, 127–128.

230 *Carter had to chase him down:* ibid.

230 *Jimmy Carter had won the nomination:* Walter Mears, AP, August 14, 1980.

231 *but not before Carter held:* Thomas Oliphant, interview by Sam Allis, July 2, 2008.

231 *In 1981, Hamilton Jordan participated:* transcript of oral history of Carter Administration, Miller Center for Public Affairs, University of Virginia, November 6, 1981, 81.

231 *"It was the single critical factor":* ibid.

CHAPTER NINETEEN

232 *"Rock bottom is a very good":* Carl Wagner, interview by Sam Allis, July 1, 2008.

232 *He'd pray by himself at St. Joseph's:* Paul Kirk, interview by Sam Allis, July 14, 2008.

232 *"There was no period":* Senator Joseph Biden, interview by Sam Allis, July 21, 2008.

232 *"It was not the worst thing":* Robert Shrum, interview by Sam Allis, July 17, 2008.

233 *"I can walk":* Joan Braden, "Joan Kennedy Tells Her Own Story," *McCall's,* August 1978, 121.

234 *"The hardest thing":* Joan Kennedy, interview by Bella English and Neil Swidey, July 2008.

234 *"It wasn't my personality":* Marcia Chellis, *The Joan Kennedy Story: Living with the Kennedys* (New York: Jove Books, 1986), 36.

235 *"They thought I'd fight it"*: Joan Kennedy, interview by Bella English, January 7, 2009.

235 *"Once you sober up"*: Sally Jacobs, "Prime Time with Joan Kennedy," *Boston Globe Sunday Magazine,* July 14, 2000.

235 *Ted found that many of his closest friends: Washington Post,* November 6, 1980.

235 *"He went from someone who was"*: David Burke, interview by Sam Allis, July 8, 2008.

235 *Tom Rollins, who served as:* Thomas Rollins, interview by Sam Allis, July 11, 2008.

236 *In 1974 the controversy over school busing:* J. Anthony Lukas, *Common Ground* (New York: Vintage Books, 1986), 259–262.

237 *His first big fight came quickly:* Ralph Neas, interview by Sam Allis, July 18, 2008.

238 *Ted reached across the aisle:* ibid.

238 *"If we had lost that battle":* ibid.

238 *"This switch was critical to Kennedy":* Anonymous, interview by Sam Allis, July 24, 2008.

238 *"The Fair Housing Bill was":* Associate Supreme Court Justice Stephen Breyer, interview by Sam Allis, July 23, 2008.

238 *Ted found that even though:* Thomas Rollins, interview by Sam Allis, July 11, 2008.

239 *For example, he beat back:* ibid.

239 *So Hatch, who was often:* ibid.

239 *"He'd say to his staff":* Associate Supreme Court Justice Stephen Breyer, interview by Sam Allis, July 23, 2008.

240 *If Republicans could persuade:* Thomas Rollins, interview by Sam Allis, July 11, 2008.

240 *"He and I were sitting around one day":* Lawrence Horowitz, interview by Sam Allis, September 6, 2008.

240 *Ted would hold the meetings:* ibid.

240 *"I'd be invited to his house":* Senator John Kerry, interview by Sam Allis, July 23, 2008.

240 *He would leave the office at night:* Jeffrey Blattner, interview by Sam Allis, July 19, 2008.

240 *"It would be 6:30 and":* Thomas Rollins, interview by Sam Allis, July 11, 2008.

241 *"There is always this congregation around him":* Senator Patrick Leahy, interview by Sam Allis, July 31, 2008.

241 *He had initially opposed:* Clymer, *Edward M. Kennedy*, 170.

241 *Likewise, before the Supreme:* ibid.

241 *A turning point was:* Eleanor Smeal, interview by Sam Allis, October 14, 2008.

242 *It bothered Ted:* Kennedy staffer, interview by Sam Allis, October 9, 2008.

242 *One of his landmark:* Ralph Neas, interview by Sam Allis, July 18, 2008.

242 *The effect of Ted's new bill:* ibid.

242 *"Senator Kennedy kept all sides":* Marcia Greenburger, interview by Sam Allis, July 28, 2008.

242 *Since 1968, he had been:* David Mixner, interview by Sam Allis, July 14, 2008.

243 *He was a cosponsor of:* ibid.

243 *"You've got to remember the times":* ibid.

243 *In 1982, Ted was the first:* ibid.

243 *"It's his character combined with":* Richard Viguerie, interview by Sam Allis, October 16, 2008.

244 *In 1983, Ted received a fund-raising letter:* Shrum, *No Excuses*, 137–139.

244 *Ted delivered the speech:* ibid.

244 *"It was so obvious":* William Carrick, interview by Sam Allis, July 29, 2008.

245 *"He was clearly positioning himself":* Anonymous former staffer of Senator Edward Kennedy , interview by Sam Allis, July 28, 2008.

245 *Ted delivered a strong speech:* William Carrick, interview by Sam Allis, July 29, 2008.

245 *The Kennedy staff's blueprint for the run:* Thomas Oliphant, "Behind Kennedy's Decision Not to Run," *Boston Globe*, December 5, 1982.

246 *On the day after Thanksgiving:* ibid.

246 *"We came on strong":* ibid.

246 *"I'd written a speech that leaned":* Robert Shrum, interview by Sam Allis, July 17, 2008.

246 *"I said to myself":* ibid.

246 *"Kennedy's announcement on December 1:* Thomas Oliphant, *Boston Globe*, December 1, 1982.

246 *Ted briefly contemplated:* Robert Shrum, interview by Sam Allis, July 17, 2008.

247 *Shrum made his last, best pitch:* Shrum, *No Excuses*, 152.

247 *Tom Rollins remembers walking:* Thomas Rollins, interview by Sam Allis, July 11, 2008.

247 *"My sense of him is":* William Carrick, interview by Sam Allis, September 26, 2008.

247 *He also knew that as long:* Robert Shrum, interview by Sam Allis, July 17, 2008.

247 *Earlier that year, for example:* ibid.

248 *"I know this decision means":* Shrum, *No Excuses*, 153.

CHAPTER TWENTY

PAGE

249 *When Ronald Reagan nominated:* Ralph Neas, interview by Sam Allis, July 18, 2008.

250 *Bork had called the provision:* Ethan Bronner, *Boston Globe*, October 7, 1987.

250 *He found no right to privacy:* ibid., 60.

250 *He also spoke out against:* Clymer, *Edward M. Kennedy*, 417.

250 *He held that the First Amendment:* ibid., 61.

250 *Back in the early 1970s:* ibid., 66.

251 *Less than an hour after:* Jeffrey Blattner, interview by Sam Allis, July 19, 2008.

251 *His speech was already in:* ibid.

251 *(When asked why):* New York Times, September 20, 1987.

251 *"Robert Bork's America is a land":* Text of speech provided by Office of Senator Edward Kennedy.

252 *"We better win":* Jeffrey Blattner, interview by Sam Allis, July 19, 2008.

252 *"There was a sense early on":* William Carrick, interview by Sam Allis, July 29, 2008.

252 *"When Ted went to the floor":* former Senator Alan Simpson, interview by Sam Allis, July 31, 2008.

253 *"Ted Kennedy had no choice":* former Senator Tom Daschle, interview by Sam Allis, August 4, 2008.

253 *"We should first address the question":* text of speech provided by Office of Senator Edward Kennedy.

253 *Ted repaired to Hyannis Port:* Ethan Bronner, *Boston Globe*, October 7, 1987.

253 *Ted called, among many other:* ibid.

254 *Ted relied on Ralph Neas:* Ralph Neas, interview by Sam Allis, July 18, 2008.

254 *"It had crumbling columns":* former Senator Alan Simpson, interview by Sam Allis, July 31, 2008.

254 *Lloyd Cutler, the prominent Washington:* New York Times, September 24, 1987.

254 *"The victory that liberals":* David Broder, *Washington Post*, October 6, 1987.

255 *"If Kennedy and Neas":* Ralph Neas, interview by Sam Allis, July 18, 2008.

255 *"Larry played Bork":* Jeffery Blattner, interview by Sam Allis, July 19, 2008.

255 *"He's a dismissive person":* former Senator Alan Simpson, interview by Sam Allis, July 31, 2008.

255 *The hearings convened on the morning:* New York Times, October 6, 1987.

255 *Over two weeks, there would be:* Office of Senator Joseph Biden.

255 *But Kennedy also made sure:* ibid.

255 *However, upon questioning from:* Ethan Bronner, *Boston Globe*, October 7, 1987.

255 *Later, the aged former:* Lyle Denniston, interview by Sam Allis, October 1, 2008.

256 *"As I understand it, under your":* transcript of Bork hearings from *Congressional Record*, Hearings before the Committee on the Judiciary, U.S. Senate, 100th Congress, First Session on the nomination of Robert Bork to be Associate Justice of the U.S. Supreme Court, p. 149.

256 *He challenged Bork on his:* Ralph Neas, interview by Sam Allis, July 18, 2008.

256 *Barbara Jordan, the respected:* ibid.

256 *"There is nothing in our constitutional":* Bork hearings, p. 157.

256 *"I believe, Mr. Bork":* ibid., 149.

256 *During Kennedy's half hour, Biden:* Ethan Bronner, *Boston Globe*, October 11, 1987.

257 *"He'd be in his den, notebook open":* Jeffrey Blattner, interview by Sam Allis, July 19, 2008.

257 *Then, at night, the Kennedy war:* ibid.

257 *The Democrats needed at least five:* Senator Joseph Biden, interview by Sam Allis, July 21, 2008.

257 *The task of persuading them:* Ethan Bronner, *Boston Globe*, October 7, 1987.

257 *What they found was surprising:* ibid. Patrick Caddell, interview by Sam Allis, August 3, 2008.

257 *"We knew we'd beat Bork":* Patrick Caddell, interview by Sam Allis, August 3, 2008.

257 *Conservative Democrat Bennett Johnston:* Ethan Bronner, *Boston Globe*, October 7, 1987.

257 *His fellow senator from Louisiana:* Ethan Bronner, *Boston Globe*, October 7, 1987.

258 *"There was tremendous sadness in":* former Senator Alan Simpson, interview by Sam Allis, July 31, 2008.

258 *The final Senate vote against him:* Linda Greenhouse, "Bork's Nomination Is Rejected, 58–42," *New York Times*, October 24, 1987.

258 *"There was a sense that we had":* Jeffrey Blattner, interview by Sam Allis, July 19, 2008.

CHAPTER TWENTY-ONE

PAGE

259 *A recent Gallup poll:* Alessandra Stanley, "Facing Questions of Private Life, Kennedy Apologizes to the Voters," *New York Times*, October 26, 1991.

259 *Instead, a few days:* Heather Campion, interview by Joseph P. Kahn, July 2008.

260 *"The temperature drops":* John Aloysius Farrell, "Comeback Kid Rising from the Ashes," *Boston Globe*, November 21, 1993.

260 *"We had a conversation":* Robert Shrum, interview by Joseph P. Kahn, August 2008.

260 *Kennedy asked that she:* Heather Campion, interview by Joseph P. Kahn, July 2008.

260 *"He's always very focused":* ibid.

261 *"I am painfully aware":* Alessandra Stanley, "Facing Questions of Private Life," *New York Times*, October 26, 1991.

261 *"To them I say":* ibid.

261 *In the* New York: ibid.

261 *While his mea culpa:* Mike Barnicle, "Dim Memories of a Dynasty," *Boston Globe*, October 27, 1991.

262 *His Senate office attracted:* Kennedy aide, interview by Joseph P. Kahn, September 2008.

262 *Asked once to name:* "Proust Questionnaire," *Vanity Fair*, May 2006.

262 *As far back as 1979:* "The Kennedy Challenge," *Time*, November 5, 1979.

262 *"The mere mention":* "Sex and the Senior Senator," *Time*, November 12, 1979, 76.

262 *A 1979 Washington Monthly:* Suzannah Lessard, "Kennedy's Woman Problem, Women's Kennedy Problem," *Washington Monthly*, December 1979.

263 *"Ted Kennedy always baffled me":* Lance Morrow, interview by Joseph P. Kahn, July 2008.

263 *"There was a sense of relief":* Kennedy aide, interview by Joseph P. Kahn, September 2008.

263 *"The trouble with Teddy is":* Anna Quindlen, "The Trouble with Teddy," *New York Times*, October 19, 1991.

264 *Whether Kennedy was an alcoholic:* Lance Morrow, interview by Joseph P. Kahn, July 2008.

264 *The senator denied it:* "Kennedy, on TV, Discusses Rape Case, Drinking," *USA Today*, June 6, 1991.

264 *"I went through a lot":* transcript, CBS, *60 Minutes*, June 7, 1998.

264 *"He seemed to have a pattern":* Lance Morrow, interview by Joseph P. Kahn, July 2008.

264 *In 1991, according to:* CBS, *60 Minutes*, June 7, 1998.

264 *"I'll tell Teddy Kennedy":* Maralee Schwartz and Paul Taylor, "A Taunt for a Taunt," *Washington Post*, August 9, 1988.

265 *After the* National Enquirer: www.politicalwire.com/archives, March 30, 2005.

265 *Girlfriends were plentiful, too:* Richard E. Burke, *The Senator* (New York: St. Martin's Press, 1992), 128.

265 *Kennedy himself characterized:* Fox Butterfield, "At Home With Ted and Vicki Kennedy: Crossed Paths, A Second Chance," *New York Times*, October 1, 1992.

265 *"He'd laugh about it":* Melody Miller, interview by Joseph P. Kahn, August 2008.

266 *"Ted came over the first week":* Edmund Reggie, interview by Joseph P. Kahn, August 2008.

266 *"There was nobody to whom":* Melody Miller, interview by Joseph P. Kahn, August 2008.

266 *Ted was such a strong:* David Burke, interview by Joseph P. Kahn, August 2008.

266 *"There's an enormously sensitive":* Nancy Korman, interview by Joseph P. Kahn, July 2008.

267 *"Ted is the reality":* Michael Kelly, "Ted Kennedy on the Rocks," *GQ*, February 1990.

267 *Kelly's withering judgment:* ibid.

267 *Arrested development "doesn't explain":* ibid.

267 *"Even after Chappaquiddick":* John Aloysius Farrell, interview by Joseph P. Kahn, July 2008.

CHAPTER TWENTY-TWO

PAGE

269 *Other dark chapters:* Larry Tye, "Edmund M. Kennedy Jr. Reports Treatment for Drinking Problem," *Boston Globe*, July 12, 1991.

270 *"Teddy had moved from the mythic":* Christopher Kennedy Lawford, *Symptoms of Withdrawal* (New York: William Morrow, 2005), 273.

270 *For more than half:* Ellen Roberts, interview by Joseph P. Kahn, July 2008.

271 *As historian Arthur:* "Kennedys Sell Family House in Palm Beach," *New York Times*, May 24, 1995.

271 *"They're not really considered":* "Kennedy Twist to an Old Plot Outline Emerges," *Boston Globe*, April 7, 1991.

272 *"just there with a weird":* ibid.

273 *"We knew that was the way":* Ellen Roberts, interview by Joseph P. Kahn, July 2008.

273 *"The press has a powerful tool":* "Bowman Lambastes Media for Invading Her Privacy," Stanford (University) New Service, April 15, 1992.

274 *Few believed, either:* John W. Mashek and Ethan Bronner, "Thomas, A Conservative, Nominated to High Court," *Boston Globe*, July 2, 1991.

274 *Doubtful that Thomas:* ibid.

275 *"Being an African American":* Faye Wattleton, interview by Joseph P. Kahn, August 2008.

275 *"Our first impression":* Alan Simpson, interview by Joseph P. Kahn, September 2008.

275 *"If we permit":* Walter V. Robinson, "2 Democrats Assail Thomas's Shifts," *Boston Globe*, September 17, 1991.

275 *"I'm a member of":* Jane Mayer and Jill Abramson, *Strange Justice* (Boston: Houghton Mifflin, 1994), 199.

276 *"Senator Kennedy was going to vote":* John Danforth, interview by Joseph P. Kahn, September 2008.

277 *Hill also said Thomas:* "Statement from Professor Hill," *Boston Globe*, October 12, 1991.

277 *"At that point I thought":* Anita Hill, interview by Joseph P. Kahn, July 2008.

277 *"It was one thing":* ibid.

277 *"Maybe the Senate needs":* Maureen Dowd, "7 Congresswomen March to Senate to Demand Delay in Thomas Vote," *New York Times*, October 9, 1991.

277 *Thomas led off:* "Statement from Judge Thomas," *Boston Globe*, October 12, 1991.

278 *"There was nothing in them":* former Senator Alan Simpson, interview by Joseph P. Kahn, September 2008.

278 *When Thomas returned:* Walter V. Robinson, "A Day of Charges and Denials," *Boston Globe*, October 12, 1991.

278 *"The issue isn't about discrimination":* Walter V. Robinson, "Hill's Friends Bolster Her Account," *Boston Globe*, October 14, 1991.

278 *He went on, "Are we":* John Aloysius Farrell, "Kennedy Becomes Target of Republican Gibes," *Boston Globe*, October 16, 1991.

278 *Sniffed Spector, "We do not need":* ibid.

279 *"I know a bridge":* ibid.

279 *"It was obvious":* Faye Wattleton, interview by Joseph P. Kahn, August 2008.

279 *"I'm not saying that's what":* Anita Hill, interview by Joseph P. Kahn, July 2008.

279 *Years later, Hill sees:* ibid.

279 *"The chance to talk to him":* ibid.

280 *Black had initially objected:* Roy Black, interview by Joseph P. Kahn, July 2008.

280 *"This really marked the beginning":* ibid.

280 *"They thought they could attack":* ibid.

280 *"after we decided":* Ellen Roberts, interview by Joseph P. Kahn, July 2008.

280 *At one point, she said:* "Diverging Details Are Key in Smith Rape Case," *Boston Globe*, December 11, 1991.

280 *After calling her:* Larry Tye, "Smith Denies Charge of Rape," *Boston Globe*, December 11, 1991.

280 *Asked if family members:* ibid.

281 *Yes, he regretted:* "Excerpts from Senator's Testimony," *Boston Globe*, December 7, 1991.

281 *"We're a very close family":* Robin Toner, "In Glare of Latest Scandal, Kennedy Defends the Dynasty," *New York Times*, December 7, 1991.

281 *"Suddenly it wasn't the Kennedys":* Roy Black, interview by Joseph P. Kahn, July 2008.

281 *"Most of all, I hope":* Larry Tye, "Smith Found Not Guilty," *Boston Globe*, December 12, 1991.

281 *In late 1993, the Kennedys:* "Kennedys Sell Family House in Palm Beach," *New York Times*, May 24, 1995.

CHAPTER TWENTY-THREE

PAGE

282 *"I could never vote":* Edmund Reggie, interview by Joseph P. Kahn, August 2008.

283 *"Last one in the pool":* Jack Thomas, "Victoria Reggie the Next Kennedy," *Boston Globe*, April 2, 1992.

283 *After Bobby died:* Edmund Reggie, interview by Joseph P. Kahn, August 2008.

283 *Photos of the event:* Harold Gonzales, interview by Joseph P. Kahn, October 2008.

283 *"If you were running for office":* Gregory Reggie, interview by Joseph P. Kahn, October 2008.

284 *He remained on the bench:* Edmund Reggie, interview by Joseph P. Kahn, October 2008.

284 *In 1952, he desegregated:* ibid.

285 *Maintaining his innocence:* Edmund Reggie, interview by Joseph P. Kahn, August 2008.

285 *"We grew up Mayberry-like":* Gregory Reggie, interview by Joseph P. Kahn, October 2008.

285 *"It was pretty cool":* ibid.

285 *Despite the close family:* Reggie family friend, interview by Joseph P. Kahn, October 2008.

286 *After a stellar:* Doris Reggie, interview by Joseph P. Kahn, October 2008.

286 *"Vicki was a real star":* Steven Engelberg, interview by Joseph P. Kahn, August 2008.

287 *"There are very few lawyers":* ibid.

287 *"What's the matter":* Laura Blumenfeld, "Victoria Reggie, Ready for Teddy," *Washington Post*, March 20, 1992.

287 *"Vicki would call":* Doris Reggie, interview by Joseph P. Kahn, October 2008.

288 *"A child calling for its mother":* Reggie family friend, interview by Joseph P. Kahn, October 2008.

288 *"His life was going":* Heather Campion, interview by Joseph P. Kahn, July 2008.

288 *At that moment:* Fox Butterfield, "At Home with Ted and Vicki Kennedy: Crossed Paths, A Second Chance," *New York Times*, October 1, 1992.

288 *"Vicki, for all her sense of humor":* Pamela Covington, interview by Joseph P. Kahn, August 2008.

288 *"There was no romance":* Edmund Reggie, interview by Joseph P. Kahn, August 2008.

289 *"I know him":* Sara Rimer, "Kennedy's Wife Is Giving Him a Political Advantage in a Difficult Contest," *New York Times*, September 24, 1994.

289 *Vicki and Ted burst out:* Reggie family friend, interview by Joseph P. Kahn, October 2008.

289 *"I want to marry Vicki":* Edmund Reggie, interview by Joseph P. Kahn, August 2008.

289 *Still, it was not until:* Clymer, *Edward M. Kennedy,* 512.

289 *Once the news broke:* Hersh, *The Shadow President* (South Royalton, Vt.: Steerforth Press, 1997), 108.

290 *Escorted by Edmund:* Mary Curtius, "Kennedy Quietly Ties Knot," *Boston Globe*, July 5, 1992.

290 *During the half-hour:* ibid.

290 *The senator's wedding gift:* ibid.

290 *They dined:* ibid.

290 *Edmund Reggie dismissed:* Jack Thomas, "Victoria Reggie the Next Kennedy," *Boston Globe*, April 2, 1992.

290 *"As good a friend":* ibid.

291 *"I told her":* Edmund Reggie, interview by Joseph P. Kahn, August 2008.

CHAPTER TWENTY-FOUR

PAGE

292 *To Burke, it was unimaginable:* David Burke, interview by Joseph P. Kahn, August 2008.

292 *It was a great record, Burke thought:* ibid.

292 *"If Democrats were thinking":* Martin F. Nolan, "At Breakfast, Democrats Look Past Their Future," *Boston Globe*, September 23, 1994.

293 *According to one focus group:* Robert Shrum, *No Excuses,* 244.

293 *"He was offended":* Kennedy aide, interview by Joseph P. Kahn, August 2008.

293 *"What he really needed":* David Burke, interview by Joseph P. Kahn, August 2008.

294 *Ranny Cooper arrived:* ibid.

294 *"It's like the Marines":* Kennedy aide, interview by Sam Allis, July 2008.

294 *"A Republican, white, male Mormon":* Mitt Romney, *Turnaround* (Washington, DC: Regnery Publishing, 2004), 14.

294 *"People in Massachusetts":* Charles Manning, interview by Joseph P. Kahn, August 2008.

295 *"He may have been":* David Burke, interview by Joseph P. Kahn, August 2008.

295 *Earlier in the campaign:* Shrum, *No Excuses,* 244.

295 *Kennedy flatly rejected:* ibid., 244.

295 *With Kiley's latest poll:* Kennedy aide, interview by Joseph P. Kahn, September 2008.

295 *More focused than agitated:* Robert Shrum, interview by Joseph P. Kahn, August 2008.

296 *"I said we should go out there":* ibid.

296 *"I would like to say":* Shrum, *No Excuses*, 246.

296 *"Labor hated Romney":* Charles Baker, interview by Joseph P. Kahn, August 2008.

296 *"Romney was toast":* Kennedy aide, interview by Joseph P. Kahn, August 2008.

297 *"I looked around and saw":* Frank Phillips and Scot Lehigh, "Poll: Kennedy Keeps Big Lead," *Boston Globe*, October 29, 1994.

297 *Local politicians including:* ibid.

297 *"We are going to board up":* ibid.

297 *"There was a sense":* Charles Baker, interview by Joseph P. Kahn, August 2008.

298 *"Think how much more difficult":* Sara Rimer, "Kennedy's Wife Is Giving Him a Political Advantage in a Difficult Contest," *New York Times*, September 24, 1994.

298 *While both campaigns:* Shrum, *No Excuses*, 247.

298 *The senator's nephew:* ibid., 247.

298 *Every time Mormonism:* Ben Bradlee Jr. and Daniel Golden, "Shaped an Epic Race: A Look Behind Kennedy-Romney," *Boston Globe*, November 10, 1994.

298 *With their candidate surging:* Kennedy aide, interview by Joseph P. Kahn, August 2008.

298 *"My argument was":* David Burke, interview by Joseph P. Kahn, August 2008.

298 *To ignore them:* Robert Shrum, interview by Joseph P. Kahn, August 2008.

299 *"Mr. Romney," Kennedy said:* ibid.

299 *Kennedy left for the JFK Library:* ibid.

299 *No problem, said Manning:* Charles Manning, interview by Joseph P. Kahn, August 2008.

299 *Ted's car pulled up:* David Burke, interview by Joseph P. Kahn, August 2008.

299 *"I just wanted to know":* ibid.

300 *With a hearty laugh:* ibid.

300 *He waited in a small room:* Kennedy aide, interview by Joseph P. Kahn, August 2008.

300 *Heavy on his feet:* Frank Phillips and Scot Lehigh, "Kennedy and Romney Blast Away," *Boston Globe*, October 26, 1994.

300 *"But Mr. Romney, that's exactly":* ibid.

300 *"The event was tied to the notion":* Robert Healy, "Kennedy—and Liberalism—Won in First Debate," *Boston Globe*, October 29, 1994.

300 *"Ted's real formula for success":* Mitt Romney, "Ted's Attack for Success," *Boston Globe*, January 30, 1995.

301 *"It was the first election":* Charles Baker, interview by Joseph P. Kahn, August 2008.

CHAPTER TWENTY-FIVE

PAGE

305 *A slimmed-down Ted:* Jon Marcus, "A Placid Ted Kennedy Settles into Life as Husband, Father, Family Man," *Los Angeles Times*, November 8, 1992.

305 *"I don't think there's any question":* ibid.

305 *"He's the flame":* ibid.

306 *"I thought the best thing":* Heather Campion, interview by Joseph P. Kahn, July 2008.

306 *The women were stunned:* ibid.

306 *His staff was learning:* Kennedy aide, interview by Joseph P. Kahn, October 2008.

306 *"She's very protective":* ibid.

306 *Ted tended to:* ibid.

306 *"Clearly Vicki was becoming":* Steve Engelberg, interview by Joseph P. Kahn, August 2008.

307 *Politics had not figured prominently:* Kennedy family friend, interview by Joseph P. Kahn, October 2008.

307 *"Vicki is a brilliant woman":* Edmund Reggie, interview by Joseph P. Kahn, August 2008.

308 *Granddaughter Caroline Kennedy:* Caroline Kennedy, "Profiles in Courage" Dinner, speech at JFK Library, Boston, May 11, 2008.

308 *"She did everything":* Edward M. Kennedy, speech at Georgetown University, October 1, 1977.

308 *"As the last of nine":* Edward M. Kennedy, ed., *Her Grace Above Gold*, 32.

309 *Knowing the depth:* Heather Campion, interview by Joseph P. Kahn, July 2008.

309 *She posted signs:* Sally Jacobs, "Prime Time with Joan Kennedy," *Boston Globe Sunday Magazine*, July 9, 2000.

309 *"I'm babysitting":* ibid.

309 *To celebrate their wedding anniversary:* Kennedy family friend, interview by Joseph P. Kahn, October 2008.

310 *It was, says one:* ibid.

310 *"Vicki and I both grew up":* John Rosenthal, interview by Joseph P. Kahn, September 2008.

310 *"The issue for her":* Phyllis Segal, interview by Joseph P. Kahn, October 2008.

310 *Beyond the passion:* ibid.

311 *"He came to the Senate":* Ross K. Baker, interview by Mark Feeney, October 7, 2008.

314 *Unlike Johnson, says Ted's:* Senator Jay Rockefeller, interview by Susan Milligan, July 18, 2008.

314 *"I'm introducing a new bill":* Representative George Miller, interview by Susan Milligan, July 23, 2008.

315 *He "wanted McCain's name":* Former Senator John Edwards, interview by Susan Milligan, July 8, 2008.

315 *He was among the first:* Senator Gordon Smith, interview by Ann Silvio, October 2008.

315 *After Joe Biden suffered:* Senator Joseph Biden, floor speech, *Congressional Record,* February 26, 2002.

315 *"He realized he would":* Senator Richard Durbin, interview by Susan Milligan, July 8, 2008.

316 *"It's flattering to have Ted":* Senator Jay Rockefeller, interview by Susan Milligan, July 18, 2008.

316 *"He was a bit green":* former Senator George McGovern, interview by Susan Milligan, July 2008.

317 *Ted, however, refused:* Kennedy aide, interview by Susan Milligan, July 2005.

317 *On St. Patrick's Day:* former Senator Peter Fitzgerald, interview by Susan Milligan, July 17, 2008.

317 *Also on St. Patrick's Day:* Kennedy aide, interview by Susan Milligan, June 2008.

318 *Kentucky's Republican Senator:* Senator Mitch McConnell, interview by Susan Milligan, July 21, 2008.

319 *"It was one of the most generous":* Senator Tom Harkin, interview by Susan Milligan, July 9, 2008.

319 *The Bush administration had:* Robert Burgdorf, interview by Susan Milligan, July 24, 2008.

320 *"He had this knee-jerk":* Senator Tom Harkin, interview by Susan Milligan, July 9, 2008.

321 *"Kennedy ate his lunch":* Senator Orrin Hatch, interview by Susan Milligan, July 14, 2008.

CHAPTER TWENTY-SIX

PAGE

322 *"Ted Kennedy, by any objective":* Senator Richard Durbin, interview by Susan Milligan, July 8, 2008.

323 *"It's really a partnership":* Senator Edward M. Kennedy, Washington, D.C., news conference, February 18, 1971.

324 *Perhaps, Ted said later:* Senator Edward M. Kennedy, interview by Susan Milligan, December 5, 2004.

324 *By the 1990s, the list:* Accomplishments of Senator Kennedy, 1962–2008, Office of Senator Edward M. Kennedy, May 2008.

325 *"The conquest of cancer":* Senator Edward M. Kennedy, statement, Office of Senator Edward M. Kennedy.

327 *Ted privately felt:* Kennedy aides, interviews by Susan Milligan and Don Aucoin, Summer 2008.

328 *Ted was intrigued:* Barry Zuckerman, interview by Susan Milligan, Summer 2008.

329 *He corralled his then chief:* Senator Orrin Hatch, interview by Susan Milligan, September 2008.

329 *"He can really belt out a song":* ibid.

329 *By the end of the evening:* Kennedy aide, interview by Susan Milligan, Summer 2008.

329 *The roadblock, as it turned out:* Senator Edward M. Kennedy, interview by Susan Milligan, March 13, 2008.

330 *The former Mormon missionary:* Senator Orrin Hatch, interview by Susan Milligan, July 14, 2008.

330 *"I thought he stood for":* ibid.

330 *First, Kennedy came:* ibid.

331 *"I can't run this committee":* ibid.

332 *"It is no secret":* Senator Orrin Hatch, Senate floor speech, *Congressional Record*, February 26, 2002.

332 *When Ted was under public assault:* Senator Orrin Hatch, interview by Susan Milligan, July 14, 2008.

333 *"A lot of my memories":* Senator Tom Harkin, interview by Susan Milligan, July 9, 2008.

333 *"Don't let that bother you":* Senator Orrin Hatch, interview by Susan Milligan, July 14, 2008.

333 *When Rose died:* ibid.

333 *And when Hatch's grandson:* ibid.

335 *The Ryan White Act:* ibid.

335 *Ted, caught unaware:* ibid.

335 *"Senator, I know you're sincere":* ibid.

336 *"Watch out for Orrin":* Anonymous U.S. senator, interview by Susan Milligan, Summer 2008.

336 *New York Senator Al D'Amato:* Senator Orrin Hatch, interview by Susan Milligan, July 14, 2008.

336 *"Orrin, I have never been":* ibid.

336 *The next day, a sheepish:* ibid.

337 *"That's his secret":* former Senator Alan Simpson, interview by Susan Milligan, Summer 2008.

337 *"I don't think he's gained":* Paul Weyrich, interview by Susan Milligan, June 2008.

CHAPTER TWENTY-SEVEN

PAGE

338 *Even though he had just lost: Boston Globe*, July 28, 1999; Anne E. Kornblut, interview by Don Aucoin, August 21, 2008.

338 *"We'll be back to fight":* CNN.com, July 15, 1999.

338 *Ted knew that the white:* Lawford, *Symptoms of Withdrawal* (New York: William Morrow, 2005), 379.

339 *"He's more than an uncle":* Caroline Kennedy, interview by Susan Milligan, August 26, 2008.

339 *After Bobby's death:* Lawford, *Symptoms of Withdrawal*, 107–108.

339 *Once, as he sipped a vodka and tonic:* ibid., 379.

340 *"He gave us a sense of continuity":* Kerry Kennedy, interview by Jenna Russell, October 7, 2008.

340 *"All that takes a tremendous amount":* Caroline Kennedy, interview by Susan Milligan, August 26, 2008.

341 *"When things are going badly":* Clymer, *Edward M. Kennedy,* 605.

342 *One of his first calls:* Margaret Carlson, Ann Blackman, and Melissa August, "Farewell, John," *Time*, August 2, 1999.

342 *"Kennedy was intimately involved":* Anonymous former aide, interview by Don Aucoin, October 7, 2008.

343 *Before he would consent:* Anonymous source close to Senator Edward Kennedy, interview by Alan Wirzbicki, October 10, 2008.

343 *Meanwhile, Caroline had returned:* ibid.

344 *After pondering the matter:* ibid.

344 *"He has always been there":* Caroline Kennedy, "Profiles in Courage" Dinner, speech at JFK Library, Boston, May 23, 1999.

345 *Ted promised Caroline that he would identify:* Christopher Andersen, *Sweet Caroline* (New York: William Morrow, 2003), 279.

345 *Ted stood stoically:* ibid.

346 *"Nobody was more amazing":* CBS News, *60 Minutes*, Gloria Borger interview with Caroline Kennedy and Ted Kennedy, May 2, 2000.

346 *"You try to live with the upside":* ibid.

348 *"For me, Williams is the classic ballplayer":* John Updike, "Hub Bids Kid Adieu," *New Yorker*, October 22, 1960.

CHAPTER TWENTY-EIGHT

PAGE

349 *"I've heard of you":* Anne E. Kornblut, "Bush Tries to Build Ties with Kennedy," *Boston Globe*, January 11, 2001.

351 *The new president, for his part:* Bruce Buchanan, interview by Susan Milligan, October 2008.

352 *Kennedy, however, was not:* Sandy Kress, interview by Susan Milligan, July 3, 2008.

352 *Bush called a meeting:* ibid.

352 *"The president was far more":* ibid.

353 *In truth, Ted hated:* Kennedy aide, interview by Susan Milligan, February 2001.

353 *During the movie night:* Anne E. Kornblut, "Bush Outreach Runs on Persistence, Charm," *Boston Globe*, February 3, 2001.

353 *But the president was happy:* Senator Edward M. Kennedy, interview by Susan Milligan, February 2006.

355 *Tom Harkin, who said:* Senator Tom Harkin, interview by Susan Milligan, Summer 2003.

355 *Ted declared that he had been:* Senator Edward M. Kennedy, interview by Susan Milligan, November 2003.

355 *And if Ted felt betrayed:* Bruce Buchanan, interview by Susan Milligan, October 2008.

355 *On September 11, 2001, Ted was in his office:* Mary Beth Cahill, interview by Don Aucoin, September 2008.

CHAPTER TWENTY-NINE

PAGE

357 *When Cindy McGinty of Foxborough:* Cindy McGinty, interview by Don Aucoin, August 5, 2008.

358 *His standing instruction:* Barbara Souliotis, interview by Don Aucoin, July 24, 2008.

358 *When he learned of a grant:* James Brett, interview by Don Aucoin, August 1, 2008.

359 *"I had not heard from one":* Sally White, interview by Don Aucoin, July 7, 2008.

360 *"He saw this from the very beginning":* Mary Beth Cahill, interview by Don Aucoin, September 2008.

361 *He walked to the front:* Cindy McGinty, interview by Don Aucoin, August 5, 2008.

361 *But as he left the meeting:* ibid.

361 *He assigned two staffers to work for a full year:* Mary Beth Cahill, interview by Don Aucoin, September 2008.

362 *When Ted learned that Christie:* Christie Coombs, interview by Don Aucoin, June 30, 2008.

363 *"To think that someone":* Carie Lemack, interview by Don Aucoin, August 26, 2008.

363 *But there was a chilling backstory:* Brian and Alma Hart, interview by Don Aucoin, July 16, 2008.

364 *"He didn't immediately dismiss":* Mary Beth Cahill, interview by Don Aucoin, September 2008.

364 *He also prodded the administration:* "Statement of Senator Edward M. Kennedy at the Senate Armed Services Committee Hearing on Iraq," Kennedy Press Office, September 19, 2002.

365 *The address drew a fiery reaction:* Susan Milligan and Elizabeth Neuffer, "Kennedy Criticizes Bush on Iraq Policy," *Boston Globe*, September 28, 2002.

365 *"We must not delegate that responsibility":* "Statement of Senator Edward Kennedy on the Military Consequences of War with Iraq," Kennedy Press Office, October 8, 2002.

365 *Ted "passionately contended":* Robert Shrum, *No Excuses*, 338.

366 *Instead, he closed by reciting:* "Floor Remarks of Senator Edward M. Kennedy Supporting Our Troops in Iraq," Kennedy Press Office, March 20, 2003.

366 *He called the war a "fraud":* Anne E. Kornblut, "Bush Calls Kennedy's Iraq Criticism 'Uncivil,' " *Boston Globe*, September 22, 2003.

366 *"The best time to visit":* Brian and Alma Hart, interview by Don Aucoin, July 16, 2008.

CHAPTER THIRTY

PAGE

370 *In fact, Ted was more willing:* David Nexon, interview by Susan Milligan, Summer 2008.

371 *Ted and the drug industry:* ibid.

371 *Some of Ted's fellow Democrats:* former Senator Tom Daschle, interview by Susan Milligan, July 2008.

372 *With the memory of:* Senator Edward Kennedy, interview by Susan Milligan, June 2003.

372 *"It was probably one of the most":* former Senator Tom Daschle, interview by Susan Milligan, July 2008.

372 *AARP leaders hadn't even told:* David Nexon, interview by Susan Milligan, Summer 2008.

372 *"We thought of this as":* Bill Novelli, interview by Susan Milligan, July 23, 2008.

373 *In the future, Ted declared:* Senator Edward Kennedy, interview by Susan Milligan, November 2003.

373 *Novelli, who says he "still":* Bill Novelli, interview by Susan Milligan, July 23, 2008.

373 *An impish grin on his face:* Mary Beth Cahill, interview by Don Aucoin, September 2008.

375 *"He's not necessarily made for the TV age":* Dan Balz, interview by Don Aucoin, August 2008.

375 *"He was effervescent":* David Yepsen, interview by Don Aucoin, August 11, 2008.

375 *"It was like going back":* Paul Pezzella, interview by Don Aucoin, July 29, 2008.

375 *Suddenly the door opened and in walked Ted:* Mary Beth Cahill, interview by Don Aucoin, September 2008.

377 *For Kennedy, who regarded undocumented:* Senator Edward Kennedy, interview by Susan Milligan, Summer 2007.

377 *The start of the 2008 campaign was:* ibid.

378 *One member of the negotiating:* former Senator Trent Lott, interview by Susan Milligan, Summer 2007.

378 *One night, he got so angry:* Susan Milligan, "Adversaries Praise a Relentless Kennedy—as Clock Ticked, Senator Pressed Sides for a Pact," *Boston Globe*, May 18, 2007.

378 *Then, at another tense negotiation:* Senator Lindsey Graham, interview by Susan Milligan, May 2007.

379 *Mel Martinez, who rarely:* Susan Milligan, "Immigration Bill Dies in Senate," *Boston Globe*, June 29, 2007.

379 *Less than an hour after the loss:* Senator Edward Kennedy, interview by Susan Milligan, June 28, 2007.

379 *"His view is":* Senator Jay Rockefeller, interview by Susan Milligan, July 18, 2008.

CHAPTER THIRTY-ONE

PAGE

380 *Less than two years later, he sought Ted's advice:* Shailagh Murray and Anne E. Kornblut, "Kennedy Will Endorse Obama in Blow to Clinton," *Washington Post*, January 28, 2008.

381 *Ted knew that Dodd's candidacy:* Anonymous sources close to Senators Edward Kennedy and Christopher Dodd, interviews by Susan Milligan, December 2007.

381 *Meanwhile, donations from members:* Carrie Budoff Brown, "Kennedy Family Split on Endorsements," *Politico*, December 17, 2007.

381 *"I've got to show you this clip":* Senator Richard Durbin, interview by Susan Milligan, July 8, 2008.

381 *In June 2003, in an address:* Huffington Post, December 18, 2007.

382 *"Oh, by the way, I'm sorry":* Anonymous source close to Senator Edward Kennedy, interview by Susan Milligan, February 2008.

382 *He flatly told the Massachusetts:* Anonymous Massachusetts political source, interview by Susan Milligan, February 2008.

382 *Meanwhile, Bill turned to Kennedy:* Clymer, *Edward M. Kennedy*, 602.

382 *When Hillary entered the Senate:* Susan Milligan, "Kennedy Smooths Senate Path for Clinton," *Boston Globe*, February 22, 2001; Susan Milligan, "Kennedy Poised to Endorse Obama, Key Democratic Nod a Setback for Clinton," *Boston Globe*, January 28, 2008.

383 *"a meeting of the man and the moment":* Mary Beth Cahill, interview by Don Aucoin, September 2008.

383 *Two days before the South Carolina:* Susan Milligan, "Kennedy Poised to Endorse Obama," *Boston Globe*, January 28, 2008.

383 *And, in a carefully planned rollout:* Caroline Kennedy, "A President Like My Father," *New York Times*, January 27, 2008.

384 *Ted called Bill Clinton that day:* Jeff Zeleny and Carl Hulse, "Kennedy Chooses Obama, Spurning Plea by Clintons," *New York Times*, January 28, 2008.

384 *The next day, three:* Kathleen Kennedy Townsend, Robert F. Kennedy Jr., and Kerry Kennedy, "Kennedys for Clinton," *Los Angeles Times*, January 29, 2008.

384 *"I've been in the family thirty years":* Jodi Kantor, "In Democratic Families, Politics Makes for Estranged Bedfellows," *New York Times*, February 4, 2008.

385 *"Women have just experienced":* New York State National Organization for Women press release, "Senator Kennedy Betrays Women by Not Standing for Hillary Clinton for President," January 28, 2008.

385 *Clinton operatives, meanwhile:* Mary Ann Akers, "Clinton LBJ Comments Infuriated Ted Kennedy," *Washington Post*, January 30, 2008; also, various anonymous Kennedy aides, interviews by Susan Milligan, January and February 2008.

385 *"Are you glad to see me, Santa Fe?":* Mark Leibovich, "Kennedy Revels in Limelight as He Stumps for Obama," *New York Times*, February 2, 2008.

386 *Ted also spoke to an audience:* Erik Siemers, "Sen. Edward Kennedy Stumps for Obama in Albuquerque," *Albuquerque Tribune*, February 1, 2008.

386 *He sang a song in Spanish:* Leibovich, *New York Times*, February 2, 2008.

386 *"A lot of us want us":* Representative Michael Capuano, interview by Susan Milligan, January 28, 2008.

387 *Christie Coombs sent:* Christie Coombs, interview by Don Aucoin, June 30, 2008.

387 *But then she rallied:* Cindy McGinty, interview by Don Aucoin, August 5, 2008.

CHAPTER THIRTY-TWO

PAGE

389 *On Wednesday, May 21, 2008, Ted left:* Karen Jeffrey, *Cape Cod Times*, May 22, 2008.

389 *Ted and Vicki offered smiles:* AP, May 21, 2008.

389 *One supporter wore a Kennedy campaign button:* Karen Jeffrey, *Cape Cod Times*, May 26, 2008.

389 *A homemade banner:* ibid.

389 *its mahogany hull:* Karl Anderson, interview by Kytja Weir, October 14, 2008.

390 *As Jack Kennedy said in a speech:* John F. Kennedy Presidential Library and Museum, online reference desk.

390 *Only a small square bandage:* Karen Jeffrey, *Cape Cod Times*, May 22, 2008.

390 *The next day he announced:* Eric Williams and Karen Jeffrey, *Cape Cod Times*, May 23, 2008.

390 *The day before the races began:* David Abel, *Boston Globe*, May 24, 2008.

390 *Yet on that Memorial Day:* Karen Jeffrey, *Cape Cod Times*, May 27, 2008.

391 *Despite his nearly lifelong exposure to doctors:* Rob Stein and Paul Kane, *Washington Post*, June 3, 2008.

391 *Ted, too, sought expert advice:* Sally Jacobs, *Boston Globe*, May 25, 2008.

391 *"Kennedy worked the other way around":* Jonathan Bor, *Baltimore Sun*, June 3, 2008.

391 *Allan Friedman, a 59-year-old:* Kristin Collins, *News & Observer*, June 29, 2008.

391 *The next day, a Saturday:* Rob Stein and Paul Kane, *Washington Post*, June 3, 2008.

392 *Ted issued a statement:* CNN.com, June 2, 2008.

392 *That Monday, June 2, hordes of reporters:* *Herald Sun*, June 3, 2008.

392 *"When you look at the brain":* Kristin Collins, *News & Observer*, June 29, 2008.

392 *"A malignant tumor is not like a cherry":* Jessica Lichter, *Chronicle* (Duke University), September 15, 2008.

392 *"It's not like you play your B game":* Kristin Collins, *News & Observer*, June 29, 2008.

392 *an avid Duke basketball fan:* Anne Blythe, *News & Observer*, June 3, 2008.

392 *Shortly after 2:00 P.M.:* Michael Levenson and Matt Viser, *Boston Globe*, June 3, 2008.

393 *But the senator kept a low profile:* Lisa Rossi, *Herald Sun* (Durham), June 5, 2008.

393 *Guards patrolled hospital hallways:* Kristin Collins, *News & Observer*, June 29, 2008.

393 *He returned home June 9:* Karen Jeffrey, *Cape Cod Times*, June 10, 2008.

393 *"I was talking to some":* Joan Kennedy, interview by Bella English and Neil Swidey, July 2008.

394 *Dodd and Kerry tried to keep fellow senators:* Senator Chris Dodd, interview by Susan Milligan, July 9, 2008.

394 *Obama was so distracted:* Susan Milligan, *Boston Globe*, July 10, 2008.

394 *on his last day of the six-week:* WBTZ.com, July 25, 2008.

395 *During the summer of 2008, Hyannis:* *Barnstable Patriot*, August 28, 2008.

395 *the Kennedy moniker to a training ship:* Letter to the Editor, *Cape Cod Times*, August 15, 2008.

395 *The* Barnstable Patriot *editorialized that a Cape:* *Barnstable Patriot*, June 5, 2008.

395 *It's a community where:* Interviews by Kytja Weir, October 13–14, 2008.

395 *Hyannis Fire Chief Harold Brunelle understands:* Harold Brunelle, interview by Kytja Weir, October 14, 2008.

397 *But Ted told Vicki and the doctors:* Adam Nagourney, "Determined to Give Speech, Kennedy Left Hospital Bed," *New York Times*, August 26, 2008.

397 *So she talked about Ted's relationship with Rose:* Caroline Kennedy, "Profiles in Courage" Dinner, speech at JFK Library, Boston, May 11, 2008.

399 *"I definitely feel a debt that has to be repaid":* Jessica Katz, interview by Don Aucoin, June 29, 2008, and September 2008.

399 *Determined to prevent more deaths like John's:* Brian Hart, interview by Don Aucoin, July 16, 2008, and December 2008.

400 *"Ted Kennedy is the most important person of the last two generations":* Bill Walczak, interview by Don Aucoin, July 30, 2008, and October 2008.

400 *"There's just nothing that keeps that man down":* Cindy McGinty, interview by Don Aucoin, August 5, 2008, and December 2008.